FAMIL'

Fathers are often neglected in histories of family life in Britain. *Family Men* provides the first academic study of fathers and families in the period from the First World War to the end of the 1950s. It takes a thematic approach, examining different aspects of fatherhood, from the duties it encompassed to the ways in which it related to men's identities. The historical approach is socio-cultural: each chapter examines a wide range of historical source materials in order to analyse both cultural representations of fatherhood and related social norms, as well as exploring the practices and experiences of individuals and families. It uncovers the debates surrounding parenting and family life and tells the stories of men and their children.

While many historians have examined men's relationship to the home and family in histories of gender, family life, domestic spaces, and class cultures more generally, few have specifically examined fathers as crucial family members, as historical actors, and as emotional individuals. The history of fatherhood is extremely significant to contemporary debate: assumptions about fatherhood in the past are constantly used to support arguments about the state of fatherhood today and the need for change or otherwise in the future. Laura King charts men's changing experiences of fatherhood, suggesting that although the roles and responsibilities fulfilled by men did not shift rapidly, their relationships, position in the family, and identities underwent significant change between the start of the First World War and the 1960s.

Family Men

*Fatherhood and Masculinity
in Britain, c.1914–1960*

LAURA KING

OXFORD

UNIVERSITY PRESS

Great Clarendon Street, Oxford, OX2 6DP,
United Kingdom

Oxford University Press is a department of the University of Oxford.
It furthers the University's objective of excellence in research, scholarship,
and education by publishing worldwide. Oxford is a registered trade mark of
Oxford University Press in the UK and in certain other countries

First published 2015
First published in paperback 2020

Published in the United States of America by Oxford University Press
198 Madison Avenue, New York, NY 10016, United States of America

British Library Cataloguing in Publication Data
Data available

Library of Congress Cataloging in Publication Data
Data available

ISBN 978–0–19–967490–9 (Hbk.)
ISBN 978–0–19–885782–2 (Pbk.)

For my dad

Preface

The history of masculinity in twentieth-century Britain remains incomplete because of the frequent omission of fathers and fatherhood. This book provides a new dimension to the social and cultural history of gender and family in the twentieth century by bringing fathers to the forefront, by examining them as individuals and considering changing family life from the perspective of men. It challenges the current assumption that the post-Second World War focus on motherhood left fathers and fatherhood in the shadows, and rejects the overriding yet narrow focus on 'domestic masculinity' and the 'domestication', or otherwise, of men.

I have many people to thank for their kind support and encouragement that has been essential to the completion of this book. Adrian Bingham has offered exemplary help and advice as supervisor of the doctoral research at the core of the book, and Clare Griffiths, Mary Vincent, and Karen Harvey also provided helpful comments at different points. I am also very grateful for Pat Thane's suggestions as external examiner of the original thesis. Colleagues at both Warwick and Leeds have also helped me develop the work further, and the supportive atmosphere at both institutions as well as Sheffield has been instrumental to the successful completion of the book. Thanks also to colleagues who have commented on various iterations of the research at numerous conferences and workshops. In particular, discussions with Helen Smith, Julie-Marie Strange, Joanne Bailey, Selina Todd, Mathew Thomson, Hilary Marland, Roberta Bivins, Daniel Grey, and Angela Davis have also been incredibly helpful in further sharpening and developing my arguments around fatherhood and masculinity, and I'm grateful to Angela for valuable comments on the full final draft. I am also grateful to the three anonymous reviewers for their very helpful suggestions, as well as the editorial team at Oxford University Press, who have been supportive and helpful throughout.

Particular thanks must go to the Arts and Humanities Research Council, for the Doctoral Award (award number 2008/140095) that allowed me to complete the doctoral research that has resulted in this book and for the Research Masters Preparation Award that supported me in completing an MA beforehand. Furthermore, the Wellcome Trust funded my postdoctoral position at Warwick where I further developed ideas for this volume. I would also like to thank Mirrorpix for giving their permission for the use of images within the book. Anyone wishing to reuse any of the images should contact Mirrorpix directly. Finally, thanks must go to the staff at the British Film Institute Archive, the British Library, the Elizabeth Roberts Archive, and the Imperial War Museum archives for their help in researching this project, and those archival institutions plus Steve Humphries and the UK Data Archive for permission to reproduce quotations from interviews and letters.

I owe a lot to various family members for their generosity with time, advice, and spare rooms at various stages, including Sylvia King, Anna Higgs, Dan Wichett, Helen, Carole, and Bill Quirk, as well as my brother Charlie, parents Phil and Alison, and most of all Joe Quirk, for their love, support, and encouragement throughout.

Contents

List of Abbreviations

BBC	British Broadcasting Corporation
BFI	British Film Institute
BMA	British Medical Association
ERA	Elizabeth Roberts Archive
IWMA	Imperial War Museum Archive
MP	Member of Parliament
NSPCC	National Society for the Prevention of Cruelty to Children
RAF	Royal Air Force
UKDA	United Kingdom Data Archive

1

Introduction

CHANGING FATHERHOOD IN A CHANGING CONTEXT

In 1956, an article in the *Daily Mirror* entitled 'Happy Families' reflected on change in recent years in terms of both fatherhood and the dynamics of family life. The anonymous writer invited opinions from readers, and noted:

> Family life is more enlightened today than it used to be. Gone (and good riddance to him) is the Victorian father who thought he was God—with a mission to hold down those perishing sinners, his offspring. Dad is no longer the Great I Am laying down the law from Way Up High.

The journalist added that 'Modern parents stay young with their children and discuss family affairs with them like good pals.'[1] This article illustrates a number of important trends in popular culture. It reflects a sense of change over time, a conscious focus on modernity, and an explicit contrast to the Victorian patriarch. The rhetoric of equality and friendship used here permeated public debates about family life. Above all, this piece situated the father at the heart of the family; numerous articles from a variety of newspapers continually reinforced fathers' importance and influential presence in their children's lives. Social researchers found this reflected individuals' behaviour and attitudes: at the end of this period, John and Elizabeth Newson concluded that the high level of participation of fathers in their children's upbringing was a 'distinctive feature of modern family life', and Ferdynand Zweig highlighted that the factory workers he studied took 'an intense, sometimes passionate, interest' in the upbringing of their children.[2] *Family Men* examines such suggestions, and provides a new contribution to the histories of family and gender. It provides the first academic history of fatherhood in this period, and considers a number of key questions. Did the father's role at this time extend much beyond breadwinning? Were fathers taking an active role in childcare and developing close relationships with their sons and daughters? Was fatherhood a prominent or celebrated aspect of culturally exalted versions of masculinity? Did change occur in this period, and why? How does this relate

---

[1] *Daily Mirror*, 2 February 1956, p. 2.
[2] John and Elizabeth Newson [1963], *Patterns of Infant Care in an Urban Community* (Harmondsworth, 1974), p. 140; Ferdynand Zweig, *The Worker in Affluent Society: Family Life and Industry* (London, 1961), p. 20.

to the wider contexts—of war and unemployment, of the increased influence of psychological ways of thinking, and of a newly national culture?

This book examines fatherhood as a cultural institution and a social role, fathering as part of the life course of most men, and fathers as actors and emotional, embodied individuals. It adopts a socio-cultural history approach by examining cultural norms and prescriptions about behaviour, feelings and identities, alongside investigating the attitudes and social experiences of men and their families. It examines men and masculinity in the context of the family, thus providing a new perspective on the history of family life in modern Britain. The fusion of social and cultural approaches emerges from a belief in the need to examine experiences, attitudes, emotions, and subjectivities as well as the social, cultural, political, and economic contexts in which these are shaped.[3] Indeed, *Family Men* responds to calls for 'more sophisticated historical knowledge' of the family, a focus on parenting as a formative experience for parents as well as children, and more research into masculinity in the twentieth century.[4] It rejects assumptions that fatherhood was somehow more clearly defined in the past, and suggests we need a more complex understanding of fatherhood in its historical context.[5] It highlights how fatherhood and individual fathers were multidimensional, complex, and often contradictory. It unpacks the actions, attitudes, emotions, and identities that constitute this concept, by analysing a wide range of sources relating to fatherhood in Britain between the First World War and the end of the 1950s.

An increased willingness of men to involve themselves in the chores of looking after children has been noted in some histories of the family, gender, and class culture in this period, particularly by the end of the 1940s and 1950s.[6] It is argued

---

[3] On this point, see Joanne Bailey, *Parenting in England, 1760–1830* (Oxford, 2012), pp. 6–11; Peter Mandler, 'The Problem with Cultural History', *Cultural and Social History* 1:1 (2004), pp. 94–117; Lyndal Roper, 'Beyond Discourse Theory', *Women's History Review* 19:2 (2010), pp. 307–19; Michael Roper, 'Slipping Out of View: Subjectivity and Emotion in Gender History', *History Workshop Journal* 59:1 (2005), pp. 57–72; Dror Wahrman, 'Change and the Corporeal in Seventeenth- and Eighteenth-Century Gender History: Or, Can Cultural History be Rigorous?', *Gender and History* 20:3 (2008), pp. 584–602.

[4] John H. Arnold and Sean Brady, 'Introduction', in J. H. Arnold and S. Brady (eds), *What is Masculinity? Historical Dynamics from Antiquity to the Contemporary World* (Basingstoke, 2011), pp. 9–10; Leonore Davidoff, Megan Doolittle, Janet Fink, and Katherine Holden, *The Family Story: Blood, Contract and Intimacy, 1830–1939* (Harlow, 1999), pp. 43, 50; Martin Francis, 'The Domestication of the Male? Recent research on Nineteenth- and Twentieth-Century British Masculinity', *Historical Journal* 45:3 (2002), p. 652; Michael Roper, 'Between Manliness and Masculinity: The "War Generation" and the Psychology of Fear in Britain, 1914–1950', *Journal of British Studies* 44:2 (2005), p. 361. Further, as LaRossa has highlighted in the American context, there is an absence of 'usable pasts' in terms of fatherhood. Ralph LaRossa, *The Modernization of Fatherhood: A Social and Political History* (Chicago, IL and London, 1997), p. 4.

[5] Burghes, Clarke, and Cronin, for example, suggest that 'Neither roles nor behaviour are as clearly or definitively socially defined as they once were', whilst Moss writes that 'While what fatherhood was is perhaps fairly clear, what it might become is less so.' Louie Burghes, Lynda Clarke, and Natalie Cronin, *Fathers and Fatherhood in Britain* (London, 1997), p. 9; Peter Moss, 'Introduction', in P. Moss (ed.), *Father Figures: Fathers in the Families of the 1990s* (Edinburgh, 1995), p. xi.

[6] For example, Lynn Abrams, ' "There Was Nobody like My Daddy": Fathers, the Family and the Marginalisation of Men in Modern Scotland', *Scottish Historical Review* 78:2 (1999), esp. pp. 226–38; Adrian Bingham, *Gender, Modernity, and the Popular Press in Inter-War Britain* (Oxford,

here that fatherhood took on a new cultural and social significance, particularly from the mid-1930s. The greater involvement of men in childcare tasks is one element of this change. The rise of popular psychological modes of thinking and raised standards of living, coupled with an emphasis on the family at the heart of post-Second World War reconstruction, led to a new stress on the father–child relationship and an increased assumption that men should focus their masculine identities on fatherhood. This shift in cultural meaning both reflected and influenced the rise in numbers of men taking their relationships with their children seriously and embracing the identity of 'family man'. Like mothers, fathers found their children to be a source of pleasure, pain, and frustration; yet, unlike mothers, their position as a parent of secondary importance meant they could choose to disassociate themselves from aspects of family life they did not enjoy.[7] Involved fatherhood could be a positive experience for many men. Many parents emphasized change between generations. Particularly in the latter half of this period, both men and women drew contrasts between their (husbands') conduct in contrast to that of their fathers and fathers-in-law.[8] We must be mindful here of the recurrent idea of change in fatherhood that can be found throughout modern history; as Charlie Lewis noted, the idea that men have recently become more involved in family life 'is as old and perhaps as prominent as patriarchy'.[9] The insistence on the novelty of fathers taking their roles seriously in popular cultural debates does not necessarily neatly reflect men's behaviour. The following chapters analyse cultural and social change, and attitudes towards change on the part of parents and children.

Fatherhood is a crucial component of men's identities and experiences, common to the vast majority of adult men at some point in their lives. As Robert Griswold notes, 'Throughout human history, most men have been fathers, and all fathers have been sons, and thus comprehending men's experiences as fathers and how fatherhood has been culturally constructed over time is fundamental to understanding human experience.'[10] Indeed, as parenting became at least notionally a choice rather than an inevitability for increasing numbers of people, with increased availability of birth control technology and knowledge about family limitation, motherhood and fatherhood were arguably situated more centrally

2004), pp. 241–2; Joanna Bourke, *Working Class Cultures in Britain 1890–1960: Gender, Class, and Ethnicity* (London, 1994), pp. 81–5; Marcus Collins, *Modern Love: An Intimate History of Men and Women in Twentieth-Century Britain* (London, 2003), p. 95; Timothy James Fisher, 'Fatherhood and the Experience of Working-Class Fathers in Britain, 1900–1939', PhD Thesis (University of Edinburgh, 2004), e.g. pp. 12–13; Elizabeth Roberts, *Women and Families: An Oral History, 1940–1970* (Oxford, 1995), pp. 38–41; Margaret Williamson, '"He Was Good with the Bairns": Fatherhood in an Ironstone Mining Community, 1918–1960', *North East History* 32 (1998), pp. 87–108.

[7] On the complexity of individual fatherhood, see Julie-Marie Strange, *Fatherhood and the British Working Class, 1865–1914* (Cambridge, forthcoming 2014), ch.1.

[8] On generational change, also see Simon Szreter and Kate Fisher, *Sex before the Sexual Revolution: Intimate Life in England 1918–1963* (Cambridge, 2010), p. 204.

[9] Charlie Lewis, *Becoming a Father* (Milton Keynes, 1986), p. 5.

[10] Robert L. Griswold, 'Introduction to the Special Issue on Fatherhood', *Journal of Family History* 24:3 (1999), p. 251.

within an individual's identity.[11] This book examines a period of political, economic, social, and cultural upheaval; what the family looked like in this period changed in the wake of a decreasing birth rate and the rise of the smaller family across all social groups.[12] Furthermore, the growing significance of a truly national culture shifted the way in which individuals negotiated norms and ideals within the context of their own family life, and this was a culture increasingly dominated by newly popular psychological ways of seeing the world and the family within it. The dramatic political and economic events of the period, most notably two world wars and the interwar economic depression, also had significant consequences for fatherhood, often in very tangible ways, such as unemployment or the splitting up of families through conscription and evacuation, but also in their reconfiguring of gender roles and ideas about identity.

THE HISTORIOGRAPHICAL LANDSCAPE

A growing literature exploring fatherhood in Britain in the nineteenth century and earlier, as well as in other national contexts such as the USA, demonstrates that this is a fruitful and significant area of history.[13] Sociologists have also researched fatherhood and family life much more extensively since the 1980s.[14] Yet only a small handful of historians have started to examine fatherhood in the twentieth century. Tim Fisher's unpublished thesis explores working-class fatherhood in early twentieth-century Britain.[15] Lynn Abrams and Margaret Williamson have

[11] On the growing dominance of motherhood as part of femininity, see Carolyn Steedman, *Landscape for a Good Woman: A Story of Two Lives* (London, 1986), p. 118.

[12] See Davidoff et al., *The Family Story*, p. 18; Diana Gittins, *Fair Sex: Family Size and Structure 1900–1939* (London, 1982).

[13] Joanne Bailey, '"A Very Sensible Man": Imagining Fatherhood in England c.1750–1830', *History* 95:319 (2010), pp. 267–92; Trev Lynn Broughton and Helen Rogers (eds), *Gender and Fatherhood in the Nineteenth Century* (Basingstoke, 2007); Davidoff et al., *The Family Story*; Megan Doolittle, 'Missing Fathers: Assembling a History of Fatherhood in Mid-Nineteenth Century England', PhD Thesis (University of Essex, 1996); Eleanor Gordon and Gwyneth Nair, 'Domestic Fathers and the Victorian Parental Role', *Women's History Review* 15:4 (2006), pp. 551–9; Claudia Nelson, *Invisible Men: Fatherhood in Victorian Periodicals, 1850–1910* (Athens, GA, and London, 1995); John Tosh, *A Man's Place: Masculinity and the Middle-Class Home in Victorian England* (New Haven, CT, and London, 1999). On fatherhood in American history, see Stella Bruzzi, *Bringing Up Daddy: Fatherhood and Masculinity in Post-War Hollywood* (London, 2005); LaRossa, *The Modernization*; Judith Walzer Leavitt, *Make Room for Daddy: The Journey from Waiting Room to Birthing Room* (Chapel Hill, NC, 2009). Many European countries remained similarly underexplored in this sense, but some historians are starting to address this, particularly focusing on the connections between citizenship, politics, and fatherhood. See Kristen Stromberg Childers, *Fathers, Families, and the State in France, 1914–1945* (Ithaca, NY and London, 2003); Till van Rahden, 'Fatherhood, Rechristianization, and the Quest for Democracy in Postwar Germany', in D. Schumann (ed.), *Raising Citizens in 'the Century of the Child': The United States and German Central Europe in Comparative Perspective* (New York, 2010), pp. 141–64.

[14] For example, Burghes, Clarke, and Cronin, *Fathers*; Brian Jackson, Fatherhood (London, 1984); Lewis, *Becoming a Father*; Lorna McKee and Margaret O'Brien (eds), *The Father Figure* (London, 1982); Moss (ed.), *Father Figures*.

[15] Fisher, 'Fatherhood and the Experience'; Tim Fisher, 'Fatherhood and the British Fathercraft Movement, 1919–1939', *Gender and History* 17:2 (2005), pp. 441–62.

employed oral history methodology to examine fatherhood in the twentieth century, in Scotland and the north-east respectively.[16] These glimpses into certain communities and sections of the population start to demonstrate that the history of fatherhood is largely an untold story and deserves more sustained attention. Fathers appear in more general histories of family life.[17] Yet the idea that there are gendered, separate spheres for men and women is still powerful and means that fathers are not usually treated as individual historical actors in histories of family life.[18] In the period in question here, a focus on the intensification of motherhood has also limited the attention paid to fathers as parents and the critical assessment of all family members. Furthermore, a focus on the process of male domestication, which can conflate men's roles as husbands and fathers and their relationship with the home, has meant fatherhood as a specific experience has been marginalized in the historical literature. This book suggests that we must examine fatherhood as separate from roles and relationships associated with being a husband, as involving more than just a potential capacity for domestic labour, and finally, as an identity, a nexus of relationships, and as a position within the family as well as a role to be fulfilled.[19] It uses the concept of a 'family-orientated masculinity' to recognize a more active fatherhood in this period alongside the strong gendered division of labour that remained intact.[20] Fatherhood here is understood to be a social construct based around biological paternity and is defined widely to encompass men who did or could fulfil this parenting position within children's lives.

Any study of fatherhood must also be concerned with masculinity to at least some extent.[21] From a twenty-first-century perspective, there remained a strong gendered differentiation in terms of male and female roles within and outside the home throughout the period in question, with more dramatic change occurring only from the 1960s and 1970s onwards.[22] Yet the twentieth century cannot be viewed as a simple progression towards the convergence of the sexes, or gender equality. Gender identities can and did shift even when the distinction between them remained strong, certainly in terms of parenting and the family. Whilst gender remains a crucial category of analysis for the family in particular,[23] focusing

[16] Abrams, 'There Was Nobody'; Williamson, 'He Was Good'.

[17] For example, David Kynaston, *Family Britain, 1951–1957* (London, 2009), pp. 595–7; Roberts, *Women and Families*, pp. 154–7.

[18] On separate spheres, see Tosh, *A Man's Place*, pp. 2–3; Amanda Vickery, 'Golden Age to Separate Spheres? A Review of the Categories and Chronology of English Women's History', *Historical Journal* 36:2 (1993), pp. 383–414.

[19] On considering emotions, authority and identity, see Joanne Bailey, 'Masculinity and Fatherhood in England c.1760–1830', in Arnold and Brady, *What Is Masculinity?*, p. 168.

[20] Laura King, 'Hidden Fathers? The Significance of Fatherhood in Mid-Twentieth-Century Britain', *Contemporary British History*, 26:1 (2012), p. 27; Laura King, '"Now You See a Great Many Men Pushing Their Pram Proudly": Family-Orientated Masculinity Represented and Experienced in Mid-Twentieth-Century Britain', *Cultural and Social History* 10:4 (2013), p. 600.

[21] On gender, identity and parenting, see Bailey, *Parenting*, pp. 10–11.

[22] Judy Giles, *Women, Identity and Private Life in Britain, 1900–1950* (Basingstoke, 1995), pp. 7–8; Roberts, *Women and Families*, p. 40; Lynne Segal, *Slow Motion: Changing Masculinities, Changing Men* (3rd edn, Basingstoke, 2007), p. 4; Szreter and Fisher, *Sex*, pp. 202–11.

[23] Joan W. Scott, 'Gender: A Useful Category for Historical Analysis', *American Historical Review* 91:5 (1986), pp. 1053–75.

too exclusively on the convergence or divergence of men and women's roles and identities can obscure change elsewhere. As John Arnold and Sean Brady high-light, ideas about masculinity and men were as frequently configured relationally between men as between men and women.[24] It became increasingly possible in this period for men to embrace fatherhood as a means to become more involved family members without challenging their masculinity.

From the First World War to the end of the 1950s, the intensified focus on fatherhood, in public debates and in individual attitudes, was connected to an increased emphasis on the family as an independent social unit. The family was in this period increasingly constructed as self-sufficient, capable of fulfilling the emotional, physical, and social needs of family members.[25] This changing notion of the family was linked to the increased prominence of 'companionate marriage' as an ideal. The importance of this concept within public discussion and to indi-viduals at the time, from various social backgrounds, has been widely debated.[26] It is argued here that there was a substantial emphasis on complementary and equal roles between mothers/wives and fathers/husbands, in evidence from popu-lar culture and individual attitudes. Another important context is the decreasing average family size in this period, as the decline in birth rate spread to families of all social classes.[27] Indeed, the family functioned as an independent social unit in its leisure time most readily if it was limited to a certain size, and in turn, the potential companionship between wife and husband both encouraged this close-ness and was encouraged by a smaller family.

Angela Davis, Simon Szreter, and Kate Fisher have argued that there was a more uniform experience of family life after the Second World War.[28] An important

---

[24] Arnold and Brady, 'Introduction', p. 3.

[25] Davidoff et al., *The Family Story*, p. 18; Giles, *Women*, p. 68; Gittins, *Fair Sex*, pp. 52–9; Kynaston, *Family Britain*, p. 582. Also see Claire Langhamer, 'The Meanings of Home in Postwar Britain', *Journal of Contemporary History* 40:2 (2005), pp. 341–62; Mathew Thomson, *Lost Freedom: The Landscape of the Child and the British Post-War Settlement* (Oxford, 2013), pp. 1–2. In the American context, see Elaine Tyler May, *Homeward Bound: American Families in the Cold War Era* (2nd edn, New York, 1999), esp. p. xxii.

[26] Historians have disagreed on the consequences and impact of this ideology. See Bingham, *Gender*, p. 237; Collins, *Modern Love*; Davidoff et al., *The Family Story*, p. 190; Angela Davis, 'A Critical Perspective on British Social Surveys and Community Studies and Their Accounts of Married Life c.1945–1970', *Cultural and Social History* 6:1 (2009), pp. 47–64; Janet Finch and Penny Summerfield, 'Social Reconstruction and the Emergence of Companionate Marriage, 1945–59', in D. Clark (ed.), *Marriage, Domestic Life and Social Change* (London, 1991), p. 7; Lesley Hall, *Sex, Gender and Social Change in Britain since 1880* (Basingstoke, 2000), pp. 150–1; Alison Light, *Forever England: Femininity, Literature and Conservatism between the Wars* (London, 1991), p. 18; Penny Summerfield, 'Approaches to Women and Social Change in the Second World War', in B. Brivati and H. Jones (eds), *What Difference Did the War Make?* (Leicester, 1993), p. 77; Szreter and Fisher, *Sex*, ch. 5.

[27] Gittins, *Fair Sex*, pp. 9, 19; Simon Szreter, *Fertility, Class and Gender in Britain, 1860–1940* (Cambridge, 1996); Szreter and Fisher, *Sex*, e.g. p. 28; Richard and Kathleen Titmuss, *Parents Revolt: A Study of the Declining Birth-rate in Acquisitive Societies* (London, 1942), pp. 9, 28.

[28] Davis, 'A Critical Perspective', p. 54; Szreter and Fisher, *Sex*, p. 29. Also see Ronald Fletcher, *Britain in the Sixties: The Family and Marriage: An Analysis and Moral Assessment* (Harmondsworth, 1962), p. 127; Geoffrey Gorer, *Exploring English Character* (London, 1955), pp. 297, 303; Richard Hoggart [1957], *The Uses of Literacy: Aspects of Working-Class Life with Special Reference to Publications*

dimension to this debate about changes to class is the notion that working-class culture underwent a process of 'embourgeoisement'. As Diana Gittins has pointed out, this period was not one of a simplistic emulation of middle-class ideals on the part of working-class communities.[29] As Jon Lawrence notes, in everyday usage class was a mutable and 'fuzzy' concept.[30] Yet in terms of family life, as John Goldthorpe et al. argued, a process of 'normative convergence' between different class groups took place, particularly in the wake of the Second World War.[31] The relationship between different class communities and class values was complex, and we should be mindful of the importance of the exchange of ideas between different classes, the overlapping and fluid nature of class identities, and the significance of middle- and upper-class control of cultural and social institutions, such as the press, and therefore the shaping of popular debate.[32] As Claire Langhamer notes, post-Second World War social conditions, and increased affluence for working-class communities particularly, allowed for a greater flourishing of ideas around mutuality, love, and domesticity that had their roots in the inter-war period.[33] Ideals of family life more common in middle-class culture became important to working-class individuals because of social conditions rather than a desire to become middle-class per se, even if the practices of love and courtship still varied according to the class of the individuals involved.[34] In this sense, the concept of class has two important, distinct, though interrelated dimensions to it: the economic and social conditions particular or common to a class group, but also the more self-conscious identity that could be associated with that group.

The First World War represents a significant moment marking the beginnings of substantial social change, relating to gender roles particularly,[35] and the starting point of a more wholeheartedly national British culture.[36] The study ends in 1960, as though there were deep continuities beyond the 1950s, the 1960s witnessed the start of a new period of social change, relating to ideas about child welfare and a questioning of the family,[37] and the start of a more wholeheartedly consumerist

and Entertainments (Harmondsworth, 1971), p. 342; Peter Willmott and Michael Young, *Family and Class in a London Suburb* (London, 1960), p. 122.

[29] Gittins, *Fair Sex*, pp. 18–19, 176.

[30] Jon Lawrence, 'Class, "Affluence" and the Study of Everyday Life in Britain, c.1930–64', *Cultural and Social History* 10:2 (2013), p. 275.

[31] John H. Goldthorpe, David Lockwood, Frank Bechhofer, and Jennifer Platt [1968], *The Affluent Worker in the Class Structure* (Cambridge, 1969), p. 163.

[32] Alston, indeed, highlights the power of children's literature in spreading middle-class ideals. Ann Alston, *The Family in English Children's Literature* (London and New York, 2008), p. 3.

[33] Claire Langhamer, 'Love and Courtship in Mid-Twentieth-Century England', *Historical Journal* 50:1 (2007), p. 179.

[34] Langhamer, 'Love', p. 184.

[35] Bingham, *Gender*, p. 2; Joanna Bourke, *Dismembering the Male: Men's Bodies, Britain and the Great War* (London, 1996), p. 13; Light, *Forever England*, e.g. p. 8; Roper, 'Between Manliness', p. 345; Elaine Showalter, 'Rivers and Sassoon: The Inscription of Male Gender Anxieties', in M. R. Higonnet, J. Jenson, S. Michel, and M. Collins (eds), *Behind the Lines: Gender and the Two World Wars* (New Haven, CT and London, 1987), pp. 61–9.

[36] Bingham, *Gender*, p. 2; Colin Seymour-Ure, *The British Press and Broadcasting since 1945* (2nd edn, Oxford, 1996), p. 16.

[37] Harry Hendrick, *Child Welfare: England 1872–1989* (London, 1994), pp. 242–4.

and permissive society.[38] As Szreter and Fisher note, this period also witnessed substantial change in intergenerational relations.[39] *Family Men* focuses on Great Britain, recognizing the important cultural, social, and legal differences between the countries of Britain. The use of Britain as a geographical entity and the subject of this study reflects an approach to understanding locality and national culture as of equal importance. Where significant, differences between these countries are recognized, but what becomes apparent within this study is that local and community-based variations in attitudes and behaviour are and were equally, if not more, important than the cultural differences between England, Scotland, and Wales. Indeed, as Abrams highlights, experiences of fatherhood and family life were 'broadly similar' in Scotland and other parts of Britain.[40] Throughout this book, examples of experience are drawn from across Britain. It is not suggested that the few hundred individual accounts and tens of surveys used here amount to a complete national picture of fatherhood; rather, that complex patterns of similarity and difference have emerged from these accounts. More research into how individual behaviours in fatherhood and family life vary across different groups is clearly needed for a fuller understanding of changing patterns of fatherhood and family life.

SOURCES AND METHODOLOGY

Combining the approaches and methods of cultural history with those of social history can result in a more comprehensive historical analysis of masculinities and femininities. As Frank Mort has argued, historians must acknowledge historical space for 'an account of the interiority of selfhood' and realize that valuable historical insights can be found in the 'gap between the social and psychic'.[41] Karen Harvey and Alexandra Shepard suggest in their survey of the historiography of masculinity that historians cannot simply research and analyse 'free-floating attributes'; they need to explore the 'grounded social and psychic contexts of experience', which are involved in a two-way interactive relationship with 'representations'.[42] In John Tosh's words, there is a need to rehabilitate older approaches to the social history of men and masculinity alongside 'questions of meaning and representation'.[43] As Joanne Bailey suggests, exploring a near universal experience, such as parenting, and using a large range of source types can result in a

---

[38] Jonathon Green, *All Dressed Up: The Sixties and the Counterculture* (London, 1999), p. 68.

[39] Szreter and Fisher, *Sex*, p. 29.   [40] Abrams, 'There Was Nobody', p. 219.

[41] Frank Mort, 'Social and Symbolic Fathers and Sons in Postwar Britain', *Journal of British Studies* 38:3 (1999), pp. 375, 383. On the importance of emotion in history, also see Roper, 'Slipping', pp. 57–72.

[42] Karen Harvey and Alexandra Shepard, 'What Have Historians Done with Masculinity? Reflections on Five Centuries of British History, circa 1500–1950', *Journal of British Studies* 44 (2005), p. 280.

[43] John Tosh, 'The History of Masculinity: An Outdated Concept?', in Arnold and Brady (eds), *What is Masculinity?*, p. 18.

more careful socio-cultural history, which gives due attention to material experience and individuals interiority.[44] In this sense, this book follows the approach of Arnold and Brady and Bailey, who highlight that discourse and reality are in a 'mutually constitutive' relationship and cannot be placed in dichotomy.[45] *Family Men* explores the relationship between ideals and individuals, and as such offers insights into the nature of this relationship as well as a social and cultural history of fatherhood in this period.

The sources selected, therefore, are diverse, to enable us to analyse cultural ideals, individual attitudes and lived experience, and the intertwined and inseparable relationships between them. Newspapers are drawn upon heavily as a rich and diverse source material, reflecting and contributing to the construction of ideals relating to the family.[46] The digital archives of five newspapers have been extensively researched: the *Daily Express, Daily Mirror, Manchester Guardian, Observer,* and *Times,* alongside a selection of magazines.[47] Four very broad keyword searches were used to research these newspapers between 1914 and 1959, yielding over 80,000 articles. These were sorted, and around 1,700 articles of relevance were identified and analysed. Over 100 magazine articles supplement this. This mass of material is of course very varied, and all types of newspaper content have been considered here, from cartoons and photographs, through court reports and opinion pieces, to advertising. Due to this, newspapers are considered here as a collection of (often contradictory) content, rather than a cohesive whole. Likewise, it is recognized that motivations for reading newspapers were also varied, as indeed was what readers actually read.[48]

From the First World War to the end of the 1950s, nearly everyone in Britain spent some time reading newspapers; by 1939, two thirds of adults saw a daily paper.[49] Between 1920 and 1939, the total circulation of the national dailies rose from 5.4 million to 10.6.[50] The circulation of national daily newspapers overtook that of the provincials near the start of this period, and peaked in 1957, at 16.71 million.[51] The *Daily Mirror* and *Daily Express* led the field in

---

[44] Bailey, *Parenting*, p. 7.

[45] Arnold and Brady, 'Introduction', p. 4; Bailey, *Parenting*, p. 8.

[46] On the importance of the press, see Adrian Bingham, *Family Newspapers? Sex, Private Life, and the British Popular Press 1918–1978* (Oxford, 2009), pp. 1–10, 15–28; Bingham, *Gender*, pp. 8–12.

[47] Due to practical restrictions, the *Daily Express* was used less extensively than the other four newspapers. Two non-consecutive months from each year within the forty-six-year period were searched in the same ways as other newspapers. The *Daily Mirror, Manchester Guardian, Observer* and *The Times* were searched throughout the whole period, from 1 January 1914 to 31 December 1959. To supplement this, the online cartoon archive (www.cartoons.ac.uk) was used.

[48] See, for example, Mass-Observation's reports on newspaper reading. Mass-Observation File Report A.11, 'Motives and Methods of Newspaper Reading' (December 1938); Mass-Observation File Report 2557, 'Attitudes to Daily Newspapers' (January 1948); Mass-Observation File Report 3063, 'Report on Newspaper Reading, 1947–1948' (November 1949).

[49] T. Cauter and J. S. Downham, *The Communication of Ideas: A Study of Contemporary Influences on Urban Life* (London, 1954), p. 170; Bingham, *Family Newspapers?*, p. 16.

[50] James Curran and Jean Seaton, *Power without Responsibility: The Press, Broadcasting and New Media in Britain* (6th edn, London, 2003), p. 40.

[51] Seymour-Ure, *The British Press*, pp. 16–18.

circulation terms, and alongside the more elite *Manchester Guardian, Observer,* and *Times* constitute a good cross-section of the British press in these decades.[52] The magazines *Lilliput, The Listener,* and *Men Only* offer examples of construc- tions of fatherhood for and by particular sections of the population: *Lilliput* and *Men Only* have been researched for their predominantly male readership;[53] *The Listener* for its insight into the culture of the BBC (as archived programmes are rare). These five newspapers, as well as the magazines, reached a very sig- nificant proportion of the British reading public in this period, across all social backgrounds.

Whilst it is difficult to find evidence relating to the production and reception of particular features or themes, the desire to sell copy and attract advertisers meant that editors and journalists had an inherent motivation to accord with popular ideals. Indeed, a Mass-Observation report of 1940 went as far as to suggest they were by and large the most important influence in terms of forming opinions.[54] The targeting of most sections of the population, furthermore, meant that ideals of fatherhood had to be largely uncontroversial and accepted. The daily presence of the newspaper in the family home contributed to this sense of normal father- hood and masculinity being presented, and the cumulative effect of its content is part of its power and influence.[55] There are limits to what newspapers can tell us; it is very difficult to ascertain exactly what place the cultural norms espoused in the press played in readers' lives. In pursuing what was newsworthy and of interest to readers, their content was focused more on social and cultural change, and the novelty of new models of fatherhood and masculinity. Hence, attention is paid here to the ideas against which articles positioned themselves, and the construc- tion of a particular sense of past and present to establish precisely how ideas about fatherhood were (or were not) shifting.

A number of other sources reflecting public debates are used here, including a small number of topical and popular films and novels, advice literature for parents, and government papers. The cinema was a particularly popular medium until the 1950s, with attendance peaking at twenty-eight visits per individ- ual per year in 1950.[56] Again, like films, novels both reflect and shape certain social norms, yet as Joseph McAleer argues, the fiction of this period tended to reinforce predominant stereotypes and ideals rather than impose new ones.[57] Children's literature in particular is utilized here as a way of fruitfully exploring

[52] For precise information about individual newspapers' circulations, see Seymour-Ure, *The British Press*, pp. 26–31.

[53] As Greenfield, O'Connell, and Reid note, *Men Only* is historically significant due to its success in this period; they note that the Hulton Readership Survey estimated its readership at 1,950,000 in 1947. Jill Greenfield, Sean O'Connell, and Chris Reid, 'Fashioning Masculinity: Men Only, Consumption and the Development of Marketing in the 1930s', *Twentieth Century British History* 10:4 (1999), pp. 459, 464.

[54] Mass-Observation File Report 126, 'Report on the Press' (May 1940), p. 5.3.

[55] Bingham, *Family Newspapers?*, p. 8.

[56] Ross McKibbin, *Classes and Cultures: England 1918–1951* (Oxford, 1998), p. 419.

[57] Joseph McAleer, *Popular Reading and Publishing in Britain, 1914–1950* (Oxford, 1992), p. 251. On the relationship between fiction and reality, also see Light, *Forever England*, e.g. p. 2.

ideas around fatherhood.[58] Advice literature aimed at parents has again been selected on the basis of its popularity; the most widely read pamphlets, books, and radio programmes by the most popular authors, such as Frederick Truby King, Winnicott, and Spock have been studied. As Denise Riley notes, analysing the process of 'popularization' is crucial, and the ways in which childcare 'experts' were presented in the press is discussed as well as the content of advice texts themselves.[59] Political and legal debates form a final context here; as well as using newspapers' coverage of political debates around parenting and family life, Hansard and cabinet documents have been used to provide further evidence of political conceptions of fatherhood, and two legal histories of this time have been examined for details on the laws relating to parenting in this period.[60]

Whilst newspapers predominantly provide a flavour of public debates about family life and fatherhood, archived interviews and contemporary social research provide evidence about individual families. The strength of these two source types lies in their use in combination: interviews are rich in relevant information and give space to an individual's voice (albeit through the mediating influence of the interviewer), whilst social research relates to greater numbers of individuals, usually focuses on a community, and can give a sense of the interaction between social, work and cultural networks. In terms of selection, this book uses evidence from the major publications on the family and related subjects, by sociologists, anthropologists, psychologists, psychoanalysts, and other experts, published between the First World War and the 1960s. Most of these studies were conducted after the Second World War, when an explosion of publishing on the family occurred. Earlier studies rarely focused on the family, but many, such as those examining unemployment, contained insights into family life. As has been noted since, the post-Second World War years in particular witnessed an optimism about the state of society which came through in social research of the time.[61] It has been suggested, not least by the researchers themselves, that the extent of change was at times exaggerated.[62] Indeed, as Martin Bulmer, Kevin Bales, and Kathryn Sklar note, the social survey has been strongly associated with social reform, and only became closely linked to academia after 1940.[63] Furthermore, social researchers were by nature interested in changes in contemporary society;

---

[58] In selecting popular and relevant children's books, Alston, *The Family*, has been particularly helpful.

[59] Denise Riley, *War in the Nursery: Theories of the Child and Mother* (London, 1983), p. 85. Furthermore, as Thane notes, we should not over-exaggerate the effect of these ideas. Pat Thane, 'Unmarried Motherhood in Twentieth-Century England', *Women's History Review* 20:1 (2011), p. 22.

[60] P. M. Bromley [1957], *Family Law* (London, 1962); Ronald Harry Graveson and Francis Roger Crane (eds), *A Century of Family Law, 1857–1957* (London, 1957).

[61] Davis, 'A Critical Perspective', pp. 48–9.

[62] Davis, 'A Critical Perspective', p. 51; Finch and Summerfield, 'Social Reconstruction', p. 15; Michael Young, interviewed by P. Thompson, 'Reflections on Researching Family and Kinship in East London', *International Journal of Social Research Methodology* 7:1 (2004), pp. 36,43.

[63] Martin Bulmer, Kevin Bales, and Kathryn Kish Sklar, 'The Social Survey in Historical Perspective', in M. Bulmer, K. Bales, and K. K. Sklar (eds), *The Social Survey in Historical Perspective, 1880–1940* (Cambridge, 1991), p. 3. Also, Davis, 'A Critical Perspective', p. 50.

like the press, the emphasis remains on what is new. However, by examining a wide range of research, from a broad variety of disciplinary perspectives and both academic and non-academic backgrounds, many useful insights can be obtained into predominant cultural attitudes as well as evidence about what families were doing. This literature can also deepen our understanding of the academic and popular debates relating to the family, as demonstrated in the work of Finch and Summerfield and of Davis.[64]

Six oral history collections have been used in conjunction with this published material. Three of these were conducted by Elizabeth Roberts, later joined by Lucinda McCray Beier, and involve men and women from Lancashire. Two such collections relate to the period 1890–1940 and were conducted in the 1970s, and the final collection relates to the period 1940–1970 and was undertaken in the 1980s.[65] Complementing this is a collection of interviews conducted for the '100 Families' sociological project led by Harold Newby and Paul Thompson in the 1980s; again, men and women were interviewed about family life stretching back to the start of the twentieth century.[66] Two further collections of interviews conducted by Steve Humphries for BBC series entitled 'A Labour of Love' and 'A Man's World' broadcast in the 1990s complete this selection. The first is held at the British Film Institute Archive, containing interviews conducted to explore the topic of masculinity between 1900 and 1960, and the second is held at the British Library and focuses on parenting from 1900 to 1950.[67]

These six collections together amount to hundreds of oral history interviews. First, the interviewees were sorted, and a small number of Humphries' interviews were discounted because only very limited biographical information could be located. Throughout all collections, the interviews that included at least some discussion of participants' fathers, husbands, or themselves as fathers were used. This resulted in 283 interviewees' testimonies researched here, together with accounts in published collections of oral history interviews, representing the perspectives of children, mothers, and fathers. Indeed, many of the interviewees reflected on their family lives as both children and parents. Interviewees were born between 1884 and 1954, with a fairly even spread throughout the period. Throughout this book, the interviewees' names, pseudonyms, or code names have been used as presented in the archive for clarity. Full names are used for the Humphries and 100 Families collections, and for Roberts' interviewees their code names are used, denoting

---

[64] Davis, 'A Critical Perspective', pp. 47–64; Finch and Summerfield, 'Social Reconstruction', pp. 7–32.

[65] For additional information about these interviews and detailed information about individual interviewees, see E. Roberts, *A Woman's Place: An Oral History of Working-Class Women, 1890–1940* (Oxford, 1984), pp. 207–13; Roberts, *Women and Families*, pp. 240–8.

[66] More information about this study and the participants can be accessed at http://discover.ukdataservice.ac.uk/catalogue?sn=4938 (accessed 30 August 2013).

[67] Where transcripts were missing or incomplete, or unable to be used for other reasons, the two books published out of these projects have also been used. Steve Humphries and Pamela Gordon, *A Labour of Love: The Experience of Parenthood in Britain, 1900–1950* (London, 1993); Steve Humphries and Pamela Gordon, *A Man's World: From Boyhood to Manhood, 1900–1960* (London, 1996).

their location.[68] Where possible, the proportion of interviews containing a partic-ular theme is given in the analysis, yet for the most part, any kind of quantitative analysis is inappropriate. The value of these interviews lies in qualitative analysis of the deep, reflective narratives of family memories around feelings, personal stories, and identities. Furthermore, the interviewees do not provide a representa-tive sample; the use of Roberts' interviews means there is an overrepresentation of what were understood to be 'respectable' working-class families. Nevertheless, the use of six collections of interviews conducted by three different research teams allows for a more in-depth understanding, as the structure, format, and research questions of each collection as well as the content of interviewees' narratives can be compared across collections.

None of these sources, of course, provides unmediated access to the lives of individuals. Archived interviews provide problematic evidence, and have been criticized because of issues of representativeness and reliability. Yet they are, however, valuable in writing the history of the family; as Thompson has noted, oral history has had 'a transforming impact' in this sense.[69] April Gallwey has emphasized the untapped potential of using archived interviews.[70] Some have taken the view that oral history is 'tainted' with modern attitudes and issues of memory: this must be remembered when using such source materials. However, as Szreter and Fisher argue, this 'dialogue with the present' can be a productive means of exploring the past.[71] Indeed, discussions of fatherhood are frequently couched in historically relative terms, on the collective level relating to ideas about family life and social change, and on an individual level across different generations of the same family. As such, the interview format, where chronolog-ical reflection is explicit, allows for a more nuanced understanding of attitudes and behaviour as they change over time. As Davis notes, it is the particular nature of the interview which invites an in-depth reflective approach to life experience, and aspects of the interview's flow, such as silences and contradictions within it, can be revealing. Interviews in this way are particularly valuable in terms of ana-lysing individual subjectivity.[72] The depth of the oral history interviews alongside the breadth provided by social research thus allows a fuller understanding of social experience.

To enhance the analysis of family life in this period, some materials have been used to supplement social research and oral history interviews. These in particular have been chosen to try to access the perspectives of fathers at the time they were parenting young children. These include a small selection of let-ters and autobiographies, including letters to Marie Stopes held at the British

---

[68] In a code name, such as Mrs B1P, the final letter denotes location: P=Preston, B=Barrow, and L=Lancaster.

[69] Paul Thompson, *The Voice of the Past* (3rd edn, Oxford, 2000), p. 8.

[70] April Gallwey, 'The Rewards of Using Archived Oral Histories in Research: The Case of the Millennium Memory Bank', *Oral History* 41:1 (2013), pp. 37–50.

[71] Szreter and Fisher, *Sex*, pp. 11–13.

[72] Angela Davis, *Modern Motherhood: Women and Family in England, 1945–2000* (Manchester, 2012), pp. 6–7.

Library and twenty collections of personal letters between fathers and families at the Imperial War Museum. As Michael Roper's work demonstrates, such letters can be invaluable in terms of understanding the emotions of family life.[73] Autobiographies, meanwhile, provide some limited testimony about family life, particularly in parts of the country not covered by social research sources.[74] This study also draws upon the research outputs of Mass-Observation, helpful particularly in gauging the reception of public debates about family life in the press, novels, and films.[75]

This wide range of source types allows for the building of a picture of fatherhood in twentieth-century Britain. The nature of the sources has led to a focus on change more than continuity, and on happier experiences more than those relating to abuse or difficult relationships or men who did not enjoy fatherhood. This is because discussions in popular culture at this time tended to focus on positive change, because social researchers sought to study what was new, and because family members were eager to talk about the happy parts of their lives. There are exceptions to this, notably the court reporting of violence and abuse in the press, and sons, daughters, and wives who highlighted that husbands and fathers made their lives difficult. Furthermore, the sources limit us to a focus on certain individuals and groups. Notably, there is an underrepresentation of ethnic minority groups within the interview collections, and so it would be inappropriate to employ this as a category of analysis here. Themes such as religion in family life and the gendered differences between the upbringings of boys and girls are also important and warrant more research.[76] Likewise, studies are needed that focus more primarily on fatherhood through the prism of class identity and regional difference, and which examine the material culture of family life or analyse this history from the perspectives of emotions, to name but a few. These are areas in which there is not enough sustained discussion in the source materials used here or which lie beyond the parameters of this study. This book, or any one study, can never present a full picture of fatherhood in these years; instead it is an examination of predominant constructions of fatherhood by public commentators and by individuals, and an analysis of the ways in which some fathers lived their lives and the meanings they gave to their actions. *Family Men* should stand as the first of many studies charting the history of fatherhood in twentieth-century Britain.

---

[73] See particularly Michael Roper, *The Secret Battle: Emotional Survival in the Great War* (Manchester, 2009).

[74] On autobiography as a historical source, see Jonathan Rose, *The Intellectual Life of the British Working Classes* (New Haven, CT, and London, 2001), pp. 1–3.

[75] On the use of Mass-Observation as a source material for historians, and the history of the organization, see Angus Calder, 'Mass-Observation 1937–1949', in M. Bulmer (ed.), *Essays on the History of British Sociological Research* (Cambridge, 1985), pp. 121–36; Nick Hubble, *Mass-Observation and Everyday Life: Culture, History, Theory* (Basingstoke, 2006); Penny Summerfield, 'Mass-Observation: Social Research or Social Movement?', *Journal of Contemporary History* 20:3 (1985), pp. 439–52.

[76] On religion and masculinity, see L. Delap and S. Morgan (eds), *Men, Masculinities and Religious Change in Twentieth-Century Britain* (Basingstoke, 2013).

SUMMARY

This book charts the changing nature of fatherhood across nearly half a century, exploring popular culture and the lives of individual families. It argues that whilst the fundamental tenets of a father's duties remained constant throughout these years and beyond, there was an increased emphasis on the significance of the father–child relationship from the interwar period. This shift was instigated by new psychological ideas about childhood and parenting, the circumstances of the Second World War, and the rising living standards of many families. The father was increasingly positioned at the heart of the family, and the identity of 'the family man' was celebrated and accepted to a much greater degree following the Second World War. A new emphasis on equal and democratic relationships between family members and a belief in the ability of the nuclear family unit to meet the emotional, psychological, recreational, and physical needs of its members shaped and was reinforced by this updated version of fatherhood. The current focus on motherhood in the twentieth century, alongside the tendency to view childcare as constituted by labour rather than a combination of labour and leisure, has obscured the substantial changes that fatherhood underwent in this period. The book examines the relationship between cultural norms and ideals, and the attitudes and experiences of family members, and suggests that this period also witnessed the growth of an increasingly prescriptive national culture. This in turn had important effects on family life, as the norms and ideals suggested by cultural authorities such as the press began to have a greater influence on the behaviour and attitudes of individuals.

Following this introduction, Chapters 2 and 3 analyse fathers' roles, in terms of breadwinning and provision, as well as within family life, including entertaining, disciplining and guiding children, and helping mothers. These two chapters together focus on expectations about men's behaviour, attitudes to this role, and evidence of what men did in terms of their parenting responsibilities. The three chapters following this consider the emotions, authority, and identity that fatherhood entailed. Chapter 4 explores relationships between men and their offspring, and examines the negative and positive emotions that were understood to be part of this relationship. Chapter 5 analyses fatherhood as a position of authority, and how men's position in the family was understood in popular cultural debate and in the practices of family life. Finally, Chapter 6 investigates fatherhood as an identity, the complex relationship between fathering and masculinity, and how being a parent could both challenge and provide a sense of manliness. Throughout this book, the wide selection of source types are used together, to reflect the inseparable relationship between cultural values and lived experience.[77] This study explores the two together to examine whether the two are aligned or otherwise, and moments of misalignment are recognized and examined in each chapter. In doing so, *Family Men* provides a full and complex study of fatherhood from the First World War to the 1950s in Britain.

---

[77] Bailey, *Parenting*, p. 14.

2

'Brought Me Anything, Dad?'
The Father as Provider

For most of the nineteenth and twentieth centuries, the fundamental tenets of a father's role remained largely constant, in both prescription and practice, centring on breadwinning, entertaining children, disciplining and guiding children's characters, and helping mother. Breadwinning formed the core of fatherhood, but as Megan Doolittle, Julie-Marie Strange, John Tosh, and others have shown, fathers also disciplined children, played with them, spent time educating them, and even nursed them.[1] Yet as Claudia Nelson has demonstrated, in the late nineteenth century fathers were, to an extent, marginalized in representation, even if they continued to fulfil and enjoy these roles.[2] As Strange has shown, family members frequently imbued breadwinning with 'affective significance'.[3] While Tosh's suggestion of a 'flight from domesticity' in these decades has been met with some disagreement, it is perhaps less controversial to suggest that, at least in public discourses, the father's role was minimized.[4] By the interwar period, in contrast, fatherhood was increasingly discussed in popular culture.

The father's role still centred on the four core elements of providing, entertaining, guiding and disciplining, and helping mothers. Yet, as Joanna Bourke argues, it is important to move away from a portrayal of the male breadwinner as an unvarying figure against which the married woman struggled.[5] This

[1] Megan Doolittle, 'Missing Fathers: Assembling a History of Fatherhood in Mid-Nineteenth Century England', PhD Thesis (University of Essex, 1996), esp. pp. 172–225; Eleanor Gordon and Gwyneth Nair, 'Domestic Fathers and the Victorian Parental Role', *Women's History Review* 15:4 (2006), pp. 551–9; Trevor Lummis, 'The Historical Dimension of Fatherhood: A Case Study 1890–1914', in L. McKee and M. O'Brien (eds), *The Father Figure* (London, 1982), pp. 43–56; Valerie Sanders, '"What Do You Want to Know about Next?" Charles Kingsley's Model of Educational Fatherhood', in T. L. Broughton and H. Rogers (eds), *Gender and Fatherhood in the Nineteenth Century* (Basingstoke, 2007), pp. 55–67; Julie-Marie Strange, 'Fatherhood, Providing, and Attachment in Late Victorian and Edwardian Working-Class Families', *Historical Journal* 55:4 (2012), pp. 1007–27; John Tosh, *A Man's Place: Masculinity and the Middle-Class Home in Victorian England* (New Haven, CT, and London, 1999), esp. pp. 79–101.
[2] Claudia Nelson, *Invisible Men: Fatherhood in Victorian Periodicals, 1850–1910* (Athens, GA and London, 1995), esp. pp. 51–4.
[3] Strange, 'Fatherhood, Providing', p. 1009.
[4] Tosh, *A Man's Place*, pp. 170–94; Trev Lynn Broughton and Helen Rogers, 'Introduction: The Empire of the Father', in Broughton and Rogers (eds), *Gender and Fatherhood*, pp. 7–8; Gordon and Nair, 'Domestic Fathers', p. 557.
[5] Joanna Bourke, *Working Class Cultures in Britain 1890–1960: Gender, Class, and Ethnicity* (London, 1994), p. 81.

chapter will go some way towards that purpose, showing that men from various backgrounds understood and enacted this role in diverse ways. It will contend that understandings of the father's provider role shifted in three key areas. The meanings attributed to and the relative importance of breadwinning shifted; the scope of provision extended to include practices such as the giving of pocket money and, as such, the bar for 'good' fatherhood was raised; and the context of this provision shifted considerably, as a range of economic, political, social, and cultural changes brought this role into question.[6] The interwar period witnessed the development of a modern consumer culture and the rise of mass, national media forms, including the press, cinema, radio, and later television.[7] Structural unemployment had crucial consequences for fatherhood and masculinity,[8] and the state intervened in private life as never before, providing services and financial contributions that were hitherto the father's responsibility.[9] Finally, female employment increased; as Adrian Bingham and Dolly Smith-Wilson have noted, the male breadwinner model was challenged by increases in women's paid employment in this period, particularly during wartime.[10] In the realm of male provision, cultural ideals and individual attitudes and behaviour were largely aligned. There was a high degree of consensus amongst public commentators and public opinion, reinforced by important cultural institutions; Alana Harris, for example, notes the role of the Catholic Church in reinforcing the centrality of stable breadwinning to fatherhood.[11] Due to the long history of the male provider role and the widespread unspoken assumption that breadwinning and fatherhood were inherently linked, there was substantial consensus in attitudes across popular culture and amongst individuals; the actions of fathers, for the most part, accorded with the picture painted in popular culture. A spectrum of behaviour remained, yet the tolerance levels for men who provided insufficiently

---

[6] Indeed, there was a shift away from limiting the father's role to provision in the late nineteenth and early twentieth centuries, and beyond in certain discourses. See for example Lynn Abrams, '"There Was Nobody Like My Daddy": Fathers, the Family and the Marginalisation of Men in Modern Scotland', *Scottish Historical Review* 78:2 (1999), p. 241; Elizabeth Buettner, 'Fatherhood Real, Imagined, Denied: British Men in Imperial India', in Broughton and Rogers (eds), *Gender and Fatherhood*, p. 184; Daniel Grey, 'Discourses of Infanticide in England, 1880–1922', PhD Thesis (Roehampton University, 2009), pp. 277–8.

[7] Adrian Bingham, *Gender, Modernity, and the Popular Press in Inter-War Britain* (Oxford, 2004), p. 4; Victoria De Grazia, 'Establishing the Modern Consumer Household: Introduction', in V. De Grazia and E. Furlough (eds), *The Sex of Things: Gender and Consumption in Historical Perspective* (London, 1996), pp. 151–61; Martin Pugh, *We Danced All Night: A Social History of Britain between the Wars* (London, 2009), pp. 94–5.

[8] Stephen Brooke, 'Gender and Working Class Identity in Britain during the 1950s', *Journal of Social History* 34:4 (2001), p. 776.

[9] On the growth of state involvement in family life, see in particular Susan Pedersen, *Family, Dependence, and the Origins of the Welfare State: Britain and France, 1914–1945* (Cambridge and New York, 1993).

[10] Bingham, *Gender*, p. 217; Dolly Smith-Wilson, 'A New Look at the Affluent Worker: The Good Working Mother in Post-War Britain', *Twentieth Century British History* 17:2 (2006), pp. 225–9.

[11] Alana Harris, '"The People of God Dressed for Dinner and Dancing"? English Catholic Masculinity, Religious Sociability and the Catenian Association', in L. Delap and S. Morgan (eds), *Men, Masculinities and Religious Change in Twentieth-Century Britain* (Basingstoke, 2013), p. 60.

for their families declined through this period as the cultural emphasis on the significance of fatherhood increased. Such men were increasingly vilified in popular culture and in individuals' accounts.

Yet one aspect of a father's position as a parent was not usually questioned throughout this period: his relative inferiority in status compared with the mother. The father was seen as secondary and as complementary to the mother, often simultaneously. In his study of working-class fatherhood from 1900 to 1939, Tim Fisher suggests change to the father's role could happen in various ways: through a convergence or divergence of the mother's and father's roles, or through a shift of emphasis within the father's accepted role. He argues that convergence or divergence of the mother's and father's roles did not take place in this period, and the evidence presented here would largely support this view.[12] However, it is a rather limited model: such roles could, and arguably did, change in scope without convergence or divergence. To put it another way, more aspects of a child's care and wellbeing could be considered as a parent's responsibility, and due to the increase in 'expert' prescription from psychologists, sociologists, and the like in the first half of the twentieth century,[13] both fathers' and mothers' roles and spheres of influence were enlarged, at least in popular imagination. There was thus an 'intensification' of parenting in this period, relating to both fatherhood and motherhood.

BREADWINNING

Newspapers frequently directly reminded fathers of their duty to provide. In the *Daily Mirror* in 1932, an editorial on fathercraft, by 'W. M.'—in fact Richard Jennings, one of the *Mirror*'s most prolific editorial writers—discussed a talk given to fathers by the Medical Officer for Health for Kensington. It was stated that fathercraft was defined as 'the art or craft of making money to keep wives and children' and that 'Father is proud of that definition.' The Medical Officer was reported to have highlighted that many fathers did not give money to their families willingly and to be a 'fathercraft father', fathers should start the following year—this article was published on 30 December—by regarding all their earnings as for their family. The writer of the article took a somewhat sceptical tone, calling the Medical Officer a 'fatherly preacher', as well as finishing on the note that a father may become a fathercraft father only 'if he wants to'. Yet the message was clear that fathers must provide for families, and the best fathers wanted to do so.[14] Whilst an ideal-type of fatherhood was discussed in the discourse of fathercraft, then, there was simultaneously an acceptance of an 'imperfect' fatherhood,

---

[12] Timothy J. Fisher, 'Fatherhood and the Experience of Working-Class Fathers in Britain, 1900–1939', PhD Thesis (University of Edinburgh, 2004), p. 50.

[13] Jane Lewis, *The Politics of Motherhood: Child and Maternal Welfare in England, 1900–1939* (London, 1980), p. 221.

[14] *Daily Mirror*, 30 December 1932, p. 11.

demonstrated by the somewhat cynical note of the writer, and the suggestion that fathers may or may not subscribe to this ideal. Which fatherhood readers should embody remained somewhat ambiguous.

This boundary between an ideal and a standard expectation could and did change, and the idea that a father would enjoy his position as breadwinner became normalized, particularly from the 1930s onwards. Letters published in *The Times* in 1941 demonstrate how newspapers praised fathers who wanted to fulfil their duty of providing. 'A Grateful Father', for instance, wrote to express his disappointment at not being able to contribute to the upkeep of his wife and children, who had been evacuated abroad, stating 'I would ask for nothing better than to be allowed to send any sum which might be approved.'[15] A letter supporting this 'grateful father' was published the next day, in which the writer claimed that many in the country must also 'heartily agree'.[16] This selection of letters and the way they were presented were arguably employed to indicate something of a consensus amongst men on this issue. The popular press, too, increasingly presented providing for children as a proud and even enjoyable aspect of fatherhood rather than one to be reluctantly accepted, as shown in an article about a letter written to advice columnist Mary Brown, published in the *Daily Mirror* in March 1952. The letter was from a wife who wanted to help her husband, a Mr Bonella, to find a way to earn a living, 'to make him feel he is still of some use in the world and to give him a chance of being a daddy to his two children'. This father was contrasted with another more seriously disabled man, to whom he was apparently introduced by the author. Yet Mr Bonella was said to be in the worse situation, because of the family for whom he could not provide. The centrality of provision to fatherhood was reiterated in the wife's question in the original letter asking if there was any way of her husband being able to be a daddy to his children again, thus linking the fulfilling of his provision role to fatherhood as a status and identity.[17]

Editors and journalists thus established the boundaries of good fatherhood across different sections of newspapers. The importance of the father's role as breadwinner was constantly made clear; it was his primary role and should be fulfilled before any other. Furthermore, the fundamental need to satisfy this role could excuse other behaviour that could, in other circumstances, be improper. This is illustrated by a short news story in *The Times* in 1921 about a father stealing milk for his hungry children. A policeman apparently verified his story that 'there was no food in the house whatsoever', and the father was portrayed in a positive light, despite his criminal actions, as he was said to have thanked the police involved for the kindness with which they treated his wife and children. In this sense, though committing a crime, he was excused by the magistrate, as well as by the newspaper and by extension the public, as he was simply fulfilling his provision role as a father, through the only means possible to him.[18]

---

[15] *The Times*, 8 May 1941, p. 5.   [16] *The Times*, 9 May 1941, p. 5.
[17] *Daily Mirror*, 14 March 1952, p. 2.
[18] *The Times*, 11 January 1921, p. 4. Also see *Daily Mirror*, 11 January 1921, p. 3.

The predominant image of father as provider permeated popular culture beyond the press. In the first of the extremely popular 'Famous Five' books by Enid Blyton, the reader is introduced to fierce Uncle Quentin, cousin George's father, who seems unfriendly, unreasonable, and perpetually bad-tempered. He is what Ann Alston terms the 'archetypal Victorian father figure'.[19] Whilst this characterization of Uncle Quentin comes across throughout the whole series of books, in the first, *Five on a Treasure Island*, the reader is given an explanation for his bad temper. Quentin explains that though he has worked hard, his occupation as an academic scientist does not bring him much money and therefore he has not been able to provide for his family as he would have liked, which has made him 'irritable and bad-tempered'.[20] Quentin's inability to fulfil his role as a father, by adequately providing, has tainted family life for himself, his wife, Fanny, and George. Now his family is financially secure, through the discovery of treasure on the family's island, Quentin can fulfil his fatherly duties, and become a father to George in other ways as well. The link between fatherhood and provision is further reinforced by Quentin's first priority, to get George whatever she wants; whilst he clearly envisions a present or similar, this turns out to be Timmy the dog, who has previously been banned from the house. This leads to George hugging her father, a very rare event, and thus, from the securing of Quentin's ability to provide comes the reconciling of father and daughter. The story ends with all children being put to bed and the narrator reminding the reader that they had plenty of holidays ahead of them, in which Quentin would be able to buy them all the little presents he wanted to.[21] Of course, the character of Quentin remained a bad-tempered and somewhat intimidating figure to the children in future books. The irresistibility of such a character for Blyton presumably outweighed the desire to provide consistency through the series, and she continued this theme for dramatic effect and as a plot device in future stories, with the explanation that Quentin acts in such a way because of stress associated with his work.

It is clear that fathers themselves felt the pressures and pleasures of breadwinning simultaneously. This was an area in which men's duties as a husband and as a father clearly overlapped, and this often meant this role was a non-negotiable one. Yet, as in other periods, there was a spectrum of what men were willing to do—some were desperate to earn as much as they could to give their family the best standard of living possible and enjoyed doing so, others handed over the minimum amount possible to their wives and kept the rest for themselves, whilst still others failed to provide for their families at all, for various reasons.[22] Most interviewees discussed whether men handed over their unopened wage packet to their wives or whether they allocated a specified sum of 'housekeeping'; as will be discussed in Chapter 5, such an action reveals attitudes about power and authority within the family. Evidence from

---

[19] Ann Alston, *The Family in English Children's Literature* (London and New York, 2008), p. 53.

[20] Enid Blyton [1942], *Five on a Treasure Island* (London, 2001), p. 236.

[21] Blyton, *Five on a Treasure Island*, p. 242.

[22] On fathers' breadwinning in the late nineteenth and early twentieth century, see Strange, 'Fatherhood, Providing', pp. 1007–27.

oral history interviews, autobiographies, and social surveys suggests that the majority of men thought they should spend a large proportion of their earnings on their families, living up to the expectations reproduced in the press and beyond. Whether they were pleased to do so or not varied, and it is difficult to estimate how many families struggled because of an unreliable breadwinner. Many individuals illustrated the centrality of economic provision to fatherhood by immediately discussing this when asked about their father's role, or fatherhood more generally. Indeed, providing properly was a sign of working-class respectability; Mrs B4L, born in 1936 and married in the mid-1950s, contrasted her own husband (a 'good' father of one son), who handed over all his wages, to her sister-in-law's husband, who took charge of his wages, meaning she was 'always short of money'. Mrs B4L spoke more generally about the Lancaster area in which she lived; handing over wage packets was 'quite common', and 'the nicest sort of men' did so.[23]

Likewise, in Margery Spring-Rice's study of working-class wives in the 1930s, whilst the author clearly believed a husband should be more than a breadwinner, the women she cited were said to have been happy with a man who provided regularly and did not worsen their situation with bad temper or drunkenness. To the women studied, receiving a fair proportion of their husband's pay packet was most important; consideration of her needs beyond this was specially commended rather than expected. An ideal husband, in the eyes of the women surveyed, was said to help his wife sometimes—by carrying heavy washing, for example, looking after the children occasionally so she could have some leisure time, or caring for her if she was ill. In this sense, Spring-Rice created an image of an ideal-type father and husband, largely in accordance with what was promoted in parts of the press, but also explored the minimum expectations of those women she studied.[24] Many men did indeed give only a limited amount of money to their wives, and kept the rest for their own needs, often cigarettes and alcohol. B. L. Coombes, in his autobiography of his life as a miner in south Wales, highlighted the fact that some of his less considerate co-workers forged their payslips to reduce the amount of money that they had to hand over to their families.[25] Mrs T5P, born in 1905, stated that her father 'would give [my mother] so much but he would spend all the other on beer'.[26] Different attitudes to money can be found within different generations of the same family; Mr K2P, a father of six from Preston, born in 1930, suggested his father did not take his breadwinner role too seriously. He 'kept a fair bit back' and 'spent more money in the pub than he ever should have done'. In contrast, Mr K2P stated that he might have a 'drink or two', but was more interested in spending his money on activities for and with his children when he became a father in the late 1950s.[27]

[23] Mrs B4L, Elizabeth Roberts Archive (ERA), 1940–70, p. 58.

[24] Margery Spring-Rice, *Working-Class Wives: Their Health and Conditions* (Harmondsworth, 1939), p. 104.

[25] B. L. Coombes, *These Poor Hands: The Autobiography of a Miner Working in South Wales* (London, 1939), p. 100, 172.

[26] Mrs D3P/Mrs T5P/Mrs M6P, ERA, Preston 1890–1940, p. 14.

[27] Mr and Mrs K2P, ERA, Preston 1940–70, p. 54.

Like Mr K2P, many men who became fathers during or after the Second World War seemed to describe breadwinning in a more positive light; as in the press, a certain pride in this role can be found from the 1940s. Whilst serving abroad, Corporal A. H. Wright wrote of his desire to 'provide all that Gillian [his daughter] needs' after the war, and allow his wife to cease her teaching post if she wished.[28] Here, the middle-class status of this family is also important; wealthier fathers had less of a stark choice between their own luxuries and their families' needs, yet Corporal Wright's suggestion that he should provide and his wife should only work if she wanted to demonstrates a persistence of the idea of the father as sole or predominant breadwinner throughout this period, and across all social levels.

The simple assumption that a father should provide is also apparent in the testimony of George Ryder, a bricklayer from Liverpool who married in 1945. He stated that he always presumed he would provide for a family: 'the whole object of the male was really to go to work to pay the rent. It was always instilled in me by my father that the main thing you did was you paid the rent, you kept the roof over your head.'[29] The language used here also demonstrates the intrinsic link between fatherhood and provision: George highlighted such a view was 'instilled' in him. The suggestion that men should have a small amount of their own money for 'beer and baccy' continued, but tolerance for those who frittered away their family's money at the pub decreased. Indeed, some individuals highlighted that they and their wives pooled all earnings and shared everything equally, such as Mr Fides, born in Luton in 1929.[30] Yet this shifting understanding of breadwinning was not universal, and contradictory impulses were at work even on an individual level. Whilst Ron Barnes wrote in his autobiography of his heartbreak at being unable to provide for his family one Christmas, and struggling with the idea of his wife providing for him when he was unemployed, he also described how his wife resorted to taking money from him because he was not generous enough with the allowance he gave her.[31] The universal norm of male provision did not allow much space for self-interest, yet, on an individual level, this could have an important influence on behaviour.

FAILING TO PROVIDE

Fathers who failed to provide for their families, or, worse, acted selfishly with the money they did earn, were consistently demonized within popular culture, presumably to instil a certain amount of guilt amongst those readers who embodied

---

[28] Private Papers of A. H. Wright, Imperial War Museum Archive (IWMA), Documents.13285, letter dated 31 December 1944.

[29] George Ryder, 'A Man's World', roll 134, pp. 43–45.

[30] Mr Fides, Int167, P. Thompson and H. Newby, *Families, Social Mobility and Ageing, an Intergenerational Approach, 1900–1988* [computer file]. Colchester, Essex: UK Data Archive (UKDA) [distributor], July 2005. SN: 4938, p. 21.

[31] Ron Barnes, *Coronation Cups and Jam Jars* (London, 1976), pp. 180, 189–90, 195.

such practices. For example, in 1953 the *Manchester Guardian* published a story about a man who, the headline stated, 'Gave Wife No Cash For 18 Years', and was fined in court as a result. The negative presentation of this man was completed by his comment that he should have 'clouted [his wife] on the head and knocked a bit of sense into her'.[32] Another article in the *Daily Mirror* in 1950 reported on a man who had been jailed for six months for failing to provide for his family. The negative presentation of this father was supported by quotations from a NSPCC official, who stated that the man was 'perfectly able-bodied', but 'sheer bone-lazy'.[33] The favourable presentation of fathers who positively fought to provide, and enjoyed doing so, was thus matched by the critical presentation of those men who completely failed in their duties as fathers. As well as strong cultural norms, the criminal justice system—through, in these cases, court fines and a prison sentence—was also crucial in enforcing men's role as breadwinners.

It is clear that a significant minority of such fathers did exist throughout the period in question here, with a weakness for spending too much on alcohol usually cited as the cause for a family's lack of income. Assessing how common such fathers were is more difficult, though cases of this were particularly prominent in older working-class areas. For many men the pub provided comfortable living space with male company, which small, poor-quality working-class homes often could not provide. Children who suffered poverty in this way often recalled this in later life, through autobiographies, interviews, and so on; the perspectives of fathers who failed to provide are harder to find. Dick Beavis, for example, born in the early part of the First World War in County Durham, wrote of his father's irresponsibility: 'old dad was working but he had an awful habit of spending the pay in the pub'. As such, amongst other hardships, Dick was forced to request free shoes through a school scheme, normally given to those whose fathers were unemployed.[34] As William Woodruff highlighted in 1920s Lancashire, mothers were frequently forced to fight for their 'housekeeping' money; they tried 'to get their husbands out of the pub late on a Friday night before the weekly earnings had all gone'.[35] Likewise, the story of Jimmy Boyle's impoverished neighbourhood when growing up in the Gorbals, Glasgow, in the 1940s was perhaps extreme by this period but by no means unique: 'On Friday kids would be at the pub doors, sent there by their mothers to tell their fathers to come home with the wages before they drank most of them.'[36] There is some evidence of change across generations in this period; Ted Cunningham spoke of his upbringing in the interwar period in north-east

---

[32] *Manchester Guardian*, 15 August 1953, p. 8.

[33] *Daily Mirror*, 22 December 1950, p. 3. Also see *Daily Express*, 4 May 1922, p. 1; *Manchester Guardian*, 29 March 1928, p. 20; *Daily Mirror*, 7 September 1954, p. 6; *Manchester Guardian*, 7 June 1957, p. 16; *Daily Mirror*, 28 February 1959, p. 12; *Daily Mirror*, 29 September 1959, p. 21.

[34] Dick Beavis, *What Price Happiness? My Life from Coal Hewer to Shop Steward* (Whitley Bay, 1980), pp. 12–13.

[35] William Woodruff [1993], *The Road to Nab End: An Extraordinary Northern Childhood* (London, 2008), p. 202.

[36] Jimmy Boyle, *A Sense of Freedom* (Edinburgh, 1977), p. 16.

England, stating that his father 'didn't care one hoot how you lived or what you eat' and that he failed to provide properly, looking after himself alone. In contrast, when Ted became a father later in the 1930s, he suggested he worked incredibly hard to provide 'everything' for his children, as 'I didn't have it and I've always made sure that my family did get what I never got.'[37] However, the discrepancy between the accounts of fathers and children here might also reflect the strength of this cultural norm; fathers were not likely to admit to failing to provide, whereas children were more likely to remember going short because of their fathers' imprudence with their income.

In the 1920s and 1930s, many fathers could not provide for their families due to high levels of unemployment, and many were out of work for extended periods. Between 1921 and 1940, the unemployment rate never fell below 1 million people, one tenth of the insured population, and this level sat at consistently over 2 million between 1931 and 1935.[38] For those men who took their provider role seriously, it was difficult to reconcile; as Woodruff wrote in his autobiography, men like his father found unemployment to be a 'demoralizing blow' as 'he felt that everybody had a duty, as well as a right, to work'.[39] Indeed, in many families, wives and daughters could find employment whilst fathers, husbands, and sons could not.[40] This could cause friction in terms of family relationships.[41] In the 1930s, due to the much-despised means test, working children frequently had to move out of the family home to allow their parents and siblings to receive the maximum unemployment allowance. This was an affront to the male bread-winner role and, for many men, this crystallized their lack of ability to act as provider. Evelyn Haythorne's older brother left their Yorkshire home for this reason: 'Dad took his departure the worst and cried bitterly for he blamed himself.'[42]

The inability of fathers to fulfil their role as breadwinners due to unemployment was frequently discussed in the press, especially the *Manchester Guardian*. Unemployment also formed the focus of numerous surveys, as various commentators sought to discover its consequences for family life. Survey writers also assumed men should be providing for their families, and throughout all these sources ran a belief that situations in which women worked and men did not were harmful and all too common. The Pilgrim Trust report, for example, highlighted the negative consequences for men and the tensions that could arise between husbands/wives and fathers/children.[43] Whilst fathers who did not provide out of laziness, or who earned plenty and failed to pass it on to their families, were consistently

---

[37] Ted Cunningham, 'A Man's World', roll 91, p. 23–6; roll 93, p. 82.

[38] John Stevenson, *British Society 1914–45* (Harmondsworth, 1984), p. 266.

[39] Woodruff, *The Road*, p. 45.

[40] Sally Alexander, 'Men's Fears and Women's Work: Responses to Unemployment in London between the Wars', *Gender and History* 12:2 (2000), p. 401; Selina Todd, *Young Women, Work, and Family in England 1918–1950* (Oxford, 2005), p. 63.

[41] Alexander, 'Men's Fears', p. 415.

[42] Evelyn Haythorne, *On Earth to Make the Numbers Up* (Castleford, 1991), p. 56. Also see Mrs A1P, ERA, Preston 1890–1940, pp. 5–6.

[43] Pilgrim Trust, *Men without Work: A Report Made to the Pilgrim Trust* (Cambridge, 1938), pp. 146–7.

criticized, unemployed fathers were, on the contrary, presented sympathetically. Commentators blamed current economic conditions and highlighted their detrimental impact in ways beyond the immediate financial situation.[44] The intentions of such fathers coupled with the external circumstances thus determined the way such fathers were presented in the press and beyond.

The discussion of unmarried fathers and divorced fathers was a common theme in the press, and again demonstrates the centrality of provision within the father's role. For example, in *The Times* in 1923, a typical article featured the difficult situation of the single mother. The unnamed author highlighted that current laws made 'the mother solely responsible for her illegitimate child', and 'the principle underlying this policy is that of deterrence'. The correspondent found a high degree of consensus amongst those familiar with the problem, regarding the need to make the father bear the burden of an 'illegitimate' child along with the mother, thereby discouraging what was termed 'irresponsible fatherhood'. The writer also suggested that public opinion favoured reform of existing laws, including ensuring better arrangements to compel the father to contribute to the upkeep of his child.[45] The idea of ensuring provision for 'illegitimate' children by their fathers demonstrates how fundamental the association between fatherhood and provision was: the simple fact of fathering a child, in any context, meant that a father should provide for that child in a material sense. Indeed, the insistence in this article that the law should be changed to ensure that all biological fathers should provide indicates the increasing importance placed on this role in the interwar years.[46]

Fatherless families formed the subjects of Margaret Wynn's 1964 study, throughout which Wynn made clear her view that economic provision for families without fathers was necessary for the avoidance of poverty. Wynn researched the numbers of fatherless families in Britain in the early 1960s, and examined legislation and official policy regarding the economic and social position of these families. In her introduction, Wynn stated that children needed their fathers for more than their income.[47] However, most of the book focused on the disadvantages a fatherless family faced in terms of economic provision: in terms of direct support to the child, and to the mother, so that she did not have to work. The core task of fatherhood was clearly thus seen to be breadwinning for a family, an assumption made in the official policy studied by Wynn as well as in her own view, whether this was explicit or not. That the book was published right at the end of the period studied here demonstrates the centrality of this role throughout

---

[44] For example, see *Manchester Guardian*, 18 February 1932, p. 6; *Manchester Guardian*, 29 August 1936, p. 10. Also see Chapter 6.

[45] *The Times*, 8 January 1923, p. 7.

[46] An insistence on the duty of fathers of any children to provide for their offspring ran throughout this period; yet it was not until the Legitimacy Act of 1959 that the rights of fathers of 'illegitimate' children were brought into line with those of separated and divorced fathers. Pat Thane, 'Unmarried Motherhood in Twentieth-Century England', *Women's History Review* 20:1 (2011), p. 22.

[47] Margaret Wynn, *Fatherless Families: A Study of Families Deprived of a Father by Death, Divorce, Separation or Desertion before or after Marriage* (London, 1964).

the first half of the twentieth century and beyond. Some individual testimonies explored the effect a father's death or desertion had had on their lives; for Molly Weir, who grew up in Glasgow in the 1910s and 1920s, and Ralph Finn, who grew up in Aldgate in the interwar period, affectionate grandparents and a working mother offset the ill effects of a father's absence.[48] For others his departure was positive, due to a previous failure to provide and other harmful behaviour, such as violence.[49] For yet others, and particularly those who were 'illegitimate' or had been deserted, the effects were lasting. Indeed, in Albert Gomes' case, his child-hood experiences shaped his behaviour when he became a father in the 1940s. Despite falling in love with another woman, who he eventually married decades later, he could not abandon his children: 'I couldn't leave them as I'd been left by my father. I'd promised myself.'[50]

The problem of 'illegitimate' and fatherless children also raised the question of the state's responsibility to provide, and, as such, to take over the father's role if he was not fulfilling it. Wynn's position on this matter was that the state was not taking enough responsibility in the late 1950s and early 1960s, and should be providing, under a 'Fatherless Child Allowance', for all such children.[51] However, the increase in state provision in place of the father did not lessen the focus on fathers as breadwinners—if anything, this pressure was increased. State provi-sion was never seen by those in power as a satisfactory alternative to a father's provision; rather, it was a last resort, such as during war or in cases of particular individual hardship. Furthermore, state policy through the interwar period and beyond was based on the ideal of a father as earner and mother as carer, and much legislation underlined fathers' duty to provide.[52] This was certainly the case dur-ing both world wars, in which the state gave allowances to families whose fathers had been sent abroad. As Sally Sokoloff suggests, the state's provision of economic support for wives of servicemen alone underlined the primary function of men as breadwinners.[53]

Debates about the state's duty to act as a provider in a father's absence, or to supplement his income, were prevalent in newspapers following both world wars, partly due to the questions raised about the status of women. This debate cen-tred on the 'endowment of motherhood', an idea promoted by Eleanor Rathbone,

[48] Molly Weir [1970], *Shoes Were for Sunday* (London, 1973), p. 10; Ralph L. Finn, *Spring in Aldgate* (London, 1968), p. 91.

[49] For example, see Pat O'Mara's relief when his father was in prison. Pat O'Mara, *The Autobiography of a Liverpool Irish Slummy* (London, 1934), p. 136.

[50] Albert Gomes, quoted in Steve Humphries and Pamela Gordon, *A Man's World: From Boyhood to Manhood, 1900–1960* (London, 1996), p. 153.

[51] Wynn, *Fatherless Families*, pp. 162–4.

[52] Leonore Davidoff, Megan Doolittle, Janet Fink, and Katherine Holden, *The Family Story: Blood, Contract and Intimacy, 1830–1939* (Harlow, 1999), p. 192; Janet Fink and Katherine Holden, 'Pictures from the Margins of Marriage: Representations of Spinsters and Single Mothers in the Mid-Victorian Novel, Inter-War Hollywood Melodrama and British Film of the 1950s and 1960s', *Gender and History* 11:2 (1999), p. 237; Fisher, 'Fatherhood and the Experience', p. 43.

[53] Sally Sokoloff, '"How Are They at Home?" Community, State, and Servicemen's Wives in England, 1939–45', *Women's History Review* 8:1 (1999), p. 28.

amongst others, after the First World War. This discussion was particularly prominent in the *Manchester Guardian*. 'H', writing in October 1918, explored the possibility of the state paying for the upbringing of children, leaving men and women to earn as much or as little as they wanted to support themselves. The likely consequences of such a policy were explored and rejected as improbable, impossible, or undesirable in turn, and thus the reader was neatly and rationally brought back to the male breadwinner model, not as a perfect solution, but because of the difficulties that alternatives would pose.[54] The newspaper published several letters from prominent advocates of the endowment of motherhood campaign in this month, yet the editorial from 'H', alongside the editor's closure of the debate after a particularly vocal letter from Emmeline Pethick-Lawrence, arguably demonstrated to readers the stance of the newspaper.[55] That the letters published were from outspoken feminists, namely Pethick-Lawrence and Ada Nield Chew, who disagreed amongst themselves in these letters, would have further served to undermine arguments for direct state allowances to mothers. Whilst the *Manchester Guardian* was by no means a conservative newspaper, it was in this case against such an endowment for motherhood, if not actively supportive of the maintenance of the male breadwinner model.

The question of state payments for families again came to the fore in the Second World War, and this time resulted in the introduction of family allowances across the United Kingdom in 1945. The government had successfully managed to resist the campaigns for family allowances for the previous two decades, yet there was substantial change during the war. Importantly, however, the needs of the economy dominated discussions about family allowances, and they were finally introduced due to the need to control inflation, avoid minimum wages, and keep wages down more generally.[56] Economic pressures had arguably outweighed the importance of prioritizing the male breadwinner model. Moreover, as Susan Pedersen highlights, by the 1930s there was a new political space which allowed for more of a consensus around aid for children.[57] The most relevant aspect of the debate about family allowances in this period was the question of to whom they would be paid; it was initially proposed that they would be paid to fathers, but after a feminist campaign led by Eleanor Rathbone pressed the issue, they were paid directly to mothers.[58]

Again, there was an explicit discussion of how the legislation reflected 'modern' attitudes; in a cabinet meeting of 1945 the Prime Minister was told that an

[54] *Manchester Guardian*, 26 October 1918, p. 5.

[55] *Manchester Guardian*, 1 November 1918, p. 8. For other examples of letters published, see *Manchester Guardian*, 28 September 1918, p. 5; *Manchester Guardian*, 18 October 1918, p. 10; *Manchester Guardian*, 21 October 1918, p. 8.

[56] José Harris, 'Social Planning in War-time: Some Aspects of the Beveridge Report', in J. M. Winter (ed.), *War and Economic Development* (Cambridge, 1975), pp. 239–56; John Macnicol, *The Movement for Family Allowances, 1918–45: A Study in Social Policy Development* (London, 1980), pp. 169–70, 199–202; Lewis, *The Politics*, p. 214; Pat Thane, *Foundations of the Welfare State* (2nd edn, Harlow, 1996), pp. 225–9.

[57] Pedersen, *Family*, p. 293.

[58] Thane, *Foundations*, p. 228.

all-party deputation recommended payment to the mother, on the basis that she was in charge of the household budget, and this would be 'in accord with modern ideas'. Winston Churchill's somewhat hostile response, retorting 'Wages will be paid to the mother next!' is evidence of the persistence of more traditional ideas amongst politicians, and a reluctance to meet the demands of women.[59] Indeed, the suggestion that such changes would reflect public opinion was largely accurate: a Ministry of Information Survey found that 59 per cent polled were in favour of payment to the mother, in contrast to only 16 per cent in favour of the father.[60] Though numerous MPs spoke in favour of paying the allowance to the mother, there was substantial resistance from the government. In 1944, Eleanor Rathbone and Edith Summerskill fiercely debated the matter with R. A. Butler in the House of Commons. The government proposed leaving the family to decide, and argued 'It would be wrong to leave out the father because, after all, he is the first breadwinner of the house and the man upon whom the children ultimately depend for a large proportion of their maintenance.'[61] Indeed, the equality of men and women was highlighted as paramount: as William Jowitt suggested when debating the bill in 1945, 'I am not a feminist. I am not a masculinist, if there is such a word. I am an equalitarian.'[62]

The debate that ensued in *The Times* about this matter is particularly indicative of the nature and outcome of this controversy. A letter from Rathbone was published in *The Times* in June 1944, arguing strongly for the payment of family allowances to the mother rather than the father. Rathbone argued that this would raise the status of motherhood and help ensure that children received the maximum amount of the allowance and the family's income more generally.[63] More significantly, the thrust and even wording of Rathbone's argument in this letter was directly reproduced in an editorial in *The Times* in March 1945, and though Rathbone was mentioned in the context of the campaign for family allowances, the editorial was presented as the view of this largely conservative newspaper. In it, it was stated that the government's reason for suggesting payment to the father was that he was responsible for the child's maintenance. Yet this was rejected, and instead it was argued that allowances should go directly to the mother, primarily because the housewives of the nation 'are in need of some clear recognition by the community of their services and of encouragement in their work of home-making and family-rearing'.[64] This was reiterated the next day in the main editorial article, in which it was stated that Britain must 'appeal specifically' to the housewife, and convince her of the 'importance it attaches to more frequent motherhood'. The

---

[59] Cabinet Meeting Minutes, W.M. 26(45), 6 March 1945, CAB/195/3. Also see War Cabinet, W.M. (45) 26th Conclusions, 6 March 1945, CAB/65/49/26, pp. 157–8.

[60] Pedersen, *Family*, p. 347.

[61] Hansard, HC, vol. 404, cc.1113–1114, 3 November 1944. Also see Hansard, HC, vol. 404, cc.987, 1025, 1029, 2 November 1944.

[62] Hansard, HC, vol. 408, c.2268, 8 March 1945. Also see Hansard, HC, vol. 408, cc.2266–2271, 2278–2279, 2287–2289, 2291–2294, 2305–2306, 2313, 2322–2324, 2350–2351, 8 March 1945.

[63] *The Times*, 26 June 1944, p. 5.   [64] *The Times*, 8 March 1945, p. 5.

state's presumption of payment of allowances to the father was said to be 'psychologically clumsy' in this sense.[65] *The Times* thus rejected the government's focus on fathers as breadwinners and economic managers of their families. The newspaper used the rhetoric of recognizing housewives for their work, a feminist principle, and obviously and directly informed by the ideas of Rathbone, to focus on the encouragement of women to bear and rear children in the face of a declining birth rate. This was, of course, an important element to discussions of family allowances, and though William Beveridge did not believe family allowances would directly help raise the birth rate, he did contend that it could bring about an atmosphere more conducive to pro-natalist measures.[66] The weight of mainstream opinion had substantially shifted since the 1920s.

Whilst the government's initial decision to pay allowances to the father indicates the importance of male breadwinning to the state, the encouragement of *The Times* and others to pay allowances to the mother instead, and the state's later change in policy, did not indicate an opposite belief. Rather, the rhetoric of recognizing mothers' work in terms of rearing families and the open desire to further encourage this reproduced existing gendered divisions of labour. As Jane Lewis has highlighted, the emphasis that the child and maternal welfare movement placed on better childcare and the importance of motherhood reinforced traditional ideas about a woman's place being in the home.[67] Pedersen suggests, furthermore, that the welfare state as envisaged in the Beveridge Report preserved men's position as breadwinners whilst alleviating child poverty, and additionally, the implementation of this plan in the post-Second World War period could be seen as the 'culmination' of the constructing of a male-breadwinner welfare state.[68] Though the state's involvement in providing for families could have threatened men's primacy as breadwinners, the framing of the public debate actually reinforced a traditional gendered division of male provision and female nurture. In this sense, though the political context was changing, the centrality of breadwinning to fatherhood and masculinity persisted, even if its meaning shifted. The emphasis on equality in difference in terms of parenting roles remained.

It is thus clear that breadwinning remained at the core of fatherhood throughout this period, and furthermore, it continued to be conceived as a father's responsibility despite women's employment and the state's increasing economic provision for families. Fathers were constantly reminded of this duty by a whole range of public voices, and there was a near-complete consensus that fathers who did not provide a minimum standard for their families should be condemned. Such men were painted as near-evil figures across popular culture, from newspaper articles

---

[65] *The Times*, 9 March 1945, p. 5.

[66] Macnicol, *The Movement*, pp. 197–9. Richard Titmuss, social researcher and co-author of the influential study *Parents Revolt*, believed the same, suggesting that they were 'no answer' to the declining birth rate but were 'urgently needed on humanitarian and social welfare grounds'. Richard and Kathleen Titmuss, *Parents Revolt: A Study of the Declining Birth-Rate in Acquisitive Societies* (London, 1942), p. 121.

[67] Lewis, *The Politics*, p. 222.   [68] Pedersen, *Family*, pp. 294, 354.

to popular fiction.[69] Indeed, an accusation of failing to provide became a means of castigating certain groups, such as in the case of racism against Afro-Caribbean men in the post-Second World War period.[70] Circumstances such as unemployment could excuse a father who was failing to provide, but in this case, it was always stated that the best outcome would be to help the fathers in question to be able to provide again, rather than the state contributing directly. Fathers' intentions became more important, and the desire to provide was idealized, and became part of even the minimum expectations of fathers, by the mid-twentieth century.

PROVIDING EDUCATION

A crucial component of the father's provider role was to secure an education for his children. This is a major way in which working-class fathers' roles differed from those of other social classes. However, though working-class fathers were not expected to provide an education in an economic sense, and were often portrayed as being uninterested in their children's education, there was much more of a spectrum of behaviour than has perhaps been recognized. Indeed, many working-class fathers, particularly in the latter half of this period, were supportive of and involved in their children's learning. One Mass-Observation report of 1944 found that fathers of all social classes were much more likely than mothers to encourage their children to read; 73 per cent were said to 'encourage' children reading as a habit, in contrast to 48 per cent of mothers. Though social class did prove a significant variable, the 'widespread indifference' to children's reading amongst the working classes was to be found much more in the attitudes of mothers. This attitude was said to be 'rather less common among the fathers'.[71] Men were actively encouraged to embrace an educational role by voices in the press, advice literature, and beyond, unlike in the nineteenth century, when men were discouraged from instructing children or interfering with school matters, despite a reality in which many fathers were involved in such ways.[72] In Fisher's study of working-class men's letters in the First World War, it is clear that many expressed concern and interest in their children's education, and explicitly advised children about this, in some cases clearly demonstrating their sense that this was a father's special responsibility.[73]

Evidence from interviews Lynn Abrams undertook with individuals from Stirling supports this, as she found many who referred to their fathers teaching

---

[69] Examples of such negative father figures can be found, for example, in the novels of D. H. Lawrence. Walter Morel is a prime example of this. D. H. Lawrence, *Sons and Lovers* (New York, 1913).

[70] Marcus Collins, 'Pride and Prejudice: West Indian Men in Mid-Twentieth-Century Britain', *Journal of British Studies* 40:3 (2001), p. 397.

[71] Mass-Observation File Report 2086, 'Childhood Reading' (May 1944), p. 4.

[72] Nelson, *Invisible Men*, pp. 51–2. On this role in the nineteenth century, also see Sanders, 'What Do You', pp. 55–67; Tosh, *A Man's Place*, esp. p. 168.

[73] Fisher, 'Fatherhood and the Experience', pp. 158–9.

them when they were young.[74] Elizabeth Roberts, furthermore, found that a growing minority of parents generally were ambitious in terms of their children's futures, and had hopes of further or higher education.[75] She also found that fathers were becoming more involved in children's education, though mothers were, she contends, more influential.[76] This fatherly role was increasing in importance through this period; as Ronald Fletcher suggested, parents were, by the 1950s, expected to support their children's educational careers in ways they were not previously.[77] Yet the educational role was much less secure than the role of bread-winning for fathers. It could be conceived as part of both father's and mother's remit, and this was certainly the case in working-class culture. For the middle- or upper-class father, the case was more clear-cut: there was a social expectation that such fathers should secure the best education possible. However, following the Second World War and the 1944 Education Act, which raised the school leaving age and created a tripartite system of grammar, technical, and secondary modern schools into which children were divided through the 11-plus test, the divisions between social classes were seemingly more permeable. Providing an education, however, went beyond financial contribution, and involved supporting children's learning in other ways.

Insurance advertising capitalized on the idea of men as providers to target them in their campaigns, whilst certain adverts highlighted this role in their promotion of educational products such as encyclopaedias.[78] Advertisements for Eagle Star and British Dominions Insurance Company from the *Daily Mirror* and *The Times* in 1919 were addressed to 'Young Married Men', who, it was suggested, would feel happiness at the arrival of a new baby, mingled with a sense of responsibility. The insurance policy offered a (middle-class) father security by assuring his income, and thus his ability to provide for the future. The inclusion of a drawing of a father in an armchair, looking thoughtful whilst his children play around him, further reinforced this message.[79] This advertisement's target audience was clearly middle-class readers, indicated by the presence of a maid in an affluently decorated room in the accompanying sketch. Both the payments and the costs secured by the policy, such as school fees, would have been beyond the means of most working-class families. Many ads frequently referred to the need to pay for an education. An advert in the *Observer* in 1931, for example, included a sketch of

[74] Abrams, 'There Was Nobody', p. 233.

[75] Elizabeth Roberts, *Women and Families: An Oral History, 1940–1970* (Oxford, 1995), p. 51.

[76] Roberts, *Women and Families*, p. 169.

[77] Ronald Fletcher, *Britain in the Sixties: The Family and Marriage: An Analysis and Moral Assessment* (Harmondsworth, 1962), p. 190.

[78] For example, *Daily Mirror*, 26 September 1922, p. 6.

[79] *Daily Mirror*, 22 July 1919, p. 15; *The Times*, 25 July 1919, p. 8; *The Times*, 8 August 1919, p. 15. Also see *Daily Express*, 18 April 1927, p. 1 (for the *Express*'s own insurance policy); *Manchester Guardian*, 29 March 1930, p. 8; *Observer*, 5 July 1931, p. 28; *Observer*, 27 January 1935, p. 15; *The Times*, 13 March 1935, p. 17; *Observer*, 22 September 1935, p. 25; *Observer*, 23 October 1935, p. 15; *Daily Express*, 30 September 1938, p. 1; *The Times*, 16 March 1949, p. 7; *Manchester Guardian*, 18 August 1949, p. 6; *Daily Mirror*, 25 March 1952, p. 11; *Manchester Guardian*, 19 January 1954, p. 11; *Manchester Guardian*, 5 October 1956, p. 2.

a father and son wrestling on the floor together, and it was stated that 'naturally Daddy wants to him to have a good upbringing and good education'.[80] The use of the word 'naturally' demonstrates an intention to induce a sense of guilt in fathers who have not yet considered the future provision of education. Yet the fact this tactic was used and clearly was effective due to its frequency indicates that fathers did feel such pressures. It was employed throughout the period: a 1959 advertisement for Prudential, for example, again highlighted the necessity of planning ahead to cope with education costs, with a photograph of a four-year-old boy included alongside a caption, 'Now is the time to provide for the education of your very young son or daughter.'[81] These two examples focused in their images on sons, yet all were careful to insist that fathers should be considering the futures of sons and daughters in the text. This most likely indicates a desire to appeal to as many potential customers as possible, but also reflects a belief that fathers should be taking care of both sons' and daughters' educations and futures. Indeed, in their parenting advice manual of 1954, Ronald and Cynthia Illingworth suggested taking out an insurance policy to secure a child's education immediately, if the reader had not done so already.[82] It is difficult to assess how many fathers took out such policies, but the frequency of this advertising technique would suggest a substantial number did so. Indeed, Corporal A. H. Wright took the time to arrange this for his daughter when he was fighting abroad during the Second World War.[83]

The association of the provision of education with fatherhood can be found in numerous opinion pieces in the press, often advising fathers on educational matters, or detailing the difficulties of choosing and ensuring a good education for children. This was such an uncontroversial aspect of middle-class fatherhood that the debate even penetrated *Men Only* magazine, in which there was otherwise very little acknowledgement that men might be parents; the focus remained on work, sports, and friends. Yet an article in November 1955, by S. P. B. Mais, instructed 'How to Choose a Public School' and advised on the relative merits of various schools and the most important factors for consideration, such as the range of sports offered and the fees.[84] Similar sentiments were present in newspapers. An article from *The Times* in 1952, for example, discussed the middle-class dilemma about choosing a child's education. A subsection entitled 'A Father's Worry', underlined the assumption that, in matters relating to education, the father should bear the economic and emotional burden of securing a good education for his children.[85] Only between 5 and 8 per cent of the population attended public schools throughout the twentieth century, and thus the practical

---

[80] *Observer*, 5 July 1931, p. 28.

[81] *Manchester Guardian*, 1 March 1959, p. 16. Also see *Manchester Guardian*, 10 March 1959, p. 10; *Manchester Guardian*, 4 October 1959, p. 13; *Manchester Guardian*, 2 November 1959, p. 5.

[82] Ronald S. Illingworth and Cynthia M. Illingworth, *Babies and Young Children: Feeding, Management and Care* (London, 1954), p. 347.

[83] Private Papers of A. H. Wright, IWMA, Documents.13285, p. 15.

[84] *Men Only* 60:239, November 1955, p. 77–80.

[85] *The Times*, 29 December 1952, p. 7. Also see *Daily Mirror*, 9 January 1928, p. 6.

application of such articles was limited to a minority.[86] However, such pieces reiterated the importance of education generally as part of a father's role. Upper- and middle-class fathers were portrayed as instrumental in achieving a good (private) education for their children, certainly before the Second World War but often afterwards as well.

The association of fathers with securing their children's education can also be seen in the relative frequency with which letters from fathers about educational matters were published in newspapers. Concerns about the standard of lessons, examinations, school meals, and so on were voiced with regularity. In 1922, a father wrote to *The Times* appealing to the editor to take seriously his concerns about 'the feeding of schoolboys'. He complained that his sons were not adequately fed at school, and it cost him a considerable amount to purchase enough extra food for them.[87] In the *Daily Mirror* in 1944, the letter of a 'Dissatisfied Father' addressed the issue of insufficient teaching staff in rural schools.[88] Another example comes from the *Daily Mirror* in 1959, written by a father voicing his opinion against the reciting of poetry in schools, as it put his son off learning poetry altogether.[89] Letter-writers and editors had no problems associating men publicly with their role in helping to provide education.

Fathers' concern about the education of their children was also explicit in a fictional context. Sorrell, an unemployed businessman in the aftermath of the First World War, and his son Kit formed the subject of Warwick Deeping's extremely popular book *Sorrell and Son*. Education is a crucial theme of this book, and is central to Sorrell's plan of working hard enough to maintain some kind of status for his son and allow him to progress in the world. Education was equated here to aspiration—Sorrell identifies spending as much time in full-time education as possible as the best way for Kit to advance himself. Additionally, class is once again important: to assure a better social position and chance in life, Sorrell wants to send Kit to a private school, despite the fact his job as a hotel porter would normally prevent him from doing so. It was stated, regarding Sorrell's ideas about class divisions, 'The obvious thing was to educate the boy above it,—and if possible to make him triumphant over it', at which point it is finally decided that Kit shall go to the public school in question.[90] However, the desire to use education in terms of achieving aspirations for one's children was not confined to the middle classes. In *The Family from One End Street*, a children's book by Eve Garnett, the importance of education is reiterated through Mr Ruggles' desire to send his daughter Kate to the local grammar school. Kate's friend also attends, paid for by money her father has won, a decision of debatable merit in the views of other neighbours, in part reflecting varied working-class attitudes, as will be discussed later in this chapter. The desirability of a good education was thus presented as

[86] George Smith, 'Schools', in A. H. Halsey (ed.), *Twentieth-Century British Social Trends* (3rd edn, Basingstoke, 2000), p. 187.
[87] *The Times*, 21 February 1922, p. 11.   [88] *Daily Mirror*, 14 October 1944, p. 2.
[89] *Daily Mirror*, 14 October 1959, p. 4.
[90] Warwick Deeping [1925], *Sorrell and Son* (Harmondsworth, 1984), p. 158.

not universally accepted, but was certainly expected to be thought of as positive by those reading, who are meant to empathize with the Ruggles family and presumably share the dreams of Kate of attending a good school.[91] Though for very different audiences, and about very different people, these two books put fathers at the forefront of decision-making regarding education, as well as reproducing positive messages about the benefits of education more generally.

For middle-class fathers, education provision was usually an assumed role, for daughters as well as sons. C. Jones, an officer serving in the First World War, felt extremely sad to be parted from his wife and young daughter, nicknamed 'Dink', for long periods. He mourned not being part of her upbringing: 'It grieves me that Dink is growing up and acquiring knowledge without me near at hand to see it.' He spent a good part of his letters instructing his wife about arrangements for her schooling, advised on allowing rest periods between learning, and discussed such matters with and advised his daughter directly.[92] Likewise, Private Butling, serving in the Army Service Corps in the First World War, wrote directly to his sons about educational matters, and in return they discussed their news and achievements and sent on their school reports.[93] Paul Johnson's autobiography of his 1930s childhood in the Midlands focused on his father's educational role. Most of the time spent together in the book is when his father was teaching him in some way, and indeed, his father is used as a narrative voice through which to impart information about the history and culture of the area, reflecting partly his father's profession as a headmaster of an arts school.[94] Richard Nesbitt, a manager for Shell and a father of two boys born in the late 1940s, discussed his desire that both of his sons receive a boarding school education, and stated 'I visited, oh, most of the boarding-schools in the area and had a good look at them.' This was linked to his determination to help them do well in life: 'a parent hopes to do as well, if not better for his young than what he enjoyed'.[95] The strong insistence on achieving a good education amongst middle-class circles particularly could prove difficult for some children, however; John Bostock, born in 1908 to a father who worked for universities and as an archaeologist in India, thought 'my father in a way was rather disappointed that I didn't get a degree or anything like that because the whole family were academic'. Partly in reaction to this, John differentiated between the pride he took in his children's education and its relative importance; their happiness was what mattered most to him.[96]

---

[91]　Eve Garnett [1942], *The Family from One End Street* (London, 1981), pp. 31–8.

[92]　Private Papers of C. Jones, IWMA, Documents.10085, pp. 344–5, also see pp. 82, 232–3, 250–1, 282, 417–18, 501–2, 507–8, 565, 568, 624.

[93]　Private Papers of G. and E. Butling, IWMA, Documents.2423, e.g. letter from George dated 17 December 1916; letter from George dated 2 January 1917; letter to George from his father dated 4 August 1918, plus other undated letters.

[94]　Paul Johnson, *The Vanished Landscape: A 1930s Childhood in the Potteries* (London, 2004), for example, pp. 23, 109–12, 192–6.

[95]　Richard Nesbitt, quoted in Humphries and Gordon, *A Man's World*, p. 194. Also see Richard Nesbitt interview transcript, 'A Man's World', rolls 144–148.

[96]　John Bostock, Int014, *Families*, UKDA, pp. 30, 44.

In this period and earlier, working-class fathers often provided their sons with a vocational education, by teaching them to take up their own line of work, though this was a declining practice. Most working-class fathers were not in a position to pay for any kind of education, but this did not mean that many did not play a role in educating their children. In the collections of oral history interviews studied, numerous men demonstrate growing aspirational tendencies regarding the education of children. This crossed class boundaries; whilst the specific aspirations differed, the desire to enhance life expectations through education grew in parts of the upper-working class at least, as well as amongst upper- and middle-class fathers. Working-class behaviour, however, deviated from predominantly middle-class standards, as promoted in popular culture and in the attitudes of social researchers, in two key ways: a vocational or technical education and the acquisition of a skilled trade was valued by many parents over an academic education, and mothers were as often involved in educational matters amongst working-class families. For some working-class fathers, their own experiences pushed them into a new appreciation for education and the opportunities it opened up. Mr D2P, in a letter to Elizabeth Roberts, wrote of the contrast between himself, born in 1910, and his children, born in the 1930s:

> My wife and self were adamant that, if possible, the children should have a reasonable education, one then could get a job with some security. I, as a tradesman, had known in the early thirties hard times. All the children won places at the grammar and Park Schools and then on to University.[97]

George Short, an unemployed miner from County Durham whose children were born in the 1930s, discussed how he taught his children not only how to read and write, but also about the importance of education itself, and how they read stories by Charles Dickens and Jack London together. Education and class were connected here: George chose such books as he felt they were 'on the side of the poor'.[98]

The importance of education was abundantly clear to these children: Joe Phillips, a merchant seaman born in 1927 to a father from Barbados, discussed his father's insistence that he and his siblings made the most of the education they received, and that he was immensely proud when they 'came out on top'.[99] For Joe's father, education was not only a way to better oneself, an idea that clearly came across strongly to his son, but was also important in disproving the racial stereotypes he thought they might face. For some, the acute difference in education levels across generations of the same family was out of practical necessity. Mr B8P was simply unable to attend school beyond the age of 13, just before the First World War, because the family did not have enough money, yet his children both went to grammar schools in the interwar period. This was partly possible because

---

[97] Mr D2P, ERA, Preston 1890–1940 (letter from Mr D2P), p. 31. Also see Robert Williamson, 'A Labour of Love', roll 161, pp. 151–5.
[98] George Short, quoted in Humphries and Gordon, *A Man's World*, p. 180.
[99] Joe Phillips, 'A Man's World', roll 31, pp. 13–18.

of their smaller family size, which would have been similar in many working-class families at the time.[100]

The years between 1914 and 1960 witnessed significant shifts in terms of the attitudes of working-class people to education and jobs. Working-class fathers had involved themselves in children's education in earlier periods.[101] Yet, by the interwar period, numerous working-class fathers were arguably becoming interested in formal education, and often wanted their children to have different and better jobs than their own.[102] By the 1950s, it is clear that there was much more emphasis placed on the benefits of education, and those who did not concur with such an opinion were criticized. There was a tension here; many working-class fathers (and mothers) saw the benefits of education for their children in ways their own parents had not. Yet this was not always recognized by public commentators who pushed forward a more middle-class academic educational route, applying their own ideas about what was best for children to those they studied. Numerous working-class families rejected such models in favour of seeking the best opportunity for their children's security and happiness, whether this was through a school or more vocational education. Such parents held different attitudes to the previous generation, yet they did not always subscribe to the middle-class stance promoted in the press and beyond.

Many recall varied reactions to children's 11-plus exam results, and conflicting views between mothers and fathers and parents and teachers. Some fathers believed a grammar school education was the best option; Mr R3B's father argued with the school at their 'very unfair' decision not to allow him to resit the 11-plus test after he failed it during the Second World War.[103] Ted Walker noted a particular conflict of interests within himself on taking the exam in the mid-1940s; his father, a carpenter, wanted him to get a grammar school education, and he knew this would be a route to becoming a *'Thousand-a-year man'*. In contrast, 'if I failed, I would be what I aspired to be: a bloke like my father, but a grave disappointment to him'. Ted's father also put part of his wages into a tin for his son's *'Start-In-Life'*, reflecting his aspirational attitudes towards his child's future.[104] Mr P5B, furthermore, born in 1950, spoke of the different reactions to his winning of a grammar school place: 'Mother was over the moon about it, about going to grammar school because she had been. Father was a bit reserved because he had been to technical school and . . . thought that would be more for me, but there was no choice in the matter.'[105] Other fathers left this role to their wives due to lack of time or interest; Mr W7B spoke of his father's overtime getting in the way of his involvement in such matters in the 1950s.[106] Mrs R1P's father was actively negative about her education and against her taking the 11-plus in the mid-50s,

[100] Mr B8P, ERA, Preston 1890–1940, pp. 3–4.
[101] Julie-Marie Strange, *Fatherhood and the British Working Class, 1865–1914* (Cambridge, forthcoming 2014), ch. 4.
[102] Fisher, 'Fatherhood and the Experience', p. 227.
[103] Mr R3B, ERA, 1940–70, p. 20.
[104] Ted Walker, *The High Path* (London, 1982), pp. 16, 105. Original emphasis.
[105] Mr P5B, ERA, 1940–70, p. 28.   [106] Mr W7B, ERA, 1940–70, pp. 26–7.

telling her she was 'more or less thick', reflecting a continuing ambivalence of many working-class parents to education for girls. Furthermore, her father left all educational matters to her mother, as 'it wasn't my dad's job'.[107] Whilst numerous fathers remained rather uninvolved, many men did have high hopes for their children. Henry Curd, for example, born in 1915, suggested that his own father, a French polisher, encouraged him to get 'the best [education] you were capable of doing' without being overly pushy, echoing his own sentiment for his own children when he became a father during the Second World War: 'The best that they were capable of taking', but 'never push 'em on anything'.[108] Indeed, parents were much more likely to have sustained contact with their children's school in the latter part of this period, though mothers were still more likely to visit schools than fathers.[109] Mrs B2B contrasted her attitudes to education in the 1950s and 1960s, with her mother's, noting:

> I think my generation we were starting to go out more, than my mother. I mean she would never go to school for anything would mother, I mean there wasn't any open nights then, but you went to school if there was anything you wanted to see the teachers about. But she used to be frightened of the hierarchy I think then yes.[110]

This increased contact was a product of the changing educational system, but also a reflection of the intensified parental role, importance placed on childhood in terms of life chances, and greater appetite and ability of working-class parents to give their children 'a better start in life'.

Indeed, conflict could also arise at the moment at which a child left school, as demonstrated by a *Daily Mirror* report of the case of a schoolboy whose father removed him from grammar school on his turning 15. The parents had the ultimate authority to do this despite the school's lack of agreement, but the father was presented negatively for exercising his authority in this manner. The case was raised at a conference of head teachers, as an indicative example of this trend.[111] In this sense, the authority of the working-class father was challenged, and his judgement questioned. In the post-war age of the welfare state, with its emphasis on education for all, equality of opportunity, and achievement based on ability, there was a sense that working-class families should be expected to value learning. Some oral history interviewees recall such a situation; Sidney Ling's father, for example, thought that becoming a clerk was the most suitable and desirable route for his son, and took him out of grammar school aged 14, in 1924, for this purpose. Sidney still understood this as the behaviour of a 'good father', as good parents 'had ideas' for their offspring.[112] Mr M12B, furthermore, spoke of his father's 'heated argument' with the school in 1949 when he was 16. Whilst

---

[107] Mrs R1P, ERA, 1940–70, pp. 50–1.

[108] Henry Curd, Int042, *Families*, UKDA, p. 37.

[109] On school contact, see for example, Mrs C8L, ERA 1940–70, p. 14; Mrs J1B, ERA 1940–70, p. 49; Mr and Mrs L3P, ERA, 1940–70, p. 91; John Buck, Int022, *Families*, UKDA, p. 56; Terrence O'Farrell, Int103, *Families*, UKDA, p. 41.

[110] Mrs B2B, ERA, 1940–70, p. 97.　　　[111] *Daily Mirror*, 4 June 1952, p. 4.

[112] Sidney Ling, 'A Man's World', roll 27, p. 79.

Mr M12B wanted to leave to start work and continue studying an accountancy course via correspondence in his spare time, his teacher disagreed, but his father won out.[113] Thus, what fathers from different class backgrounds did for their sons cannot be judged in the same way, and the varying values ascribed to education and to different career paths must be taken into consideration. A similar kind of aspiration for one's children could look very different depending on social and educational circumstances.

During the First World War, a group of researchers in Sheffield analysed how 'well equipped' workers were in cultural and social terms. Educational aspirations for children were present in some men, yet those who wanted to keep their children in education often could not do so for economic reasons. Furthermore, such desires were a sign of being 'well equipped', whereas the working-class observers who conducted the research judged those men who wanted their children to earn as soon as possible negatively.[114] In contrast, social research evidence from late 1950s and 1960s indicates that although there remained diversity in fathers' involvement in education and their aspirations for their children, families were more able to realize such ambitions. Brian Jackson and Dennis Marsden spoke to numerous men who had high hopes for their children and sought to keep them in education as long as possible, even though many working-class families did not have much knowledge of the education system.[115] Some took great pleasure in their children's new experiences of grammar school and found it 'a new extension of living for themselves too'.[116]

The middle-class attitudes of the researchers differed from those they were studying in some ways, and, at times, influenced their analysis. In surveys by Ferdynand Zweig and Michael Young and Peter Willmott in the 1950s, education was again presented as part of a father's, rather than mother's, role. Zweig found that many of the male factory workers he interviewed in 1958 and 1959 took an 'intense' interest in their children's education, were proud of their achievements, particularly if they attended grammar school, and had strong aspirations for them.[117] Young and Willmott found an increasing interest of men in their children's education, and again, the desire for the children to do better than they had, through gaining white-collar employment. They suggested that this was not the case for all manual workers—some were hoping for a good technical education for their children.[118] However, arguably the middle-class prejudices of the researchers affected their analysis here, as they dismissed those fathers who hoped for a good apprenticeship or trade for their children as having lesser aspirations than those

---

[113] Mr M12B, ERA, 1940–70, p. 50. Also see Mr K1B, ERA, 1940–70, p. 2.

[114] St Philip's Settlement Education and Economics Research Society, *The Equipment of the Workers* (London, 1919), pp. 143, 153, 161, 165, 229, 233, 236, 243, 249.

[115] Brian Jackson and Dennis Marsden [1962], *Education and the Working Class* (Harmondsworth, 1970), pp. 31, 97, 129.

[116] Jackson and Marsden, *Education*, pp. 129, 131.

[117] Ferdynand Zweig, *The Worker in Affluent Society: Family Life and Industry* (London, 1961), pp. 20–2. Also see Jackson and Marsden, *Education*, esp. p. 134.

[118] Michael Young and Peter Willmott [1957], *Family and Kinship in East London* (Harmondsworth, 1967), pp. 28–9.

who hoped for white-collar jobs. Gaining a skilled trade, however, would have been a reasonable and sensible ambition for many families in this period, and thus the aspirations of these fathers too can be detected from the survey. The evidence from the interviews and surveys together form a picture of increasing aspirations for children, of working-class mothers and fathers being able to provide the tools necessary for children to fare better than their parents, many of whom had suffered unemployment or underemployment, or experienced bad working conditions. It is clear, then, that many fathers staked a lot on both their daughters' and their sons' education and future chances. This went beyond the economic provision of education by middle- and upper-class fathers, and many helped provide the education by teaching their offspring directly, as well as more general encouragement. Yet working-class aspirations could appear unambitious to middle-class observers, and working-class mothers remained as or more involved as fathers in comparison to their middle- and upper-class counterparts.

PROVIDING FOR THE FUTURE

Fathers, then, were portrayed as, to a degree, responsible for the education of their children, and this differed along class lines, in both the expectations placed on the father and in terms of how men behaved. For all fathers, regardless of what children's expectations were in terms of careers, there was an obligation to help children provide for themselves in the future, through gaining skills and knowledge to be successful in their chosen career. As Fisher noted in terms of working-class fathers, many felt that equipping their offspring for life beyond the parental home was one of their most important duties.[119] This was clearly most relevant in the case of sons, though for middle-class families particularly, as well amongst some working-class communities, the education of daughters was seen as increasingly important.[120] In her research into London in the interwar period, Sally Alexander found that fathers taught both sons and daughters a range of skills for future employment.[121]

The father's duty to ensure future provision for his daughters could also be enacted through the encouragement of an appropriate marriage, and throughout the period, a daughter's choice of husband continued to be scrutinized by fathers of all social backgrounds.[122] This is demonstrated by the traditional authority of a father over his daughter's actions and conduct in terms of courtship; as John Gillis notes of the late nineteenth and early twentieth centuries, fathers were often quite strict in their control of their daughters' romantic relationships, enforcing curfews

---

[119] Fisher, 'Fatherhood and the Experience', pp. 225–7.
[120] For example, see Mrs S6L, ERA, 1940–70, p. 7.
[121] Alexander, 'Men's Fears', p. 413.
[122] On the provision for daughters' future in the nineteenth century, see Nelson, *Invisible Men*, pp. 67–70; on the shifting legal rights of fathers regarding their children's marriages, see Fisher, 'Fatherhood and the Experience', p. 80. One or two men discussed dealing with their prospective

and interrogating potential partners.[123] Though such strictness was declining by the mid-twentieth century, a respect for fathers' authority over their daughters' futures remained. This was reflected in part by the tradition of a man asking a girl's father for her hand in marriage before asking the girl herself, a custom that Gillis suggests only became 'of real significance' by the middle of the twentieth century.[124] Fathers also helped children maintain or better their social status. This was arguably more important in the Victorian and Edwardian eras, yet the potential for fathers to provide the means to achieve a certain position—through a private education for example—meant this role remained important.[125]

Fathers' duty to ensure future provision for their children was consistently reinforced in the popular press. Finding jobs for sons formed a fruitful topic of discussion. Paternal ambitions for sons (and daughters) to take up a specific career path did appear to be declining, but were replaced with the desire for children to do well generally and to make their own decisions in order to achieve happiness. In March 1922, for example, numerous letters were published in *The Times* on the theme of choosing careers for sons. A letter from 'A Father', published under the subheading 'The Modern Father's Problem', posed the question 'What can we do with our sons?', as 'One hears on every hand that the professions are overcrowded, that the Army, the Navy, and the Civil Service are being reduced.'[126] The topic was said to have received 'widespread attention' even by the next day.[127] Many correspondents agreed with the letter-writer, and other contributors suggested solutions, with the perspectives of those in the civil service, law, clergy, education, and others given. The letters were also matched with editorials and articles, and several editions included features relating to this theme on more than one page.[128] The debate also moved on to discuss daughters' futures, which was, in an article of 13 April, said to be as important as that of sons.[129]

The length and nature of this debate indicates the significance attributed to fathers in the decision-making process about children's careers. Such debate continued through the period, but shifted slightly by the 1940s and 1950s to discussing fathers' (and mothers') ambitions for their children more generally, with much talk of giving children 'a good start' or a 'chance in life', and helping by

---

father-in-laws: Glyn Davies interview transcript, 'A Man's World', roll 54, pp. 17–18; Kenneth Davies Int047, *Families*, UKDA, p. 31; Edward Blishen, *Shaky Relations: An Autobiography* (London, 1981), p. 41.

[123] John R. Gillis, *For Better, For Worse: British Marriages, 1600 to the Present* (Oxford, 1985), p. 264.

[124] Gillis, *For Better*, p. 283.

[125] Carol Dyhouse, 'Mothers and Daughters in the Middle-Class Home, c.1870–1914', in J. Lewis (ed.), *Labour and Love: Women's Experiences of Home and Family, 1850–1940* (Oxford, 1986), p. 27; Christine Heward, 'Like Father, Like Son: Parental Models and Influences in the Making of Masculinity at an English Public School, 1929–1950', *Women's Studies International Forum* 13:1/2 (1990), p. 140.

[126] *The Times*, 16 March 1922, p. 8.   [127] *The Times*, 17 March 1922, p. 12.

[128] Numerous letters were printed between 17 March 1922 and 1 May 1922.

[129] *The Times*, 12 April 1922, p. 12. Also see, for example, *The Times*, 17 April 1922, pp. 6, 10; *The Times*, 18 April 1922, p. 12; *The Times*, 19 April 1922, p. 12; *The Times*, 24 April 1922, p. 7; *The Times*, 25 April 1922, p. 7.

providing them with the skills and education necessary to choose for themselves. A letter published in the *Daily Mirror* indicates this, in which 'Father of Three' states that 'A father's duty is to give his children a good start in life: it is in fact a debt which he has contracted through having brought them into the world.'[130] Advertisers, particularly those selling insurance, exploited this idea. Such advertisements were increasingly aimed at men of the working classes as well as their upper- and middle-class counterparts—an advert for Home Service Insurance in the *Daily Mirror* in 1952 is a prime example. A boy is pictured mending his bicycle, with the explanation that his father thinks he will be some kind of fitter, so is saving up to pay for his training through the insurance plan. That this might have been difficult for some fathers financially is recognized, but brushed aside: '[saving] isn't always easy, but Dad knows that it's worth a bit of a struggle to get his boy into a job with a future to it'.[131] Fathers were increasingly expected to have high ambitions for their children as well as ensuring provision for them in the future, no matter what their social class.

Those fathers who were engaged with their children's education were also much more likely to be involved in their choice of career path, though for some working-class men, their responsibilities only began when their child—most likely, their son—left school. In the first decades of the twentieth century, and earlier, boys frequently followed their fathers' footsteps into the family career, particularly in certain jobs and areas, such as mining and farming, and in middle-class occupations such as stockbroking or within a family business. Other fathers simply chose a job for their children.[132] Whether sons did take up their fathers' trades or professions seems to have depended largely on the area in which they lived and on their father's job. Some interviewees discussed how they did follow their father in their work: Sam Clarke, born 1907, decided to follow his father into cabinet-making; Joe Crofts became a miner like his father in 1927, as this was expected by his father's boss, at the potential cost of his job; and Dundas Hamilton took up his father's profession of stockbroking in 1946.[133] In some communities dependent on one main occupation, this was entirely natural; for Robert Morgan, who started work in the mines in south Wales in 1935 under the guidance of his father, 'My father, his father and grandfather had all been coal miners, so it seemed natural that I should become one.'[134] James Littlejohn noted that most sons followed their fathers into farming in the rural Scottish borders, in his anthropological survey conducted between 1949 and 1951, though he did believe that this was changing.[135] Young and Willmott found that only dockers' and porters' sons regularly followed

---

[130] *Daily Mirror*, 24 January 1935, p. 13.   [131] *Daily Mirror*, 25 March 1952, p. 11.

[132] For example W. H. Barrett, *A Fenman's Story* (London, 1965), p. 3.

[133] Sam Clarke, *Sam, an East End Cabinet-Maker* (London, n.d., c.1983), p. 15; Joe Crofts, quoted in Humphries and Gordon, *A Man's World*, pp. 57–8; Dundas Hamilton, quoted in Humphries and Gordon, *A Man's World*, p. 130.

[134] Robert Morgan, *My Lamp Still Burns* (Llandysul, 1981), p. 7.

[135] James Littlejohn, *Westrigg: The Sociology of a Cheviot Parish* (London, 1963), pp. 5–7, 117. For an example of this, see Andrew Purves, *A Shepherd Remembers: Reminiscences of a Border Shepherd* (East Lothian, 2001), p. 72.

their fathers' trades in late 1950s Bethnal Green, in contrast to previous generations in which this had happened in numerous occupations. They attributed this to the growing geographical mobility of Bethnal Green residents, and to the proliferation of types of employment in the area.[136] Indeed, the disruptions of both world wars and mass unemployment, as well as increasing geographical and social mobility, encouraged fathers and sons to consider different career paths. Many men discussed their ambitions for their children's careers in negative terms; they simply did not want them to take the same path as them. George Ryder became a bricklayer in the 1930s because his father, a docker, insisted he gain a skilled trade; Ron McGill started work for the Post Office in 1944 because of his father's belief that it represented secure employment, in contrast to his own unemployment in the 1930s.[137] In Coombes' autobiography, a final reflection, when the book was published in 1939, was on his son's own entry into the labour market in a couple of years' time: 'if any sacrifice on my part will prevent it, he shall not go into the mines. I would rather he did anything else than work under the ground.'[138] Many men from various social backgrounds, then, had greater ambitions for their children than themselves, and this often meant departure from a traditional family trade or profession.

The decline in sons following their fathers' career paths was exacerbated by the full employment following the war; wartime work experience also broadened the horizons of many young people. Young and Willmott found a decrease in sons following their fathers' trades in the early 1950s, and by the late 1950s, Zweig found that fewer than 13 per cent of men interviewed worked in the same or a similar trade than their father.[139] Colin Rosser and Christopher Harris, furthermore, noted that in Swansea there could be found a great degree of mobility between occupational grades, as well as between trades. This occurred in the most part 'upwards', with men moving towards more skilled and professional jobs, though there was a substantial amount of movement 'downwards' as well, attributed to the desire for more money regardless of the skill level needed.[140] Though a father was clearly expected to help his children provide for themselves in the future, and fathers lived up to this expectation, the means through which this was achieved were thus changing.[141]

The post-Second World War context of a changing educational landscape and full employment, coupled with the previous generation's memories of difficult times during unemployment, meant that many working-class fathers expressed higher but vaguer hopes for their children's careers; in this sense, retrospective

---

[136] Young and Willmott, *Family and Kinship*, pp. 97–103.

[137] George Ryder, 'A Man's World', roll 133, p. 2; Ron McGill, 'A Man's World', roll 41, p. 1. Also see Mr R3B, ERA, 1940–70, p. 22; Mr S9P, ERA, 1940–70, p. 9; Harry Tillett, Int140, *Families*, UKDA, p. 41.

[138] Coombes, *These Poor Hands*, p. 240.

[139] Young and Willmott, *Family and Kinship*, pp. 101–3; Zweig, *The Worker*, p. 139.

[140] Colin Rosser and Christopher Harris, *The Family and Social Change: A Study of Family and Kinship in a South Wales Town* (London, 1965), pp. 96–9; Zweig, *The Worker*, pp. 139–46.

[141] Some press articles were nostalgic about previous patterns: for example, *Daily Mirror*, 9 October 1925, p. 7; *Daily Mirror*, 5 January 1940, p. 11; *Daily Mirror*, 14 February 1940, p. 11; *Daily Mirror*, 17 October 1941, p. 5.

testimonies certainly reflected the rhetoric of the press, which promoted a newly aspirational working-class culture. Increasing numbers of fathers expressed a desire to help their children choose a path better than their own, but this meant they were less able to fulfil their traditional role of finding a job for their son. As such, the ambitions expressed were uncertain and focused on security and happiness more generally, rather than a specific route. Moreover, education became an increasingly attractive possibility. It provided new opportunities at a time when working-class parents and children were more receptive to them. As Julia Brannen and Ann Nilsen found in interviews with different generations of the same family, for those born in the 1940s onwards, what was passed on from parents to children was 'the freedom to choose a different way of life'.[142] Frank Jonston, a factory worker born 1933 and from Llanelli in Wales, contrasted three generations of his family, focusing particularly on his children born in the late 1950s and 1960s:

> When I was younger, it was different then . . . down here. I suppose [my parents] would have liked to have seen me go to university or gone further. But I don't think that worried em really. I think it's a bit different from today; it's different for myself and my children. I want my children to go as far as they can. Well, try and do their best, don't expect wonders out of them. But in them days it was different.[143]

Many parents, reflecting on their own experiences and considering their children's educational chances in a shifting social and cultural context, believed much more strongly that their children had a chance at a better 'start in life' than they had experienced.

POCKET MONEY, PRESENTS, AND SWEETS

The father's role as provider was also expected to encompass the giving of pocket money, sweets, and presents. The giving of pocket money as a matter of course was a relatively new development; as Siân Pooley notes, the idea of pocket money for children was not present in the late nineteenth century.[144] This was a substantial break from the past, as the concept of children's pocket money went from unknown to widely accepted within a short space of time. Indeed, understandings of the term 'pocket money' previously referred to the money that was available to the father, or other wage earners, after household expenses had been met, an understanding that continued into the twentieth century for some time, alongside its more recent definition of money for children. By the interwar period, the expectation that even the poorest fathers should give their children a 'Saturday penny' was illustrated by Joseph Toole, Labour MP for Salford South, in a House of Commons debate of 1931. He attacked the government's tax policy on this

---

[142] Julia Brannen and Ann Nilsen, 'From Fatherhood to Fathering: Transmission and Change among British Fathers in Four-Generation Families', *Sociology* 40 (2006), p. 341.

[143] Frank Jonston, Int076, *Families*, UKDA, p. 11.

[144] Siân K. Pooley, 'Parenthood and Child-Rearing in England, c.1860–1910', PhD Thesis (University of Cambridge, 2009), pp. 154–5.

basis, suggesting that the hard line taken would mean poor fathers would no longer be able to fulfil this 'common practice'.[145]

Toole was largely justified in this claim; many fathers gave pocket money. This habit crossed class boundaries, though clearly the manner in which fathers gave differed. The scale and regularity with which pocket money was given varied between different income levels; for some fathers with an uncertain or particularly low income, the giving of pocket money was by necessity sporadic, and some did not meet the weekly standard set by Toole. In Lancashire, many fathers gave small amounts of money to their children; Mr D2P, born 1910, recalled on his birthday 'Father always gave us coppers and when we got older, somehow managed a shilling.'[146] For Mrs C5P, born 1919 and who, like Mr D2P, lived in Preston, her regular penny was given out on Fridays, that being payday in the region:

> On a Friday night we used to come home and we used to stand by my dad. He used to say, 'What are you stood there for?' I'd say, 'Nothing.' Then he'd turn round and he'd put his hand in his pocket and he'd say, 'That's one, two, three.' . . . That were our Friday penny.[147]

Bert Healey, born 1908, received four pence from his father, a driver, who was granted custody of Bert but not his other three children after a split with his wife; Bert, who lived in Brighton, considered this 'a lot of money in those days'.[148] Phyllis Willmott recalled her father's generosity with mixed feelings as she was growing up in interwar London; her father would regularly give her and her siblings half-crowns, but this reflected that he was 'by temperament incapable' of saving money.[149] Such practices continued throughout the period, but children could expect a more generous allowance by later decades; Mrs M12B, born 1936, received from her father 'half a crown a week, which was a lot really' when she was at school.[150] Mr Y1P, born 1948, was lucky enough to have two parents in work; he received 'something like five shillings' a week in the late 1950s and early 1960s.[151]

Providing pocket money and presents was important to men serving away from their family homes in both world wars. Forces pay could be meagre, but many fathers writing to their families referred to sending home pocket money, toys, and sweets where possible, and feelings of frustration when impossible. For those fighting in France in the First World War, this was often very difficult, but men found ways to fulfil their role as a gift-giver, and indeed it was one of the few roles they could still enact. Some sent drawings and sketches of their own doing as a small token for their children; two letters from P. A. Wise, a gunner serving on the Western Front, to his young daughter are filled with light-hearted drawings of all

[145] Hansard, HC, vol. 256, c.1078, 17 September 1931.
[146] Mr D2P, ERA, Preston 1890–1940 (letter from Mr D2P), p. 11.
[147] Mrs C5P, ERA, Preston 1890–1940, p. 9.
[148] Bert Healey, *Hard Times and Easy Terms and Other Tales by a Queen's Park Cockney* (Brighton, 1980), p. 27.
[149] Phyllis Willmott, *Growing Up in a London Village: Family Life between the Wars* (Halifax, 1979), p. 95.
[150] Mrs M12B, ERA, 1940–70, p. 11.   [151] Mr Y1P, ERA, 1940–70, p. 17.

aspects of his life in France.[152] E. G. Buckeridge, likewise serving in France in the First World War, filled letters with sketches of his son playing, on a train, in bed, and various other light-hearted drawings of animals and the like, as well as of himself. His letters home ceased in May 1917, at which point his wife was told he was missing.[153] Others managed to send presents; C. Jones sent toys, handkerchiefs, and regular picture cards to his daughter whilst stationed in Britain, and sent money for his wife to buy her a birthday present when he could not find anything, with specific instructions to 'let Dink have it in bed when she wakes up'. When in France, he described how he was saving pictures from cigarette packets but there was little to buy.[154] The letters of George and Eric Butling demonstrate the pleasure with which children received these small gifts, and the letters themselves.[155]

Fathers largely behaved in the same way in the Second World War, reflecting the continuity of this role and the consistent pleasure many men derived from it. C. D. Fuller, for example, sent home Canadian dollars and presents. In June 1941, he wrote to his elder son, David, 'I hope you will enjoy some sweets or ice-cream with the $1 bill enclosed', whilst in a letter of September 1942, he suggested they use the enclosed dollar for a trip to the cinema.[156] F. I. Williams, who fought in Egypt and then became a prisoner-of-war in Italy, enjoyed his role as a present-giver whilst he was training in England: 'I am going to buy Susan some more clothes. It is fun going round the shops, hunting for them.' He also sent shoes and clothes from Egypt and expressed a similar sentiment in a letter to his wife, which was all the more poignant as it was sent from the prisoner-of-war camp in which he now resided: 'I do hope you had as much pleasure in receiving them as I had in buying & packing them.'[157] A. H. Wright wrote extensively of his love and devotion to his baby daughter, and was disappointed he could not provide properly for her. Stationed in China, he found it near-impossible to find presents to send home: 'Tell G[illian] her Daddy is so sorry Chungking has so little to offer for little girl babies, else he would buy her lots of things.'[158] Children were delighted with any presents that could be sent and disappointed when some inevitably went missing; Mrs Dockrill, for example, wrote to her husband, who was serving with the RAF in India, that their son was 'watching every post for the book' his father had sent, and decided not to tell him that his father had sent presents in the future to avoid any disappointment.[159] This role mattered to fathers living nearer

---

[152] Private Papers of P. A. Wise, IWMA, Documents.1131.

[153] Private Papers of E. G. Buckeridge, IWMA, Documents.13267, numerous undated letters.

[154] Private Papers of C. Jones, IWMA, Documents.10085, pp. 48, 103, 140, 210, 451.

[155] Private Papers of G. and E. Butling, IWMA, Documents.2423, e.g. letter dated 2 January 1917, 19 February 1917, 9 April 1917.

[156] Private Papers of Mr and Mrs C. D. Fuller, IWMA, Documents.16408, letter to wife dated 29 June 1941; letter to David dated 1 September 1942.

[157] Private Papers of F. I. Williams, IWMA, Documents.17022, letter to wife dated 27 May 1941; letter to wife postmarked 22 December 1942; also see letter to daughter postmarked 28 December 1942.

[158] Private Papers of A. H. Wright, IWMA, Documents.13285, p. 23.

[159] Private Papers of Mrs H. L. Dockrill, IWMA, Documents.11743, letter to Warwick dated 7 January 1943; letter to Warwick dated 20 May 1943.

home too: M. Canty worked as an insurance agent during the Second World War, and was separated from his evacuated family; he tried to get hold of chocolates and sweets for his family despite shortages of such items.[160] Likewise, men abroad on service delighted in receiving gifts and photos from their families.[161] This evidence, of course, represents the most generous fathers; the nature of this source material means that those who did not write home, with or without the enclosure of small gifts, are not represented in such archives. Robert Williamson, who fought in the Second World War, highlighted this, noting that though he 'spent most of my evenings writing letters given the chance', 'Some fellows never bothered if they didn't have a letter you know because they didn't want to write one back.'[162]

For working-class fathers, making toys for their young children seems to have been a common, cheaper way of providing gifts, and was an important theme in accounts from both fathers and children. Again, this theme was prominent in the press, as fathers' achievements were celebrated.[163] Abrams' working-class Stirling interviewees noted that their fathers made them various toys, and would often bring sweets home for them after work.[164] Other oral history interviews indicate this was commonplace. Mr M14B, born 1931, spoke about his father making many toys for him; he even went as far as selling them for a small amount to other parents.[165] Ted Cunningham, a father in the 1930s, took a lot of pleasure in giving his children presents. He said, 'my ears were always open to whatever they were talking about, whatever they wanted', thus indicating that this role was one enjoyed by fathers as well as children.[166] Others, such as Alf Short, a father in 1930s Sussex, used to hoard presents away in time for Christmas.[167] Mrs H3P, born 1931, explicitly contrasted her mother and father here: 'my dad would give me the odd halfpenny to go to the shop for a ha'porth of wine gums. But my mum would never give any, I could ask until I was blue in the face!'[168] Some fathers used this role to get what they wanted; Mrs J1P, born 1912, spoke about her father, who gave her threepence for sweets to keep her happy whilst he went to the pub on Sundays. Furthermore, those fathers who failed to provide would have been unlikely to fulfil this role.[169] There is little evidence about fathers giving or making toys and presents in the social surveys used here. Arguably, this indicates the

[160] Private Papers of M. Canty, IWMA, Documents.13575, undated letters to wife.

[161] In the First World War, see Private Papers of G. and E. Butling, IWMA, Documents.2423, pp. 42, 62, 73; Private Papers of J. W. Mudd, IWMA, Documents.1174. In the Second World War, see Private Papers of D. E. Parker, IWMA, Documents.1926; Private Papers of A. H. Wright, IWMA, Documents.13285, esp. pp. 13, 16, 18, 19, 23. Also see the papers of D. S. Cave, a father who wrote and sent many parcels to his prisoner-of-war son. Private Papers of D. S. Cave, IWMA, Documents.6443.

[162] Robert Williamson, 'A Labour of Love', roll 159, p. 28.

[163] For example, see *Daily Mirror*, 25 November 1935, p. 19; *Daily Mirror*, 11 January 1947, p. 11; *Manchester Guardian*, 17 June 1949, p. 3.

[164] Abrams, 'There Was Nobody', p. 232.   [165] Mr M14B, ERA, 1940–70, p. 65.

[166] Ted Cunningham, 'A Man's World', roll 93, p. 81.

[167] Alf Short, 'A Labour of Love', roll 212, p. 5.

[168] Mrs H3P, ERA, 1940–70, p. 61.

[169] Mrs J1P, ERA, Preston 1890–1940, p. 21. Also see Mrs D3P/Mrs T5P/Mrs M6P, ERA, Preston 1890–1940, pp. 31–2; Miss T4P, ERA, Preston 1890–1940, p. 30; Mr N3L, ERA 1940–70,

apparent insignificance of the practice in the eyes of researchers; for them, investigating what fathers did in terms of caring for their child more directly, as well as whether they provided material necessities, seemed to have been more important. Yet, by examining the testimonies of both fathers and children, it is clear that the custom of present-giving was, in many families, much more meaningful than the spending of a few pennies at the weekend, or receiving a bag of sweets. It could have real emotional importance.

These practices were reinforced by a clear expectation within newspapers that fathers should provide pocket money to all their children, no matter what they earned. Some articles asserted this explicitly, though often the role of the father as the provider of pocket money was simply assumed without question. Such a belief was clear in debates about how much pocket money was appropriate. A commentator, L. F. Ramsey, argued in the *Daily Mirror* in 1927 that children were not being taught the value of money. He contended that pocket money should be a regular affair, given in proportion to a father's income, and should not be supplemented by 'teasing' more money out of father occasionally.[170] In another article of the same year, Winifred Philips suggested children were given too much money, and so did not comprehend its value.[171] Both writers agreed that it was reasonable for a child to expect pocket money from their father, but that fathers would be wise to accompany the provision of pocket money with lessons in economic sense; this educational role regarding the management of money again demonstrates the father's role in teaching and guiding his children. The idea was taken further in an article from the women's pages of the *Mirror* in 1934, in which the author, 'Jennifer', wrote about a young boy who had to submit weekly balance sheets to his father, detailing the spending of his pocket money.[172] While the aim of the article was to amuse and it was likely exaggerated for comic effect, the writer highlighted that the same boy became a successful businessman, who retired comfortably at an early age.

Numerous articles throughout the period detailed court cases in which fathers of children caught stealing were reprimanded for their lack of generosity or ability to give pocket money, and were blamed for their children's crimes. This indicates that some fathers at least did not see this as part of their role, or failed to fulfil it, and that this became both legally and culturally unacceptable. For example, an article from the front page of the *Daily Mirror* in 1948 detailed the case of a little girl who waited outside the court, 'timid and apprehensive', to hear her punishment for stealing a rattle and socks for her baby sister, as she had no money with which to buy such items. The chairman of the juvenile court criticized her father for keeping two pounds a week for himself and never giving his daughter any

---

p. 25; Lily Felstead, quoted in Steve Humphries and Pamela Gordon, *A Labour of Love: The Experience of Parenthood in Britain 1900–1950* (London, 1993), pp. 137–8; Winifred Foley [1977/1978/1981], *Shiny Pennies and Grubby Pinafores: How We Overcame Hardship to Raise a Happy Family in the 1950s* (London, 2010), p. 239.

[170] *Daily Mirror*, 8 July 1927, p. 7.   [171] *Daily Mirror*, 12 August 1927, p. 7.
[172] *Daily Mirror*, 15 March 1934, p. 27.

pocket money. He promised from then on to give his daughter half a crown a week, which the chairman thought reasonable.[173] A 1952 case reported in the *Daily Mirror* also illustrates this expectation: the writer of the article, entitled 'The girl who had no pocket money', emphasized the amount the father, a shipyard worker, was earning in overtime payments, and quoted the judge, who suggested that the father was wrong for buying cigarettes instead of giving his daughter money. The judge was also reported as saying that a father could afford one shilling a week for pocket money, however poor he may be.[174] Similarly, in the *Manchester Guardian* in 1958, a father whose son had been stealing was quoted as admitting to responsibility for his son's crimes, stating: 'If I had done what a father should have done he would not be here to-day.'[175] Pocket money was thus constructed as part of every father's role, and coverage of such cases served to remind fathers of this.

Cultural representations of fatherhood also reinforced the idea of fathers as a source of sweets and presents.[176] The father's role as gift-giver was frequently underlined in advertising, with the recurrent suggestion to 'ask father' for toys or sweets, or the appeal to the father himself to treat his children to the advertised product. In an advertisement for bicycles in the *Daily Mirror* in 1956, father is told, 'Give the gift that brings happiness every day.' A small illustration of a son and father, with the son saying 'thanks daddy', further reinforced both the desirability of this item, and the perceived obligation for fathers to provide presents.[177] This was also a common theme for advertising sweets and small treats for children; for example, an advertisement for date dainties in the *Daily Mirror* in 1929 with the caption 'Brought me anything Dad?' indicates this expectation. The advertisement highlighted that this was a common greeting as father returned from work, and reminded father of the 'happy moments' that could be had as he watched his children's faces fill with 'sheer delight'. The drawing of a jovial father and daughter reinforced this message.[178] Across the press could be found a greater investment in the pleasures of provision. Advertisers also noted a change to the father's role; in an advert for the toy department in Selfridges, published in *The Times* in 1928, for example, the writer, 'Callisthenes', suggested that now the 'heavy father' was disappearing, men could enjoy buying toys for their children. Whilst 'the heavy father could never have been really happy in a toy department, even if he would have entered it', 'modern fathers' were to be seen enjoying their shopping.[179] Throughout the popular press, there was thus an emerging image of a father who enjoyed providing such gifts and presents.

The emotional importance of breadwinning and giving presents took on greater significance during both world wars and also gained in prominence as the century progressed, with increasing numbers of men feeling the need to work hard to

[173] *Daily Mirror*, 23 January 1948, p. 1.   [174] *Daily Mirror*, 28 March 1952, p. 6.
[175] *Manchester Guardian*, 30 December 1958, p. 2.
[176] This was emphasized by Enid Blyton, as noted above. Blyton, *Five on a Treasure Island*, p. 242.
[177] *Daily Mirror*, 8 November 1956, p. 19.
[178] *Daily Mirror*, 17 December 1929, p. 6.   [179] *The Times*, 1 December 1928, p. 10.

achieve a good standard of living for their families. The discussion of the emotional resonance of provision in popular culture arguably helped create a more explicit recognition of this amongst families—this will be further explored in the context of men's relationships with their children in Chapter 4.[180]

CONCLUSION

The father's role as provider was thus relatively uncontroversial and widely accepted in the period in question. A growing emphasis on a father taking pride in and pleasure from this role can be found from the 1930s onwards. Alongside this positive affirmation of the father's role as provider was the continual reprimanding of fathers who did not provide, whether they were married to the child's mother or not. It is clear there remained a spectrum of behaviour on the part of fathers, with other family members remembering men's lack of consideration for their material needs. It became seen as less acceptable, by both commentators in the public sphere as well as amongst individual communities, for men to spend their spare money on themselves; choosing to buy sweets and presents for children was increasingly positioned as more acceptable than the purchase of alcohol and tobacco for oneself.

In the 1930s, the idea of the father as more than just a breadwinner was continually reiterated, with numerous examples of writers explicitly suggesting this idea and warning fathers to make sure they did more than hand over their wages each week. Class was significant here: the image of the father of whom such pieces disapproved tended to be working-class, and there was arguably an unspoken assumption that middle-class fathers would have been taking more of an interest in their children anyway. In an article in the *Daily Mirror* from 1955 for example, John Thompson looked 'Behind the Headlines', and reported on a recently published book on children in Liverpool. The writer highlighted 'masculine selfishness', whereby a man thought 'his responsibility comes to an end when he has given his wife the housekeeping money'. The article, and the book on which it was based, focused on children growing up in Liverpool's dockland area, and thus this was clearly a warning for working-class men—it was noted that boys who go to public schools would get their 'bottoms tanned' there, and 'that's that'. The danger presented when men failed to act as more than providers was reiterated at the end of the article, when the writer highlighted that sons would tend to follow their fathers' bad example.[181]

Conversely, the idea that fathers should be more than breadwinners was also positively affirmed, such as in the *Daily Mirror* in 1938, where resident agony aunt

---

[180] This notion of breadwinning does have a longer history, as demonstrated in the research of Doolittle and Strange, in the late nineteenth century. See Megan Doolittle, 'Time, Space and Memories: The Father's Chair and Grandfather Clocks in Victorian Working Class Domestic Lives', *Home Cultures* 8:3 (2011), p. 250; Strange, 'Fatherhood, Providing', p. 1008.

[181] *Daily Mirror*, 8 January 1955, p. 7.

Dorothy Dix gave advice to an 'Unhappy Father' whose wife would not let him be involved with his children. He wrote of his wife, 'She apparently thinks that all I am good for is to pay the bills.' Dorothy Dix advised this man to stand up for his 'rights as a father', suggesting not only was it perceived as good for a father to be more than a breadwinner—stating that every child at some point needs the 'strong and tender hand of a father to guide him'—but that this was part of a father's rights.[182] The idea of a father's role as more than a simple provider of material necessities is thus clear, and this theme was increasingly emphasized through the period. The provision of treats and pocket money beyond the necessities was part of this notion, alongside the idea of a father as an entertainer for children, as a helper or secondary parent to the mother, and as a disciplinary figure to guide his children, help them develop, and chastise or punish them if necessary. This will be explored in Chapter 3.

---

[182] *Daily Mirror*, 17 January 1938, p. 26.

3

'Wait Till Your Father Gets Home'?
The Father's Roles in the Family

The centrality of provision to the father's role has been made clear by Chapter 2; yet this centrality should not be mistaken for sole importance. Steve Humphries and Pamela Gordon suggest, in their oral history project on parenting between 1900 and 1950, that men were stereotyped as breadwinners in society and culture, and consequently as not very involved in the day-to-day running of the household.[1] Yet numerous fathers they interviewed highlighted the other roles they played within family life. Though the centrality of breadwinning is clear, the limitation of fatherhood to provision is an inaccurate picture of this period, in terms of both representation and experience. There were other dimensions of fatherhood that were understood to be valuable and worthwhile, mostly to be undertaken when his role as provider had been satisfied. Indeed, there could be a tension here as, for many fathers of all social backgrounds, providing to a satisfactory standard could limit the time they had available to fulfil other responsibilities. This chapter will explore these roles, of 'entertaining', 'guiding', and 'helping', all of which were understood to be components of fatherhood prior to the twentieth century. As John Tosh states of the nineteenth century, 'Above all, fathers were licensed to play.' Furthermore, guiding and disciplining children were important aspects of Victorian fatherhood, and some fathers, particularly those of the 'middling sort', were involved in the nursing of children too.[2] Yet the status of the father was also perceived to be under threat by the late nineteenth century, and as Tosh highlights, 'Procreating and providing were practically the only paternal functions left unscathed', as the mother's status was increased and the state's intervention grew.[3] Simon Szreter also suggests that having children was of decreasing importance to men by the end of the nineteenth century, and it became less possible for men to participate in child-rearing.[4]

---

[1] Steve Humphries and Pamela Gordon, *A Labour of Love: The Experience of Parenthood in Britain 1900–1950* (London, 1993), pp. 84–5. Also see Lynn Abrams, '"There Was Nobody Like My Daddy": Fathers, the Family and the Marginalisation of Men in Modern Scotland', *Scottish Historical Review* 78:2 (1999), p. 241; Lynne Segal, *Slow Motion: Changing Masculinities, Changing Men* (3rd edn, Basingstoke, 2007), p. 23.

[2] John Tosh, *A Man's Place: Masculinity and the Middle-Class Home in Victorian England* (New Haven, CT, and London, 1999), pp. 87–90.

[3] Tosh, *A Man's Place*, p. 160.

[4] Simon Szreter, *Fertility, Class and Gender in Britain, 1860–1940* (Cambridge, 1996), p. 462.

The first half of the twentieth century witnessed significant developments in the understanding of the father's role. As the help available to women to run their homes decreased, through the lack of residential domestic servants or the growing distance between the nuclear family and wider kinship networks, particularly for working-class families, fathers helped around the home more.[5] By doing so, they were enacting a role as a good husband as well as helpful father. Entertaining children and guiding and shaping their characters became increasingly intertwined, as the seemingly light-hearted duty of a father to play with his children became imbued with a new psychological importance in certain popular cultural discourses by the mid-twentieth century. The absence of large numbers of men during both world wars brought fathers' disciplinary roles into focus, as fears about juvenile delinquency escalated. Yet, at the same time, a father's role as a guiding figure in the shaping of children's characters expanded to include gentler modes of moral education, beyond an initial focus on rules to be followed and discipline and punishment to be meted out when they were not. This could include the religious socialization of children, bringing them up in a (usually) Christian spirit, as Lucy Delap has highlighted.[6] Additionally, more responsibility for children's welfare was placed on the father as well as the mother. Motherhood was being continually raised in status in the first half of the twentieth century and, as such, pressures on mothers grew in intensity.[7] Yet this also occurred in terms of fatherhood, as the psychological significance placed on childhood experience rendered parenting more important.[8] The father's role was expanding, albeit along traditional lines, and his roles were increasingly seen as significant.

ENTERTAINING

Fathers were frequently associated with fun, and it was often suggested that they should play with children, and take them for holidays and outings. Men were often happy to participate in the more pleasurable aspects of child-rearing, and cultural

[5] Joanna Bourke, *Working Class Cultures in Britain 1890–1960: Gender, Class, and Ethnicity* (London, 1994), pp. 82–7.

[6] Lucy Delap, '"Be Strong and Play the Man": Anglican Masculinities in the Twentieth Century', in L. Delap and S. Morgan (eds), *Men, Masculinities and Religious Change in Twentieth-Century Britain* (Basingstoke, 2013), p. 134.

[7] Abrams, 'There Was Nobody', pp. 219–42; Ann Alston, *The Family in English Children's Literature* (London and New York, 2008), p. 22; Leonore Davidoff, Megan Doolittle, Janet Fink, and Katherine Holden, *The Family Story: Blood, Contract and Intimacy, 1830–1939* (Harlow, 1999), p. 210; Janet Finch and Penny Summerfield, 'Social Reconstruction and the Emergence of Companionate Marriage, 1945–59', in D. Clark (ed.), *Marriage, Domestic Life and Social Change* (London, 1991), pp. 7–12; Daniel Grey, 'Discourses of Infanticide in England, 1880–1922', PhD Thesis (Roehampton University, 2009), p. 26; Jane Lewis, *The Politics of Motherhood: Child and Maternal Welfare in England, 1900–1939* (London, 1980); Diane Richardson, *Women, Motherhood and Childrearing* (Basingstoke, 1993), pp. 29–48.

[8] Davis makes this point in terms of family life in general. Angela Davis, 'A Critical Perspective on British Social Surveys and Community Studies and Their Accounts of Married Life c.1945–1970', *Cultural and Social History* 6:1 (2009), pp. 47–64.

constructions placed increasing emphasis on the idea that men should and could enjoy fatherhood. This can be seen most clearly in the father's role as a playmate, which was not a chore like numerous other childcare tasks, and, as Margaret Williamson notes, could easily be completed within a man's leisure time.[9] It was also easier for men to take on this task in the home, which for them was predominantly a space of leisure, unlike for their wives. There is ample evidence that fathers genuinely enjoyed their role as the 'playing parent'. Clearly, this was not the case for all men, but by the end of this period a majority of fathers played with their children fairly regularly. As Elizabeth Bott highlighted in her intensive but small-scale study of twenty families in London in the late 1950s, there was in several families 'a recognized tendency for fathers to specialize in entertaining the children'.[10] John and Elizabeth Newson's study of over 700 Nottingham families with a 1-year-old infant provides additional compelling evidence. In measuring fathers' participation in childcare through interviews with their wives, they dismissed playing with a child as a 'useless' criterion for assessing involvement levels, as it was so universal: 83 per cent of those assessed were found to play with their 1-year-old child 'often', and another 16 per cent did so 'sometimes'.[11]

Evidence from oral history interviews and other testimony material further illustrates the enjoyment fathers gained from this role; the majority of fathers seemed to have spent some time at least playing with their offspring. Of the children's accounts in interviews, fifty-four discussed this role: forty-four said they played with their fathers at least occasionally, with ten stating this never happened. Of seventy-seven fathers, twenty-one highlighted playing with their children; no father explicitly said he did not do this. T. D. Laidlaw wrote of this in letters to his wife at home in Glasgow when he was serving in the Army Service Corps on the Western Front in the First World War. He sent postcards to his children as well as his wife, and wrote in hope of returning home after the war had ended in spring 1919, instructing her to 'Give me wee kiddies my love, tell them it won't be very long now until they will have their Dad every Sunday to play with.'[12] Ivy Summers, a working-class mother of twelve children born between 1920 and 1942, discussed how fond her husband was of all of them, saying that he used to sing to them and play with them whilst she was at work.[13] Mr S4P, an only child born to a Preston family in 1915, noted that 'my father played with me much more than mother did' and described how they watched cricket and football matches together, and when he was younger, 'we played on the sands, my father helped me to make sand-castles, as fathers all over do'.[14] In this description, Mr S4P universalized the

[9] Margaret Williamson, '"He Was Good With the Bairns": Fatherhood in an Ironstone Mining Community, 1918–1960', *North East History* 32 (1998), p. 98.

[10] Elizabeth Bott [1957], *Family and Social Network: Roles, Norms, and External Relationships in Ordinary Urban Families* (London, 1971), p. 81.

[11] John and Elizabeth Newson [1963], *Patterns of Infant Care in an Urban Community* (Harmondsworth, 1974), pp. 137–40.

[12] Private Papers of T. D. Laidlaw, Imperial War Museum Archive (IWMA), Documents.11018, transcript p. 110.

[13] Ivy Summers, 'A Labour of Love', British Library, roll 2, pp. 22–3.

[14] Mr S4P, Elizabeth Roberts Archive (ERA), Preston 1890–1940, pp. 26–7, 41.

father's role as playmate from his own father, and presumably himself, to an experience to be found within all families. Martin Jack, from Oldham and born in 1931, also contrasted his mother with his father; whilst his father played numerous board games with him, his mother was 'not that way inclined'.[15] Robert Williamson, a working-class father of one from Bradford, discussed how he used to enjoy playing games as a family in the evening, and how he used to 'croon a bedtime tune' to his daughter, born 1932.[16] Furthermore, one of the main benefits he valued in a new house on an estate was having a proper garden as a playground for his daughter.[17] This was an important theme for interviewees living in modern, spacious housing; play was possible here, unlike in older, cramped working-class housing in which children were forced to play in the streets.

Some fathers were impatient with their children, whilst others did not recognize play as particularly beneficial for their children in relation to other roles; time playing together served the purpose of amusing that father momentarily, perhaps whilst waiting for a meal. Henry Curd, for example, born 1915 and from Surrey, spoke of his father's emphasis on him getting an apprenticeship and on educational matters, but 'I never used to sort of play with [my father], not [that] I remember', though later he used to play with his own children born in the 1940s.[18] Ron Barnes contrasted his grandfather, who fought in the First World War, and his own father, born around 1910: 'Dad's father was not a man to amuse kids in his young days, perhaps through being too exhausted after a day's work. So Dad took over here, also', by inventing games for his younger siblings, something he continued when he became a father to Ron, although their relationship was not always an easy one.[19] For some, it was a question of time, or lack thereof; Mr L4B, for example, born in 1931, spoke of his father's dedication to the family shop and, as a result, the fact that he 'just didn't have the opportunity' to play in the way that other fathers did.[20]

Even when some fathers did have spare time for leisure, hobbies could be more important to them; Mr M12B's father used to dedicate his free hours to politics and gardening, and so Mr M12B had 'no recollections of my mother and father playing with me a lot, no'.[21] The interplay between Harry Tillett, from the West Midlands and born 1929, and his wife in their interview underlines the idea that playing with children was seen as a leisure activity for men who enjoyed time with their children. After speaking about how Mrs Tillett did most of the childcare chores:

---

[15] Martin Jack, Int075, P. Thompson and H. Newby, *Families, Social Mobility and Ageing, an Intergenerational Approach, 1900–1988* [computer file]. Colchester, Essex: UK Data Archive (UKDA) [distributor], July 2005. SN: 4938, p. 27. Also see Mathew Meret, Int089, *Families*, UKDA, p. 26.

[16] Robert Williamson, 'A Labour of Love', roll 161, pp. 47–8, 56.

[17] Robert Williamson interview recording, 'A Labour of Love', British Library, number C590/01/412.

[18] Henry Curd, Int042, *Families*, UKDA, pp. 14, 33.

[19] Ron Barnes, *Coronation Cups and Jam Jars* (London, 1976), pp. 90–1.

[20] Mr L4B, ERA, 1940–70, p. 23.   [21] Mr M12B, ERA, 1940–70, pp. 3, 21.

INTERVIEWER: When they got older then, was there something particular you did with them? Would you read to them?

SUBJECT: Oh yeah—I used to read or play with them in the garden or . . .

WIFE: Yeah, he always played with 'em—he always played with children, anybody's children he'd play with. Used to roll about and gambol and fight and that. Always played with them.[22]

Playing with children was, in this instance, positioned as Harry Tillett's choice; he would play with 'anybody's children', highlighting that it was for his own enjoyment more than his children's particular benefit.

In a more middle-class family context, Rose Luttrell suggested that her children, born in the late 1910s and early 1920s in Wiltshire, were in many ways closer to their nanny than herself and her husband. Yet, though her husband was 'much too frightened' to feed the children or anything particularly practical, he played with them regularly. As Rose stated, 'All he did was to enjoy them, he loved the children.'[23] This hints at the different meanings of the act of playing with children; some discourses emphasized the benefits of play for children, yet for men, it could be an amusing distraction or way to spend leisure time, whereas for their wives, men's entertainment of children allowed them to complete other domestic work. Other men did position their playtime as more about their children than themselves: Leonard Canning, for example, from Aldershot, discussed how he took care of bedtime for his only son, born in 1945: 'he always liked me to put him to bed because we used to have a bit of a romp on the bed, you know. Throw him up and that sort of thing. He liked that.'[24] From a child's perspective, fathers thus represented the more 'fun' side of parenting; for most men, whilst at home they were at leisure, whereas the home represented a place of work for women. That fathers were the parent who played and entertained underlines the fact that child-care as a chore remained the responsibility of mothers; parenting was part of men's leisure time rather than labour in itself. Such a conception did not change significantly across families from all class backgrounds, even though parents increasingly spoke of the shared responsibility of child-rearing as the period progressed.

Throughout different sections of newspapers, fathers' role as playmates was reinforced and encouraged. Many commentators saw playing with children as a positive aspect of good fatherhood, and fathers who did this were praised. For example, an article of 1921 in the *Daily Mirror* highlighted that father was a specialist in this area, and a more interesting holiday companion for children, as he was never too busy to play, unlike mother, was an 'authority' on ice creams, and 'has a way with a spade that would win the respect of the most blasé four-year-old'.[25] Similarly, an article by Evelyn Smith from the *Manchester Guardian* in 1928 established fathers' superiority over mothers as playmates, noting 'Father is always playmate-in-chief.' Smith also highlighted that parents in the 1920s were much more involved in playing with their children than the previous

[22] Harry Tillett, Int140, *Families,* UKDA, p. 79.

[23] Rose Luttrell, quoted in Humphries and Gordon, *A Labour,* p. 92.

[24] Leonard Canning, Int025, *Families,* UKDA, p. 23.

[25] *Daily Mirror,* 27 July 1921, p. 2.

generation. A father's tirelessness and energy was also reiterated, again in compari-son to the less fun mother:

> It is father who races and chases and growls and howls and bumps and jumps about
> the nursery; father who draws the pictures of cottages with rabbits on the lawn and
> birds flying over the chimneys, and of demons and Chinese idols with thrust-cut
> tongues; father who breaks the mechanical toys on Christmas Eve and generally sets
> them going again on Christmas morning.[26]

Advertisers capitalized on this idea: advertisements for soap and other family prod-ucts highlighted the idea of playtime between father and child to promote their product throughout this period; in an advert in *The Times* in 1945, it was said that a 'romp with Peggy is a nightly custom' for father, before she washed with Pears Soap.[27] An article about Errol Flynn in the *Daily Mirror* in 1954 further illus-trates the commonality of such an idea by the end of this period. His wife, Patrice Wymore, was interviewed and quoted as saying Errol Flynn was a 'grand father'. She supported this statement by saying, 'You should see the way he plays with Arnella—icky-ing, oogy-ing and iddy widdy-ing like any other father.'[28] Through his wife's statement, and the quoting of it by the journalist Donald Zec, it was established not only that good fatherhood required playing with one's children, but also that most fathers did this, including Errol Flynn. This was typical of the post-Second World War years, in which journalists increasingly insisted that most fathers were 'good fathers'.

Articles from the children's pages of the *Daily Mirror* throughout the period also reinforced the role of the father as a playmate and entertainer of his chil-dren, this time from a child's perspective. Children were encouraged to tell Daddy jokes, ask for his help with small projects, and play tricks and riddles on him. A section of the children's page in a 1922 edition of the *Daily Mirror* instructed children to 'Tell Daddy These!' and also featured 'Some Funny Little Stories That Will Make Him Laugh'.[29] 'Referring to father' was a frequent instruction to chil-dren in these pages, and he was portrayed as a fun parent. A trick of removing a waistcoat whilst leaving the jacket on was explained in the children's page in 1952, and it was suggested that children try it on Dad.[30] In the 'Famous Five' books, by Enid Blyton, the children sometimes wish that Quentin was not the somewhat fierce and preoccupied man he is, and rather that he was like Julian, Dick, and Anne's father, or other ordinary fathers, and would play with them. At times, Blyton hints that a more ready interest in the children's fun and games was characteristic of normal fathers—and that Quentin is unusual in this respect. For example, in *Five Have Plenty of Fun*, Blyton narrates, 'George sometimes wished that [Quentin] was a more *ordinary* parent, one who would play cricket or tennis with children, and not be so horrified at shouting and laughter and silly

[26] *Manchester Guardian*, 24 January 1928, p. 8.
[27] *The Times*, 20 March 1945, p. 3. Also see *Daily Express*, 11 December 1935, p. 2; *Observer*, 2 November 1924, p. 19; *The Times*, 23 December 1925, p. 14
[28] *Daily Mirror*, 28 June 1954, p. 2.   [29] *Daily Mirror*, 3 August 1922, p. 11.
[30] *Daily Mirror*, 18 October 1952, p. 4.

jokes.'[31] E. Nesbit personified perfect fatherhood in her characterization of the father in *The Railway Children*: he was described as 'just perfect—never cross, never unjust, and always ready for a game'.[32] *The Railway Children* was published in 1906, fifty years before *Five Have Plenty of Fun*, and just before the start of this period. Yet children read it throughout the whole twentieth century, and the idea of a father being always ready for a game was a persistent theme in the ideal father, from a child's perspective. The role of the father as a playmate was thus represented and understood in a range of media and contexts throughout and beyond this time frame. Yet there was also change in these discourses, and by the mid-twentieth century the willingness of a father to participate in games with his children became more of an expectation than an ideal.

DEVELOPING CHARACTERS

Play, then, was important to both children and fathers, and was celebrated by a range of social commentators. In popular culture, it took on a new significance in this period, as play was seen as extremely important for the healthy development of the child.[33] This meant the father's role, as a specialist in entertaining, was, in some circles, regarded more seriously. Fathers were, in general, held responsible for their children's emotional, intellectual, and physical development, through formal education but also informal interaction. This emphasis on fathers' obligation to provide a more informal education in terms of emotional rather than intellectual development became increasingly prominent. Though it was not entirely new, the explicit terms in which this was discussed were a result of the greater prominence of psychological modes of thinking in popular debate.

As Adrian Bingham notes, throughout the press from the 1930s journalists frequently underlined the crucial role that men had to play in their children's lives, and many commentators suggested that fathers were happy to be involved in such a way.[34] Mathew Thomson highlights, furthermore, that play increasingly became understood as a positive part of childhood, to be encouraged rather than repressed from the early twentieth century.[35] On the radio, for example, a talk in 1930 by Cyril Burt focused on the 'psychology of play'.[36] By the mid-1930s, the psychological importance of play was an established theme, certainly in the *Daily Mirror*. In April 1935, for example, the *Daily Mirror* featured an article

---

[31] Enid Blyton [1954], *Five Have Plenty of Fun* (London, 1991), p. 8–9. Original emphasis.

[32] E. Nesbit [1906], *The Railway Children* (London, 1995), p. 2.

[33] Timothy J. Fisher, Fatherhood and the Experience of Working-Class Fathers in Britain, 1900–1939, PhD Thesis (University of Edinburgh, 2004), p. 126.

[34] Adrian Bingham, *Gender, Modernity, and the Popular Press in Inter-War Britain* (Oxford, 2004), p. 241.

[35] Mathew Thomson, 'Psychology and the "Consciousness of Modernity" in Early Twentieth-Century Britain', in M. Daunton and B. Rieger (eds), *Meanings of Modernity: Britain from the Late-Victorian Era to World War II* (Oxford and New York, 2001), p. 108.

[36] *The Listener*, III:70, 21 May 1930, p. 901.

entitled 'Holidays are Here Again', with the subtitle 'Do You Find Time to Play with Your Children? Asks a Child Psychologist', which encouraged both parents to play with their children during school holidays.[37] There were numerous articles that urged men to get involved in their children's lives, such as one in the *Daily Mirror* in 1955, entitled 'Hey, Dad, Get Down On Your Knees!' In it, Ronald Bedford reported on the comments of an American psychiatrist, who believed 'the antics of a playful father are as important as his pay packet'. British experts were quoted in support of such a view, and it was emphasized that, by playing with their children, fathers were helping prevent juvenile delinquency. Another expert was cited who suggested that 'wayward children' frequently experienced little involvement from their fathers when they were young—'either Dad wasn't there to take an interest in him, or her, or, if he was, he just didn't care'.[38] In this way, the non-provider aspects of a father's role became viewed as equally important in some contexts, although this was never a consistent theme, even within the same publication.

Play was reiterated as crucial to a child's development in various texts written by psychologists and paediatricians. In Susan Isaacs' *The Nursery Years*, first published in 1929, for example, fathers' influence was noted. Yet when the father was mentioned, or even when the word 'parent' was used instead of 'mother', it was most often in reference to such matters as play, rather than any more direct, caring aspect of parenting.[39] This did not mean, however, that fathers were unimportant, in Isaacs' view. The second chapter of this book was dedicated to 'Play and Growth', in which Isaacs highlighted, for example, that 'Play is indeed the child's work, and the means whereby he grows and develops.'[40] Many childcare experts recognized the father's importance in terms of play: Mrs Sydney Frankenburg, for example, in her text for parents entitled *Common Sense in the Nursery*, first published 1922, named him 'the best romping instructor'.[41] D. W. Winnicott, a paediatrician and child psychologist in the 1940s and 1950s, also highlighted the importance of fathers' participation in their children's play in his BBC broadcasts in 1944, which were published in a one-shilling pamphlet the following year. He stated:

> if father sometimes joins in their play, he is bound to bring valuable new elements that can be woven in to the playing. Moreover, father's knowledge of the world enables him to see when certain kinds of toys or apparatus would help the children in their play without hindering the natural development of their imagination.

He did, however, suggest that some fathers were apt to spoil their children's games by becoming too controlling.[42] Benjamin Spock, the most popular US writer

[37] *Daily Mirror*, 24 April 1935, p. 23.

[38] *Daily Mirror*, 30 May 1955, p. 5. Also see *Daily Mirror*, 18 September 1935, p. 23; *Daily Mirror*, 2 October 1935, p. 27.

[39] Susan Isaacs [1929], *The Nursery Years: The Mind of the Child from Birth to Six Years* (London, 1956).

[40] Isaacs, *The Nursery Years*, p. 9.

[41] Mrs Sydney Frankenburg [1922], *Common Sense in the Nursery* (Kingswood, 1954), p. 201.

[42] D. W. Winnicott, *Getting to Know Your Baby* (pamphlet, London, 1945), p. 19; D. W. Winnicott, *The Child and the Family: First Relationships* (London, 1957), p. 84. For a similar

on child-rearing in the 1950s, also supported fathers' involvement in play, but doubted their interest. Because of this, he recommended 'Better to play for 15 minutes enjoyably . . . than to spend all day at the zoo, crossly', though argued that if 'he understands how valuable his companionship is, he will feel more like making a reasonable effort'.[43] Here, authors hinted at the ambivalence men might feel at taking this role in their children's lives, and the potential tedium of such involvement, a theme rarely touched upon in the press. Such texts focused mostly on the mother's role, a theme of particular importance after the Second World War and culminating in the work of John Bowlby on attachment; yet a small corner of this literature allowed for fathers' involvement in the easy task of entertainment.

Some key writers on child psychology thus focused on the importance of play and, through this, allowed for the father's influence, though they maintained the mother's superiority as a parent throughout. However, whilst commentators in the press were optimistic about fathers' willingness to embrace their duties, child-care experts were much less so. In oral history interviews and other testimony material, there is little evidence of fathers citing the psychological benefit in their reasons for greater interaction with their children—but this absence is perhaps to be expected. It indicates the limits of childcare advice literature and its diffusion by the press. As such, the reiteration of play as a significant role for men could be considered as more of a reflection of behaviour than an instigator of change in itself. What can be found is a greater number of fathers engaging with their children in a meaningful way through play, as discussed earlier in this chapter, and in terms of developing a fuller emotional relationship, as will be discussed in Chapter 4. However, relating to their role as providers of education, numerous fathers conceived moral leadership and education as part of their particular parental specialism. This could become part of play or entertainment; for example, Doreen Angus, born 1940, answering the interviewer's question as to whether her parents played games with her, stated:

> Yeah, they used to play well as I say, again, it was all sort of educational. Dad used to read to us. Read us stories. Like Tom Sawyer and that sorta thing. We used to play tiddlywinks, I can remember playing that. Jigsaw puzzles we used to do. And like hangman and things like that. But that was because I'm such a rotten speller. And that is to spell.[44]

Many fathers put more emphasis on their role as a guide and example to their children than their influence in their children's psychological development. For some, this meant ensuring a religious education; Edward Byrne, for example, born 1904, spoke of his father's strict regime: 'we had to go to church morning, afternoon and evening'.[45] Others introduced religious teaching into the home;

view, see Ronald S. Illingworth and Cynthia M. Illingworth, *Babies and Young Children: Feeding, Management and Care* (London, 1954), pp. 139–40.

[43] Benjamin Spock, *Baby and Child Care* (London, 1955), p. 235.
[44] Doreen Angus, Int001, *Families,* UKDA, p. 46.
[45] Edward Byrne, Int019, *Families,* UKDA, p. 10.

Andrew Purves, in his autobiography of life in the Scottish borders in the 1910s to the 1940s, wrote of his father's habit of saying grace before meals and, furthermore, noted 'The *Christian Herald* came into our house every week and father would read parts of it aloud to us on Sunday evenings.'[46] At the start of the twentieth century, Jim Bullock's father used to lead his family to chapel through their Yorkshire mining village: 'We usually all went together, my father and mother first, with father just slightly in the lead.' When a 7-year-old Jim refused to say his prayers one Christmas, his father 'coaxed, then threatened and finally became violent'.[47] Here, men's involvement in family life could be a difficult or unpleasant experience, for both children and parents. Yet the conception of fatherhood as enacting religious authority, apparent in the late nineteenth and early twentieth century, was arguably waning throughout this period,[48] partly due to a more general dismantling of the hierarchical conception of the nuclear family, as will be discussed in Chapter 5. Interviewees parenting in the latter part of this period were much less likely to discuss this aspect of fatherhood.

Others highlighted the importance of teaching their children to conduct themselves in terms of manners and morality. There was arguably something of a shift in the way this role was enacted within families in the first half of the twentieth century. Fathers and children from various social groups discussing the earlier decades focused on particular rules to be followed, and a strict regime of punishment in the case of mistakes. For Mr B7P, born 1904, there was an 'Orderly Table Bill', featuring twenty-one rules for the children. Forbidden activities ranged from the specific 'Not saying "Please"' and 'Eating big pieces of bread or potatoes' to the vaguer 'Acting silly' and 'Picking'. A system of fines was in place to enforce this, with all proceeds going towards a prisoner-of-war fund.[49] Mr P6B, born 1909, noted his father 'always used to say never, ever let me catch you up town without a tie on and a clean face and clean boots, he said, I'll kill you'.[50] An active fathering role was not a positive part of family life for these children. Mr R3B, born in 1931, noted that the strict rules his parents set out were indeed intertwined with their religion:

> I think it was basically because of the church background, they were Wesleyan Methodists and there was no drink in the house, no swearing. You had to do as you were told, if you went anywhere visiting you had to keep quiet, they [sic] old Victorian virtues of don't speak unless you are spoken to, and when you are spoken to, speak nicely. So it was strict.

In contrast, Mr R3B suggested he was much less strict with his own children, born in the late 1950s and early 1960s, and whilst still ensuring he taught them good

[46] Andrew Purves, *A Shepherd Remembers: Reminiscences of a Border Shepherd* (East Lothian, 2001), p. 35.

[47] Jim Bullock, *Bowers Row: Recollections of a Mining Village* (Wakefield, 1976), pp. 20, 23.

[48] Trev Lynn Broughton and Helen Rogers, 'Introduction: The Empire of the Father', in T. L. Broughton and H. Rogers (eds), *Gender and Fatherhood in the Nineteenth Century* (Basingstoke, 2007), p. 16.

[49] Mr B7P, ERA, Preston 1890–1940, pp. 9–10.   [50] Mr P6B, ERA, 1940–70, p. 36.

manners, he 'let them lead their own lives out of the house'.[51] In this latter part of the period, there was a greater sense of gentle guidance towards an independent understanding of the principles of good manners and the meaning of right and wrong in more general terms. George Short, a miner who was unemployed for most of the 1930s and who held socialist political views, went to great efforts to teach his children about his values regarding education and self-improvement.[52] Mathew Meret from Oldham, whose first child was born in the late 1950s, high-lighted the need to give his children 'a basic grounding' in manners and morality, a common theme amongst fathers of this period.[53]

For others, again particularly in the latter part of the period, encouraging their children's development came through supporting their education and even direct help with homework. Harry Tillett, growing up in the West Midlands in the 1930s, discussed his parents' insistence on his completing homework, noting that 'You had to do it if your dad told you to do it.'[54] Furthermore, Doreen Angus, born 1940, highlighted that homework was part of her father's domain and he used to 'make me sit and he really used to ladle into me. Make me read out loud and what have you', an unwelcome activity for Doreen.[55] Some fathers found this to be a chore, and children did not welcome their fathers' participation for this reason. Others saw this as a positive opportunity. Mr N2L, who became a father in the mid-1950s, discussed the importance of helping children to help them-selves. He emphasized that if his children 'looked to me for help, I would try to help but I wouldn't try to solve the problem. I would try to help by giving them the key, but I certainly wouldn't do the sum.'[56] Terrence O'Farrell, speaking of his children's schooling in the 1960s, similarly noted: 'I wouldn't do the homework for them, but if they had a problem then I would help 'em. With a crossword, I would help 'em with crosswords, anything like that. It would help their educa-tion.'[57] In these descriptions can be found hints at a newer mentality towards providing the tools to formulate a basic sense of morality and an independent intellect. Mathew Meret explicitly noted the generational change in attitudes towards homework: when asked if his parents encouraged him to do schoolwork when he was growing up in the 1930s and 1940s, he answered 'Not the same as we do today', reflecting on his parenthood from the late 1950s onwards.[58]

Such a development was largely paralleled in press discussions. The normality of men helping children with homework, and contributing to their education through informal teaching, was such that many cartoonists satirized this theme, often mocking fathers. Some suggested that father would rather not help, such

[51] Mr R3B, ERA, 1940–70, p. 34.

[52] George Short, quoted in Steve Humphries and Pamela Gordon, *A Man's World: From Boyhood to Manhood, 1900–1960* (London, 1996), pp. 179–80.

[53] Mathew Meret, Int089, *Families*, UKDA, p. 75.

[54] Harry Tillett, Int140, *Families*, UKDA, p. 38.

[55] Doreen Angus, Int001, *Families*, UKDA, pp. 57–8.

[56] Mr N2L, ERA, 1940–70, p. 46.

[57] Terrence O'Farrell, Int103, *Families*, UKDA, p. 41.

[58] Mathew Meret, Int089, *Families*, UKDA, p. 42.

such as a cartoon in the *Daily Mirror* in 1935, in which the idea of a homework hour on the radio was jokingly proposed.[59] Here, we can see recognition of the lack of interest fathers might feel in their children's education and lives more generally. Others claimed that father's help was often limited by his lack of knowledge, to father's chagrin and the child's displeasure.[60] Articles discussed this idea with varying degrees of seriousness; some highlighted father's lack of knowledge of modern teaching methods, and how this could be overcome, whilst others discussed the desirability of parental intervention in homework. The discussion shifted to considering such help more seriously, such as examining how parental help could be better facilitated.[61]

Two other aspects of ensuring children's healthy development were seen as the duty of fathers: acting as a role model and disciplining children. Fathers were told they should set an example to children of both sexes. As Tim Fisher highlights, fathercraft authors placed great emphasis on this aspect of the father's role and, from the interwar period, commentators suggested that it was important from a very early age.[62] Fathers were said to have a crucial role to play in helping their sons to achieve manhood, and it was often implicit that debates about juvenile delinquency related to boys. Yet the example set by fathers was seen to be of importance to daughters too, and this idea was frequently found in all newspapers. For example, in 1954, an article on the front page of the *Daily Mirror* reported that the Home Secretary commented on fathers' responsibilities, appealing to all fathers to demonstrate moral standards to their daughters. Again, fathers were portrayed as responsible for upholding the morality of society through guidance given to their children. By treating daughters with courtesy and respect, it was said that they could learn about the importance of such values, and in turn come to expect them in their boyfriends. The Home Secretary was also reported as highlighting that it was 'the custom' for the upbringing of daughters to be left to mothers. These comments from the Home Secretary were part of a 'campaign' against immorality and, as a footnote, it was observed that he himself spent as much time with his daughter as he could.[63] The newspaper and its editors endorsed the Home Secretary's comments. On the next page, he was 'cheered' for encouraging fathers to be involved in their daughters' lives, and it was said that 'Sir David Maxwell Fyfe is right in believing that a girl's best friend can be her father.'[64]

This idea was also common in advice literature: as Illingworth and Illingworth suggested in 1954, a father should set a 'good example' to his children, 'in the way of love, honesty, unselfishness and politeness'.[65] Fathers and children also noted this aspect of men's parenting; it could be linked to fathers' educative role, as men felt it was important to help their sons develop their masculinity. Many

---

[59] *Daily Mirror*, 22 January 1935, p. 11.
[60] For example, see *Daily Mirror*, 26 April 1958, p. 8; *Daily Mirror*, 10 April 1937.
[61] *Daily Express*, 30 April 1951, p. 3.
[62] Fisher, 'Fatherhood and the Experience', pp. 130–3.
[63] *Daily Mirror*, 25 January 1954, p. 1.   [64] *Daily Mirror*, 25 January 1954, p. 2.
[65] Illingworth and Illingworth, *Babies*, p. 159.

fathers, particularly those from the working classes, taught their sons to box, as it was seen as vital for boys to be able to defend themselves and to become tougher as they grew older.[66] Others were very aware of the example they were setting to their children: Mr S9P, for example, who became a father in the late 1940s, spoke about teaching his children manners and respect, suggesting 'I didn't make them do it, I just told them what I used to do.'[67] Men often spoke of wanting to grow up to be like their fathers; David Swift mentioned how much he wanted to emulate his father, who was 'a smart man', despite the fact that his father was rather violent and even abusive.[68] John Buck, born 1935, also highlighted how he 'modelled myself, and still do, on my father'.[69] This particular role, of moral guidance and the development of children's characters, which became increasingly infused with psychological meaning as this period progressed, became particularly notable when men were, for some reason, absent.

THE ABSENCE OF PATERNAL INFLUENCE

During both world wars, the lack of male influence on boys and girls was seen to be detrimental, and often blamed as the root cause of juvenile delinquency, along with the absence of mothers. For numerous journalists, fathers' long-term separation from their children was as or more troubling than their lack of time with mothers, through war work or children's evacuation. Indeed, many children did still have male authority figures present in their lives even if their fathers were away, in the form of uncles, grandfathers, and others. Yet the perception of this absence, and the importance placed on a father's influence, is revealing. During the First World War, a 1915 article in the *Manchester Guardian* noted that though crime had fallen generally, instances of juvenile crime had actually increased in Manchester and beyond. This was attributed to the fact that there were

> thousands of fathers away from Manchester fighting their country's battles, and in the ordinary case the father is, of course, the chief disciplinarian at home. With the wife naturally preoccupied with the war news and with the excitement running through the family it is not much to be wondered that the children sometimes get out of hand.[70]

In *The Times* too, commentators strongly linked juvenile misbehaviour with paternal absence, noting this was the 'first and foremost' reason for increased crime levels.[71] This debate continued well after the end of the war. An article from *The Times* in 1929, for example, reported the comments of the court Recorder of

---

[66] See Tom Hopkins, 'A Man's World', British Film Institute Archive, roll 50, p. 3; Mr T1P, ERA, Preston 1890–1940, p. 15. This also took place in the novel *Sorrell and Son*. Warwick Deeping [1925], *Sorrell and Son* (Harmondsworth, 1984), p. 94.

[67] Mr S9P, ERA, 1940–70, p. 12.   [68] David Swift, 'A Man's World', roll 85, p. 6.

[69] John Buck, Int022, *Families*, UKDA, p. 42.

[70] *Manchester Guardian*, 18 November 1915, p. 9. Also see *Daily Mirror*, 8 April 1916, p. 5.

[71] *The Times*, 5 October 1916, p. 3.

Leeds, who noted the 'wave of youthful crime' which 'seemed general throughout the country'. He suggested that the causes of this were difficult to discover but that the children involved grew up 'without the discipline of the father'. However, it was thought that 'there was reason to hope that it would pass with the present generation', as younger children were now growing up with the benefit of a father's guidance.[72]

During and after the Second World War, such fears about juvenile delinquency were heightened, and a mother's absence was often noted as a contributing cause, as many children were evacuated from their parental homes.[73] Many commentators at the time were again equally fearful about the effect of fathers' prolonged absence. Juvenile delinquency was related strongly to discipline in the *Manchester Guardian*, where the absence of fathers was again cited as a primary cause of great rises in youth crime.[74] The *Daily Mirror* featured articles sympathetic to mothers who were 'being father and mother' to a child.[75] As the war went on, fears about the effects of fathers' absence on children became more urgent, and when the conflict ended, calls for the prioritization of 'family men' in demobilization could be found in the *Mirror*.[76] The *Daily Express* also supported servicemen's families, suggesting on a front page in 1944 that 'Family men should get home first', and supported this headline with an opinion poll. Forty per cent of those asked were in favour of prioritizing men with children, a result which the anonymous writer of the article described as 'a majority vote'. The statement that 'Some mothers complained that their children were urgently in need of their father's disciplinary influence' further supported this argument.[77] The *Times*, too, showed some favour for this idea, in particular printing letters from MP and Air Commodore J. A. Cecil Wright, who was campaigning for the prioritized demobilization of fathers of young children.[78] Indeed, this case was also made in House of Commons debates, by various MPs,[79] though family considerations did not, in the end, have any sway in demobilization priorities.[80]

Such debates persisted beyond wartime. An article from *The Times* in 1945 reported that the president of the National Association of Schoolmasters

---

[72] *The Times*, 23 January 1929, p. 5.

[73] For example, Dolly Smith-Wilson, 'A New Look at the Affluent Worker: The Good Working Mother in Post-War Britain', *Twentieth Century British History* 17:2 (2006), p. 210. Of course, the standards were very different for men and women; whilst the wholesale absence of fathers from their children's lives for prolonged periods was judged to be detrimental, commentators such as John Bowlby felt even hours or days away from the 'warm, intimate, and continuous relationship' with a mother could be harmful. John Bowlby, *Child Care and the Growth of Love* (Harmondsworth, 1953), p. 11.

[74] *Manchester Guardian*, 7 March 1941, p. 6; *Manchester Guardian*, 16 June 1943, pp. 5, 6.

[75] *Daily Mirror*, 19 September 1940, p. 9; *Daily Mirror*, 20 April 1942, p. 7.

[76] *Daily Mirror*, 15 October 1942, p. 7; *Daily Mirror*, 25 June 1942, p. 2; *Daily Mirror*, 25 October 1945, p. 7.

[77] *Daily Express*, 18 September 1944, p. 1.

[78] *The Times*, 16 June 1943, p. 5; *The Times*, 14 September 1944, p. 5.

[79] Hansard, HC, vol. 404, cc.2408, 2056, 2057, 15 November 1945.

[80] Alan Allport, *Demobbed: Coming Home after the Second World War* (New Haven, CT, and London, 2009), pp. 23–6.

emphasized the need for male schoolteachers for boys. A lack of 'male influence' was seen to be detrimental, and whilst male schoolteachers were said to be able to somewhat negate the effects of the absence of boys' fathers, the president highlighted how a shortage of male teachers was further exacerbating the problem.[81] This belief that the lack of male influence had a negative impact on boys, and the wider community, grew in the 1950s, and the rise in juvenile delinquency, or at least the reporting of it in the press, was often linked to the absence of the fathers of such delinquents during the war. Psychologist John Nash drew attention to this relationship, and his views were reported in an article in the *Daily Mirror* from 1952. He was quoted as saying too much 'mothering' was bad for boys, and that their father was more important to their development after infancy. He was also quoted as telling the *Daily Mirror*, 'If only fathers realised how vital it is to a boy's development they would spend more of their leisure time with their sons.' Too much mothering, furthermore, was said to explain the greater numbers of delinquent boys than girls.[82] Geoffrey Gorer's research suggests this view was also widely accepted by the public: he found that 26 per cent of men and 20 per cent of women believed a father in the Forces was an important factor in the rise in juvenile delinquency.[83]

Unlike psychological conceptions of play, which had a somewhat limited reach in their influence on behaviour and attitudes, more generalized concerns about fathers' absence were expressed through the language of discipline and character development. Children like Danny Slattery recognized the relative freedom they had because of their lack of a father. Danny suggested that because his father died when he was four, in the 1930s, he had 'a bit of a free run, a bit of a free [h]and'.[84] Mr B4B, born in 1920, noted that his father's absence due to the Second World War and his work at sea meant that he and his siblings were 'running wild', and his mother 'would say sometimes, I wish to Hell he was home'.[85] Mr S9P directly blamed the Second World War for 'a lot of the trouble today', noting that many children brought up during or just after the war by their mothers alone 'didn't have true discipline[,] it wasn't the mother's fault, it was just that, it was just the nature. A child doesn't seem to take as much notice [of the mother].'[86] Kenneth Davies had a slightly different take on his father's absence during the Second World War when he was growing up, pondering that 'I think we grew up rather more quickly because there was only one parent than if—than today. I think my own children are not as old in their ways as I was.'[87] Yet mothers were frequently as or more involved in discipline and punishments, as will be discussed further later in this chapter.

---

[81] *The Times*, 5 April 1945, p. 2. Also see *Manchester Guardian*, 19 July 1948, p. 4.

[82] *Daily Mirror*, 8 January 1952, p.6.

[83] Geoffrey Gorer, *Exploring English Character* (London, 1955), p. 208.

[84] Danny Slattery, 'A Man's World', roll 29, p. 33; also quoted in Humphries and Gordon, *A Man's World*, p. 32. For an example pre-dating this period, see George Hewins, *The Dillen: Memories of a Man of Stratford-Upon-Avon*, ed. A. Hewins (London, 1981), p. 18.

[85] Mr B4B, ERA, 1940–70, p. 44.   [86] Mr S9P, ERA, 1940–70, p. 11.

[87] Kenneth Davies Int047, *Families*, UKDA, p. 17.

Comparing letters from the First and Second World War, parents in the latter conflict were slightly more explicit in their articulation of the potential negative effect a father's absence could have on their children. In First World War letters there was less serious discussion of the absent father's role, and more attention paid to how fathers were missing out. Through these letters, many men expressed general encouragement that their children be 'good' in their absence.[88] T. D. Laidlaw focused on the idea of his family's lack of discipline in his absence in a jokey manner in a letter to his wife in September 1918, noting, of their new baby, 'My wee Berthette seems to be an awful tyrant, I can quite see I am going to have a h—l of a time with you all when I come back, just breaking you in.'[89] A. J. Butling was the only father of this period within the sample who wrote to his sons at length about their behaviour and disciplinary matters.[90] The devoted H. W. Hicks was in raptures about becoming a father to his new baby son in early 1915 and spoke of wanting to help his wife on his return. In a letter of August 1917 he addressed his wife's worries about managing their toddler's behaviour, yet he was ambivalent about the assistance he could provide: 'hang on a bit longer, I shall be coming along soon to give you a hand, or will it be to give you extra worry, you will have two boys to manage instead of one?'[91]

A number of fathers separated from their families in the Second World War were more explicit about the difficulties their absence might present. This may reflect the central role they were playing in family life, but may also have been part of a particular kind of self-presentation that emphasized their own importance. M. Canty, for example, worked in London whilst his family was evacuated to Oxfordshire. As early as November 1939, he noted how well his wife was coping with the changes she had been through without him, including her 'self-sacrifice for the kiddies' sake', and as such, 'as the weeks go by, I have thought much more of you for it', indicating an initial expectation that the family would not manage well without him.[92] C. D. Fuller meanwhile, serving mostly in Canada during the war, discussed various aspects of his sons' behaviour with his wife, giving advice about discipline and so on, even when the delay between sending and receipt of letters was some weeks. When his elder son tried to run away from home, he speculated 'I guess it all is part of this cussed war that causes men to leave home and kids to grow up unchecked . . . I am sure David would not have behaved like this had I always been at hand.' He also discussed his behaviour with his son directly, noting 'Mummy tells me that your present behaviour at school and at home still leaves much room for improvement, although it has been

---

[88] Private Papers of T. D. Laidlaw, IWMA, Documents.11018, for example postcard to son, transcript p. 15; Private Papers of G. and E. Butling, IWMA, Documents.2423, for example letter to George, p. 42.

[89] Private Papers of T. D. Laidlaw, IWMA, Documents.11018, letter to wife, transcript pp. 85–6.

[90] Private Papers of G. and E. Butling, IWMA, Documents.2423, for example letter to Eric, p. 73.

[91] Private Papers of H. W. Hicks, IWMA, Documents.15335, letter to wife dated 21 August 1917.

[92] Private Papers of M. Canty, IWMA, Documents.13575, letter to wife, p. 4.

a little better since our chat when I was home.'[93] J. S. Mathews, writing to his son who had been evacuated to the USA with his siblings, noted how he had 'lost most of my hair worrying about you all', as well as advising him how to keep his sisters in check in their foster home. In turn, Cliff appreciated the advice from his father, emphasizing he read one letter from his father 'over and over', as it was 'the kind of letter I'd like to get more often for it really helps a boy who worries quite a bit about the future'.[94]

This concern about men's absence can be seen in survey evidence, and indeed, the study of 'fatherless families' during and after the war demonstrates the perception of fathers' importance, as well as the marginalization of single mothers.[95] Much of this literature focused on financial provision, but the rise of juvenile delinquency was also strongly linked to fathers' absence and subsequent inability to set moral standards for their children. In a booklet aimed at bereaved mothers, for example, Isaacs argued that providing for children's psychological needs in the face of losing their father was incredibly difficult in comparison to the 'simple' task of providing for them financially. Furthermore, she cautioned, 'Even when the background of life remains secure, the loss of the father's affectionate guidance may lead to far-reaching changes in the child's emotional development and in his attitudes to other people.' The father was thus a crucial role model.[96] In the same pamphlet, psychoanalyst Ella Freeman Sharpe suggested that the formative influence of the father was essential in helping children develop stable gender identities, and that, in the absence of a father, other male influences should be sought. Sharpe claimed that the presence of a father was vital for sons: 'To the growing boy, father is the model to copy.' As was reiterated in the press, the importance of the father–daughter relationship was also highlighted; if fathers had set a good example to daughters, they would demand the same standards from their husbands in later years, a theme also emphasized by the popular childcare specialist Benjamin Spock.[97] Psychologist Agatha Bowley, moreover, in her study of 'problem families', found that delinquency was uncommon when children had a satisfactory relationship with their fathers, whereas those whose fathers were in the Forces, or absent for some other reason, were much more likely to become delinquent, a finding echoed in Wynn's research.[98] Finally, a study of juvenile delinquency itself, in a deprived area of Liverpool, found that 'the disturbance of the parent–child relationship' was, 'beyond all reasonable doubt', the most important

---

[93] Private Papers of C. D. Fuller, IWMA, Documents.16408, letter to wife dated 'Tuesday evening', letter to David dated 'Sunday afternoon'.

[94] Private Papers of J. S. Mathews, IWMA, Documents.16403, letter to Cliff dated 12 December 1943; letter to Cliff dated 26 March 1944; letter to parents from Cliff dated 4 August.

[95] For example, Susan Isaacs (ed.), *Fatherless Children: A Contribution to the Understanding of Their Needs* (London, 1945); Margaret Wynn, *Fatherless Families: A Study of Families Deprived of a Father by Death, Divorce, Separation or Desertion before or after Marriage* (London, 1964).

[96] Susan Isaacs, 'Fatherless Children', in S. Isaacs (ed.), *Fatherless Children*, p. 1.

[97] Ella Freeman Sharpe, 'What the Father Means to the Child', in S. Isaacs (ed.), *Fatherless Children*, pp. 23, 27–8; Spock, *Baby and Child Care*, pp. 235–7.

[98] Agatha H. Bowley [1946], *Problems of Family Life: An Environmental Study* (Edinburgh, 1948), pp. 107–14; Wynn, *Fatherless Families*, pp. 140–50.

cause of criminality and delinquency.[99] Through their prescriptive writing and research, then, such researchers both found evidence of and encouraged the idea that fathers were important guiding figures in their children's lives.

DISCIPLINING AND PUNISHING

The role of a father as a disciplinary figure was closely related to this belief in the importance of paternal influence. Claudia Nelson, in her study of representations of fatherhood, contended that the father's disciplinary role was of decreasing importance through the Victorian period, as softer, more motherly models of discipline became favoured by the end of the nineteenth century.[100] Yet during both world wars, as discussed earlier in this chapter, the father's importance as a disciplinary figure was reasserted, and mothers were, to an extent, marginalized in this sense in popular discourse. As Sally Sokoloff suggests, there was a constant assumption in the Second World War that women were unable to maintain discipline. Indeed, she contends that to admit families could function without men 'offended the patriarchal construct of the family'.[101] Both world wars brought fathers' disciplinary roles back into focus, as the absence of men apparently resulted in unruly children. Perhaps more importantly, however, discourses surrounding the war arguably had to assert the importance of men to family life, to reinforce the reasons for them fighting, for their families, and to help ensure their easy return to civilian life.

A father's duty to discipline was rarely presented as more important than the 'softer' aspects of helping children develop. Certainly in the latter half of this period, in popular cultural discourses guiding a child, helping him or her understand moral standards and setting him or her a good example were highlighted as being as central to a father's role of punishment and physical discipline. A *Listener* article from 1956 observed, for example, that it was now normal that naughty children were not simply 'spanked', but instead the reasons for their naughtiness were explored, indicating that psychological modes of understanding were crucial to bringing up children.[102] Discipline was important, though, and was prominent in accounts of fathers' behaviour, perhaps because its more tangible nature made it easier for parents to articulate this role.

Ideas about the nature and limits of a father's disciplinary role were debated across various genres, and throughout the period. In *Sally in our Alley*, a Gracie

---

[99] John Barron Mays [1954], *Growing Up in the City: A Study of Juvenile Delinquency in an Urban Neighbourhood* (Liverpool, 1964), p. 158. On masculinity and juvenile delinquency more generally, see Abigail Wills, 'Delinquency, Masculinity and Citizenship in England 1950–1970', *Past and Present* 187 (2005), pp. 157–85.

[100] Claudia Nelson, *Invisible Men: Fatherhood in Victorian Periodicals, 1850–1910* (Athens, GA, and London, 1995), pp. 62–7.

[101] Sally Sokoloff, '"How Are They at Home?" Community, State, and Servicemen's Wives in England, 1939–45', *Women's History Review* 8:1 (1999), p. 28.

[102] *The Listener*, LV:1421, 21 June 1956, pp. 850–1.

Fields film of 1931, Sally takes in a young girl who is beaten by her father. Though the girl steals and lies, Sally tries to help her and strongly criticizes her father's violent approach to discipline, a sentiment with which the audience are clearly meant to agree.[103] The plotline of the 1940 film *The Briggs Family*, furthermore, centred on the son's involvement in a drunken car crash. Mr Briggs takes him to the police station to hand himself in, though he was an innocent party, and thus the father's role to uphold punishments in a wider context than the family was reinforced. However, Mr Briggs also fights his son's case in court, and wins, demonstrating that his disciplinary role was also accompanied by love and a prioritization of his children's best interests.[104] *The Scamp*, a British film of 1957, also explored this theme of a father's duty to discipline and uphold the morality of his children. The father of this film fails completely in this duty to his son, Tod, and as such is portrayed in an unsympathetic light. In contrast, Tod's teacher Stephen Leigh, played by Richard Attenborough, quickly takes on this role in Tod's life and the boy comes to live with him and his wife. Whilst there is some disagreement as to how to deal with Tod's behaviour, Mr Leigh's approach, to issue stern but fair punishments and use no corporal punishment, is proved to be effective. The suitability of Mr Leigh as a substitute father is cemented at the end of the film; he and his wife take Tod away with them, as Tod's biological father has died in an accident.[105]

Characterizations of fathers as stern authority figures, associated with discipline, were clear in various sources, and particularly those that presented fathers from the child's perspective. Whilst men saw their disciplinary roles as important to children's well-being, the discipline meted out by fathers could render them a figure of fear to their offspring. This is true of Quentin from the Famous Five stories—in *Five Go Adventuring Again*, for example, he punishes George's disobedience to her tutor by forbidding her from seeing Timmy the dog, and he is the only authority that the unruly George will heed.[106] In contrast, in Blyton's 'Adventure' series, Bill Cunningham, a stepfather to the fatherless children, is always fair and just. If any of the children do wrong, he chastises them, but in a much friendlier and more cheerful way than Uncle Quentin. In *The River of Adventure*, for example, Bill is cross with the two boys for leading their sisters into trouble. He explains their misbehaviour in a reasonable way, and both boys are 'red in the face', as they realize Bill is right.[107] These two figures, designed by Blyton to appeal to children's imaginations, represent the opposite ends of the spectrum of fatherhood, with Quentin as a fierce father, whom the children wish

---

[103] *Sally in Our Alley* (Maurice Elvey and Basil Dean, 1931).

[104] *The Briggs Family* (Herbert Mason and A. M. Salomon, 1940).

[105] *The Scamp* (Wolf Rilla and James Lawrie, 1957).

[106] Enid Blyton [1942], *Five Go Adventuring Again* (London, 1993).

[107] Enid Blyton [1955], *The River of Adventure*, published with *The Circus of Adventure* (London, 2002), p. 238. Mr Bargery, the kind and generous father of the family in Ballard's *The Bargerys*, was similarly fair: he advises his son who has broken a window, that he must do the 'right thing', and as such, the son offers to pay. Mr Bargery, however, will not help him pay, suggesting he must 'bear your punishment like a man'. Philip Boswood Ballard, *The Bargerys* (London, 1934), pp. 42–4.

was different, contrasted with Bill, who treats the children with respect, though
his guidance is always forthcoming. Indeed, the fact that he is not the children's
real father but a friend, and then stepfather, further reinforces his position as an
ideal-type. The children have some input in him becoming their stepfather, as
they introduce him to Dinah and Philip's mother, and even suggest they get married. Thus, Bill has been, from the children's perspective, chosen for his admirable
fatherly qualities. A cartoon from the children's pages of the *Daily Mirror* also
illustrates the assumption of the father as a disciplinary 'bogeyman'. The human-
ized animals that regularly appeared in the cartoon on the children's pages were
depicted playing 'Mothers and Fathers'. Wilfred played 'Father' and was strict
and caned 'his children' for making too much noise. 'Uncle Dick', in his regular
letter, observed that most fathers were probably less stern than Wilfred's version
of a father, though he did advise children to be nice to their fathers and not to
make too much noise.[108] At least from a child's perspective, the father was thus
frequently described as a disciplinary figure, whether this discipline was delivered
in a stern or affable manner.

Various opinion pieces advised or commented on fathers disciplining and punishing their children, and the necessity of this was also established in the reporting of court cases. For example, a judge's pronouncements on a case of a boy who
had stolen from his employers were quoted in the *Daily Mirror* in 1927. The title
'Spare the Rod and—' established the theme of the piece, that children must be
punished and disciplined, and the judge's comments made it clear that this was
the father's responsibility. The judge was reported to have told the father of the
boy that he ought to be ashamed of himself, as he had never 'struck' any of his
five children.[109] Whilst the position of the father as a disciplinary figure in children's lives was always positively affirmed in the press, the acceptability of various
punishments changed over the period. Corporal punishment was often endorsed
in articles from the 1920s and early 1930s, but caused greater controversy by the
1950s, and a more understanding type of discipline was promoted in some of
the more progressive newspapers, such as the *Guardian*. The changing social and
political mood was indeed demonstrated by the ending of judicial birching and
flogging in 1948.

Furthermore, the uncertainty of what exactly constituted appropriate punishment for children was also present in features that engaged readers more
actively in current debate. For example, the letter of an 'Anxious Father' was
published in a 1932 edition of the *Daily Mirror*. The father wrote asking how
parents should discipline their children, as in the 'old days' disobedient children
were beaten, but now parents and teachers were 'liable to be punished by law
if they adopt the old-fashioned method against bad behaviour'.[110] There was a

---

[108] *Daily Mirror*, 30 November 1922, p. 13. Indeed, Hugh Cudlipp, who was later editor of
the *Mirror*, insisted that this particular cartoon had extremely wide appeal amongst adults as well
as children, and could count politicians, bishops, and authors amongst its fans. Hugh Cudlipp,
Publish and Be Damned! The Astonishing Story of the Daily Mirror (London, 1953), p. 70.
[109] *Daily Mirror*, 25 March 1927, p. 2.   [110] *Daily Mirror*, 19 April 1939, p. 9.

tension between diversity in public attitudes to corporal punishment and the editorial line of the *Daily Mirror*, which largely condemned such practices. For example, in response to a father's letter which called for a stop to 'all this bunk' about treating difficult children through psychological methods and advocated instead caning and other physical punishments, a *Daily Mirror* writer wrote in 1937 that 'Flogging a child isn't the best way' and suggested that this man's children might have been simply scared of him, rather than 'happy and obedient' as he claimed.[111] Some articles directly discussed shifting ideas about punishing children. For example, in the *Mirror* in 1939, one writer noted that 'Father's slipper is becoming out of date' and that special sessions on how to tackle naughty children were being held for fathers at the Tavistock Child Guidance Clinic in London.[112] As in films like *Sally in Our Alley*, there was a strong current of opinion against those who employed excessively strict and violent methods of discipline, certainly amongst those largely middle-class individuals writing in the press.

There was thus a degree of uncertainty about the limits of punishment permitted, both in terms of the law and in terms of public opinion. Furthermore, the law could be ambiguous, as it was stated that a parent could inflict 'moderate and reasonable corporal punishment' in order to correct or punish a child, though opinion clearly differed in both legal and popular opinion as to what 'reasonable' and 'moderate' actually meant.[113] Throughout the period, however, there was a constant reminder of the limits of fathers' rights in terms of punishment in the reporting of court cases detailing cruel parents, many of whom claimed they were merely trying to teach their children a lesson. In a *Times* article of 1919, for example, George Smillie, a father charged with cruelty to his daughters, was held up for contempt in articles detailing his trial, particularly as he used 'more force than reasonable'.[114] In the reporting of such cases, fathers and their solicitors were often cited as suggesting that the cruel act was a legitimate part of fatherhood, as a case from the *Daily Mirror* in 1950 also demonstrates. After beating his 15-month-old daughter, her father, who was sent to prison, was quoted as stating that he always tried to stop his children from being 'unruly' and that he was 'only doing what a father should'. The headline, 'Baby howled—he hit her with a belt', and the attention paid to the extent of the ensuing injuries to the young child demonstrates the paper's disapproval of this attitude.[115] The reporting of such cases in all newspapers served as a reminder of the limits of a father's authority regarding discipline, and the lengths to which he could legitimately go. Though there was a degree of debate and lack of consensus as to where exactly this boundary lay, in legal and social terms there was a constant rejection and denouncing of fathers who were cruel, whether they acted in the name of discipline or not. The constant coverage

---

[111] *Daily Mirror*, 4 June 1937, p. 14.   [112] *Daily Mirror*, 24 February 1939, p. 11.
[113] P. M. Bromley [1957], *Family Law* (London, 1962), p. 329; Women's Group on Public Welfare, *The Neglected Child and His Family* (London, 1948), pp. 76–7.
[114] *The Times*, 7 November 1919, p. 7; *The Times*, 14 November 1919, p. 4.
[115] *Daily Mirror*, 3 October 1950, p. 3.

of these kind of court cases illustrates that some fathers bordered on cruelty when disciplining their children.

In terms of the experiences of families, it is clear that there was a substantial range of paternal behaviour. For some men, as Abrams highlights, it was a duty from which they shied away.[116] The operation of discipline varied in two key ways: who was believed to be the most appropriate dispenser of discipline and beliefs surrounding the most effective nature of punishment. Fathers were viewed as the ultimate authority in terms of discipline, but mothers quite frequently handled disciplinary matters on a day-to-day basis. However, an increasing stress on the sharing of this role emerged in this period, as did a growing emphasis on 'softer' disciplinary methods. Distaste for very harsh physical punishment could be found within many families by the post-Second World War period, echoing sentiments in the press and popular culture more broadly. In his survey of juvenile delinquency in Liverpool in the 1950s, John Barron Mays discovered that most working-class families he studied believed that men were the 'ultimate source of authority and disciplinarian', though their wives did also act independently.[117] John Mogey, in his study of the effects of new estates on family life in Oxford, also in the 1950s, found that in the older, inner-city working-class area, men did not usually punish their children but did act as a 'court of appeal', whereas in the new housing estate, women wanted their husbands to share in the disciplining of the children.[118] Gorer, in his questionnaire study of England, found some variety in attitudes across different regions. Overall, 61 per cent of English parents felt that the father should be the 'chief source of authority' and 35 per cent argued the mother should hold this position. The emphasis on the father's authority was found to be most prominent in the north and north-east, whereas those in the north-west and south-west highlighted this least. Furthermore, paternal authority was claimed to grow alongside income levels, although ideas about who should punish a child did not fall easily along class boundaries.[119] This directly contrasts with Mays' findings with regards to Liverpool (in the north-west), perhaps because of his focus on a specific group of families with problems.

The complexity and variety in terms of behaviour relating to disciplining children is also apparent in oral history evidence. It is clear that corporal punishment continued in numerous families, particularly those from the most traditional working-class backgrounds. As Robert Roberts highlighted of the early part of the twentieth century, corporal punishment could be severe and even brutal in areas like Salford.[120] Gorer highlighted that corporal punishment continued amongst many families in the 1950s, and found that fathers with young children especially favoured a 'spanking' as punishment.[121] Mr D2P, born 1910,

---

[116] Abrams, 'There Was Nobody', p. 229.   [117] Mays, *Growing Up*, p. 86.
[118] John M. Mogey, *Family and Neighbourhood: Two Studies in Oxford* (Oxford, 1956), p. 62.
[119] Gorer, *Exploring*, p. 170.
[120] Robert Roberts, *The Classic Slum: Salford Life in the First Quarter of the Century* (Manchester, 1971), p. 28.
[121] Gorer, *Exploring*, pp. 191–2.

discussed his regular punishment from his parents, receiving 'Backhanders from mum, with folded daily papers from dad' when he misbehaved.[122] Some fathers only hit their sons; Mrs M1P, born 1913, highlighted how strict her father was with her brothers, who 'got smacked, yes. With the back of the hand, mind.'[123] Many spoke of harsh discipline on the part of their own fathers, and some interviewees were beaten in the name of discipline.[124] How the interviewees felt about this depended on their judgement of the justice of their punishments: Frank Davies, for example, who was born in 1921, was only punished by his father if a neighbour complained about his behaviour, and was quite accepting of this, stating with regard to being beaten across the backside, 'that was normal then, most of the kids got that'. He himself was a very different sort of father, however, rejecting such a strict regime.[125] Others, too, felt that this sort of behaviour was 'normal'; as Denis Parsons and Verna Brennan, for example, agreed in their joint interview about their childhoods in the 1920s, 'All fathers were strict.'[126] The perspectives of parents and children could differ dramatically here; whilst fathers' involvement in discipline could be seen as a positive engagement in family life by mothers and fathers, for children punishment was often quite naturally unwelcome.

Not surprisingly, no interviewee discussed being cruel to their child, though some did refer to corporal punishment in a positive light: Lord Riverdale, for example, a rare example of an upper-class father amongst the interviews used, became a father in 1927. He spoke of administering a 'wallop' if necessary, though added, 'it wasn't the formal wallop it was more a sharp smack'. His ideas about discipline were in other ways rather progressive, however, as he spoke of how he would not hit his second son, as he was more sensitive, and thus required a different sort of punishment.[127] Mr N2L's father was particularly strict when he was growing up in the 1930s, to the extent that to 'get a good hiding was really a good hiding. To get a good hiding to the point where you couldn't walk to school the following day, you couldn't move the following day.' In contrast, though Mr N2L also thought he was something of a strict father, he differentiated his behaviour from his father's:

> Yes I was pretty strict and I believed in smacking if it was necessary, I didn't like doing it you know. But if it was necessary it certainly happened.

LB: Well you had been smacked yourself as a child so . . .

R: No I'd been beaten, there's a hell of a difference. I would never get too . . . I never did to my children the way I was beaten.[128]

---

[122] Mr D2P, ERA, Preston 1890–1940 (letter from Mr D2P), p. 9.

[123] Mrs M1P, ERA, Preston 1890–1940, p. 37.

[124] For example, Frank Davies, 'A Man's World', roll 75, pp. 6–7; David Swift, 'A Man's World', roll 85, p. 5.

[125] Frank Davies, 'A Man's World', roll 75, p. 6.

[126] Verna Brennan, 'A Labour of Love', British Library, roll 146, p. 8.

[127] Lord Riverdale, 'A Man's World', roll 177, p. 110.

[128] Mr N2L, ERA, 1940–70, pp. 10, 42.

Here again we see a strong difference in the account of a father and child, but this also reflects changing social attitudes and practices. Indeed, an emphasis on smacking rather than using instruments to beat a child became increasingly common, and in this sense, testimony evidence was in tune with public debates: the harshest forms of punishment were rejected. As Gorer noted, in the 1950s parents differentiated between corporal punishment with an open hand (slapping or spanking) and corporal punishment as inflicted with another item, or a foot or fist.[129]

In some families, particularly those in working-class areas, only the mother administered corporal punishment. Indeed, of eighty interviewees who were explicit about the delivery of punishment in their childhood, thirty-four noted that their mothers administered punishment, twenty-one their fathers, and twenty-five said both parents did so. Ivy Summers, who had children in the 1920s and 1930s, hit her children sometimes even though her husband refused to do so. This was in part because she noted that a man's hand was too hard to inflict punishment on children, reflecting the potential risks of fathers becoming too involved in this aspect of child-rearing.[130] Mrs O1B, parenting in the 1940s, noted that 'I would smack [my daughter]. My husband never did . . . just one word from dad was enough.'[131] Indeed, though popular cultural discourses at this time emphasized the father as the parent who meted out discipline, a theme reinforced by both world wars, in many families women were as or more important in terms of this role.[132] Mrs M3P, for example, who had five children following her marriage in 1922, spoke about how both her and her husband would give their children a smack if they thought it necessary, but she felt she was the stricter parent, suggesting 'I did the bossing of the children.'[133] Lucy Bayliss, who brought her children up during the First World War whilst her husband was away from home, noted how she remained in charge of discipline when he returned, telling him 'I said, don't you smack em please'; she had used a cane merely as a threat until this point. Like Ivy, she thought a man might be too violent if punishing a child, and insisted that hitting was not necessary in any case.[134]

Mr W6L discussed the impact of his father's absence during the Second World War, noting that because his mother had handled disciplinary matters during the war, she remained in charge afterwards, like Lucy Bayliss, in direct contrast to discourses which were attempting to reinforce this aspect of men's roles.[135] In contrast, Mr B4B noted that his father resumed his position as boss when he returned from serving in the same war, not least because he was 'used to commanding men and expected you to do what you were told'.[136] Mothers' involvement in this part

---

[129] Gorer, *Exploring*, p. 191.

[130] Ivy Summers, 'A Labour of Love', roll 2, pp. 22–3; roll 8, pp. 11; roll 9, pp. 17–18.

[131] Mrs O1B, ERA, 1940–70, p. 42. Also see Mrs R3P, ERA, 1940–70, pp. 12, 71; Herbert Allen, 'Leicestershire', in Nigel Gray (ed.), *The Worst of Times: An Oral History of the Great Depression in Britain* (London, 1985), p. 144.

[132] Also see Simon Szreter and Kate Fisher, *Sex before the Sexual Revolution: Intimate Life in England 1918–1963* (Cambridge, 2010), p. 207.

[133] Mrs M3P, ERA, Preston 1890–1940, p. 18.

[134] Lucy Bayliss, 'A Labour of Love', roll 121, p. 11

[135] Mr W6L, ERA, 1940–70, p. 23.   [136] Mr B4B, ERA, 1940–70, p. 49.

of childcare persisted in many families throughout the period; Mr F2L, born 1946, discussed how 'in general it was mother who sorted you out', though his father took charge 'if it was serious'.[137] Mr M10L, born 1948, likewise noted that his 'mother was the organiser, the disciplinarian' and would issue a 'good hiding' if necessary.[138] For some, like Mrs O1B's husband, this was because words were enough to make the point, whereas for others, like Mrs F1L's husband, they feared they would not know their own strength and therefore at what point to stop.[139] These accounts, then, hinted at the greater physical strength and potentially over-aggressive nature of fathers' punishments.

In total, eighty-four children spoke of being hit or smacked at least occasionally, with others remembering only one or two occasions when this happened. Only fourteen children noted that their parents never used corporal punishment. Parents were more likely to speak of a rejection of corporal punishment entirely. This, of course, has to be read in the context of change over time. When the interviews were conducted, between the late 1970s and mid-1990s, such punishment had become less acceptable. However, a number of fathers (and mothers) insisted they never or only extremely rarely resorted to corporal punishment, suggesting that the acceptability of severe corporal punishment was decreasing in at least some families.[140] Mr B4B, born in 1920, noted how he would 'get a crack' if he misbehaved as a child, and though he also brought up his own children, born in the 1940s and 1950s, in line with similar principles of good manners and so on, he would only 'tell them off'; he 'never hit them, never struck them in my life'.[141] However, the numbers of parents still relying on the threat or practice of smacking, hitting, or even caning indicate that there remained some discrepancy between attitudes in the popular press and the wider population in this period and beyond. In many families the use of corporal punishment remained, though it was less heavy-handed than in previous generations, and its practice, in terms of who administered it and how it was enacted, demonstrates that this particular parenting role was dictated by internal family dynamics as much as wider cultural values. As will be discussed in Chapter 4, these relationships were changing, and a less hierarchical relationship between parent and child in time affected the practice of and meanings associated with corporal punishment. Mr M7P's discussion of discipline is particularly revealing here: his three sons, born after his marriage in 1952, challenged his threat of 'clobbering them' if they were disobedient, telling him 'All three of us were going to set about you' if the threat was carried out, something at which they all laughed.[142]

Many still felt the father's role was to 'police' the family. One way to investigate this theme is to examine the idea behind the phrase 'wait till your father gets home', a threat used in Mr M7P's family even though he never resorted to corporal punishment and felt his wife was the stricter of the two.[143] This arguably

---

[137] Mr F2L, ERA, 1940–70, pp. 10, 35.   [138] Mr M10L, ERA, 1940–70, p. 135.
[139] Mrs O1B, ERA, 1940–70, p. 42; Mrs F1L, ERA, 1940–70, p. 61.
[140] For example Mrs C5P, ERA, Preston 1890–1940, p. 18.
[141] Mr B4B, ERA, 1940–70, p. 65.   [142] Mr M7P, ERA, 1940–70, p. 28.
[143] Mr M7P, ERA, 1940–70, p. 28.

reflects the idea that day-to-day disciplinary matters were dealt with by mothers, with fathers used as a last resort and threat. As Bingham highlights, there was a rejection of this mode of discipline in the press in the interwar period and beyond, though some writers believed it was still widely used.[144] In their influential child advice book of 1954, Illingworth and Illingworth cautioned against using this method of discipline, stating:

> It is always wrong for the mother to say 'Wait till Daddy comes in; he will give you a good hiding.' The child is kept in suspense all day, and regards the father as a man to fear. The father should refuse to have anything to do with this sort of thing. On the other hand, he should take part in punishment, if punishment is necessary. It is always wrong to leave all punishment to the other parent in order to court the child's affection.[145]

Here, then, they rejected the simple role of father as a bogeyman (and provider), and suggested that disciplining children should be a shared parenting duty.

Yet as noted earlier in this chapter, Mogey found that, in Oxford, fathers remained the 'court of appeal'.[146] The idea of the father as supreme disciplinary power was certainly understood in this period, as a means by which mothers commanded obedience. Interviewees were both questioned about this idea and mentioned it spontaneously in their interviews. Ray Rochford, born in 1925 in Salford, discussed his mother's use of this threat, describing the wait for his father's return as 'mental torture', and added he was glad this was 'all gone now'.[147] For some children, the fear of fathers' disciplinary power could be all-encompassing. When asked about this idea, George Ryder agreed with this sentiment, observing that, in general, 'I think mother used to use father as the whipping stick.' However, he rejected the interviewer's suggestion that he was, as a parent himself, 'remote' and a 'bogeyman', adding, 'It's very difficult to explain to people who are younger, in this age, you didn't feel remote.' He highlighted that he felt more relaxed and involved than his own father.[148] Richard Nesbitt, a headmaster from Devon, also felt he played this role. In response to a comment by the interviewer that 'it was kind of wait till your father gets home', Richard laughed and replied: 'I was the policeman [laughs] or what have you, because I don't know what went on during the week except I would hear if there'd been trouble.' However, he also insisted that this 'didn't stop affection in any way', and indeed, he described his loving relationship with his sons in other parts of the interview.[149] For fathers at least, coupling a disciplinary overseeing of the family with affection was not problematic. Even where fathers were used as a final threat, this frequently came

---

[144] Bingham, *Gender*, p. 241. See *Daily Mirror*, 20 April 1942, p. 7; *Daily Mirror*, 18 October 1949, p. 4.

[145] Illingworth and Illingworth, *Babies*, p. 160. Also see Frankenburg, *Common Sense*, p. 194.

[146] Mogey, *Family*, p. 66.

[147] Ray Rochford, 'A Labour of Love', roll 48, pp. 10–11. Also see Sidney Ling, 'A Man's World', roll 26, p. 60; Mr R3B, ERA, 1940–70, p. 34; J. R. Ackerley [1968], *My Father and Myself* (New York, 1999), p. 103.

[148] George Ryder, 'A Man's World', roll 135, pp. 53–4, 59.

[149] Richard Nesbitt, 'A Man's World', roll 145, pp. 18–19.

to nothing and it was still the case that many children viewed the mother as the stricter, disciplinary parent.[150] For some families, this mode of discipline worked in a different way; Mrs A2B highlighted that in her childhood in the first two decades of the twentieth century, her parents both referred to each other: 'One would say, "I'll tell your dad," and the other say, "I'll tell your mum." '[151] Some adhered to more progressive parenting ideals; Mrs W6L, parenting in the 1960s, challenged her husband when he suggested she used him as a 'final say', stating 'I never used to say, Just wait until your dad comes home.'[152]

The notion that fathers were the ultimate 'policemen', then, had many contested meanings in this period, and though the father was associated with discipline in all evidence examined, the nature of the discipline dispensed by him, and how much the mother was involved in this, varied to a great degree in both prescription and practice. In popular culture and in childcare advice literature, there was a concerted rejection of strict discipline of harsh corporal punishment, and of the construction of the father as a 'bogeyman' figure. Yet this did not match what was happening in many families. In numerous cases, mothers were consistently the key disciplinary figures in their children's lives, in part because, as Mrs T2L highlighted, women were 'at home most you see'.[153] The internal dynamics of individual families appear to have been particularly important in mediating how shared cultural attitudes were adopted or rejected. Indeed, whilst working-class mothers were arguably more responsible for disciplinary matters than their middle-class counterparts, attitudes and behaviour in terms of enacting this parenting role did not fall along traditional class lines. The balance of power between a married couple could dictate how discipline was administered, with little attention paid to cultural norms. Yet, as the father's authority was increasingly challenged and more equal parent–child relationships valued, harsher regimes of punishment were starting to become outmoded.

HELPING

The final key aspect of a father's role as understood in popular culture and by individuals was that of a helper, in terms of childcare and domestic labour. In many ways this differed from other duties explored, as, by its nature, it remained a voluntary task. As Angela Davis notes of the second half of the twentieth century, women frequently welcomed the help of their husbands, yet childcare remained the mother's key responsibility in both prescription and practice.[154] However, the amount of evidence that points to men being both expected to and indeed

---

[150] For example, Mr M10L, ERA, 1940–70, p. 135; Mr R1P, ERA, 1940–70, p. 58.

[151] Mrs A2B, ERA, Barrow/Lancaster 1890–1940, p. 51. Also see Kenneth Davies Int047, *Families,* UKDA, pp. 21–2.

[152] Mr and Mrs W6L, ERA, 1940–70, p. 120.   [153] Mrs T2L, ERA, 1940–70, p. 63.

[154] Angela Davis, *Modern Motherhood: Women and Family in England, 1945–2000* (Manchester, 2012), p. 163.

actually helping with domestic work and childcare warrants attention. As Joanna Bourke highlights, most men did do housework of some kind in this period.[155] Helping brought together men's familial roles as husbands and fathers, and men were frequently more willing to take on childcare tasks than domestic housework per se. Fathers were portrayed as 'spare mothers', there to look after children and help with certain chores, often in particular circumstances, such as the mother's illness or pregnancy. As Fisher notes, the message promoted within fathercraft texts and lessons suggested that fathers should be capable of all childcare chores, but that they would only take on such duties if the mother was in some way indisposed. He also contends that there was a shift to an understanding of the father's carer role as possible and acceptable, if not desirable, by the interwar period.[156] It can also be argued that this role was augmented during the period, across different class groups, if for different reasons. Amongst the middle classes, the employment of residential domestic servants was decreasing, though many families still paid for some help in the home.[157] For working-class families, moving to new areas further away from wider kin networks reduced the amount of help available to wives from other female relatives.[158] Both developments meant that husbands were often needed to assist in domestic work. Perhaps more importantly, however, the growing emphasis on the importance of fatherhood was accompanied by an increasing pride in the home on the part of many (working-class) men, due partially to the improvement of housing and the increase in available consumer goods after the Second World War, as well as the greater attention paid to do-it-yourself and home improvement in popular culture.[159]

In the press, articles, cartoons, advertisements, and the like referred implicitly to the possibility of a father taking on childcare. There were serious calls for fathers to help, as well as comic examinations of what happened when they did embark on traditionally 'female' duties. The emphasis on help shifted in this period, from a focus on the benefits for wives to that of children as well. This links to the growing importance attributed to the father's influence on his child's development, as discussed earlier in this chapter. A man's help as a father was becoming as important as that as a husband. For example, an article from the *Daily Mirror* in 1919 instructed men to work at becoming good husbands after marrying, and praised

---

[155] Bourke, *Working Class Cultures*, p. 83.

[156] Fisher, 'Fatherhood and the Experience', pp. 119, 121.

[157] As Coleman and Gallie note, by 1951, only 1 per cent of houses employed a residential servant, and the proportion of the occupied population employed in 'personal services' declined from 11.6 per cent in 1921 to 7.6 per cent in 1951. David Coleman, 'Population and Family', in A. H. Halsey (ed.), *Twentieth-Century British Social Trends* (3rd edn, Basingstoke, 2000), p. 76; Gallie, 'The Labour Force', p. 282.

[158] Bourke, *Working Class Cultures*, pp. 82–7; Chris Harris, 'The Family in Post-War Britain', in J. Obelkevich and P. Catterall (eds), *Understanding Post-War British Society* (London, 1994), pp. 54–5.

[159] Bourke, *Working Class Cultures*, p. 82. Many books were published catering for this market—see, for example, Colin Willcock (ed.), *The Man's Book* (London, 1958). Regarding the press, Bingham highlights the 'Man about the house' column in the *Daily Express* from the mid-1930s. Bingham, *Gender*, p. 241.

fathers who spent their free time helping out their wives, such as those who make 'excellent use of their leisure time by taking out baby in the perambulator'.[160] An article by writer Vera Brittain published in the *Manchester Guardian* in 1928 noted that the division of work between husband and wife was more equitable in America than Britain, and that British families were worse off because of this. Like many of the articles cited earlier in this chapter, Brittain's highlighted the idea that father's 'presence in the nursery' was wholly positive, and had a 'cheerful and stimulating effect' for children. She also condemned the father who did a 'comparatively light' eight-hour day and simply sat and relaxed in his chair whilst his pregnant wife worked hard throughout the evening, suggesting that this type of father was 'by no means as uncommon as he ought to be'.[161]

The possibility of fathers helping with the personal care of their children was brought into focus by high unemployment levels. In the early 1930s, when unemployment was at its worst, there was some recognition in the press, and particularly the *Manchester Guardian*, that unemployed men were becoming more involved in housework and childcare. A 1931 article about welfare centres, for example, observed that fathers often brought in their babies whilst their wives worked,[162] and an article from 1932 reflected that some unemployed men were 'filling in their time by studying mothercraft'. The writer argued that public opinion had changed, and now the 'amateurishness' in childcare that was previously seen as an 'admirable male characteristic' was no longer true of the 'modern father', who wheeled a pram with 'assurance and dignity' and took his responsibilities seriously.[163] The circumstances of unemployment had thus, in the opinion of such writers, helped men to see that they must take responsibility for childcare. Another article from 1936 suggested, in the context of mothers' holidays, 'It is true that unemployed men are showing an increasing aptitude and willingness to deal with domestic matters', and in support of this the writer cited the case of a woman who was leaving the house and children to her husband whilst she went away. The woman was quoted as saying 'He baths them and dresses them and makes their dinner.' It was recognized that there was a substantial degree of diversity in men's responses to the opportunity of more involved fatherhood presented by unemployment. In general, the article pointed out the difficulties faced by mothers who had to mind their children without any help.[164]

Numerous historians have discussed how unemployed men rarely took on a more extensive role in the home; Bourke contends that 'Inter-war unemployment menaced many forms of masculine housework.'[165] Sally Alexander too notes that the family and home could not provide the employment men wanted.[166] Neil

[160] *Daily Mirror*, 4 July 1919, p. 7.
[161] *Manchester Guardian*, 13 September 1928, p. 6.
[162] *Manchester Guardian*, 26 March 1931, p. 6.
[163] *Manchester Guardian*, 30 June 1932, p. 8.
[164] *Manchester Guardian*, 25 April 1936, p. 10.
[165] Bourke, *Working Class Cultures*, p. 95.
[166] Sally Alexander, 'Men's Fears and Women's Work: Responses to Unemployment in London between the Wars', *Gender and History* 12:2 (2000), p. 411.

Penlington found that in south Wales, though men were encouraged to take on new domestic duties, most did not.[167] Yet, though men did not embrace house-work and share duties equally with their wives, Penlington found many were willing and happy to do 'manly' chores, such as making fires. Furthermore, as long as those men did housework on their own terms, and the traditional power relationship of the man as the dominant partner remained, this was largely seen as acceptable.[168] Fisher reached similar conclusions: men were willing to help in the home with certain tasks that could be defined as help. Childcare was a possibility, as, if the children were older, this was not a domestic chore in the same way that cleaning or cooking could be. Indeed, Fisher concludes that many men were eager to become more involved in childcare, to compensate for their inability to fulfil their paternal duty of providing.[169] Additionally, John Burnett found in research into working-class autobiographies that most men were willing to help their wives more when unemployed, repairing and decorating the house, gardening, cutting children's hair, and undertaking a whole range of tasks, some of which crossed traditional gender boundaries.[170]

A small number of oral history interviewees and autobiographers discussed fathers' reactions to unemployment. In W. H. Barrett's autobiography, he described long periods of unemployment during and after the First World War because of his health; he took on housework whilst his wife worked as a midwife in East Anglia.[171] George Short, from County Durham, was unemployed for most of the 1930s. He discussed the anger and demoralization experienced by himself and others in his situation, but also mentioned how much time he spent with his children as a result. He took his daughter with him, for example, when he used to give talks to other unemployed men.[172] Robert Williamson similarly described looking after his daughter so his wife could go to work, and in particular high-lighted taking her to and picking her up from school.[173] Norah Austin, born 1927 and from Manchester, noted that though her father was irresponsible with his earnings and dole money and was even abusive, he 'saw to us kids' when he was not in work.[174] Mr B9P, born 1927, discussed his father's attitude to domestic work in gendered terms: 'That was a woman's work. Except in the sense that when he wasn't working he would do the thing fulltime. As far as I can remember he did it quite well.'[175] Other fathers, even if unemployed, were not any more involved in their children's lives; Mrs L3B, born 1920, discussed how her father 'was out most

[167] Neil Penlington, 'Masculinity and Domesticity in 1930s South Wales: Did Unemployment Change the Domestic Division of Labour?', *Twentieth Century British History* 21:3 (2010), p. 284.
[168] Penlington, 'Masculinity and Domesticity', p. 286.
[169] Fisher, 'Fatherhood and the Experience', pp. 260–9.
[170] John Burnett, *Idle Hands: The Experience of Unemployment, 1790–1990* (London, 1994), pp. 237–8.
[171] W. H. Barrett, *A Fenman's Story* (London, 1965), p. 128. Also see Hewins, *The Dillen*, pp. 91–2.
[172] George Short, quoted in Humphries and Gordon, *A Man's World*, pp. 108, 179–82.
[173] Robert Williamson, 'A Labour of Love', roll 161, pp. 46–8.
[174] Norah Austin, Int003, *Families*, UKDA, pp. 4–5.
[175] Mr B9P, ERA, Preston 1890–1940, p. 21.

of the time looking to see if he could get any jobs or anything', and picking up any little bits of work he could.[176] Mr S4B likewise spoke of how his father used to spend time smoking with his unemployed friends rather than in the house.[177]

Interwar research can give further detail as to men's helping role during periods of unemployment. Authors of the Pilgrim Trust study, for example, focused on six representative towns across England, and noted that many men were reluctant to help with domestic work if their wives were employed, and in many families women did not work because of their husbands' unhappiness about such a situation.[178] In E. Wight Bakke's *The Unemployed Man*, however, a survey of unemployed men in Greenwich and other parts of England, it was noted that children were the focus of the worker's attention, and this was intensified by a lack of work, which could otherwise form a source of satisfaction in a man's life. Furthermore, unemployed men spent an average of five hours a day at home, excluding time spent sleeping.[179] Children and childcare arguably gave life meaning for some men, and unemployment could constitute the special circumstances in which it became permissible to undertake domestic labour. Reactions differed significantly, though; whilst some men undertook childcare in order to be of some use, others did not want to threaten their masculinity further.

The majority of social research in the post-Second World War period highlighted that fathers were increasingly helping. Young and Willmott, in reporting their research in the 1950s, were optimistic, noting that the segregation between men's and women's work in the home was becoming less rigid, that the majority of men helped their wives on a regular basis, and that the 'old style' of working-class family was disappearing, particularly in the new housing estate they surveyed.[180] The men questioned from the estate were said to help their wives more, spend more on their homes, and felt their families to be the focus of their lives.[181] Likewise, Young and Willmott suggested in their 1960 study of Woodford that wives 'wouldn't stand for it' if husbands left all the domestic work to them. In their Woodford sample, 82 per cent regularly helped their wives with the housework.[182] Gorer, furthermore, found a 'marked change' in terms of the expectations of husbands' help, and suggested the young middle-class husband in particular was expected to help more than his father had been.[183] A more varied picture emerged from other research: Bott structured her analysis around the degree of 'conjugal

---

[176] Mrs L3B, ERA, 1940–70, p. 36.

[177] Mr S4B, ERA, 1940–70, p. 53. Also see Phyllis Willmott, *Growing Up in a London Village: Family Life between the Wars* (Halifax, 1979), p. 144.

[178] Pilgrim Trust, *Men without Work: A Report Made to the Pilgrim Trust* (Cambridge, 1938), p. 147.

[179] E. Wight Bakke, *The Unemployed Man: A Social Study* (London, 1933), pp. 201, 246–7.

[180] Michael Young and Peter Willmott [1957], *Family and Kinship in East London* (Harmondsworth, 1967), pp. 27–30.

[181] Young and Willmott, *Family and Kinship*, pp. 145–6.

[182] Peter Willmott and Michael Young, *Family and Class in a London Suburb* (London, 1960), pp. 21–2. Also see a *Mirror* article on this research, which painted this change in men's behaviour as positive. *Daily Mirror*, 26 April 1957, p. 9.

[183] Gorer, *Exploring*, p. 131.

segregation', finding a broad range of experience in this sense that correlated, albeit only very loosely, to class boundaries, with greater segregation amongst working-class couples on the whole.[184] Mogey, in his study of two areas of Oxford, noted that husbands did help, but only at certain times: many assisted after tea and at weekends, though only providing 'supplementary help'. Mogey suggested that 'The fact that husbands are praised for helping in the house shows that such performances are not a routine expectation.' In terms of expectations, wives from both the old working-class area and the new housing estate expected help if they asked for it.[185] It is clear that, despite the optimism of prominent researchers such as Young and Willmott, a substantial diversity in behaviour remained.

Other research indicated that, in many working-class areas, husbands were still not expected to help, particularly before the Second World War. In Caerphilly in the interwar period, one memoir writer suggested that because it was a 'man's world', men did not look after children.[186] Margery Spring-Rice's 1939 account of the difficulties faced by working-class wives recorded that only a 'good husband' would help on a Sunday, and many women felt their husbands did not realize how hard they worked.[187] In some areas, such as Govan in Glasgow and the mining town of 'Ashton' in Yorkshire, social researchers suggested that men's involvement in childcare remained almost completely unacceptable.[188] Richard Hoggart reflected that a man was 'not really expected to help about the house. If he does, his wife is pleased; but she is unlikely to harbour a grudge if he does not.' Amongst some younger husbands, however, Hoggart noted 'signs of striking change', as 'Some wives press for it and find their husbands ready to modify the outlook they inherited from their fathers.'[189] The pace of change did vary from region to region, and amongst different class groups, as Bott noted. Yet the expectation that fathers and husbands should help to at least some degree had become more widely accepted by the end of this period.

Those researchers that examined childcare specifically discovered an increase in men's help. Newson and Newson's study of over 700 Nottingham families recorded a substantial degree of participation of men in at least some childcare tasks, as Table 3.1 demonstrates.

They suggested a rapid degree of change over the last generation, arguing that 'the old joke about henpecked husbands doing the washing up is no longer a sign of henpeckery, but something to be taken for granted'.[190] John Goldthorpe and David Lockwood found the same: amongst their Luton factory workers, 48 per

---

[184] Bott, *Family*, esp. pp. 53–6.   [185] Mogey, *Family*, pp. 27, 56, 62.
[186] Kenneth Maher, 'Caerphilly', in Nigel Gray (ed.), *The Worst of Times: An Oral History of the Great Depression in Britain* (London, 1985), p. 33.
[187] Margery Spring-Rice, *Working-Class Wives: Their Health and Conditions* (Harmondsworth, 1939), p. 100.
[188] Tom Brennan, *Reshaping a City* (Glasgow and London, 1959), p. 105; Norman Dennis, Fernando Henriques, and Clifford Slaughter [1956], *Coal is Our Life: An Analysis of a Yorkshire Mining Community* (London, 1969), p.234.
[189] R. Hoggart [1957], *The Uses of Literacy: Aspects of Working-Class Life with Special Reference to Publications and Entertainments* (Harmondsworth, 1971).
[190] Newson and Newson, *Patterns*, p. 133.

Table 3.1 Proportions of fathers undertaking various activities in the care of 1-year-olds (%)

	Feed him	Change nappy	Play with him	Bath him	Get to sleep	Attend in the night	Take out alone
Often	34	20	83	15	31	18	29
Sometimes	44	37	16	24	49	32	39
Never	22	43	1	61	20	50	32

From John and Elizabeth Newson [1963], *Patterns of Infant Care in an Urban Community* (Harmondsworth, 1974), p. 137.

cent were involved in putting their children to bed, and 55 per cent read or told stories to their children. They surmised that duties such as washing-up and shopping remained segregated by sex, but this was less apparent in terms of childcare.[191]

A few fathers were relatively involved in all housework and childcare tasks, even in the early part of this period. It is clear that a number of men took on such roles throughout this period and earlier: Mr G1P's father cooked the Sunday dinner and cleaned, both before and after his mother died in 1920.[192] Fathers were more likely to stress the help they gave in comparison to children's accounts of their fathers' behaviour; Mr T3P married in 1909, and felt he was relatively helpful, especially in contrast to his own father who did 'nothing' around the house. Mr T3P baked bread and would sit rocking his baby in a cradle 'many a time', for example, but did not help with washing and cleaning.[193] Mrs B3B, who had three children in the 1950s and early 1960s, contrasted her own experience with her daughter's:

> I notice a big difference between my daughter's attitude to her husband, yet she quite expects that he will take an equal share in the work of the house or whatever they were doing. Whereas if my husband did, it was quite a bonus, I didn't expect him to you know.[194]

She did describe her husband's help with preparing meals and washing-up, suggesting that even if help was not always expected, it was often forthcoming.[195] There are signs of generational change amongst the interviews, particularly in the light of increasing female employment following the Second World War.[196] As Mrs A1P, a millworker, noted, her own mother had not worked, which in her view explained her father's lack of help in her childhood in the 1910s and 1920s; in contrast, her husband was involved in shopping and cooking, though not cleaning.[197] The post-war period seems to have represented a moment in which the balance

[191] John Goldthorpe, David Lockwood, Frank Bechhofer, and Jennifer Platt [1968], *The Affluent Worker in the Class Structure* (Cambridge, 1969), pp. 105–6. Also see Ferdynand Zweig, *The Worker in Affluent Society: Family Life and Industry* (London, 1961), p. 176.
[192] Mr G1P, ERA, Preston 1890–1940, p. 48.
[193] Mr T3P, ERA, Preston 1890–1940, pp. 64, 70.
[194] Mrs B3B, ERA, 1940–70, p. 39.   [195] Mrs B3B, ERA, 1940–70, p. 48.
[196] Elizabeth Roberts, *Women and Families: An Oral History, 1940–1970* (Oxford, 1995), p. 37.
[197] Mrs A1P, ERA, Preston 1890–1940, pp. 52–3.

between help as a bonus and an expectation, in terms of childcare at least, seems to have been starting to shift.

Indeed, women's accounts portray a change in the level of men's help in this period, or at least an appreciation of it. Of those women born after 1925, only eight of thirty-six did not mention their husbands' help with the children, whereas of the sixty women born before 1925, only fifteen women mentioned husbands helping. Just under half the fathers, thirty-one of seventy-seven, discussed how they helped with childcare. It is clear that, within the Lancashire area, the amount of housework that husbands took on remained minimal, though this was increasingly questioned. Yet there was a shift in the involvement of fathers in their children's lives; as Elizabeth Roberts argues, whilst men's participation in housework changed little, they did take on some childcare tasks.[198] As Newson and Newson and other researchers noted, men were increasingly happy to play with children, feed them, put them to bed, and so on, with bathing and nappy-changing remaining less popular. As Mrs Y1L, born 1927, explained, her father 'never did much housework but he always helped with us you know, he was always a good dad'.[199]

This had clear limits; Mr D2P discussed how his father, who was living with him and his wife when they started a family in 1936, advised him to curb his interest in the details of childcare, as it was tiring his wife. He agreed, and so said to his wife, 'I think if I help with the nappies and assist with David's bath (he was big enough for me to risk holding now), I'll leave it all to you. After all, you are so good at it.'[200] Helping in the physical care of infants was particularly acceptable if it related to another aspect of the father's role. Fathers were frequently associated with bedtime rituals, and though putting children to bed at night could certainly be seen as a chore, by portraying it as an entertaining experience, through bedtime stories and the like, it could become part of fathers' roles as playmates and entertainers to their children. Men's roles as husbands and fathers were inextricably intertwined, yet should not be conflated; the shift in men's involvement in domestic tasks largely occurred within their role as fathers. Not only could looking after children be enjoyable for men, but it was often a preferable task in terms of adhering to gendered norms, in comparison to cooking or cleaning, especially as children grew older.[201] It was also largely positive for women; discussing his post-Second World War childhood (during an interview with his mother present), Mr Y1P said that his father was 'always involved with the children'. His mother added that 'he took the load off me because he looked after the children for me'.[202]

Mr K2P became a father at the end of this period, and noted how much he enjoyed certain childcare tasks: 'I found it very relaxing when you had finished work, to be able to sit in the chair, and if Mrs had other jobs to do I'd say, "You know, give me the baby and I'll feed them", you know. It's kind of relaxing, you know.'[203] Mrs B2B, born 1931, had her first child in 1955, and highlighted how

---

[198] Roberts, *Women and Families*, pp. 154–7.   [199] Mrs Y1L, ERA, 1940–70, p. 8.
[200] Mr D2P, ERA, Preston 1890–1940 (letter from Mr D2P), p. 61.
[201] For example, see Mrs F1L, ERA, 1940–70, p. 62; Mrs H3P, ERA, 1940–70, p. 52.
[202] Mr Y1P, ERA, 1940–70, p. 16.   [203] Mr K2P, ERA, 1940–70, p. 13.

men's roles as fathers had changed in terms of childcare in her lifetime. When asked if her own father ever looked after her, she said 'No. No as I say he was very much a man's man.' In contrast, her own husband had 'always been very good' and would readily help and take care of the children during her long spells of illness. At a different point in the interview, Mrs B2B emphasized how greater affluence, changing attitudes to education, and ideas about authority had led her to bring her children up somewhat differently to her own parents.[204]

This generational shift around the time of the Second World War, indicated by Roberts' interviews, crossed class and regional boundaries. Those interviewed for other studies had largely similar attitudes and suggested similar patterns of behaviour. Some men simply had very little time available to help in any way, such as Mr Fides' father, an electrician and trade union official who worked long night shifts in Mr Fides' childhood in the interwar period.[205] Others did not trust their own abilities, particularly with babies; Frank Jonston, a driver in a factory from Llanelli who became a father in the late 1950s, explained he was 'frightened I would interfere', particularly because he felt his wife was such a 'wonderful mother'. Discussing the particular example of bathing, he said he 'was there and helped sort of thing, but I wouldn't do it on my own'.[206] It is clear that a proportion of fathers still felt happy with their relatively low levels of involvement in childcare.

Some men were more involved in housework and childcare, particularly those from more upper-working- or middle-class backgrounds, though class background did not always dictate behaviour. Barrett took on a lot of housework, as his wife was a midwife, and he highlighted the 'gaping on-lookers' who witnessed him pegging out washing in the First World War and afterwards.[207] Likewise whilst Leonard Small, a church minister from the Edinburgh area, was delighted to take care of his children, by bathing them and winding them and so on, his wife did not like him being seen doing so by neighbours, as this would make him look like 'a big Jessie'.[208] Yet men's involvement in some domestic tasks became increasingly acceptable, particularly following the Second World War. Peter Coverley, born 1915 and married in 1944, initially trained as a joiner and then became a teacher in Liverpool after the Second World War, and recalled that he 'used to take the two youngsters out of the way on a Saturday to do the Saturday morning shopping—that sort of thing'.[209] Mathew Meret, an electrical engineer, who became a father in the late 1950s, discussed in detail how much he did for his children as babies:

> if I could do anything, I did it. I've had everything on my knee, from coming home at dinnertime, just to jog her up and down and getting covered in it, wiping her off and cleaning her off and doing it again and—blow me, she did another lot.[210]

[204] Mrs B2B, ERA, 1940–70, pp. 14, 71, 97.
[205] Mr Fides, Int167, *Families*, UKDA, pp. 8–9.
[206] Frank Jonston, Int076, *Families*, UKDA, p. 31.
[207] Barrett, *A Fenman's Story*, p. 128.
[208] Leonard Small, quoted in Humphries and Gordon, *A Man's World*, p. 173.
[209] Peter Coverley (Snr), Int037, *Families*, UKDA, p. 30.
[210] Mathew Meret, Int089, *Families*, UKDA, p. 65.

In many ways, the post-war era can be seen as an intermediate period between an earlier time in which father's involvement was limited by a number of different factors, and the latter decades of the twentieth century, in which fully involved fathering practices became increasingly common amongst at least some social groups. A number of fathers throughout history have been incredibly involved, whilst others have separated themselves entirely from family life. In this period, there was a new acceptability in terms of men taking on certain forms of child-care. Their activities still had to fall within certain gendered boundaries, but men were arguably more likely to engage with their children and get involved in some infant-care chores as this became seen as increasingly acceptable within local and national cultural norms. In terms of the dynamic between husband and wife, the amount of time spent interacting with children mattered; to be helpful and a good husband, time was needed to complete these tasks. As working hours generally decreased in the 1940s and 1950s, men were able to spend more time at home. Those that helped to a greater degree than their fathers had done tended to do so through childcare rather than domestic work such as cleaning. Yet, as Chapter 4 will explore, time was not a principal consideration for the value and importance of the father–child relationship; as Mrs W6L noted, her husband worked from 7am until 7pm, and so barely saw his children. This did not mean Mr W6L was an unimportant part of his children's lives; she noted how they would always 'run up the street to meet him when he was walking down from work. Always waiting for daddy coming home.'[211] This highlights the importance of differentiating between men's positions as husbands and fathers, and between father's roles and relationships with children.

CONCLUSION

In conclusion, it can be seen that the father was expected to participate in child-rearing beyond financial provision. These roles, of entertaining, guiding, and helping, could vary in their construction and the way they were understood by individuals. Playing with children took on a new significance in this period, and, furthermore, a growing emphasis on helping children develop beyond the narrower idea of discipline emerged in both prescription and practice. Yet there remained something of a discrepancy here, as alongside this shift in attitudes could be found a continuation of corporal punishment within many families. Mothers were also far more involved in children's discipline than some popular cultural discourses acknowledged. One important context of this changing significance of fatherhood was the rise in 'fathercraft', lessons for fathers in a range of parenting skills, which are thought to have started in 1920 in London. A number of fathers' councils were set up to complement the services provided for mothers, and, as well as educating fathers, the movement promoted certain

---

[211] Mrs W6L, ERA, 1940–70, pp. 84–5.

messages about active fatherhood in popular culture. In many ways, the rhetoric of this movement fitted in with contemporary social norms: motherhood and fatherhood remained distinct. As Fisher notes, the main aim of the movement was to find a way for fathers to engage more with their children without challenging gendered norms.[212] The fathercraft message supported and influenced the growing importance of the father–child relationship more broadly: Fisher goes as far as to say that its 'most striking aspect' was the stress placed on a 'loving, friendly and affectionate relationship between father and child', a theme that will be explored in Chapter 4. Further, this emphasis had a psychological aspect, as the father was thought responsible for his child's psychological development.[213] Fisher does not study the press in this article, but had he done so he would have also found some coverage of this movement, usually in a positive light, at least in the highbrow press.[214] Thus, whilst the fathers' councils themselves had a limited impact, their message gradually began to permeate the media, and their significance lies in their illustration of the contemporary status of fatherhood. Indeed, the establishment of Father's Day in the early 1950s also suggests a new recognition of the importance of fatherhood, though this was arguably brought about by companies seeking to generate business, rather than to celebrate fathers per se.[215]

At first glance it could be suggested that there was a contradiction inherent in the different types of roles a father was meant to enact. By fulfilling the role of disciplinarian, his more friendly and affectionate role as an entertainer could be threatened, and vice versa. Yet it is clear that this was by no means a problem for many fathers, and indeed, interviewees such as George Ryder and Richard Nesbitt explicitly stated that this was not a difficulty for them.[216] What is clear is that the father's role was multifaceted, and that this was acceptable to both fathers and children. Furthermore, the father's roles as playmate and disciplinarian could actually complement and balance each other. The father's roles in this sense lay at the extreme ends of a parenting spectrum, of the most pleasant and unpleasant tasks respectively, with mothers attending to the more everyday childcare. Indeed, in examining fathers' roles, we must be wary of anachronism. Some historians

---

[212] Tim Fisher, 'Fatherhood and the British Fathercraft Movement, 1919–1939', *Gender and History* 17:2 (2005), pp. 441, 450–1.

[213] Fisher, 'Fatherhood and the British', pp. 453, 455.

[214] *Manchester Guardian*, 7 July 1926, p. 12; *The Times*, 7 July 1926, p. 21; *Manchester Guardian*, 10 March 1927, p. 8; *Manchester Guardian*, 13 September 1928, p. 6; *Daily Mirror*, 30 December 1932, p. 11; *Manchester Guardian*, 30 December 1932, p. 2; *The Times*, 30 December 1932, p. 12; *Manchester Guardian*, 4 July 1935, p. 8; *Daily Mirror*, 3 July 1936, p. 13; *Daily Mirror*, 10 October 1938, p. 13; *Daily Mirror*, 24 February 1939, p. 11; *The Times*, 21 June 1939, p. 21; *Daily Mirror*, 1 March 1949, p. 1; *Observer*, 6 July 1952, p. 2.

[215] Indeed, many articles about the subject explicitly linked this development with consumerism. On the importance or otherwise of Father's Day, see *Daily Express*, 17 March 1950, p. 7; *Daily Mirror*, 28 March 1951, p. 6; *Daily Express*, 18 June 1951, p. 2; *The Times*, 20 June 1951, p. 7; *The Times*, 13 June 1952, p. 7; *Daily Express*, 20 June 1953, p. 6. On adverts for Father's Day presents, see *Daily Express*, 17 June 1951, p. 3; *Daily Express*, 17 June 1953, p. 4; *Daily Mirror*, 18 June 1954, p. 2; *Daily Mirror*, 18 June 1955, p. 2.

[216] George Ryder, 'A Man's World', roll 135, p. 54; Richard Nesbitt, 'A Man's World', roll 145, pp. 18–19.

have not adequately recognized either fathers' participation in children's lives or the changes that were occurring, arguably because of a too-great emphasis on how fatherhood in this period relates to today. By placing the father's role in its historical context, and being aware of the shifting meanings associated with the roles men did have, we can identify and understand these developments in greater depth. There was a new acceptability to fathers' involvement in childcare within this period; playing with children, setting them a good example, and disciplining them all took on a different and newly significant emphasis. Whilst men's actual participation in domestic work remained rather limited, they were becoming more involved in some childcare tasks, and this took on a new acceptability at a national and community level. There were limits in the reach of new ideas within the press and other discourses; for working-class families particularly, corporal punishment remained widely used, although severe beatings were tolerated less. Moreover, whilst commentators often suggested disciplining children was a male role, mothers frequently took on this responsibility in everyday life. The shift in framing fathers' roles in popular culture reinforced the idea of their importance. The effects of such a shift were variable in individual attitudes and behaviour, but it is clear that many men were engaging with their children through play, moral education, and childcare by the end of this period. This was increasingly accepted as positive in both national discourses on family life and the attitudes of individuals.

4

A Good Pal? Fathers' Emotional Relationships

The fundamental components of a father's role, as Chapters 2 and 3 have illustrated, remained largely constant in this period and beyond, whilst the context in which they were understood and framed changed considerably. The father–child relationship was imbued with greater social, cultural, and psychological meaning. The new meaning given to fatherhood could be found in the press from the mid-1930s, as commentators regularly called for a greater status for fathers.[1] This was reinforced by the Second World War and its aftermath. Successful family life lay at the heart of peacetime reconstruction, and within this a positive family-orientated masculinity was emphasized alongside the suggestion that fathers and children were of great importance to each other.[2] The numerous difficulties that Alan Allport has highlighted with regards to demobilized men's return to family life were, to an extent, smoothed over, at least at a discursive level, by a reiteration of fatherhood as central to men's lives and identities and the positioning of the family as central to Britain's successful future.[3] There is a good deal of evidence, from both fathers and children, suggesting that men were investing more in relationships with their children, and enjoying the pleasures that time spent with children could bring. There remained a certain degree of emotional distance in many cases, and a lack of physical intimacy between fathers (and mothers) and their children. Yet we should be wary of judging the changing nature of this relationship by today's standards. An important theme in the testimony of many individuals who were children in the first half of this period and parents in the latter part is the insistence that their relationships with

---

[1] Laura King, 'Hidden Fathers? The Significance of Fatherhood in Mid-Twentieth-Century Britain', *Contemporary British History* 26:1 (2012), pp. 25–46. Regarding the lack of significance attributed to fatherhood in the nineteenth century, see Claudia Nelson, *Invisible Men: Fatherhood in Victorian Periodicals, 1850–1910* (Athens, GA, and London, 1995), p. 54.

[2] On the focus on the family in reconstruction, see Angela Davis, 'A Critical Perspective on British Social Surveys and Community Studies and Their Accounts of Married Life c.1945–1970', *Cultural and Social History* 6:1 (2009), pp. 57–8; Janet Fink and Katherine Holden, 'Pictures from the Margins of Marriage: Representations of Spinsters and Single Mothers in the Mid-Victorian Novel, Inter-War Hollywood Melodrama and British Film of the 1950s and 1960s', *Gender and History* 11:2 (1999), p. 237; Martin Francis, 'The Domestication of the Male? Recent Research on Nineteenth- and Twentieth-Century British Masculinity', *Historical Journal* 45:3 (2002), p. 644; Michael Peplar, *Family Matters: A History of Ideas about Family since 1945* (London, 2002), pp. 25–6.

[3] Alan Allport, *Demobbed: Coming Home after the Second World War* (New Haven, CT, and London, 2009), pp. 8, 50–80. Also see Barry Turner and Tony Rennell, *When Daddy Came Home: How Family Life Changed Forever in 1945* (London, 1995).

their children were different from their relationships with their parents. Many claimed that they had a more friendly, open, and informal relationship with their offspring, indicating at least a discourse of change. As Lynn Abrams notes of her Stirling interviewees, there was an assumption that there had been a 'sea-change' in the 1930s and 1940s, and that men were encouraged to become much more involved with their own children than their fathers had been with them.[4] This reiteration of change recurs throughout the twentieth century and beyond, and it is important to investigate the difference between change in rhetoric and a change in behaviour.[5] This chapter suggests a strong emphasis on positive change within popular culture discourses and in individual attitudes, and some limited evidence of changing behaviour.

This chapter will explore understandings of the relationship between child and father in cultural constructions and evidence of the experiences of families. It will argue that there was a much stronger emphasis on the importance of the father in general terms in this period, caused in part by the growing popular influence of psychological theory, related normalization of involved fatherhood in the press, and the rising living standards of many families. These developments meant the parent–child relationship was seen as increasingly important but also that the particular conditions of the post-war period allowed individuals to develop such a relationship.[6] As Ronald Fletcher suggested in the early 1960s, 'the family is now responsible for the fulfilment of *more* functions than hitherto'.[7] An exploration of father–child relationships of course relates strongly to a father's role; yet by separating the emotional meanings of actions and behaviour from what men were doing, we can benefit from a more nuanced understanding of parenting in this period, and a clearer appreciation of patterns of change and continuity.[8]

From a father's perspective, time was (and is) a key factor in terms of men's roles and relationships—whilst additional time would have been needed for men to take on more significant parenting roles in terms of childcare, a shift in the conception of the emotional bond between father and child did not require substantial changes in patterns of behaviour. It might encourage men to spend their time in different ways, but a shift in leisure activities was a *result* of a change in

---

[4] Lynn Abrams, '"There Was Nobody Like My Daddy": Fathers, the Family and the Marginalisation of Men in Modern Scotland', *Scottish Historical Review* 78:2 (1999), p. 233. Also see Margaret Williamson, '"He Was Good with the Bairns": Fatherhood in an Ironstone Mining Community, 1918–1960', *North East History* 32 (1998), p. 95.

[5] Charlie Lewis, *Becoming a Father* (Milton Keynes, 1986), p. 5; Ralph LaRossa, 'The Historical Study of Fatherhood: Theoretical and Methodological Considerations', in Mechtild Oeschsle, Ursula Müller, and Sabine Hess (eds), *Fatherhood in Late Modernity: Cultural Images, Social Practices, Structural Frames* (Leverkusen, 2012), pp. 38–9.

[6] King, 'Hidden Fathers', p. 37.

[7] Ronald Fletcher, *Britain in the Sixties: The Family and Marriage: An Analysis and Moral Assessment* (Harmondsworth, 1962), pp. 53, 177. As Mort notes, there emerged a more 'expansive blueprint' of the human personality at this time. Frank Mort, 'Social and Symbolic Fathers and Sons in Postwar Britain', *Journal of British Studies* 38:3 (1999), pp. 363–4.

[8] On this point, see Strange's exploration of provision and its emotional meanings in an earlier period. Julie-Marie Strange, 'Fatherhood, Providing, and Attachment in Late Victorian and Edwardian Working-Class Families', *Historical Journal* 55:4 (2012), pp. 1007–27.

the conception of the father–child emotional relationship, whereas more time or a change in the use of it would be *prerequisite* to new enactments and understandings of men's roles. In other words, whilst time spent together was needed for parents and children to cultivate good relationships, there was (and is) less of a correlation between men's time available and men's relationships, as opposed to men's time available and men's roles within the family. Indeed, as will be seen later in this chapter, less time that children spent with their fathers could render the father–child relationship more special.[9] From a father's perspective at least, the emotions they felt for their child were to an extent unaffected, and, indeed, in the case of war or prolonged periods of absence, could even be intensified, by time spent apart. This did not apply to all fathers, of course; yet this illustrates how men's involvement was changing.

A NEW PSYCHOLOGICAL MEANING TO THE PARENT–CHILD RELATIONSHIP

From the First World War onwards, there was increased stress on the importance of ensuring the healthy development of children's minds as well as their bodies, encouraged by new educational, medical, and criminological thinking, as well as the growth of social services for the family.[10] As noted in Chapter 4, fathers were, in particular, seen as a crucial influence in children's moral and social development; yet this discussion of fathers' importance went beyond a consideration of the role he must fulfil. The increased visibility and influence of psychological thought was further reinforced by the focus on children brought about by evacuation during the Second World War, and became newly and more widely significant following the war. Furthermore, the child guidance movement in particular underlined the importance of childhood as a formative period.[11] This in itself put greater weight on the importance of strong emotional bonds with children.[12] As Mathew Thomson notes, the Second World War provided a particular context in which 'psychological subjectivity' became a matter of national debate, and in the years that followed psychological ideas about children's development became mainstream.[13] The presentation of academic and medical expertise in the press

---

[9] See Paul Johnson, *The Vanished Landscape: A 1930s Childhood in the Potteries* (London, 2004), p. 24; Ted Walker, *The High Path* (London, 1982), pp. 14–18.

[10] See Cathy Urwin and Elaine Sharland, 'From Bodies to Minds in Childcare Literature: Advice to Parents in Inter-War Britain', in R. Cooter (ed.), *In the Name of the Child: Health and Welfare, 1880–1940* (London and New York, 1992), pp. 174–99.

[11] Harry Hendrick, *Child Welfare: England 1872–1989* (London, 1994), pp. 131, 221; Deborah Thom, ' "Beating Children Is Wrong": Domestic Life, Psychological Thinking and the Permissive Turn', in L. Delap, B. Griffin, and A. Wills (eds), *The Politics of Domestic Authority in Britain since 1800* (Basingstoke, 2009), pp. 261–83; Urwin and Sharland, 'From Bodies', pp. 174–99.

[12] Diana Gittins, *Fair Sex: Family Size and Structure 1900–39* (London, 1982); Diane Richardson, *Women, Motherhood and Childrearing* (Basingstoke, 1993), pp. 38–40.

[13] Mathew Thomson, *Psychological Subjects: Identity, Culture, and Health in Twentieth-Century Britain* (Oxford, 2006), p. 225, 253.

was perhaps more influential than the texts themselves, due to the much higher circulations of newspapers than parenting manuals and the like.

Childcare advice literature placed great importance on the influence of parents on their children. The importance of considering a child's emotional as well as physical development became a prominent theme in the latter half of this period. Whilst Frederick Truby King's books, arguably the most influential of their kind in the interwar period, focused predominantly on physical development, those written during and after the war explored the conditions necessary for healthy mental and emotional development.[14] Psychologist C. W. Valentine's 1953 book for parents, for example, was entitled *Parents and Children: A First Book on the Psychology of Child Development and Training*. This is indicative of a deviation in this literature towards a more psychological emphasis on child-rearing. The father's importance was clear in many parts of this book, as Valentine considered the popularity of the father with his children, especially from age 2 onwards. Furthermore, the father's interest was made acceptable by the constant reference by the writer to his own children and his influence on them.[15] Benjamin Spock and D. W. Winnicott, two of the most influential childcare experts of the 1950s, also focused as much or more on emotional than physical development in their books and broadcasts.[16]

As numerous historians have highlighted, mothers were subject to a new level of scrutiny following the Second World War.[17] This focus on the mother within advice texts, however, should not blind us to their discussion of fatherhood, limited though it was, and the general significance of parenting and children's psychological development could apply to fathers too. Moreover, we should place such texts in their wider context of messages about parenting in popular culture. Whilst commentators such as Bowlby continually reiterated that the father played 'second fiddle' to the mother in terms of young children,[18] others writing in the press increasingly placed emphasis on his important role, and his part in his children's healthy development was at the forefront of this. The greater attention paid to the father could be a result of the male-focused and patriarchal

---

[14] Frederick Truby King, *The Expectant Mother and Baby's First Month* (London, 1924); Frederick Truby King, *Feeding and Care of Baby* (London, 1937); Mary Truby King [1934], *Mothercraft* (Sydney, 1937).

[15] C. W. Valentine, *Parents and Children: A First Book on the Psychology of Child Development and Training* (London, 1953).

[16] Benjamin Spock, *Baby and Child Care* (London, 1955/1958); D. W. Winnicott, *Getting to Know Your Baby* (pamphlet, London, 1945); D. W. Winnicott, *The Ordinary Devoted Mother and Her Baby: Nine Broadcast Talks* (pamphlet, London, 1949); D. W. Winnicott, *The Child and the Family: First Relationships* (London, 1957).

[17] Abrams, 'There Was Nobody', pp. 219–42; Ann Alston, *The Family in English Children's Literature* (London and New York, 2008), p. 22; Leonore Davidoff, Megan Doolittle, Janet Fink, and Katherine Holden, *The Family Story: Blood, Contract and Intimacy, 1830–1939* (Harlow, 1999), p. 210; Janet Finch and Penny Summerfield, 'Social Reconstruction and the Emergence of Companionate Marriage, 1945–59', in D. Clark (ed.), *Marriage, Domestic Life and Social Change* (London, 1991), p. 15; Jane Lewis, *The Politics of Motherhood: Child and Maternal Welfare in England, 1900–1939* (London, 1980); Richardson, *Women*, pp. 29–48.

[18] John Bowlby, *Child Care and the Growth of Love* (Harmondsworth, 1953), p. 15.

nature of the press and the producers of it.[19] Yet the presentations of mother-hood and fatherhood and their respective importance in the press are arguably more a result of the generalized emphasis on the significance of parents to their children. The more subtle messages of these experts arguably got lost, whilst the more general ideas were incorporated in popular culture, as they fitted in with the need to promote men's role in their families and the importance of those families to Britain's future. This, then, indicates the danger of focusing on spe-cialist advice literature aimed at the middle classes, without further investigat-ing its trajectory to a more mainstream audience. There is limited evidence on the place of the newspaper commentary in influencing individual attitudes, and the transient nature of the medium may have limited its impact on behaviour. Yet it provided a conduit for the consumption of expert thinking, and by explor-ing both of these discourses and the testimony of individuals, we can start to explore the extent of change in thinking about fatherhood. Indeed, the way in which individuals used these ideas was complex; as Angela Davis demonstrates in terms of mothers, parents took on aspects from different theories and ideas and co-opted them in ways that would work for themselves.[20] Furthermore, whilst parenting advice literature was largely aimed at women, newspapers had a more mixed audience.

In the interwar period, some articles in the press reinforced the father's influence on his children's psychological development, and this was particularly prominent in *The Times* and the *Manchester Guardian*. However, while a father's presence was portrayed as advantageous to the child, it was not seen to be as necessary as it came to be in the 1940s and 1950s. In 1929, an article in *The Times* reported on a lecture by Dr Alice Hutchinson on the psychology of the mother, which suggested the mother needed some time each day away from her child. This, it was said, could be achieved if the children spent time with father. Dr Hutchinson recommended that 'If a father only took [the child] for a walk sometimes, or talked to him alone, it would lead to the more normal development of the child.' As with much press discussion about fathers' help in the interwar period, this article focused on help for the mother and doubted fathers' willingness to get involved.[21] Similar articles regarding children's psychological development were also published in the *Manchester Guardian*. In 1929, a series of lectures for moth-ers on child psychology were reported, and here the focus was on the mother, though the father was briefly mentioned: 'The importance of the father's active co-operation in the upbringing of his children even in infancy was another factor specially emphasised.'[22] In this sense, the father–child relationship was conceived mostly in terms of his role as a helper and entertainer.

[19] Laura King, 'The Perfect Man: Fatherhood, Masculinity and Romance in Popular Culture in Mid-Twentieth-Century Britain', in Alana Harris and Timothy Jones (eds), *Love and Romance in Britain, 1981–1970* (Basingstoke, forthcoming 2014)
[20] Angela Davis, *Modern Motherhood: Women and Family in England, 1945–2000* (Manchester, 2012), p. 62.
[21] *The Times*, 3 January 1929, p. 7.
[22] *Manchester Guardian*, 21 November 1929, p. 8.

This discussion of the father's influence on the child's psychological development was increasingly highlighted, and spread to the tabloid press, and working-class readers, by the 1940s. Sociologists, psychologists, and other medical experts were frequently cited in articles. In the *Daily Mirror* in 1935, an article suggested the fundamental importance of mothers, especially to young children, and in contrast minimized the role of the father as an occasional entertaining diversion for young children. Fathers were fun for toys and sweets and to 'play with you sometimes, but mother means much more than this'.[23] The constant emphasis on the paramount importance of the mother remained. Yet there was a shift in the mid-1930s to a more consistent and serious focus on the father's impact on children's emotional states; the quality of the relationship in itself became important, alongside the father's role and the time spent together. An article in 1940 from the *Daily Mirror*, for example, considered the circumstances in which it was acceptable for a wife to nag her husband, one of which was if he ignored his children. If he was too tired after work, or busy with hobbies on days off, it was said to be a wife's 'duty' to nag him, as he was 'starving his son for affection'.[24] In this article, a healthy and developed father–child relationship was not an ideal, but portrayed as an expected part of fatherhood.

The influence of experts on family life was also normalized and accepted; in his regular column for the *Daily Mirror* in 1952, Noel Whitcomb included an anecdote about trying to read a psychology text entitled 'The Importance of the Father's Influence on a Toddler'. Though his view was rather sceptical—it was said to be his wife's book, and a 'line of flannel'—and his influence was ironically absent, as his 2-year-old daughter knocked the book out of his hand and gave it to her teddy bear, this was somewhat undermined by the fact he wrote about reading it.[25] In this sense, the father–child relationship was conceived as important whilst a disdain for advice literature (for men) was maintained, allowing for the combination of male authority with emotional engagement in a gender-appropriate way. Furthermore, in an article on the front page of the *Daily Mirror* in 1951, the research of educational psychologist Hubert Child was discussed. Child found that fathers were losing their traditional authority within the family home, a 'good thing' according to both Child and the *Mirror* writer.[26] Indeed, the father himself was portrayed as a legitimate subject for psychological investigation by the end of this period, as demonstrated by a short article in the *Mirror* summarizing a paper from *The Lancet*. It was said that by getting fathers to draw pictures, psychiatrists could better understand 'hidden worries about fatherhood'.[27] The reporting of

---

[23] *Daily Mirror*, 2 October 1935, p. 27.   [24] *Daily Mirror*, 31 January 1940, p. 17.
[25] *Daily Mirror*, 14 October 1952, p. 7.   [26] *Daily Mirror*, 12 April 1951, p. 1.
[27] *Daily Mirror*, 10 September 1955, p. 5. Also see *Daily Mirror*, 12 April 1951, p. 1; *Daily Mirror*, 30 May 1955, p. 5; *Observer*, 22 July 1956, p. 4; *Observer*, 9 December 1956, p. 2; *Observer*, 23 December 1956, p. 9; *Daily Mirror*, 26 April 1957, p. 9; *Manchester Guardian*, 4 January 1958, p. 3.

an article from a medical journal by a psychiatrist is notable in itself, further demonstrating the growing influence and infiltration of psychological academic thought into the popular press.

As such, an increased emphasis on psychological approaches to child-rearing can be found in this period. Whilst in the interwar period it was limited to the higher or more middlebrow press, the popularity of such theories became widespread, as the tabloid press highlighted the importance of psychologists' ideas and drew on their evidence to inform and justify the newspaper's stance. The BBC also focused on this theme, broadcasting a range of talks on children's psychological development from the 1930s onwards.[28] Journalists tended to focus on the general importance of both mothers' and fathers' influence, and the quality of parent–child relationships, rather than the intricacies of particular theories. Another important difference between specific advice literature and general discussion in the press was that, by the 1950s, journalists were optimistic about how seriously fathers were taking this role, whereas child advice commentators did not generally believe they were doing so.

AN IMPORTANT EXPERIENCE?

As Michael Roper argues, it is vital to focus on emotions and subjectivity in writing social history.[29] Men's constructions of their experiences as fathers in interviews or autobiographies years later, and also the construction of those experiences into an academic narrative by social researchers, provide somewhat problematic evidence in investigating the understandings of the emotional relationship between parent and child. In this period, both cultural commentators and individuals themselves increasingly invested in the significance of this relationship. The variety of emotions that men felt as fathers are extremely hard to analyse, yet what can be noted in their testimonies is their growing active interest in this relationship. However, as will be discussed later in this chapter, interviewees struggled to articulate the meaning of their relationships, perhaps because they had had little chance to examine their emotions before, or due to gendered constraints in the ways in which men were permitted to voice such feelings. There were limits to fathers' emotional engagement in family life.

It is very difficult to trace how important the ideas of psychologists and other experts were to individuals' experiences. Indeed, though we can arguably link

---

[28] Speakers included psychologists Cyril Burt, W. E. Blatz, and Emmanuel Miller. See *The Listener* magazine for full texts: *The Listener* III:69, 7 May 1930, pp. 797–8; *The Listener* III:70, 14 May 1930, pp. 849–50; *The Listener* III:71, 21 May 1930, pp. 900–1; *The Listener* III:72, 28 May 1930, pp. 947–8; *The Listener* XXVII:724, 26 November 1942, pp. 693–4; *The Listener* XXXV:887, 10 January 1946, p. 40; *The Listener* LV:1418, 31 May 1956, pp. 719, 722; *The Listener* LV:1419, 7 June 1956, pp. 762–3; *The Listener* LV:1420, 14 June 1956, pp. 793–4; *The Listener* LV:1421, 21 June 1956, pp. 850–1, 854.

[29] Michael Roper, 'Slipping Out of View: Subjectivity and Emotion in Gender History', *History Workshop Journal* 59:1 (2005), pp. 57–72.

the general psychological emphasis on parenting and childhood to the growing involvement of fathers, this is almost always implicit in the evidence of individuals' experiences. The more complex messages debated by childcare experts were rarely explicitly discussed or enacted by individuals. However, one important aspect of individuals' testimony that can deepen understandings of men's perception of their importance as fathers is the language they used to frame their roles, and the emotional meanings they gave to their actions as parents. As discussed in Chapter 2, the meanings associated with providing for a family changed, and, in the testimony evidence used here, a number of men were inclined to associate their breadwinning role with their feelings for their children. As Julie-Marie Strange notes, both men and children invested men's work with 'affective significance'. Her article on this theme examines working-class life in the late Victorian period, but uses autobiographies written and published from the 1920s to the 1960s, the period of study of this book. The investment that Strange identifies, then, is, in its explicit articulation, a product of the twentieth century. In her use of examples such as Jack Lawson's autobiography, published in 1932, Strange effectively demonstrates both the emotional life of working-class families in the late nineteenth century, and the change in how this was articulated in the twentieth. As Strange notes of Lawson's account, he 'interpreted his father's labour as evidence that the older man cared about and for his children'.[30]

This relates to an important finding of Fisher and Szreter's oral history study of sexual relationships in the middle decades of the twentieth century. They emphasized 'emotional caring' balanced with 'sharing' and discovered that many interviewees thought a man who provided economically but spent his evenings at the pub did not achieve the emotional sense of caring.[31] In this period, there was a new understanding of an engaged and caring provider, which allowed for a continuation of the traditional male role of breadwinning alongside a new emotional context of fatherhood. This does not reflect a vast change in the behaviour of fathers, but a shift in attitudes about what was and was not acceptable practice. A small number of autobiographies included such a construction of fatherhood. In J. R. Ackerley's autobiography, published in 1968, the author reproduced a letter from his father written during his last term at Cambridge, where he studied in the early 1920s after fighting in the First World War. The idea of an emotional meaning was present in both the letter and Ackerley's discussion of it. In the letter, his father mentioned that he believed his son to be short of funds, and this need not be so, as 'all I have is at your disposal' because 'My faith in you is as my affection for you.' Ackerley in turn described this as demonstrating his father's feelings for him, and highlights that 'no sweeter letter' was possible.[32] Moreover, a colliery banksman, from a contrasting social background and in a situation of unemployment, wrote of his pain at being unable to provide for his family, as part

---

[30] Strange, 'Fatherhood, Providing', esp. pp. 1014–15.
[31] Simon Szreter and Kate Fisher, *Sex before the Sexual Revolution: Intimate Life in England 1918–1963* (Cambridge, 2010), ch. 5, esp. pp. 214, 225.
[32] J. R. Ackerley [1968], *My Father and Myself* (New York, 1999), p. 136.

of H. L. Beales and R. S. Lambert's collection of accounts of joblessness. This man discussed 'the bitterness, the irritation and gloominess' at being unable to provide for his family, noting 'these feelings are emotional'.[33]

Most male oral history interviewees felt this responsibility keenly, and a small but significant number directly associated their provider role with caring for and loving their children, reflecting a strengthening of the link between love and provision as the century progressed.[34] These men most likely represent a more active side of fatherhood, as those who were not engaged in family life would have been less likely to participate in an interview. Terrence O'Farrell, who became a father in 1959, strongly associated love and provision. When asked how he 'showed love and affection' to his children, he discussed how his daughter had recently noted that she and her brother 'never wanted for anything' when they were young, and had plenty of love and affection.[35] There could be a tension between different aspects of men's roles, as provision came first. The choice men made regarding how to dedicate their time could reflect their individual weighing up of which of their roles was most important. Some men interviewed in the 1970s and onwards were uncomfortable at the lack of time they had spent with their children, noting that their role as breadwinners constrained such quality time together. Others were more single-minded in their provider role, and their strong feelings towards their children were used to explain why they spent so many hours earning money for the family. Indeed, some were explicit about how values had changed in the intervening decades.

Lord Riverdale, an upper-class father whose first child was born in 1927, stated he prioritized his work at the expense of family time together: 'I was conscious of not doing as much as I would have liked with the family. But then you can't do everything.' He also highlighted that he felt more able to develop a relationship as his children grew older, a feeling common to many, particularly before the Second World War.[36] Likewise, Alf Short quite obviously felt uncomfortable about a similar experience in the interview, stating that it was still difficult for him to think and talk about the lack of time he had to spend with his children because of his long hours of employment. He said, 'I don't even like it now to think ta tell you about it . . . I never did 'ave the love of my children I ought to 'ad, cause I was always at work.' Alf's testimony suggests how more recent shifts in attitude can influence the process of reflection in an oral history interview.[37] Indeed, other men explicitly reflected on their behaviour through the prism of contemporary attitudes. George

---

[33] A Colliery Banksman, 'Frustration and Bitterness', in H. L. Beales and R. S. Lambert (eds) [1934], *Memoirs of the Unemployed* (Wakefield, 1973), p. 94.

[34] Of 75 accounts from fathers, 14 discussed this explicitly. See for example Geordie Todd, 'A Man's World', British Film Institute Archive, roll 100, pp. 135–6; Martin Jack, Int075, P. Thompson and H. Newby, *Families, Social Mobility and Ageing, an Intergenerational Approach, 1900–1988* [computer file]. Colchester, Essex: UK Data Archive (UKDA) [distributor], July 2005. SN: 4938, p. 75; Frank Jonston, Int076, *Families*, UKDA, p. 33.

[35] Terrence O'Farrell, Int103, *Families*, UKDA.

[36] Lord Riverdale, 'A Man's World', roll 178, p. 118.

[37] Alf Short, 'A Labour of Love', British Library, roll 212, pp. 7–8.

Ryder, a father in 1940s Liverpool, expressed regret about his prioritizing of work when interviewed in the 1990s. He stated, 'I don't know whether they think I was remote from them, but it was a different way of life and maybe the kids, my kids, don't understand it, they think Dad was cool and cold but he wasn't, he loved his kids.' As noted elsewhere, he voiced frustration at younger people's lack of understanding of older attitudes.[38] There is evidence here of how a discrepancy between fathers' and children's attitudes could emerge; fathers might feel they were doing their best for their families by working hard for long hours, whilst children could perceive the lack of time available for them as remoteness.

Others framed this problem differently, noting their love for their children led them to work an increased number of hours, behaviour which perhaps would have taken on even more significance in the post-war period, at which time standard working hours were decreasing. John and Elizabeth Newson noted a shift in experiences in this sense, suggesting that the 'advent of the forty-hour week' either led to more family time for men or the money for labour-saving devices for the home.[39] Henry Curd, for example, recalled that he took on overtime when he had a family in 1940s Surrey: 'If I had the chance to earn money I used to think oh, you must earn money, you gotta family, so you can give 'em a better standard of life.'[40] Mathew Meret, married in 1956, noted he used to spend all his overtime money on his wife or children.[41]

For some men, however, investing time in their relationships was not a high priority, particularly in contrast with other aspects of their lives. Lord Riverdale explained that his wife gave him a 'mild reproof' for not spending enough time with his children, despite the fact he said it was important to him.[42] Other fathers were explicitly indifferent to family life. It was other family members who were more likely to point to this rather than fathers themselves. Mary Siddall discussed her husband's near-complete lack of interest in his children. She met him in 1918 whilst working at a textile mill in Oldham and, after marrying in 1921, the couple had ten children. She noted that he freely admitted how little his children interested him, stating 'he'd say I'm not bothered about them'. Mary suggested this was because of jealousy, a theme discussed later in this chapter. Mary's daughter was also interviewed, and agreed that her father was ambivalent towards family life, though she described him as 'marvellous'. Her father's apparent lack of participation and interest in his children did not stop him from being 'good' in her eyes, demonstrating that the standards for being a good father were not particularly high in the 1920s.[43] This evidence of a complete lack of interest

[38] George Ryder, 'A Man's World', roll 135, pp. 37–8, 43–8.
[39] John and Elizabeth Newson, *Patterns of Infant Care in an Urban Community* (Harmondsworth, 1963), p. 243.
[40] Henry Curd, Int042, *Families*, UKDA, p. 43. Also see Leonard Canning, Int025, *Families*, UKDA, p. 19.
[41] Mathew Meret, Int089, *Families*, UKDA, p. 26.
[42] Lord Riverdale, 'A Man's World', roll 178, p. 118.
[43] Mary Siddall, 'A Labour of Love', roll 42, pp. 20–1; roll 46, p. 8. Also see Mrs J1B, Elizabeth Roberts Archive (ERA), 1940–70, p. 31.

in children can be found in families of all social classes. A nanny, Charlotte Huggett, highlighted how, in one of the first families she worked for in the 1920s and 1930s, the children were strangers to their parents, particularly the father. She described the short periods of time he spent with the children, and the mishaps that occurred when they were in his charge. They fell in the pond, for example, and Charlotte described how 'one day the children came up with handfuls of gold sovereigns which he'd given the children to play with because he didn't know what to do with the children there. They were, sort of, quite strangers to him.'[44]

A minority of the social research conducted in this period also points to fathers' indifference in certain communities. In their research into a mining community in Yorkshire in the 1950s, for example, Norman Dennis, Fernando Henriques, and Clifford Slaughter found that men lacked interest in family life.[45] Similarly, in John Barron Mays' study of problem families in Liverpool in the 1950s, it was noted that fathers did not spend much time with their children: 'All too often the husband sheds his responsibilities and places them on his wife's shoulders.' Yet Mays saw good parent–child relationships as the key to solving the problems he studied.[46] The growing emphasis on the importance of fatherhood and the father–child relationship in popular culture, and the press in particular, inspired a variety of views. It is clear that, for a minority of men from various social backgrounds, family life was not of much importance, and many remained indifferent to their role within it.

Nonetheless, both interviewees and social researchers pointed to change in this area, and an awareness of it. A shift in male attitudes was prominent in both Abrams' and Williamson's oral history studies, noted earlier in this chapter. Young and Willmott surveyed families in Debden, a housing estate in Essex, who had moved from Bethnal Green. These families had clearly experienced a dramatic alteration in their lifestyles, yet those who remained in Bethnal Green also emphasized changes to family life. The authors stated 'People are well aware of the change which has come upon them in the course of a few decades', and highlighted how contrasts between past and present informed the mentality and framework of reference of interviewees.[47] Many of Newson and Newson's respondents also mentioned changing social trends with varying degrees of approval.[48] A number of male oral history interviewees suggested they made active decisions to become different parents from their own fathers; of the seventy-five accounts from fathers themselves, ten discussed this in explicit terms, and others made more implicit

[44] Charlotte Huggett, quoted in Steve Humphries and Pamela Gordon (eds), *A Labour of Love: The Experience of Parenthood in Britain 1900–1950* (London, 1993), p. 175.

[45] Norman Dennis, Fernando Henriques, and Clifford Slaughter [1956], *Coal Is Our Life: An Analysis of a Yorkshire Mining Community* (London, 1969), pp. 180–7, 234. This research is, to an extent, challenged by Williamson's oral history study. Williamson, 'He Was Good', pp. 87–108.

[46] John Barron Mays [1954], *Growing Up in the City: A Study of Juvenile Delinquency in an Urban Neighbourhood* (Liverpool, 1964), pp. 86, 158.

[47] Michael Young and Peter Willmott [1957], *Family and Kinship in East London* (Harmondsworth, 1967), p. 19.

[48] Newson and Newson, *Patterns*, pp. 246–8.

comparisons.[49] One or two highlighted the fact that their parental relationships were similar to those of the previous generation, and others felt it had changed in some respects but had remained the same in others.[50] Ted Cunningham, who married in 1932 in the north-east of England, stressed that his own father did not care about his family and stated that 'in my mind my father wasn't a father'. In contrast, Ted wanted to give his children 'everything they wanted', as 'I didn't have it and I've always made sure that my family did get what I never got.' He said he did not mind working very long hours 'as long as they were happy', highlighting an emotional sense of breadwinning as outlined earlier in this chapter.[51] Frank Davies, a father in 1950s Salford, also stressed the differences between himself and his own father. Whilst his father was one of the 'old school', Frank described the very conscious decision he made to take responsibility for his child, to make sure his daughter 'knew him as a father'.[52] This rhetoric of change reflects both a shift in attitudes around the middle of the twentieth century and since, and hints at the different perspectives of fathers and children.

The meaning attributed to 'being a father' gained a new significance in such men's analysis of their own emotional relationships with their children. Some men invested in these interactions and believed that their presence and relationships with their children were very influential and significant. Such men actively chose to behave differently from their own fathers, and indeed, such a reaction against the previous generation was one way in which change occurred in this period. Particularly for working-class families such as Frank's and Ted's, increased employment levels and rising standards of living in the latter half of this period enabled them to put this change into practice. Here the conditions in which families of different class backgrounds lived were all important; a shifting cultural emphasis on fatherhood alongside a desire to act differently to one's parents encouraged many men to put greater value on their relationships with their children. This became more possible in the 1950s, when new housing and greater levels of affluence began to bring benefits to working-class families, particularly after years of hardship and shortages.[53] However, as demonstrated earlier in this chapter, the emotional engagement men had with their children did not fall along class lines; both emotionally involved and distant fathers could be found amongst all social classes. Where substantial shifts occurred within working-class communities, there is little evidence that individuals wanted to emulate the middle classes per se. Instead there occurred a moving together of the conditions in which

---

[49] For example, see Edward Byrne, Int019, *Families*, UKDA, p. 50; Vera/Leonard Spencer, Int134, *Families*, UKDA, p. 26; Edward Winn, Int159, *Families*, UKDA, p. 22.

[50] For example, see Ernest Shiell, Int131, *Families*, UKDA, pp. 27–8; Ron Vincent, Int146, *Families*, UKDA, p. 19.

[51] Ted Cunningham, 'A Man's World', roll 91, pp. 23–4; roll 93, pp. 80–3.

[52] Frank Davies, 'A Man's World', roll 75, pp. 1–2; roll 158, p. 35.

[53] On affluence, see Claire Langhamer, 'The Meanings of Home in Postwar Britain', *Journal of Contemporary History* 40:2 (2005), pp. 341–62; Jon Lawrence, 'Class, "Affluence" and the Study of Everyday Life in Britain, c.1930–64', *Cultural and Social History* 10:2 (2013), pp. 273–99; Selina Todd, 'Affluence, Class and Crown Street: Reinvestigating the Post-War Working Class', *Contemporary British History* 50:1 (2008), pp. 501–18.

working- and middle-class families lived, which could enable closer relationships. Class differences in terms of the ways in which father–child relationships operated were important, but, as in numerous aspects of family life, class was not a prime determinant of behaviour.

DIFFICULT EMOTIONS AND RELATIONSHIPS

A significant number of men, however, remained not only uninterested in family life, but also a difficult and unpredictable element within it. It is clear that a minority of fathers throughout this period were also violent and abusive, as was highlighted in Chapter 3 in the context of discipline.[54] In discussing parenting, a small number of wives and children raised incidents of physical abuse and drunkenness.[55] Sean Smith, born in 1927 in Manchester, and one of five children, was brutally beaten by his father, and Sean felt this was 'to make you cry and to humiliate you and to break you down and to make you nothing, so that you were destroyed'. He dreamt of a proper family life, which came into conflict with what he described as this 'awful reality'.[56] Elizabeth Arnold, born 1935, spoke about the sexual abuse she endured from her stepfather, which resulted in her joining the Army and leaving home.[57]

Researchers such as Bowley insisted on the good intentions of most parents: she stated that 'I think neglectful parents are now in the minority. Most parents that I have met are genuinely interested in their offspring, and are most grateful for advice and help.'[58] However, many families clearly experienced difficult and even abusive relationships in this period. Newspapers reported on cases of abuse throughout these decades, and legislation, such as the Children's Act 1948, brought such problems to public notice. In the post-war age of state social services, the continued preoccupation with the family as a positive unit is notable. New legislation focused on keeping the family together and preventing problems rather than curing them. However, debates about rising levels of juvenile delinquency and 'problem families' revealed the ambivalence that lay behind such ideas.[59] At least in the press, however, the positive post-war mood persisted, and faith in the family as the basic unit of social order, with the father at the head and heart of it, remained strong. It was not until the 1960s that a renewed focus on child abuse emerged, particularly with the publication of the Kempe Report on 'battered baby syndrome'.[60]

---

[54] David Kynaston, *Family Britain, 1951–57* (London, 2009), pp. 595–6.

[55] Nine of the accounts from children and three accounts from mothers explicitly indicated this sort of abuse. For example, see Mrs O1P, ERA, Preston 1890–1940, pp. 11,13; Norah Austin, Int003, *Families*, UKDA, p. 4; Albert Handley, Int062, *Families*, UKDA, p. 49.

[56] Sean Harold Smith, 'A Man's World', roll 48, p. 46.

[57] Elizabeth Arnold, Int002, *Families*, UKDA, p. 40.

[58] Agatha H. Bowley [1946], *Problems of Family Life: An Environmental Study* (Edinburgh, 1948), p. 52.

[59] Hendrick, *Child Welfare*, pp. 217–22.   [60] Hendrick, *Child Welfare*, pp. 242–4.

Whilst there was a tension between the constant assertion that fathers were taking their duties seriously and the continual stream of articles on abuse and neglect cases, the newspapers studied here mostly used these cases to underline the limits of behaviour. The *Manchester Guardian* portrayed the most negative perspective on such matters, arguing that the rise in child abuse cases since the war was due to fathers' return.[61] In 1950, furthermore, an article was published positing that 'delinquent families' were to blame for the rise in child crime.[62] Alongside its greater acceptance of the difficult and abusive situations children faced, however, remained an acknowledgement of the potential good of the family, with calls for more education for families and the importance of a secure family environment for children. Other articles across the press insisted on the important influence of parents in tackling problems such as juvenile crime, and held those parents with delinquent children responsible for society's problems.[63] Whether it was functioning properly or not, the family remained the basis for treating such problems. An article in *The Times*, for example, noted that too many fathers were a 'negative quantity' in their children's lives, yet contended that the remedy to this was a greater focus on the influence of fathers on their children's development, whilst an article in the *Manchester Guardian* focused on 'treating the minds of parents' to combat child cruelty.[64] The *Daily Mirror*, meanwhile, concentrated on castigating what it portrayed as unusual and untypical cases of cruelty, even when such cases appeared on a weekly or even daily basis.[65] In 1959, this depiction was reinforced in a story about a man being subjected to violence in prison at the hands of other prisoners, as they had been horrified at his crime of cruelly abusing his daughter.[66] However, whilst such coverage in the press constantly reiterated the limits of parents' and in particular fathers' spheres of influence, it was not until after the period studied here that a renewed focus on the problem of abuse emerged.

Throughout the years between 1914 and 1960, there was a continued acknowledgment of the potential for fear within the father–child relationship. The coverage in the press of cases of abuse clearly recognized this, and a small number of children interviewed highlighted this aspect of their family life. A relatively small number, only fourteen of nearly 250 accounts, explicitly highlighted they were actually afraid of their fathers. Three explicitly rejected this idea.[67] Mrs P2P, for example, born 1907, recalled that even her father's voice 'frightened us to death' and he 'was very bad tempered in drink'. She described him as 'Victorian', a description frequently used, as will be discussed in Chapter 5.[68] Ella Carey, born

[61] *Manchester Guardian*, 20 February 1948, p. 3.

[62] *Manchester Guardian*, 11 May 1950, p. 4.

[63] See *Daily Express*, 15 February 1949, p. 2; *The Times*, 21 April 1949, p. 5; *Daily Express*, 20 May 1952, p. 3.

[64] *The Times*, 12 April 1957, p. 13; *Manchester Guardian*, 1 June 1956, p. 12.

[65] This was even the case in more general feature and comment pieces, as well as individual news items. For example, *Daily Mirror*, 11 August 1955, p. 4.

[66] *Daily Mirror*, 13 March 1959, p. 7.

[67] For example, see Mrs M1P, ERA, Preston 1890–1940, p. 65; Mary Moran, Int092, *Families*, UKDA, p. 6; Mr F2L, ERA, 1940–70, p. 36.

[68] Mrs P2P, ERA, Preston 1890–1940, p. 15.

1915, similarly noted that her father was 'Very domineering. In fact I think—I don't know about the others, but I was terrified of him. I was terrified of him.'[69] More women than men highlighted experiences of fear as children, perhaps indicating either a difference in the treatment of girls and boys or, alternatively, a difference in the acceptability of recounting certain experiences along gendered lines. This emotion was less prominently discussed in popular culture as the period progressed. In the *Daily Mirror* in 1950, for example, a study of children's fears was reported. It was stated that not one child was afraid of their father, 'a complete and very welcome reversal of the state of affairs . . . in the Victorian era' according to Reverend Jinks, the director of the research.[70]

Within even the happiest families, both individuals and public voices recognized that the father–child relationship could involve negative emotions. Jealousy of the children's place in their mother's affections in particular was recognized as a danger, as highlighted by Mary Siddall earlier in this chapter. Overall, this was referred to even less frequently than fear, but some people did think it was significant in terms of their relationships. Humphrey Gillett, for instance, described what happened when his children were born: 'I felt that [the children were] what really mattered to her and that probably happens in most cases—once the first child is born you've really lost your wife.' He did also state that he was 'very fond' of the children, though whether this was borne out of his emotions or a perceived pressure to appear a loving father in the context of the interview is very difficult to ascertain.[71] Likewise, Lily Felstead, a mother in Cheshire in the 1930s, spoke of her second husband, whom she had been forced to marry to secure some kind of income. Their relationship was a difficult one, in part, Lily stated, because 'He really was jealous of the kids.'[72] It was commonly assumed that fathers were capable of this jealousy, but that by becoming more involved in their children's lives it could be avoided. Bowley, in her study of problem families, reflected that:

> Normally, affection is the parents' first response to the child; the desire to comfort, assist, to please or to make secure is a natural response of the parent. But it is equally true to say that a certain amount of jealousy is almost bound to arise. A child first turns to his mother, and the husband may feel neglected or resentful. The careful wife does not allow the child to displace the husband, and is quick to stimulate the child's interest in the father.

She also believed that positive relationships between family members could ensure that children did not become jealous of either parent, avoiding the Oedipus complex, an idea popular amongst some psychologists at this time.[73] In their study

[69] Ella Carey, Int027, *Families*, UKDA, p. 8. Also see Doreen Angus, Int001, *Families*, UKDA, p. 26; Nigel Gray, *The Worst of Times: An Oral History of the Great Depression in Britain* (London, 1985), pp. 179–80.

[70] *Daily Mirror*, 13 September 1950, p. 3.

[71] Humphrey Gillett, 'A Man's World', roll 44, pp. 55–7.

[72] Lily Felstead, quoted in Humphries and Gordon, *A Labour*, pp. 140–1.

[73] Bowley, *Problems*, p. 3. Sharpe also discussed the possibility of jealousy and how to deal with it in her essay of 1945. Ella Freeman Sharpe, 'What the Father Means to the Child', in S. Isaacs (ed.), *Fatherless Children: A Contribution to the Understanding of Their Needs* (London, 1945), p. 26. Many

of infant-care practices, Newson and Newson highlighted how most literature aimed at mothers-to-be included a section on involving fathers from the start, 'so they do not feel excluded and become jealous'. In light of this concern, they measured what fathers did do for their children, and argued that 'The willingness of so many fathers to participate actively in looking after such young children is, we believe, a very distinctive feature of modern family life in England.' They did not refer to jealousy in this relationship when discussing their research findings.[74]

In the press, jealousy was again a common theme, but portrayed as a problem that could be overcome, at least from the perspective of contributors and editors. In this sense, there was an ongoing promotion of an ideal version of fatherhood and a repeated positivity about fathers, alongside the acknowledgement that many men did not live up to such a standard. Analysing this negative emotion, however, could provide a means to promote more involved parenting for men, and fathers' jealousy of their children became increasingly unacceptable in the positive portrayal of family life after the Second World War. In 1920, for example, an article was printed in the *Daily Mirror*, which started 'Children are the invaders of the kingdom of marital happiness.' The subheading read: 'Fathers who must expect to be neglected', and it presented the cause of the neglected father sympathetically.[75] The *Manchester Guardian* presented a different viewpoint around the same time, suggesting that the emotion of jealousy was a natural consequence of overcrowded living conditions for working-class families, and sympathized with wives negotiating the needs of husbands and sons.[76] By the 1950s, the *Daily Mirror*'s agony aunts at least had little sympathy for jealous fathers.[77] In 1955, for example, 'The case of the jealous father' was featured in 'Sister Clare's Clinic'. Such jealousy was described as 'tragic' and 'hard to understand', and the reader was told that this relationship should be one of 'wonderful comradeship—not rivalry'. Whilst fathers received little sympathy here, women were reminded not to leave father out of their babies' lives.[78] Likewise, Mary Brown, another regular advice writer, responded in 1959 to a letter from a wife whose husband was jealous of their son and refused to have more children. The subtitle similarly read 'the case of the jealous husband', thus problematizing such a situation into a 'case' to be dealt with, rather than a common occurrence. That she suggested the husband in question might need 'expert help' further isolated this as a psychological or medical issue rather than a minor and common difficulty.[79]

Another aspect of the father–child relationship frequently highlighted was irritation. It was assumed that children could disrupt the 'peace and quiet' fathers enjoyed. This could certainly be the case for men who worked night shifts, such

psychologists remained sceptical of Freudian theory: Valentine, for example, noted the evidence for the Oedipus complex was lacking. Valentine, *Parents*, p. 162.

[74] Newson and Newson, *Patterns*, pp. 134, 139–40.

[75] *Daily Mirror*, 25 November 1920, p. 7. Also see *Daily Mirror*, 29 December 1937, p. 18.

[76] *Manchester Guardian*, 22 June 1923, p. 6.

[77] For example, see *Daily Mirror*, 1 May 1948, p. 2; *Daily Mirror*, 5 October 1949, p. 8; *Daily Mirror*, 3 October 1956, p. 19.

[78] *Daily Mirror*, 18 August 1955, p. 4.   [79] *Daily Mirror*, 5 October 1959, p. 21.

as Dave Bowman, a train driver.[80] Most interviewees did not refer to such emotions. Yet the use of this subject in other contexts, such as satire and cartoons, demonstrates that this aspect of the father–child relationship was a recognized part of family life. There was a substantial degree of sympathy for fathers in the press in this respect. In a cartoon entitled 'Why does father ask that question?', in the *Daily Mirror* in 1933, for example, a father was portrayed tripping over his son's belongings and being disturbed whilst reading, and in response asking 'And when did you say you were going back to school?'[81] In a similar vein, in 1936 the paper published a verbatim recording of a child asking his father a vast number of questions and generally being unable to remain quiet. The story was introduced by the comment that such conversations were 'exquisite agony' and could 'make you mad', and ended with father emitting 'something very like a sob'.[82]

This sort of relationship between father and child was also a feature of some novels: Uncle Quentin of the 'Famous Five' books was continually enraged by the children's noisiness and the disruption they caused.[83] Furthermore, the 'Just William' books were centred on the chaos that William caused for his family, amongst whom his father is the most irritable. This is explored to great comic effect in all the books. In *Just William*, first published in 1922, the first story, 'William Goes to the Pictures', detailed Mr Brown's irritation at his family and William in particular. William crashes into him, is reprimanded for eating sweets, and is found out to have been lying, for which his father accuses him of being 'mad'. William reflects on his day: 'he had been brutally assaulted by a violent and unreasonable parent. Suddenly William began to wonder if his father drank.'[84] In other stories in the book, Mr Brown looks forward to dining out as it provided 'a short rest from William', thanks the heavens when the rain stops so that William can play outside, and tells his wife to be 'thankful for small mercies' when William has recovered from illness and is able to leave the house.[85] Other books continued the theme: in *More William*, for example, the family quickly hide William's efforts at 'cleaning' from his father, as 'It was felt—and not without reason—that William's father's feelings of respect for the sanctity of Christmas Day might be overcome by his feelings of paternal ire.'[86] In addition, Mr Brown is disappointed at William's presence on their holiday, stating he thought 'it was to be a *rest* cure',[87] whilst 'what will your father say?' becomes a repeated response to William's antics in the book.[88] Although the stories were written very much for

---

[80] Dave Bowman, quoted in Steve Humphries and Pamela Gordon (eds), *A Man's World: From Boyhood to Manhood, 1900–1960* (London, 1996), p. 176.

[81] *Daily Mirror*, 17 January 1933, p. 11.

[82] *Daily Mirror*, 8 September 1936, p. 10. Also see *Daily Mirror*, 30 March 1936, p. 14.

[83] For example, Enid Blyton [1942], *Five on a Treasure Island* (London, 2001), p. 98; Enid Blyton [1949], *Five Get into Trouble* (Leicester, 1975), p. 13; Enid Blyton [1956], *Five on a Secret Trail* (London 1985), p. 8.

[84] Richmal Crompton [1922], *Just William* (London, 1990), pp. 18–31.

[85] Crompton, *Just William*, pp. 59, 121, 214.

[86] Richmal Crompton [1922], *More William* (online, 2005, available at http://manybooks.net [last accessed 30/08/2013]), p. 6.

[87] Crompton, *More William*, p. 75.   [88] Crompton, *More William*, pp. 8, 41.

children, and, as such, from William's perspective, it could certainly be argued that a parental audience was also in mind, and adults reading these stories to children might have greeted the exasperation of Mr Brown with familiarity. In this sense, whilst there was a consistent emphasis on a positive version of fatherhood in popular culture, there was a simultaneous sympathy for parents in terms of the more trying aspects of bringing up children.

LOVE AND AFFECTION

Numerous interviewees spoke about more positive emotions in relation to the father–child relationship. Fathers, mothers, and children hinted at the love and fondness between men and their sons and daughters. These emotions were particularly notable amongst the interviews conducted for Thompson and Newby's '100 families' project, as one core question was 'how did you/your parents show affection?', whereas the interviews conducted for Elizabeth Roberts' projects tended to focus more on behaviour than feelings. Out of nearly 250 accounts in total from children, around a quarter explicitly described positive emotions such as love, affection, fondness, and closeness in this relationship, and over a third of the seventy-five accounts from fathers did so. Marion Thomas, for example, born 1909, felt fortunate in her relationships with her parents, noting 'I mean they both made me feel . . . that I meant everything to them. I think in that way I was lucky, I never doubted their affection for me. Well they must have felt like that, or they wouldn't have put themselves out . . . putting me first you know.'[89] Even so, whilst there is evidence of strong feelings between fathers and children, many interviewees found it difficult to articulate these emotions, to give them a name, or to give examples of how they demonstrated them. Furthermore, it was even less likely that these emotions had been explicitly discussed between parents and children at the time, particularly in the earlier part of this period. This reticence did not vary significantly along class or regional lines, and it appears that internal family dynamics and personalities were most influential. Mrs J1P, for example, born 1911 to a working-class family in Preston, noted that her parents did not show any affection beyond a routine kiss at bedtime.[90] May Welham, born 1913 to a lower-middle class family in Manchester, was asked whether her parents were affectionate, and responded, 'They were because they were fond of us, very, very fond of us, but they didn't show—they weren't always loving and kissing you and that kind—we've always been pretty matter of fact, you know. We've never been a sloppy sort of family.'[91]

[89] Marion Thomas, Int168, *Families*, UKDA, p. 15. Also see J. Mann, Int087, *Families*, UKDA, p. 9; Patricia Dowden, Int051, *Families*, UKDA, p. 14.
[90] Mrs J1P, ERA, Preston 1890–1940 (notes from Mrs J1P). Also see Margret Hallum, Int060, *Families*, UKDA, p. 32; Joyce Mary Pounds, Int114, *Families*, UKDA, p. 15; Mrs Schlarman, Int128, *Families*, UKDA, p. 11.
[91] May Welham, Int155, *Families*, UKDA, p. 20. Also see Martin Byrne, Int020, *Families*, UKDA, p. 9; John Dennis, Int049, *Families*, UKDA, p. 13; Barbara Hirbert, Int066, *Families*, UKDA, p. 6; Diana Kellard, Int077, *Families*, UKDA, p. 26; Jean Nedwell, Int098, *Families*,

There was a sense among a number of families that too much affection was indeed undesirable in some way; Lord Riverdale, an upper-class father from Sheffield, felt he was a more tactile and demonstrative father than most, but stated with regard to the lack of discussion of feelings: 'I don't think you talk to them about how much you love them. That's surely something they take for granted.'[92] Indeed, displays of affection could be embarrassing; Geoffrey Turner, born 1929, felt that his father, an engineer, 'was a bit bluff and hearty really. I think he would have been embarrassed by too much shows of emotion.'[93] Roy Hubbard, born 1939, likewise reflected on the attitudes of men like his father, a miner: 'It's almost as if it was regarded by men as being unmanly to show real affection.'[94] Others discussed the difference between fathers and mothers; some mothers were more openly affectionate. Peter Coverley (Snr), born 1915, explicitly contrasted his parents. Although he described both as 'loving and easy-going', he added that 'my father was very undemonstrative. You'd never see him kissing one of his daughters until later on when he was getting older. Whereas my mother would always take you in her arms, you know. As mothers do.'[95] Pamela Pittuck, born 1930, spoke about how she was close with her mother, but found her father somewhat distant. She was more forgiving in retrospect, stating, 'It isn't everyone that can put their arms round you and say I love you, but it doesn't mean to say that they don't.' She contrasted the fear she felt as a child with the growing realization of the love between her and her father as she grew older.[96] Indeed, these accounts suggest that open emotion could be seen as much more appropriate between fathers and daughters than fathers and sons.

Though physical affection was not common amongst fathers and children, this did not mean that the relationship between father and child was not about bodily experiences. Fathers' bodies were important to children when they recollected their relationships. A small number did remember kisses and cuddles with fathers and mothers, or with their children.[97] For some, this was only when the child was ill or upset.[98] For other fathers, this behaviour was only

UKDA, p. 7; Michael Wall, Int150, *Families*, UKDA, p. 12; Edward Winn, Int159, *Families*, UKDA, p. 5.

[92] Lord Riverdale, quoted in 'A Man's World: The Father', cassette no. 8.031587 AA, broadcast on BBC 2, 27 March 1996.

[93] Geoffrey Turner, Int145, *Families*, UKDA, p. 16.

[94] Roy Hubbard, Int069, *Families*, UKDA, p. 15. Also see Alan Parks, Int106, *Families*, UKDA, p. 15; Glenda Speed, Int135, *Families*, UKDA, p. 15.

[95] Peter Coverley (Snr), Int037, *Families*, UKDA, p. 13. Also see Frank Jonston, Int076, *Families*, UKDA, p. 11; Terrence Walter, Int152, *Families*, UKDA, p. 8; Arthur Winn, Int160, *Families*, UKDA, p. 8.

[96] Pamela Pittuck, Int108, *Families*, UKDA, pp. 24–5. Also see Doreen Angus, Int001, *Families*, UKDA, p. 39; Kathleen Murray, Int095, *Families*, UKDA, pp. 21–2.

[97] Leonard Canning, Int025, *Families*, UKDA, p. 23; Patricia Dowden, Int051, *Families*, UKDA, p. 14; Mary Lear, Int084, *Families*, UKDA, p. 20; Lord Riverdale, A Man's World', roll 177, p. 106; G. A. W. Tomlinson, *Coal-Miner* (London, c.1937); Walker, *The High Path*, p. 14.

[98] John Burrell, Int024, *Families*, UKDA, p. 19; Ian Canning, Int026, *Families*, UKDA, p. 11; Margret Hallum, Int060, *Families*, UKDA, p. 32; Sean Harold Smith, A Man's World', roll 48, pp. 49–50.

appropriate when the child was very young; Leonard Canning, for example, remembered the rough affection with his son, born 1945, as he put him to bed, which included 'Kiss and a cuddle and all this sort of thing.'[99] Yet his son Ian, interviewed separately, suggested that physical affection and bodily contact was rare, noting 'I had some illness as a child and that is the only time I can recall him picking me up and sort of hugging me with any real sort of feeling.'[100] Here again, it is clear that the different expectations of fathers and children could leave fathers feeling involved and emotionally engaged, with children feeling this was not quite the case. Whilst most fathers did not regularly cuddle or kiss their children, the rough and tumble of games could provide a close physical intimacy. Harry Daley in his autobiography wrote of how he and his siblings used to play with their father when he returned home from sea, and described how 'He was strong enough for us to climb about on, and we crawled sniffing over his lovely, warm, drowsy body.'[101] William Woodruff also recalled the particular 'rasp' of his father's beard against his young cheek.[102] Ted Walker noted how he 'would nuzzle at his [father's] own essential fragrances—sweat and Nut-Brown shag at the nape of his neck—when he carried me through to the living-room table'.[103]

Furthermore, reflecting on the emotions of fatherhood, many interviewees pointed to their embodied experiences whilst interacting with their children. The experience of childbirth could be particularly emotional. Alf Jenkins, a miner from South Wales, first became a father in 1924, and recalled fainting in response to his wife's distress. After regaining consciousness 'some hours after' (in Alf's words), Alf experienced 'feelings of elation' when presented with his baby.[104] John Caldwell, who had two children in Leeds in the 1940s, described his emotional response to becoming a father. He remembered, 'I just filled up. I didn't properly cry or that, I just filled up you know, with emotion.'[105] His wife, Hilda, gave a different account. Describing John's response when he first saw the new baby, she stated, 'Thanks lovey, he says, it's wonderful and he cried. There was tears in his eyes.'[106] Whilst Hilda was happy to admit to John crying, he suggested he 'filled up' and did not 'properly cry', reluctant to admit to displaying emotion in such a visible way. Richard Nesbitt, a headmaster from Devon, also highlighted the bodily nature of his emotional response to his son hurting himself. He stated that 'the howl of agony that went up went straight to my heart [laughs] it was real, a cry of despair and I picked him up and hugged him and hugged him'.[107] Likewise, fathers away from their families during wartime could

[99] Leonard Canning, Int025, *Families*, UKDA, p. 23.
[100] Ian Canning, Int026, *Families*, UKDA, p. 11.
[101] Harry Daley, *This Small Cloud: A Personal Memoir* (London, 1986), p. 18
[102] William Woodruff [1993], *The Road to Nab End* (London, 2008), p. 105. For an example from literature, see Radclyffe Hall [1928], *The Well of Loneliness* (London, 1983), p. 39.
[103] Walker, *The High Path*, p. 14.
[104] Alf Jenkins, quoted in Humphries and Gordon, *A Man's World*, p. 170.
[105] John Caldwell, 'A Labour of Love', roll 69, p. 7.
[106] Hilda Caldwell, 'A Labour of Love', roll 67, p. 6.
[107] Richard Nesbitt, 'A Man's World', roll 146, p. 36.

admit to their devastation at leaving their families; C. Jones in the First World War and F. I. Williams in the Second both admitted to tears when being parted from their families.[108]

Though many interviewees suggested the mother–child relationship was closer and more affectionate, a small minority suggested this not always the case. Mr Fides, born 1929, compared his mother and father's personalities, and his relationship with them, suggesting that 'I loved me father more than me mother, but I love me mother, you know.'[109] Florence Warner, born at the start of the period in 1906, described how her position within her family led to her close relationship with her father: 'I think I got on better with me father than me mother, you know, I think, with being the only girl, I probably was made more fuss of.'[110] Similarly, Alec Gunn also felt that sons and daughters could have different relationships with parents, noting of his childhood in the 1930s, 'my sister was closer to my father and I was closer to my mother, but my father was extremely kind and nice to me'.[111] Mathew Meret, born 1931, spoke of the difference between his own and his sisters' view of their father. When asked whether his father was affectionate, he answered 'I think he was in his own way. Me sisters think he was a bit of a tyrant, you know . . .'[112] Harry Stainer, born 1949, thought his parents were especially affectionate to him as he was the only son.[113] Likewise, others reflected on how their relationships changed as children got older. George Sadler, for example, who was born in 1929, noted that he did not see much of his father when he was young as he worked long hours, but they grew 'very close' when George reached age 12 onwards, a sentiment which his father echoed.[114] Mr W7B, born 1945, and Brian Welham, born 1949, similarly talked about becoming closer to their fathers as they got older.[115]

A few interviewees spoke of more open emotional exchanges; this was slightly more common as the period progressed and in more upper- and middle-class families. Ruth Tilley, for example, born 1933, spoke of the 'affectionate and loving letters' she received whilst at school from her father, who worked in the RAF and for Scotland Yard.[116] Elaine Rickwood, a teacher born in 1946, remembered her father as 'a cuddly sorta man' who would touch, cuddle, and chat with his children.[117] Likewise, Martin Jack, a physiotherapist who became a father in the mid-1950s, highlighted that his children 'got plenty of TLC, I s'pose—Tender

[108] Private Papers of C. Jones, Imperial War Museum Archive (IWMA), Documents.11085, p. 493; Private Papers of F. I. Williams, IWMA, Documents.17022, letter to wife dated 20 September 1940.
[109] Mr Fides, Int167, *Families*, UKDA, p. 16.
[110] Florence Warner, Int153, *Families*, UKDA, p. 7.
[111] Alec Gunn, 'A Man's World', roll 35, p. 6.
[112] Mathew Meret, Int089, *Families*, UKDA, p. 16. Also see George Cook, *A Hackney Memory Chest* (London, 1983), p. 3.
[113] Harry Stainer, Int137, *Families*, UKDA, p. 13.
[114] George Sadler, Int127, *Families*, UKDA, p. 15; Sidney Sadler, Int126, *Families*, UKDA, p. 19. Also see Laura Millard, Int090, *Families*, UKDA, p. 10.
[115] Mr W7B, ERA, 1940–70, p. 15; Brian Welham, Int158, *Families*, UKDA, p. 14.
[116] Ruth Tilley, Int142, *Families*, UKDA, p. 27.
[117] Elaine Rickwood, Int117, *Families*, UKDA, p. 10.

Loving Care' and that 'we always were pretty close, you know, as a family'.[118] Yet the more openly emotional style of fathering that became more prominent in the latter decades of the twentieth century was only hinted at in this evidence.[119] Indeed, some interviewees reflected explicitly on this change; Robert Williamson, for example, though he spoke movingly about his love for his daughter, recalled that he rarely kissed or cuddled her, and contrasted that with his relationship with his grandchildren, noting 'I kiss and cuddle me grandchildren as soon as I see them—I can't leave them alone. It's a different way of life now you see, we didn't do it then you know.'[120]

As such, a particular emphasis on love within the oral history interviews can be discerned, yet at the time, the expression of such emotions was more restrained. The autobiographies and social research studied support such a finding. As Jack Lawson noted of County Durham miners in the 1930s, they 'loved and were loved—though [they] would laugh at the word'.[121] Newson and Newson, researching over 700 families in Nottingham, found it difficult to assess change in this matter, contending that the ease with which parents demonstrated love for their children depended as much on individual personality as social context. One key consideration was the more equal relationship between parent and child, as they argued that 'The fact that parents nowadays do not feel so strongly the need to elevate themselves on to a different plane from their children, to *enforce* "respect", must also help to foster the atmosphere of love within the home.' Again, there are signs here of a reaction against previous generations, though this is very difficult to ascertain. The authors quoted several female interviewees who, together with their husbands, were determined to show more love to their children than their own parents had shown to them. Such a finding led Newson and Newson to suggest that 'It does not seem over-optimistic to hope that an investigation thirty years hence would arouse fewer memories of childhood loneliness and rejection.'[122] Their proposition, however, applied more to mothers than fathers, whose gendered identities could limit the extent to which they could display their emotions.

FEELING AND FRAMING EMOTIONS

Men also demonstrated their emotions for their children in reaction to particularly traumatic events. The impact of war had important consequences for the emotional relationships between fathers and children, particularly if the former were sent abroad on service. As Tim Fisher discussed in his study of fatherhood in

---

[118] Martin Jack, Int075, *Families*, UKDA, p. 75.

[119] On the later period, see Esther Dermott, *Intimate Fatherhood: A Sociological Analysis* (London, 2008), esp. ch.8.

[120] Robert Williamson, 'A Labour of Love', roll 161, p. 50.

[121] Jack Lawson [1932], *A Man's Life* (London, 1949), p. 66.

[122] Newson and Newson, *Patterns*, pp. 246–8. Original emphasis.

the First World War, the unique circumstances of wartime could intensify emotional experiences.[123] For some, communicating through letters arguably allowed them to express their emotions more freely, whilst others felt compelled to do so because they were frequently facing the possibility of death. Letters provide a useful way into the intimacy of relationships, yet by nature those letters preserved represent more engaged fathers; we cannot know about those who did not write. Along with the formal expressions of affection to be found in correspondence of the time, letters sent from Private Arthur James Butling to his children during the First World War were full of kisses and declarations of love, sentiments which they matched in their replies.[124] The letters of C. Jones to his family in the First World War initially focused on his experience of military service, but his emotions for his family and his concern with his daughter's development became more prominent as the war progressed. In March 1916, for example, he sent his daughter in written form 'more love than you can ever think of'; in November that year he noted in a letter to his wife that his 'separation from you and Dink [his daughter] always has been the most distressing feature of this business'; and in March 1918 he sent his daughter 'Such a big love my darling. I shall be soon home to give you a big hug.'[125] In both the First and Second World War, numerous men explicitly sent kisses and hugs to their children, beyond the usual sentiments in signing off from a letter.[126] In J. S. Mathews' case, in the Second World War, his letters to his three children evacuated to America were humorously tailored to gendered ideals, yet betrayed a loving relationship. He wrote to his son, Cliff, in January 1942, and signed off with loving messages from himself, his wife, and their youngest child, who had stayed in Britain: 'Mummy and Jo both send their love and kisses, as do I minus the kisses *of course.*' Likewise, a letter from Cliff dated 3 March, most likely of the same year, ended 'Lots of love and kisses for Mummy and Jo and a *hearty* handshake for Pop. *Of course.*'[127]

The letters of Corporal A. H. Wright to his wife and young child during the Second World War contained lengthy descriptions of his strong feelings of

[123] Timothy J. Fisher, 'Fatherhood and the Experience of Working-Class Fathers in Britain, 1900–1939', PhD Thesis (University of Edinburgh, 2004), p. 169.

[124] Private Papers of G. and E. Butling, IWMA, Documents.2423, pp. 1, 2, 15, 42, 61, 65, 120. Also see Private Papers of P. A. Wise, IWMA, Documents.1131.

[125] Private Papers of C. Jones, IWMA, Documents.11085, pp. 297, 444, 568.

[126] In the First World War, see Private Papers of C. Jones, IWMA, Documents.11085, e.g. pp. 31, 103, 160, 207, 286; Private Papers of H. W. Hicks, IWMA, Documents.15335, transcript e.g. pp. 25, 57 [inconsistent page numbering]; Private Papers of J. Evans, IWMA, Documents.16621, transcript pp. 32, 33, 34; Private Papers of P. A. Wise, IWMA, Documents.1131, pp. 1, 2; Private Papers of S. Bensinger, IWMA, Documents.16579, pp. 2, 3, 10, 20, 24; Private Papers of T. D. Laidlaw, IWMA, Documents.11018, pp. 15, 52, 76, 78, 217. In the Second World War, see Private Papers of C. D. Fuller, IWMA, Documents.16408, e.g. letters to wife dated 30 April 1940, 15 December 1942; Private Papers of J. S. Mathews, IWMA, Documents.16403, letters to Sheila/Dinah dated 12 December 1943, 12 January 1944; Private Papers of J. Mott, IWMA, Documents.15587, e.g. letters to wife dated 19 August 1942, 1 September 1942, 26 September 1942; Private Papers of F. I. Williams, IWMA, Documents.17022, letters to wife dated 25 September [1940?], 31 October 1941, 30 June 1942, letter to Susan dated 22 September 1942.

[127] Private Papers of J. S. Mathews, IWMA, Documents.16403, letter to Cliff dated 31 January 1942; letter to parents from Cliff dated 3 March [1942?]. Original emphasis.

love and affection, such as the 'thrill' he felt when he saw his baby for the first time.[128] C. D. Fuller similarly told his sons directly that he loved and missed them, and described to his wife how 'I am so hungry for the sight of them . . . and long to hold them in my arms again, I am always wondering what they look like after so long and know I am going to be a very proud husband and father.'[129] Frank Williams discussed very openly the painful emotions of separation, telling his wife that 'I am well on my way now & very unhappy. I feel very tearful. I wept a bit when I said good-bye to Susan [his daughter] & again when I said good bye to you', in a letter of September 1940 as he left them after a visit home.[130] The profundity of this experience remained with many men: in Woodruff's autobiography, he wrote of how the thought of his family 'sustained' him when fighting, and the 'bottomless depth of bliss' he felt when he met his son.[131] Interviewee Robert Williamson had one daughter when he went away to serve in the Second World War: he recalled how 'despondent' he felt if he did not receive letters from his family, and the joy he experienced on being reunited with them. In his interview, his voice wavered and was full of emotion when he remembered what he missed in terms of his daughter growing up. He also spoke of how he cried with joy when he first saw her again.[132] Whilst it is impossible to gauge how representative such sentiments were, these letters and accounts demonstrate the strength of emotional experience fatherhood entailed for at least some men.

In a number of interviews and autobiographies, sons and daughters described how the death of a child was a particular moment in which the emotions of parenting could override any normative gender ideals. Various individuals highlighted that the death of a sibling was one of the only times they saw their fathers shed tears. Jim Bullock, for example, born 1903, described his father's reaction on being told his eldest son had died in a mining accident, in the early twentieth century: 'Tears were running down his cheeks and he looked like a man mortally wounded.'[133] Doris Bailey similarly described her sister's death in 1925, from meningitis, and how she 'could hear the most unusual noise and it was a man crying. I'd never heard such a thing and I got out of bed, opened the door and went and stood on the landing and I could hear my dad crying.'[134] George Hitchin and William Woodruff both had siblings who died in infancy, in the

---

[128] Private Papers of A. H. Wright, IWMA, Documents.13285, esp. pp. 3, 6, 7, 11, 12, 13, 15, 16, 17, 18, 19, 23. Also see private Papers of D. E. Parker, IWMA, Documents.1926; Private Papers of D. S. Cave, IWMA, Documents.6443; Private Papers of H. W. Hicks, IWMA, Documents.15335.

[129] Private Papers of C. D. Fuller, IWMA, Documents.16408, letter to David dated 11 February 1942; letter to wife dated 24 November 1942. Also see Private Papers of J. Mott, IWMA, Documents.15587, e.g. letters to wife dated 19 August 1942, 3 September 1942.

[130] Private Papers of F. I. Williams, IWMA, Documents.17022, letter to wife dated 20 September 1940.

[131] William Woodruff [2003], *Beyond Nab End* (London, 2008), pp. 300, 309–10.

[132] Robert Williamson, 'A Labour of Love', roll 159, pp. 28–32; Robert Williamson interview recording, 'A Labour of Love', British Library, number C590/01/412.

[133] Jim Bullock, *Bowers Row: Recollections of a Mining Village* (Wakefield, 1976), pp. 177–8.

[134] Doris Bailey, quoted in Humphries and Gordon, *A Labour*, p. 134.

early part of this period; George, born 1910, noted that when his youngest sibling died, his 'father took the blow badly but undemonstratively. He was silent for long periods, he stopped whistling, and had the appearance of a man whose spirit had been crushed. Soon afterward he fell ill with double pneumonia.'[135] William, born 1916, likewise described seeing his father desperately trying to warm up his stillborn sibling in front of the fire.[136] Glyn Davies' experience of fatherhood also demonstrates the incredibly painful emotions of the death of a child. After his daughter's death just a few minutes after she was born in 1956, Glyn described the envy he felt when he saw other men with their daughters, and how he had 'a sort of nervous breakdown' in response.[137] Indeed, for some children, experiences of illness often opened up the possibility for more emotional moments with their fathers. Mr M10L, for example, born 1948, remembered how when he was in hospital with an inflamed gall bladder, his father would 'always come and give me a love [a cuddle] before he went, which was quite unusual for him. He wasn't a very demonstrative man.'[138]

Despite the strong emotions parenting could clearly induce in an everyday context or when facing a traumatic event, codes of normative masculinity prevented men from displaying these emotions. For example, as discussed earlier in this chapter, John Caldwell insisted that he did not 'properly cry' when his child was born in the late 1940s.[139] The nervous breakdown of Glyn Davies was in part due to his inability to show emotion, which he linked to his subsequent job loss and divorce.[140] The gendered nature of emotions and the constraints of displaying felt emotion as a man were explored in depth in Warwick Deeping's 1925 novel, *Sorrell and Son*. Christopher's understanding about his father's lack of employment takes Sorrell by surprise. Sorrell thinks, 'How was it that he understood? It was almost womanish, a kind of tenderness, and yet manly, as he had known manliness at its best during the war.' That father and son love each other dearly is made clear in their thoughts, as portrayed by the narrator. For example, Deeping wrote, 'Christopher could not analyse all that lay behind his father's eyes, but he felt the warmth of the love in them.' Their intimacy as father and son is described as very deep, yet their love is not expressed to each other, at least verbally. Sorrell's efforts in helping his son progress in his career succeed, and when Christopher wins prizes at university, 'Sorrell felt an inward glow, a mother and father pride mingled.'[141] The reasserted difference between mothering and fathering can thus be seen as the result of a tension between the newly significant father–child bond, and the continued importance of conforming to gendered norms of behaviour.

---

[135] George Hitchin, *Pit-Yacker* (London, 1962), p. 56.

[136] Woodruff, *The Road*, pp. 58–9. Also see Mrs R3P, ERA, 1940–70, p. 63; Mrs P2P, ERA, Preston 1890–1940, p. 8.

[137] Glyn Davies, 'A Man's World', roll 55, pp. 30–6.

[138] Mr M10L, ERA, 1940–70, p. 48.

[139] John Caldwell, 'A Labour of Love', roll 69, p. 7. Also see Richard Nesbitt, 'A Man's World', roll 144, pp. 6–7; Alf Jenkins, quoted in Humphries and Gordon, *A Man's World*, p. 170.

[140] Glyn Davies, 'A Man's World', roll 55, pp. 27–8.

[141] Warwick Deeping [1925], *Sorrell and Son* (Harmondsworth, 1984), pp. 18–19, 34, 253.

Whilst Sorrell is the sole carer for his son and can be both mother and father to him, this difference is always maintained.[142]

The emphasis on a father's pride was part of this understanding of gendered norms, and was a prominent theme in the press, where discussions of fatherhood were, by nature, public. Being a 'proud' father was constructed differently to being a 'loving mother', therefore preserving gender difference through parenting, and reinforcing masculinity. Numerous advertisements used this theme, tying their product to the emotions of fatherhood. Charities, for example, exploited this parental emotion to evoke sympathy for their cause. The Waifs and Strays Society ran a campaign around Christmas 1929 with the slogan 'Daddy's pride but Daddy's died', which accompanied a picture of a small child, whilst in 1958 the RNIB campaigned for donations under the heading 'The proud eyes of a father'. This, with the picture of the father and child, linked donations to the RNIB to the facilitation of the natural emotion of paternal pride.[143] Specific products were promoted on the basis that they could deepen this emotion. Two advertisements focused on fathers serving in India, and the pride they would feel on their return. The beautiful skin that Pears soap could ensure in a girl was said to guarantee the pride of her father, whilst another father was said to be 'very proud' of his 'fine-looking son' who had been fed on Trufood.[144] Middle or lowbrow newspapers, particularly the *Daily Mirror*, also featured numerous photos of 'proud fathers' and particularly focused on celebrities. These 'proud fathers' included a wide range of men, such as David Lloyd-George, pictured with his daughter in 1922; Gordon Richards, a jockey, in 1930; a Captain Bannan during the Second World War, comedian Ted Ray, pictured watching his son on military parade in 1953; and bandleader Edmundo Ros with his newborn child in 1956.[145] The association of such men with fatherhood in this way furthered the idea that paternal pride was a wholly positive emotion.

This theme was also reinforced in various features and human-interest stories from the mid-1930s, with the *Daily Mirror* leading the field. In 1948, for example, it featured two stories that celebrated the pride of fathers in their children, as part of the promotion of a family-orientated masculinity for men after the war.[146] A photograph of a 2-year-old boy was printed in August with a short story explaining that 'his daddy is entitled to be even prouder than usual of a son like this', as he had taken care of his child while his wife was unwell. Although this was an exceptional story, the message was sent out that all fathers were usually proud of

[142] Deeping, *Sorrell*, pp. 253, 360.

[143] *Manchester Guardian*, 11 December 1929, p. 8; *Manchester Guardian*, 20 January 1958, p. 1; *The Times*, 27 January 1958, p. 11.

[144] *Daily Mirror*, 28 April 1933, p. 8; *Daily Mirror*, 9 May 1947, p. 3.

[145] *Daily Mirror*, 27 October 1922, p. 5; *Daily Mirror*, 26 August 1930, p. 11; *Daily Mirror*, 17 February 1942, p. 8; *Daily Express*, 5 December 1953, p. 5; *Daily Mirror*, 5 July 1956, p. 5. For a more in-depth discussion of celebrity fathers in this period, see King, 'The Perfect Man'.

[146] King, 'Hidden Fathers', pp. 26–27; Laura King '"Now You See a Great Many Men Pushing Their Pram Proudly": Family-Orientated Masculinity Represented and Experienced in Mid-Twentieth-Century Britain', *Cultural and Social History* 10:4 (2013), pp. 602–3.

their children.[147] Other stories focused on very proud fathers of large families, an increasingly unusual occurrence in this period. In April of 1948, for example, a large photograph of a father and his new daughter was published, with the headline 'It's that fatherly feeling!' The caption below explained this further: 'How it feels to be a father—of seven. Mr. Tom Phillips . . . smiles with good-humoured pride at six-month-old Lucille', demonstrating that fatherhood was still about proving virility and masculinity, as will be discussed in Chapter 6.[148] Similarly, an article in the same newspaper from the previous year featured a father of six, Tom Hardcastle, who had apparently written the piece entitled 'The More the Merrier'. The tagline read 'This proud father of six children now finds himself the envy of his childless friends'.[149] Furthermore, in 1956, 'Proud father M.G. Morby' had allegedly written in to the *Mirror* simply to tell other readers about how early his daughter had started speaking. The five-and-a-half-month-old had 'distinctly said "Dad" three times'.[150]

While the emotions attributed to fatherhood by individuals and in public forums such as the press were constrained by norms of masculinity, there was a concurrent growth in the acceptability of men professing strong emotions towards their families, particularly after the Second World War. This was especially the case in the *Daily Mirror*, which had a more sentimental editorial line. Men were actively associated with a range of different emotions towards parenting, and were the subject of advice features. For example, in a response to a letter from a 'worried father' in the *Daily Mirror* in March 1953, agony aunt Sister Clare suggested that the father was overly anxious about his shy toddler.[151] However, the pleasures of parenting were also widely associated with fatherhood. Many articles were credited to fathers, in which they wrote of the enjoyment they took in their children's company and their amusement at their children's antics. The tone of such articles was frequently amusing yet sincere. A prime example is an article from the *Daily Mirror* in 1943, in which an unnamed 'proud father' wrote of his son's amusing behaviour, and described their shared Sundays as 'the day to which we both look forward'.[152] Indeed, such a trend even permeated the ultimate masculine space of the men's magazine by the end of this period: in 1958, *Men Only* featured an article entitled 'Darling daughter', which described the fondness of a father for his daughter and how he missed her when she went away to college.[153]

An emphasis on the affection and fondness of fathers for their children was also present in the reporting of court cases by the end of the period. A new theme in this reporting, and perhaps even in the court cases themselves, was the need for fathers to be demonstrative towards their children. In 1952, for example, a story was printed in the *Daily Mirror* about a trial of a young girl who had been caught

---

[147] *Daily Mirror*, 9 August 1948, p. 4.   [148] *Daily Mirror*, 7 April 1948, p. 5.
[149] *Daily Mirror*, 12 March 1947, p. 2.   [150] *Daily Mirror*, 10 April 1956, p. 14.
[151] *Daily Mirror*, 10 March 1953, p. 12.
[152] *Daily Mirror*, 3 June 1943, p. 7. Other examples of fathers recounting their toddlers' endearing behaviour can be found in *Daily Mirror*, 13 January 1937, p. 10; *Daily Mirror*, 28 August 1941, p. 7.
[153] *Men Only* 68:269, May 1958, pp. 82–6.

shoplifting. Her father was told by the chairman of the juvenile court that 'This girl needs to be shown that you love her about three times as much as any other children. Lay it on with a trowel—do make a great fuss of her.' This was further highlighted in the headline 'Father told—"Lay your love on with a trowel" '.[154] Conversely, fathers who were affectionate, even if they were in the wrong, were presented in a positive light. In the *Manchester Guardian*, for example, the case of a man charged with 'contempt of court' was reported in 1954. He had made contact with his daughter despite being forbidden to do so under a divorce nego-tiation. The father was said to have offered 'sincere apologies' to the court but 'could not apologise for sending a message of love to his daughter at Christmas'. Although the judge ruled to prevent this father interacting with his daughter in this way, a subsection entitled 'Very Human' and the discussion of the father's strong love for his child suggested that the newspaper's stance was different.[155] A similar tale also featured in the *Daily Mirror* in September 1954, in which a father had taken his daughter away from her foster home without permission. Again, his plight was portrayed in a positive way, due to his obvious strong love for his child.[156] Here we see evidence that, by the end of this period, a father's instrumental role as a provider, disciplinarian, playmate, and helper was not in itself enough: an emotional connection between father and child was prized in these discussions, even in difficult circumstances.

There were thus contradictory messages promoted in the press and in popu-lar culture more widely. Whilst men were encouraged to show their emotions more openly, and discuss their fatherhood with pride, this was limited by certain gendered norms. In this sense, a strong differentiation between motherhood and fatherhood remained. Whilst both were undergoing change at this time, the dis-tinction between mothers' and fathers' roles remained intact, as has been demon-strated in previous chapters. Moreover, the emotions associated with relationships with children were subtly gendered, with more emphasis on pride and fondness in terms of fathers rather than the more feminine love. However, in line with the shifting psychological significance of the father–child relationship came a grow-ing acceptance that fathers could feel strongly about their children. It was also accepted that they would discuss this, if not demonstrate it in more physical ways, such as crying or kissing their children too often.

A NEW BALANCE—FRIENDSHIP

The shifting significance of the father–child relationship, alongside the decline in paternal authority as discussed in Chapter 5, influenced and was influenced by a growing rhetoric of friendship, at least in popular culture. This trend began at the end of the nineteenth century; as John Tosh notes, some advice writers suggested

---

[154] *Daily Mirror*, 6 February 1952, p. 3.
[155] *Manchester Guardian*, 13 January 1954, p. 4.
[156] *Daily Mirror*, 1 September 1954, p. 1.

father should be a 'chum'.[157] Furthermore, as Ann Alston argues at the turn of the century, in children's literature this relationship was increasingly portrayed as more informal, as children freely conversed with their parents.[158] Friendship was also a common theme in the American press; as Ralph LaRossa argues, the idea of fathers as companions or 'pals' to their children, particularly their sons, increased in influence from the 1920s.[159] In Britain, this development intensified around the time of the Second World War. More egalitarian and democratic relationships between parents and children were celebrated, in part perhaps because of a wider rejection of the traditional hierarchies of authority after the war.[160] Furthermore, ideas about friendship depended strongly on the age of the child, with boys particularly enjoying an easier friendship with fathers once they had entered the adult world of work.[161] Alongside this rhetoric of friendship, the mutual benefits of the relationship for father and child were frequently reiterated.

This emphasis on companionship can be found in the interwar period, but was much more widely discussed in the 1940s and 1950s, and was increasingly advocated in the popular press as well as more progressive middle-class titles. Many articles discussed this relationship using the language of friendship and equality, whilst others touched on this theme in discussing children's involvement in more 'adult' aspects of family life. There was ongoing debate as to whether this was a desirable development. Numerous articles posited that many families were already treating this relationship as more of a friendship, indicating a notion that this was common practice in many families. For example, in a *Times* article of 1936, the writer argued that 'children to-day probably treat their parents more as friends and companions than heretofore'.[162] Stories about individuals tended to paint such a relationship in a positive light: a bus driver and his bus conductor daughter, for example, were said to be 'good mates' in an article in the *Daily Mirror* in 1941, and in 1949 a similar article celebrated the friendship of a father and son who were both miners.[163] The desire to condemn those fathers who tried to be a 'friend' to their children also reveals a presumption that it was becoming increasingly common. For example, the disapproval of councillor and education expert Dorothy Archibald was reported in an article from 1947 in the *Daily Mirror*. She believed that there was something to be said for the 'Victorian papa', and that the modern father who expected his children to adopt him and his wife

---

[157] John Tosh, *A Man's Place: Masculinity and the Middle-Class Home in Victorian England* (New Haven, CT, and London, 1999), p. 163. Burgess suggests the image of the father as confidante and pal was 'relentlessly promoted' in the first half of the twentieth century. Adrienne Burgess, *Fatherhood Reclaimed: The Making of the Modern Father* (London, 1997), p. 18.

[158] Alston, *The Family*, p. 40.

[159] Ralph LaRossa, *The Modernization of Fatherhood: A Social and Political History* (Chicago, IL, and London, 1997), pp. 130–43.

[160] Such an emphasis could also be found in post-war Germany. See Till van Rahden, 'Fatherhood, Rechristianization, and the Quest for Democracy in Postwar Germany', in D. Schumann (ed.), *Raising Citizens in 'the Century of the Child': The United States and German Central Europe in Comparative Perspective* (New York, 2010), p. 142.

[161] Strange, 'Fatherhood, Providing', p. 1020.   [162] *The Times*, 3 March 1936, p. 24.

[163] *Daily Mirror*, 28 August 1941, p. 3; *Daily Mirror*, 22 June 1949, p. 7.

as 'casual friends' was to be condemned.[164] In a more positive article in the *Daily Mirror* in 1956, an unnamed writer suggested again that such a friendly relationship was common: 'Modern parents stay young with their children and discuss family affairs with them like good pals.' The article invited readers to consider whether children should participate in the more adult aspects of family life and, for example, witness their parents arguing.[165]

This conception of the father–child relationship as one of companionship was thus increasingly common but remained controversial. In a section of *Baby and Child Care* entitled 'The father as companion', Spock painted it in a wholly positive light, suggesting 'Boys and girls need chances to be around with their father, to be enjoyed by him, and if possible, to do things with him.' Yet he was not convinced that fathers understood their importance in this sense.[166] A warm relationship between father and son was explored in the novel *Sorrell and Son*, and indeed, the idea of a genuine friendship included a son more often than a daughter. Early in the book, father and son speak frankly to each other about their situation, a moment which is described as 'the beginning of a great comradeship between them'.[167] Their discussions, indeed, are frequently referred to as between friends, rather than father and son, both implicitly and explicitly, and the narrator and the characters repeatedly highlight their comradeship and companionship.[168]

Evidence from social research also suggests that the investigators thought this companionship was common. Newson and Newson, for example, observed that many respondents welcomed the greater freedom of speech between themselves and their children, in contrast to their relationships with their parents, as it allowed 'a relationship of real friendship between them'. Mothers also claimed that there was 'a new warmth and companionship in the present-day relationship between parents and children'.[169] The subjects of Young and Willmott's research also alluded to such a relationship.[170] Yet this change was not a prominent theme in the interview evidence. Whilst, as noted earlier in this chapter, some interviewees highlighted a more informal relationship between parents and children, an explicit rhetoric of friendship was rarely used.[171] George Ryder, for example, though feeling that his relationship with his child was not particularly close in

---

[164] *Daily Mirror*, 24 April 1947, p. 3. Also see *Daily Mirror*, 5 December 1934, p. 12.

[165] *Daily Mirror*, 2 February 1956, p. 2. This idea is also supported in other articles. See: *Daily Mirror*, 2 March 1934, p. 25; *Manchester Guardian*, 14 May 1935, p. 18; *Daily Mirror*, 30 September 1946, p. 5; *Daily Mirror*, 17 May 1948, p. 2; *Daily Mirror*, 26 May 1948, p. 2.

[166] Spock, *Baby and Child Care* (2nd edn, London, 1958), pp. 319–22.

[167] Deeping, *Sorrell*, p. 18.

[168] Deeping, *Sorrell*, pp. 124, 188–9, 195, 207, 217, 228, 272–3.

[169] Newson and Newson, *Patterns*, pp. 237, 243.

[170] Young and Willmott, *Family and Kinship*, p. 28.

[171] Rare examples of this are in Mr W5L's interview, in which he and his wife discuss their son's upbringing just after the end of this period, in the 1960s, and in letters from C. D. Fuller to his wife, in which he describes how he and his son are 'great pals'. Mr W5L, ERA, 1940–70, pp. 61–2; Private Papers of C. D. Fuller, IWMA, Documents.16408, letters to wife dated 9 August 1942, 27 September 1942. Also see Tomlinson, *Coal-Miner*, p. 177; Joseph Farrington, 'Manchester', in Gray, *The Worst*, p. 26.

comparison with contemporary attitudes when interviewed in the 1990s, noted that family time when he was a parent was more relaxed. Whilst his could be characterized as a 'seen and not heard' childhood, he refuted the suggestion that this was the same for his own children, born in the late 1940s: 'No. When I became a father no, when I became a father it became more relaxed.' He highlighted that, in contrast to his childhood, the family used to eat meals in front of the television.[172] As Elizabeth Roberts argued, the norms of family conduct at mealtimes changed considerably in the mid-twentieth century. This became a time of family discussion rather than silence on the part of children, and indeed, more 'companionable' relationships were common.[173] Edward Winn, born 1917, reflected upon this change. He said that that ideas were different when his two sons were growing up in the late 1940s and 1950s to when he was a child. When asked whether he was as strict as his own parents had been, he said, 'I think it was just the times, the times you live in you know, things . . . Things were easier in a way, end of the war, there was a sort of relaxation, I suppose, in some ways.'[174]

In general, the benefits of a more involved relationship for both father and child were increasingly cited in popular cultural debates. Claudia Nelson highlights that Victorian periodicals encouraged men to become more active fathers for their own good rather than that of their children.[175] Similarly, discussing the early twentieth century Fisher notes that children were viewed as an enjoyable part of home life, and home as a place where men could recuperate and take pleasure from their families.[176] In the press, too, the healing nature of the home was discussed throughout the period, and men who were shut out from family life were treated sympathetically. During the war, the positive effects children had on the recovery of men from war injuries were often mentioned. In the *Mirror* in 1940, for example, a photograph of a man on crutches kissing his child, accompanied by the headline 'Daddy's tonic—once a week!' spelled this out very clearly.[177] The positive effects fathers had on their children were also noted. Another *Mirror* article of 1940 reported how one father's return from France encouraged the recovery of his two young children from serious illness.[178] The *Mirror*, in 1954, continued this theme in a problem page feature by Mary Brown. To a wife deciding whether to move abroad with her children to be with her husband, Brown advised her to go: 'Children need a good father's love and influence. And their father needs them.'[179] In another piece two years later, Brown advised a father excluded from family life by his wife, who was said by the agony aunt to be making a 'terrible mistake'. Furthermore, she reminded readers that 'When a wife forgets to remember that her husband is the father of her children she hurts something deep

---

[172] George Ryder, 'A Man's World', roll 135, pp. 58–9.
[173] Elizabeth Roberts, *Women and Families: An Oral History, 1940–1970* (Oxford, 1995), pp. 43, 156.
[174] Edward Winn, Int159, *Families*, UKDA, p. 22.
[175] Nelson, *Invisible Men*, p. 204.
[176] Fisher, 'Fatherhood and the Experience', p. 207.
[177] *Daily Mirror*, 29 April 1940, p. 9.   [178] *Daily Mirror*, 9 January 1940, p. 8.
[179] *Daily Mirror*, 17 February 1954, p. 10. Also see *Daily Mirror*, 3 December 1956, p. 12.

within him.'[180] As has been demonstrated through this chapter, a father's love for and influence over his children were increasingly portrayed as valuable and even irreplaceable. The discourse around this relationship remained insistently positive within popular culture and amongst individuals. With the explicit emphasis on the importance of fatherhood came a greater exploration of the positive and negative consequences of this relationship or the lack of it for both father and child.

Understandings of this relationship influenced and were influenced by the language of fatherhood. As LaRossa notes in his study of interwar American fatherhood, 'father' and 'dad' could have different meanings.[181] He suggests that the use of 'dad' as opposed to 'father' in the magazines he studied correlated closely with the focus on men as 'pals' to their children.[182] In this sense, the term 'dad' was linked to the more friendly relationship that emerged in the twentieth century, in both Britain and America. As Tosh highlights, the term 'dad' entered common usage in the late nineteenth century.[183] By the interwar period, its meaning had become understood as symbolizing an informal and positive version of fatherhood. In the *Daily Mirror* on 10 April 1937, three letters addressed this theme, responding to a letter of the previous day, which criticized adults who still called their parents 'Mummy' and 'Daddy'.[184] The three letter-writers did not agree, arguing that men should be proud of being called 'Daddy' as it demonstrated an affectionate relationship, and that it was better than previous terms such as 'guv'nor', 'the old man', and 'pater', or calling parents by their Christian names.[185] A *Times* editorial in 1948 was more sceptical, suggesting that 'Mummy' and 'Daddy' were the current preferred forms of address, but 'Mother' and 'Father' were preferable. The article ended with the thought, 'Let Mummy and Daddy rejoice while they may in the sunshine of popularity now beating full upon them. Mother and Father may yet come back to put them in the shade.'[186] In contrast, an editorial in the paper six years later lamented that children did not know their parents' Christian names, and contended that 'Mum' and 'Dad' were here to stay.[187]

These terms of address were also imbued with meanings of class, as 'Mum' and 'Dad' were more frequently associated with working-class families, with middle- and upper-class equivalents being 'Mummy' and 'Daddy' or 'Mother' and 'Father'.[188] In the children's series about Milly-Molly-Mandy, for example, the eponymous protagonist calls her father 'Farver' or 'Father', whilst other, working-class, children such as Billy Blunt call their fathers 'Dad'.[189] In contrast, in Ella Monckton's children's novel, *The Gates Family*, the four young middle-class children call their father 'Daddy', reflecting their informal relationship with him.[190] However, the class-based nature of these

---

[180] *Daily Mirror*, 3 October 1956, p. 19.
[181] LaRossa, *The Modernization*, p. 17.   [182] LaRossa, *The Modernization.*, p. 137
[183] Tosh, *A Man's Place*, p. 163.   [184] *Daily Mirror*, 9 April 1937, p. 15.
[185] *Daily Mirror*, 10 April 1937, p. 13.   [186] *The Times*, 13 February 1948, p. 5.
[187] *The Times*, 28 September 1954, p. 9.
[188] Raymond Firth, Jane Hubert, and Anthony Forge, *Families and Their Relatives: Kinship in a Middle-Class Sector of London: An Anthropological Study* (London, 1969), p. 305.
[189] Joyce Lankester Brisley [1928], *Milly-Molly-Mandy Stories* (Harmondsworth, 1972), e.g. p. 11.
[190] Ella Monckton, *The Gates Family* (London, 1934), e.g. p. 14. Blyton also used this term as a reflection of a warm, close relationship in the 'Family' series. Enid Blyton [1945], *The Caravan Family*; Enid Blyton [1947], *The Saucy Jane Family*; Enid Blyton [1950], *The Pole Star Family*; Enid

terms arguably became less prominent. Interestingly, Raymond Firth, Jane Hubert, and Anthony Forge, in their study of middle-class London families, found that 'Mother' was much more common than 'Father', and around two thirds of their subjects addressed their fathers as 'Dad', 'Daddy', or a special term. The authors stressed the apparent desire for more informal terms that did not suggest a relationship of authority.[191] The shifting language of fatherhood thus tied into increasingly informal and friendly relationships that were both promoted and experienced in this period.

CONCLUSION

The growing psychological emphasis on parenting, fatherhood, and the father–child relationship is a crucial feature of this period in terms of family life. Whilst it is very difficult to measure the effect this had on people's lives, the evidence used here indicates that more men were aware of their responsibilities as fathers and realized the enjoyment this relationship could bring. Amongst families, a lack of engagement of some type was becoming less acceptable. Yet it is clear that a significant minority of men remained uninvolved in their children's lives, that the press arguably overemphasized an idealized version of fatherhood, and that social researchers were often overly optimistic in their reading of fatherhood. Additionally, the maternal relationship was still seen as of primary importance. There was not a sustained mass change in all fathers' behaviour. Yet more informal relationships between parents were becoming common, though open declarations or displays of love and affection remained unusual. A whole gamut of emotions, both negative and positive, was associated with men's relationships with their children throughout the period, but a number of factors made it easier for a more friendly relationship to develop. These involved practical considerations, such as more spacious housing and gardens for some families and smaller family sizes, as well as shifts in cultural ideals that promoted the importance of involved fatherhood and reconnected fatherhood with normative masculinity.[192] In this way, whilst the specific focus on equality and friendship and the particular psychological language of child development was not to be found within the testimony evidence, there is evidence that understandings and practices of this relationship was changing.

In general, the father was seen as more important to his children, and many men from all social backgrounds began to approach this relationship with greater seriousness than their own fathers had done. Throughout this period, and before the First World War, those from lower-middle-class families reported close family relationships. Richard Church, for example, suggested in his autobiography that it was his family's lower-middle-class position that meant he was close to his parents, noting 'Above that level, parents were, usually, kept somewhat more at

Blyton [1950], *The Seaside Family*; Enid Blyton [1951], *The Queen Elizabeth Family*; Enid Blyton [1951], *The Buttercup Farm Family*, all published in *The Family Collection* (London, 2002).

[191] Firth, Hubert, and Forge, *Families*, pp. 306–8.
[192] King, 'The Perfect Man'; Roberts, *Women and Families*, pp. 154–5.

arm's-length from their children.'[193] As the period progressed, such relationships could be found throughout most social classes. Historians such as Joanna Bourke, Stephen Brooke, and Elizabeth Roberts have touched upon the general changes to working-class men's attitudes in their wider research into the family in this period, and this research indicates that this shift also applied to men of other classes.[194] Indeed, expectations placed upon men were as high as those of women, a fact often overlooked in the historiography.[195]

What arguably emerged throughout this period was the weakening of the clear division between working- and middle-class lifestyles. Instead, what emerged was a spectrum of class experience, rather than a strong division between working- and middle-, or 'new' and 'old' working-class communities. As Roberts notes, it is perhaps more accurate to speak of working classes in the plural than as a singular group by the mid-twentieth century.[196] In some particularly deprived or traditional areas, such as those described by Mays and Dennis and colleagues, older attitudes persisted, and clearly some men remained distant from family life. But those men from more affluent working-class families, who constituted most of Roberts' samples, were more engaged with family life than previous generations, even if they did not take on equal responsibility for housework and childcare.[197] These families were enjoying better living standards, created by high employment levels, smaller family size, shorter working hours, and improved housing. These conditions were similar to those enjoyed by more affluent middle-class families in the interwar period, but historians should be careful here to differentiate between class as related to income and living standards, and class as an identity. As Jon Lawrence notes, exaggeration of the divisions between various class groups can lead to an overemphasis on sudden change in the mid-twentieth century.[198] There was little evidence of an explicit desire to emulate the middle classes amongst interviewees, but what can be found is some degree of convergence of lifestyles and living standards. As Langhamer and Lawrence have noted, shifts towards more family-centric or domestic ways of living for the working classes were enabled rather than transformed by the changing living standards and expectations in an era of affluence.[199] As Geoffrey Gorer noted, by the 1950s there was remarkable consensus on ideas about child-rearing that overrode class and regional difference and other social variables.[200] In terms of men's increased involvement and investment in their relationships with their children, this had become common amongst large swathes of British society by the end of this period.

[193] Richard Church, *Over the Bridge: An Essay in Autobiography* (London, 1955), p. 18.
[194] Joanna Bourke, *Working Class Cultures in Britain 1890–1960: Gender, Class, and Ethnicity* (London, 1994), esp. pp. 81–6; Stephen Brooke, 'Gender and Working Class Identity in Britain during the 1950s', *Journal of Social History* 34:4 (2001), esp. pp. 783–6; Roberts, *Women and Families*, pp. 38–41.
[195] Davis, 'A Critical Perspective', p. 58. King, 'Hidden Fathers', p. 34.
[196] Roberts, *Women and Families*, p. 237.   [197] Roberts, *Women and Families*, p. 38.
[198] Lawrence, 'Class', pp. 288–9.
[199] Claire Langhamer, 'Love and Courtship in Mid-Twentieth-Century England', *Historical Journal* 50:1 (2007), p. 179; Lawrence, 'Class', p. 289.
[200] Geoffrey Gorer, *Exploring English Character* (London, 1955), p. 162.

5

Master of the House? The Father's Position, Power, and Authority

The shifting understandings of a father's status in relation to his family, in both public and private, are indicative of broader changes in the conceptualization of fatherhood, and the involvement of men in family life, in both ideal and actual terms. A substantial amount of research has been conducted into paternal authority in nineteenth-century Britain. From a wide range of perspectives, and in contexts as diverse as literature, material culture, and census returns, the Victorian father was invested with a great deal of authority within his family and within society more generally.[1] Yet some suggest that this position of authority was less secure by the end of the nineteenth century; John Tosh, for example, argues that both the sphere of authority and expertise credited to the father were diminishing, as the middle-class father's role within the home was reduced to procreation and provision and as the law gave increasing powers to the mother, particularly in terms of the custody of children.[2] As Trev Lynn Broughton and Helen Rogers note, the ways in which paternal authority were experienced in families could differ according to class.[3] Indeed, it was largely accepted throughout the years from the First World War to the end of the 1950s, if only implicitly, that the working-class father was and could be accepted as the 'master' of the family and home, whereas a sense of partnership and genuine equality between middle-class couples was most often represented as the ideal. Working-class fathers were also

---

[1] Leonore Davidoff, Megan Doolittle, Janet Fink, and Katherine Holden, *The Family Story: Blood, Contract and Intimacy, 1830–1939* (Harlow, 1999), p. 156; Megan Doolittle, 'Time, Space and Memories: The Father's Chair and Grandfather Clocks in Victorian Working Class Domestic Lives', *Home Cultures* 8:3 (2011), p. 250; Carol Dyhouse, 'Mothers and Daughters in the Middle-Class Home, c.1870–1914', in J. Lewis (ed.), *Labour and Love: Women's Experiences of Home and Family, 1850–1940* (Oxford, 1986), p. 30; Christopher Parker, 'Introduction', in C. Parker (ed.), *Gender Roles and Sexuality in Victorian Literature* (Aldershot, 1995), p. 15; Siân K. Pooley, 'Parenthood and Child-Rearing in England, c.1860–1910', PhD Thesis (University of Cambridge, 2009), pp. 57–8.

[2] John Tosh, *A Man's Place: Masculinity and the Middle-Class Home in Victorian England* (New Haven, CT, and London, 1999), pp. 159–60. Also see Ann Alston, *The Family in English Children's Literature* (London and New York, 2008), p. 18; Trev Lynn Broughton and Helen Rogers, 'Introduction: The Empire of the Father', in T. L. Broughton and H. Rogers (eds), *Gender and Fatherhood in the Nineteenth Century* (Basingstoke, 2007), pp. 1–28; J. M. Mogey, 'A Century of Declining Paternal Authority', *Marriage and Family Living* 19:3 (1957), pp. 234–9; Claudia Nelson, *Invisible Men: Fatherhood in Victorian Periodicals, 1850–1910* (Athens, GA, and London, 1995), p. 43.

[3] Broughton and Rogers, 'Introduction', pp. 7–8.

subject to more involvement from bodies of the state than their middle-class counterparts, which perhaps exacerbated their need to be seen as a master within their home.[4] Yet alongside this, fathers of all classes were both ridiculed for their declining authority and simultaneously praised for becoming more equal and accessible parents. Though in some ways the father was still exalted as the head of the family, Stella Bruzzi has highlighted that, in the case of Hollywood films, the questioning of fathers' authority continued and increased in the twentieth century.[5] In practice too, Elizabeth Roberts has demonstrated how young people in Lancashire increasingly challenged authority, both parental and otherwise, by the middle decades of the twentieth century.[6]

The 1925 Guardianship Act removed the legal preference for fathers when awarding custody of children, and, as such, this period is an important one in terms of the legal position of fathers. The Act in theory gave equality to male and female parenting, to reflect social practice and legal, academic, and public opinion. It limited the rights of fathers to a greater extent, and bolstered the position of mothers in terms of both custody and decision-making about children's upbringing.[7] As Katherine Holden has shown, this led to a situation in which fathers had limited rights, and unmarried fathers, in consequence, often evaded their responsibilities.[8] The early part of the twentieth century can thus be seen as one of consistent scrutiny and questioning of the father's authority. Indeed, those forces supporting the unquestioned authority of the father were also subsiding in power. As traditional religious authorities were increasingly, if not always successfully, challenged, the authority invested in fathers by religious conceptions of the family became less significant. In the nineteenth century, as Tosh notes, the authority endowed in the father was symbolized by his leading of family prayers, an idea of less importance and significance by the twentieth century.[9] The links between authority and religion are also explored by Siân Pooley, who suggests that obedience to parental authority was fundamentally linked to obedience to divine authority, a construction that again was less prominent by the twentieth century.[10] For Broughton and Rogers, the relationship between religious beliefs and fatherhood was becoming 'less harmonious' at the end of the nineteenth century.[11] Yet, as Alana Harris notes, Christian religious ideas were also, by the mid-twentieth

---

[4] On fathers and the state in an earlier period, see Megan Doolittle, 'Missing Fathers: Assembling a History of Fatherhood in Mid-Nineteenth Century England', PhD Thesis (University of Essex, 1996), esp. chs 3 and 4.

[5] Stella Bruzzi, *Bringing Up Daddy: Fatherhood and Masculinity in Post-War Hollywood* (London, 2005), p. xviii.

[6] Elizabeth Roberts, *Women and Families: An Oral History, 1940–1970* (Oxford, 1995), p. 47.

[7] Timothy J. Fisher, 'Fatherhood and the Experience of Working-Class Fathers in Britain, 1900–1939', PhD Thesis (University of Edinburgh, 2004), pp. 63–92.

[8] Katherine Holden, *The Shadow of Marriage: Singleness in England, 1914–1960* (Manchester, 2007), pp. 113–15.

[9] Tosh also notes the significance of religious language, such as the emphasis on the 'Heavenly Father', in further supporting the father's authority. Tosh, *A Man's Place*, pp. 83–4, 90. Also see Broughton and Rogers, 'Introduction', p. 16.

[10] Pooley, 'Parenthood', pp. 64–8.   [11] Broughton and Rogers, 'Introduction', p. 16.

century, encouraging a masculinity which was 'home-based, if not house-trained'.[12] Relating to fatherhood and Christianity, the twentieth century was a period of contradictory trends. This was not a period of straightforward secularization, though the authority invested in religious institutions was increasingly questioned. Furthermore, hierarchical relationships were challenged more generally as egalitarian relations were celebrated, particularly in the post-Second World War period. For example, a new emphasis on classlessness, as has been discussed elsewhere, flattened traditionally hierarchical relationships, at least in their discursive construction. In addition, on an international scale decolonization provided another example of a move away from vertical power relationships, as the traditional paternal relationship between colonizer and colonized was seriously challenged.[13] In the words of Jon Lawrence, by the 1950s 'Britain's paternalist traditions began to crumble' as events like the Suez crisis encouraged a wider questioning of traditional structures of authority.[14] Likewise, the 'breaking down' of the authority of the Victorian patriarch was increasingly portrayed positively as this period progressed, with the scope for more open, equal, and consequently close relationships between fathers and children deemed to be a result.

THE DISTANT FATHER OR HEAD
OF HOUSEHOLD?

Various representations of the father throughout this period continued to situate him as a distant figure. That the father had separate interests to those of his wife and children, and wished to maintain this situation, was a common theme of numerous light-hearted items in the press throughout this period. In the *Daily Mirror* in 1922, for example, a W. K. Haselden cartoon contrasted a father 'in the days of spacious houses' and his contemporary counterpart. Whilst previously a father could seclude himself in the peace of his study, space now had to be shared with the rest of the family, who were apparently a source of irritation.[15] The traditional association of men with the pub and alcohol in general was illustrated in a cartoon printed in the *Daily Mail* in 1946, in which a wife noted of her husband, 'This beer shortage should give me an opportunity of introducing him to the children.'[16] A similar theme dominated a cartoon published as part of the 'London

---

[12] Alana Harris, '"A Paradise on Earth, a Foretaste of Heaven": English Catholic Understandings of Domesticity and Marriage, 1945–1965', in L. Delap, B. Griffin, and A. Wills (eds), *The Politics of Domestic Authority in Britain since 1800* (Basingstoke, 2009), p. 167.

[13] On the idea of the 'empire of the father' and the links between such imperial language and broader understandings of authority, see Broughton and Rogers, 'Introduction', esp. p. 8. On the conception of the colonizer/colonized relationship as paternal, see Elizabeth Buettner, 'Fatherhood Real, Imagined, Denied: British Men in Imperial India', in Broughton and Rogers (eds), *Gender and Fatherhood*, p. 180.

[14] Jon Lawrence, 'Class, "Affluence" and the Study of Everyday Life in Britain, c.1930–64', *Cultural and Social History* 10:2 (2013), p. 288.

[15] *Daily Mirror*, 10 January 1922, p. 5.

[16] *Daily Mail*, 25 June 1946. From the cartoon archive (www.cartoons.ac.uk), reference number NEB0422 [accessed 30/08/2013].

Laughs' series by Joseph Lee in the *Evening News* on Christmas Eve in 1951. That father turned up at all, even if he was depicted as rather grumpy and dishevelled, was suggested to be surprising in the caption and comment by the daughter, 'Oh Mum! Christmas Eve and Daddy's home . . . under his own steam!'[17] This theme of fathers prioritizing other interests was common in men's magazines as well as the more traditional, conservative newspapers. In an early article in *Men Only* in 1936, for example, a 'man's paradise' was described by Captain Hugh MacKay as an island in the Seychelles free from 'the clutterings of wives and children'.[18] Some advertising also suggested that fathers disassociated themselves from family life. For example, an advertisement for Edward's Soups in 1927 recommended that, by using their product to create a 'lovely dinner', father might be persuaded to refrain from going out for the evening.[19] This was also a theme in some literature of the period. In Virginia Woolf's *To the Lighthouse*, for example, it is explicit that Mr Ramsay cares more for his work than his family: 'The truth was that he did not enjoy family life.'[20]

The distance and lack of interest was thought to be due to fathers' wishes, but this was also portrayed as positive for other family members. The idea of the (working-class) father as a potential danger was an undercurrent in discussion about men's potential and actual participation in family life. This was demonstrated through news pieces about fathers abusing, attacking, and even killing their wives and children, as discussed in previous chapters. These were portrayed as exceptional cases, but were regularly present, particularly in popular newspapers, reminding readers of the constant potential threat of men. Though abuse by mothers was also reported, the inherently caring traits associated with women meant such cases were often explained through some particular circumstance. As Daniel Grey notes, women who killed children could be partially excused through their alleged temporary insanity following childbirth or the extreme shame associated with bearing an 'illegitimate' child. In consequence, newspapers were more likely to be sympathetic to mothers in these circumstances.[21] From the Victorian patriarch to the modern 'dad', via the violent father, a wide spectrum of behaviour was portrayed throughout the press. There was a tension in these representations of fathers, though, as however much newspapers praised men, the

[17] *Evening News*, 24 December 1951. From the cartoon archive (www.cartoons.ac.uk), reference number JL4682 [accessed 30/08/2013].
[18] *Men Only* 2:5, April 1936, pp. 86–7.
[19] *Daily Mirror*, 1 December 1927, p. 16. Also see advertising for Will's Gold Flake tobacco, *Daily Express*, 16 September 1938, p. 17.
[20] Virginia Woolf [1927], *To the Lighthouse* (Harmondsworth, 1964), p. 103. As detailed elsewhere, this prioritization of work and lack of enjoyment of family life can also be found in the very different context of Enid Blyton's 'Famous Five' books. Enid Blyton [1952], *Five Have a Wonderful Time* (London, 1986), p. 11; Enid Blyton [1949], *Five Get into Trouble* (Leicester, 1975), p. 17; Enid Blyton [1954], *Five Have Plenty of Fun* (London, 1991), pp. 8–9; Enid Blyton [1956], *Five on a Secret Trail* (London, 1985), p. 13.
[21] Daniel Grey, 'Discourses of Infanticide in England, 1880–1922', PhD Thesis (Roehampton University, 2009), pp. 64–5; Daniel Grey, 'Women's Policy Networks and the Infanticide Act 1922', *Twentieth Century British History* 21:4 (2010), pp. 442–3.

discursive undercurrent of their potential danger meant the situation of men at the heart of their families could be somewhat uncomfortable: a contradiction that was rarely addressed.

Indeed, it is clear that the power invested in the position of father and head of household was abused by a significant number of men. Jim Bullock highlighted how his father, 'undisputed head' of the house and family, 'often resorted to physical action' if 'he did not get his own way'.[22] Mrs B1P, born 1900, noted that her father 'was the head, the boss and you didn't get to saying anything', and would disapprove of almost everything they did.[23] Yet more seriously, Mary Moran, born 1928 to an Irish family in Glasgow, noted how she 'detested, loathed and feared' her father and the abuse of his position in beating her mother and sexually abusing her sister.[24] Similarly, Mr N2L, born 1931, noted how his father would give him 'a good hiding to the point where you couldn't walk to school the following day, you couldn't move the following day' in the name of discipline.[25] Doreen Angus, born 1940, spoke about how her stepfather's strictness and insistence on perfection from his children stemmed from experience with the Navy in the Second World War.[26]

The patriarchal organization of society remained intact, if not unchallenged, in this period and extended to the private sphere of the family, with the father at its head. Despite a perception of declining power, the long history of men's authority within and outside the home meant the idea of fathers as heads of their families stayed strong throughout this period in individual attitudes and popular culture. However, most fathers involved themselves in everyday family life more than the previous generation had done, as previous chapters have demonstrated, and for many, the retention of the idea of 'master' could be little more than a ceremonial conception of position. The father's status as 'master' and his potential separation from his family could be mutually reinforcing: earning money outside the home for a family not only meant fathers were separated from their families temporally and geographically, but also invested them with economic power and thus authority over other family members.[27] However, the legal position of fathers was changing and in this sense their rights were being curtailed, challenging their innate authority. The social status that fathers had consequentially enjoyed as heads of their households was thus also altered, as it was increasingly argued that the father had to earn his position and maintain it with benevolence and active care. This

---

[22] Jim Bullock, *Bowers Row: Recollections of a Mining Village* (Wakefield, 1976), p. 23.

[23] Mrs B1P, Elizabeth Roberts Archive (ERA), Preston 1890–1940, p.22. Also see Irene/Albert Handley, Int062, P. Thompson and H. Newby, *Families, Social Mobility and Ageing, an Intergenerational Approach, 1900–1988* [computer file]. Colchester, Essex: UK Data Archive (UKDA) [distributor], July 2005. SN: 4938, p. 49.

[24] Mary Moran, Int092, *Families*, UKDA, pp. 6, 20. For other examples of (potential) sexual abuse, see Elizabeth Arnold, Int002, *Families*, UKDA, p. 40; Derek Benjamin, Int011, *Families*, UKDA, p. 11.

[25] Mr N2L, ERA, 1940–70, p.10.

[26] Doreen Angus, Int001, *Families*, UKDA, pp. 25–6.

[27] One interviewee made this link explicitly: Ray Rochford, 'A Labour of Love', British Library, roll 48, pp. 11–12.

pattern could and did vary according to class in terms of both prescription and practice. Furthermore, ideas about fathers' loss of authority shifted dramatically over the course of this period. It was, then, a period of confused and contradictory trends, in which attempts to combine men's historical power with more equal relationships between parents and children met with varying success.[28]

The most important legislative change in terms of fatherhood and parenting in this period was the Guardianship of Infants Act of 1925, part of a series of legislation that was arguably brought about by the impact of female suffrage and women's movements more broadly.[29] As Fisher notes, the introduction of the Act forced lawmakers to consider the father's authority and importance in explicit terms, though little agreement was reached about the extent and nature of his responsibilities.[30] Yet, as Fisher also acknowledges, the aim of the Act was to equalize the rights and responsibilities of parents and prioritize children's welfare, rather than to curtail fathers' authority.[31] As Viscount Cave, the Lord Chancellor, noted in 1926, 'the purpose of the Act of last year was not to extend the father's rights; it dealt with the mother's rights'.[32] Indeed, in debates in both the Houses of Commons and Lords, there was an emphasis on securing the equality of parents, both in terms of the preparation of the legislation and in proposed amendments for it afterwards.[33] As Major Entwistle highlighted in the Commons as early as 1919, putting mothers in an equal position to fathers in terms of the guardianship of their children was 'long overdue'.[34] Others reiterated the suggestion that the Act would bring the law in line with public opinion and the state of the family.[35] Whilst some MPs disagreed with the principle of equality between men and women, and others were concerned about the consequences of the Act, the priority within these debates was to secure the child's best interests.[36]

---

[28] On this theme in the context of romance literature, see Laura King, 'The Perfect Man: Fatherhood, Masculinity and Romance in Popular Culture in Mid-Twentieth-Century Britain', in Alana Harris and Timothy Jones (eds), *Love and Romance in Britain, 1918–1970* (Basingstoke, forthcoming 2014).

[29] Pat Thane, 'Women and Political Participation in England, 1918–1970', in E. Breitenbach and P. Thane (eds), *Women and Citizenship in Britain and Ireland in the Twentieth Century: What Difference Did the Vote Make?* (London and New York, 2010), p. 19.

[30] Fisher, 'Fatherhood and the Experience', p. 64.

[31] Fisher, 'Fatherhood and the Experience', p. 70. Also see Nigel V. Lowe, 'The Legal Status of Fathers: Past and Present', in L. McKee and M. O'Brien (eds), *The Father Figure* (London, 1982), p. 29; P. H. Pettit, 'Parental Control and Guardianship', in H. Graveson and F. R. Crane (eds), *A Century of Family Law, 1857–1957* (London, 1957), p. 72.

[32] Hansard, HL, vol. 63, c.178, 17 February 1926.

[33] Major Entwistle's speech, Hansard, HC, vol. 114, cc.1590, 1591, 4 April 1919; Lord Askwith's speech, Hansard, HL, vol. 49, c.250, 1 March 1922; Lord Askwith's speech, Hansard, HL, vol. 56, c.631, 26 March 1923; Viscount Haldane's speech, Hansard, HL, vol. 57, cc.791, 792, 3 June 1924; Under-Secretary for the State for the Home Department, Mr Godfrey Locker-Lampson's speech, Hansard, HC, vol. 181, cc.533, 4 March 1925; Lord Southam of Banbury's speech, Hansard, HL, vol. 63, c.178, 17 February 1926.

[34] Hansard, HC, vol. 114, cc.1590, 1591, 4 April 1919.

[35] Lord Askwith's speech, Hansard, HL, vol. 49, c.250, 1 March 1922; Viscount Haldane's speech, Hansard, HL, vol. 49, cc.254, 255, 1 March 1922.

[36] For example, see Lord Askwith's speech, Hansard, HL, vol. 49, c.250, 1 March 1922; Viscount Haldane's speech, Hansard, HL, vol. 57, cc.791, 792, 3 June 1924; Under-Secretary for the State

Whilst this piece of legislation was certainly significant, its effects on the status of fatherhood were incidental rather than central to the aims of lawmakers. This legislation necessitated a more explicit discussion of the meanings of fatherhood, but its principal aim was to make mothers and fathers more equal in legal terms and to ensure the best interests of children.[37]

The Act was discussed widely in the press throughout the 1920s and similar themes dominated the debate, such as the emphasis on the child's best interests, equality between parents, and the need to bring legislation in line with the social circumstances of the time. In 1921, for example, an article in the *Manchester Guardian* introduced the subject by considering how surprising it was that the mother had so few legal rights with regard to her children. Doubts about the efficacy of the legislation were discussed, and it was highlighted that some believed that the bill would not work because 'a man must be master in his own house'. However, such doubts were quickly dismissed, as 'Fortunately we no longer look upon the relation between husband and wife as one between master and servant, but as one of equal partnership.'[38] This language of equality permeated debates in all newspapers; in the *Daily Mirror* in 1925, for example, the Act was described as 'seek[ing] to give the mother exactly the same rights with regard to the guardianship of children as the father', though the difficulties this could create for judges were raised here too.[39] Such sentiments were also apparent in the more conservative *Times*. Indeed, it published letters from feminist campaigner Eva Hubback, who wrote in support of the bill, and an appeal by women's societies to extend the power of the bill to ensure women's equality.[40] However, there was a recognition of other views too: letters were published from Claud Mullins, for example, a lawyer who argued against the bill, on the basis that it had detrimental effects to the promotion of child welfare.[41]

Whichever view was supported, the child's welfare was said to be the priority. Such sentiments, along with an emphasis on equality, were also at the forefront of debates about family allowances in the 1940s, as discussed in Chapter 2, and continued after the legislation had come into force, when criticisms were made on the basis that mother and father were not, in actuality, equal in their rights and responsibilities. Indeed, the father's status was defended and said to be in peril, but this came only when it was felt that he was in an inferior position to the

---

for the Home Department, Mr Godfrey Locker-Lampson's speech, Hansard, HC, vol. 181, cc.533, 4 March 1925.

[37] P. M. Bromley [1957], *Family Law* (London, 1962), p. 306.

[38] *Manchester Guardian*, 2 May 1921, p. 5. Indeed, it was this period in which there were substantial debates about whether marriage vows should include the promise for wives to obey their husbands. Timothy Jones, 'Love, Honour, and Obey? Romance, Subordination and Marital Subjectivity in Interwar Britain', in Alana Harris and Timothy Jones (eds), *Love and Romance in Britain, 1918–1970* (Basingstoke, forthcoming, 2014).

[39] *Daily Mirror*, 27 March 1925, p. 9.

[40] *The Times*, 8 February 1924, p. 15; *The Times*, 13 January 1925, p. 8; *The Times*, 17 April 1924, p. 14.

[41] *The Times*, 7 April 1924, p. 8. Also see *The Times*, 5 April 1924, p. 12.

mother.[42] In 1926, this matter was discussed in the Lords, and as well as noting the potential need for an amendment to the legislation, the fact that the consequences of the Act had been criticized by magistrates and in the press was highlighted by Lord Raglan. The potential inequality brought about by the legislation formed the basis of the discussion.[43] For the most part, the equality of parents was portrayed as a positive development, and criticism of the law usually lay in its failure to guarantee this.

The legal position of fathers was thus frequently debated in the press, and clearly had consequences for the representation of the father more generally. Alongside the more negative depictions of the father as distant from his family, various elements in the press sought to rebrand the father's position, suggesting he could and should earn his status as head of the family, and within this, his presence could be entirely positive. Many writers portrayed the ideal father as a benevolent head of the family, different from his Victorian counterpart in his justice and accessibility to children, but still the 'boss'. In this way, he was depicted and understood as the centre of the family and of the highest status within it, though still separate in some sense because of this difference. In an article about fathercraft in *The Times* in 1926, it was claimed that it was still the case, at least in working-class families, that the father remained 'the head of the house'.[44] In 1932 the *Manchester Guardian* printed a very similar article, again highlighting the reverence that should be given to fathers by those teaching fathercraft, as emphasized in the subtitle of the article: ' "Head of the House" tradition'.[45] In 1946, it was reported on the front page of the *Mirror* that the fathers' dignity was in peril, as indicated by the London County Council Education Committee. Little was actually being reported here: the story merely covered a meeting in which fathercraft classes were discussed. Though these were deemed to be positive, it was thought that the dignity of the 'head of the family' was endangered by the terminology.[46] These debates about fathercraft thus carefully negotiated the possible problem of emasculating men, and accepted the working-class man's prerogative to view himself as the 'master' of his home and family.

In an article published in the *Daily Mirror* in 1930, Grant Richards discussed the need for each home to have their own strong man, though he hastened to add, 'I do not mean bad-tempered men, men who rule their homes by the exercise of force and terror.' A kind, understanding, but authoritative father was thus portrayed as the ideal, though not the reality, for most fathers of the time, as it was stressed that 'it is not fashionable to be strong'.[47] The possible benevolence of fathers' authority was also demonstrated in a *Mirror* article in 1958, which advised that a father must earn his status as 'happy king in his home' through giving 'love, admiration and respect'.[48] This condition was further illustrated by

---

[42] See, for example, *The Times*, 8 January 1925, p. 9; *The Times*, 21 January 1926, p. 7; *Daily Mirror*, 15 March 1926, p. 3; *Daily Mirror*, 10 March 1927, p. 2.

[43] Hansard, HL, vol. 63, cc.176, 177, 17 February 1926.

[44] *The Times*, 7 July 1926, p. 21.   [45] *Manchester Guardian*, 30 December 1932, p. 2.

[46] *Daily Mirror*, 24 October 1946, p. 1.   [47] *Daily Mirror*, 31 October 1930, p. 7

[48] *Daily Mirror*, 29 April 1953, p. 4. Also see *Daily Mirror*, 2 May 1953, p. 9.

condemnations of those who abused their authority; in the *Daily Mirror* in 1946, for example, an article entitled '"Master of the house" issue—father fined' discussed the case of a father charged in court for physically abusing his daughter in order to feel like a 'master in his own house'. The negative portrayal of this father was strongly reinforced throughout the article, particularly in its demonstration of the highly questionable reason for beating his child, simply to feel like a 'master', as the title reiterated.[49] The connotations associated with being a 'head' of a family were thus mixed: it was assumed that men would want to retain this status, but it must be enacted with care and respect for his family.

AUTHORITY WITHIN THE FAMILY

Social researchers were somewhat divided in their studies of working-class families. Whilst some found that the working-class man was still thought of as 'master', others asserted that he had been removed from this position, willingly or unwillingly, and instead was a humble and ordinary family member. Through careful readings of these studies, it can be seen that the differences in findings, though real and important, could often be exaggerated by the researchers' own interpretations and analyses. As Lawrence notes, researchers in the mid-twentieth century focused too readily on perceived dramatic change, ignoring the range of behaviour to be found amongst working-class communities across the century and before.[50] Interviews too add to this picture of a wide variety of attitudes and behaviour. The idea of 'the master of the house' was strong amongst interviewees, yet again the conception of him within this as a just and kind 'ruler' was frequently insisted upon. A balancing of authority with fairness in its enactment was to be found in both individual attitudes and popular cultural discussions.

Some researchers contended that the father remained the head of the household: Robert Roberts, reflecting back on the first quarter of the twentieth century, noted the gulf between parents and children and highlighted that, in Salford at least, the labourer 'played king at home'.[51] Richard Hoggart, in *The Uses of Literacy*, considered that father was still 'master', though there were signs of change.[52] Those studies focusing on small, rural communities also found evidence of a traditional conception of the father's status as 'master'; for example, in James Littlejohn's study of a Cheviot parish in the 1950s he suggested that 'the dominance of the male' could be found amongst working-class families, where a husband might chastise his wife in front of the children, in contrast to upper- and upper-middle-class families, in which extreme deference was shown to the woman

---

[49] *Daily Mirror*, 14 March 1946, p. 5. Also see advertising which tapped into this discourse; for example, *Daily Mirror*, 22 December 1954, p. 6.

[50] Lawrence, 'Class', pp. 285–6.

[51] Robert Roberts, *The Classic Slum: Salford Life in the First Quarter of the Century* (Manchester, 1971), p. 33.

[52] Richard Hoggart [1957], *The Uses of Literacy: Aspects of Working-Class Life with Special Reference to Publications and Entertainments* (Harmondsworth, 1971), pp. 48–51.

of the house.[53] Again, Littlejohn also highlighted a general sense of change in relations between the sexes, particularly in the working classes.[54] However, such findings were not confined to rural communities; John Barron Mays also discovered a strong deference to the father/husband as wage-earner and traditional head of the family in the problem families he studied in Liverpool.[55] Likewise, in Oxford, John Mogey also found that in the old, working-class part of the city that he studied, the man of the house remained a 'shadowy figure . . . in the background of the life of the woman and her children'. He took up an 'established position', and the running of the household was orientated around his work day.[56] Yet in the new housing estate he studied, the situation was very different: the women interviewed discussed the importance of sharing the responsibility for home and children between husband and wife, and, as such, men were established as equal parents and family members to women, within accepted yet partially flexible gendered divisions of labour—a difference that Mogey believed had been brought about by the new environment and way of life of the suburban housing estate.[57] However, fathers in all families studied were described as 'the final court of appeal on matters of discipline'.[58]

John and Elizabeth Newson, who concluded that the middle of the twentieth century witnessed quite significant changes to fatherhood generally, also found a class-based division in terms of the status of the father. Referring to working-class fathers, they stated that 'However subordinate may be his position at work, in his own house he is the "mester" [master]', whilst within middle-class couples men and women were described as being on 'an equal footing'. In terms of the household routines, working-class households revolved around the father's work schedule, whereas a middle-class man was expected to fit into an established routine.[59] As just quoted, Newson and Newson linked this to working-class men's subordinate position in the workplace, and this may indeed have had a bearing on the sense of status of individuals; if they felt inferior and unimportant at work, organizing the household to suit their needs could enhance their sense of masculine dignity, status, and importance.[60] Geoffrey Gorer also found that most people still insisted on the father as the 'chief source of authority', but did not believe this was incompatible with close family relations. He suggested there were class differences, as people of the upper-working classes were more likely to emphatically stress paternal authority.[61] Ferdynand Zweig, meanwhile, noted that around three quarters of factory workers he interviewed in the late 1950s said that

---

[53] James Littlejohn, *Westrigg: The Sociology of a Cheviot Parish* (London, 1963), pp. 126–8.

[54] Littlejohn, *Westrigg*, p. 135.

[55] John Barron Mays [1954], *Growing Up in the City: A Study of Juvenile Delinquency in an Urban Neighbourhood* (Liverpool, 1964), p. 89.

[56] John M. Mogey, *Family and Neighbourhood: Two Studies in Oxford* (Oxford, 1956), pp. 59–61.

[57] Mogey, *Family and Neighbourhood*, p. 62–3.

[58] Mogey, *Family and Neighbourhood*, p. 66.

[59] John and Elizabeth Newson [1963], *Patterns of Infant Care in an Urban Community* (Harmondsworth, 1974), pp. 218–19.

[60] Also see Roberts, *The Classic Slum*, p. 33.

[61] Geoffrey Gorer, *Exploring English Character* (London, 1955), pp. 170, 299.

they shared an equal or near-equal status and relationship with their wives.[62] The idea that the head of household should earn his position was also insisted upon in many working-class households. Hoggart thought, for example, that though there was an inherent respect for the father as the head of the house, 'this does not mean that he is by any means an absolute ruler or that he gets or expects his own way in everything. It often accompanies a carefulness, a willingness to help and be "considerate", to be "a good husband".'[63] Indeed, many men shied away from the aspects of their roles that required them to act in a dominant and authoritative fashion, such as when they meted out discipline.[64] This could mean they remained a benevolent presence, but could also reflect a lack of active taking of responsibility within family life. Holding ultimate authority within a family did not necessarily mean the enacting of a particular role.

A number of fathers simply saw themselves as an outsider to their families: Mrs H8P, born 1903, noted that 'It wasn't a case of being boss, my dad wasn't, because he couldn't have cared less.'[65] Dave Bowman, a train driver who had two sons in Dundee in the 1940s, believed that the hours he worked meant he was unable to have much contact with his children. This was why, he said, 'my wife took charge of the kids, that's why I gave her the pay packet. This was because I was outside, I was the fellow who was doing the work, I was bringing in the money, so she must be the organizer for the family. I accepted that.'[66] Humphrey Gillett, who was born in 1927, spoke of his own father as 'distant' and more engaged with local politics than with his family. When Humphrey himself married and started a family during the Second World War, he was initially quite distant with his children, partly as he was sent abroad to fight. When he returned, he claimed that he felt that the children came to 'dominate the marriage', a fact he resented.[67] Fatherhood was not a positive part of his life.

Some interviewees explicitly discussed whether father was the 'boss' within their family; many described how their father was the 'boss' or 'master', or even 'captain of the ship'.[68] A minority claimed that their mother was a more dominating figure, or, less commonly, that parental authority was evenly split between mother and father.[69] This picture did not vary according to when those

[62] Ferdynand Zweig, *The Worker in Affluent Society: Family Life and Industry* (London, 1961), p. 31.

[63] Hoggart, *The Uses*, p. 54.

[64] Lynn Abrams, '"There Was Nobody Like My Daddy": Fathers, the Family and the Marginalisation of Men in Modern Scotland', *Scottish Historical Review* 78:2 (1999), p. 229.

[65] Mrs H8P, ERA, Preston 1890–1940, p. 20.

[66] Dave Bowman, quoted in Steve Humphries and Pamela Gordon (eds), *A Man's World: From Boyhood to Manhood, 1900–1960* (London, 1996), p. 176.

[67] Humphrey Gillett, 'A Man's World', British Film Institute Archive, roll 44, pp. 55–60.

[68] For example, see Mr T2P, ERA, Preston 1890–1940, pp. 27, 28, 51; Mr B7P, ERA, Preston 1890–1940, p. 23; Mr M12B, ERA, 1940–70, p. 27; Kathleen Lunan, Int086, *Families*, UKDA, p. 27; J. R. Ackerley [1968], *My Father and Myself* (New York, 1999), p. 10; Bullock, *Bowers Row*, p. 3.

[69] For examples of mothers as the 'boss', see Mrs N3L, ERA, 1940–70, p. 6; Mrs S3B, ERA, 1940–70, p. 82; Mr W6L, ERA, 1940–70, p. 22; for examples of more joint arrangements, see Mr F1P, ERA, Preston 1890–1940, p. 33; Mrs C5P, ERA, Preston 1890–1940, p. 24.

interviewees were growing up, indicating that there remained a diverse range of understandings of parental power across this period. Mr S1P, for example, born 1900, noted that his mother was 'the ruling character in our house', to the extent that she intervened when his father beat him as a punishment.[70] Here, authority was constructed around discipline and punishment. Likewise, Mrs B1P, born the same year, recalled that her father was the 'boss' and a 'disciplinarian', enacting this through strictness with his children. As her mother died when she was 3 years old, this position was not determined in relation to her.[71] Mrs P2P, born 1907, and Mr I2L, born 1930, said their fathers were heads of the family and linked this with their 'Victorian' attitudes.[72] Arthur Wood, furthermore, born 1912, suggested his father did not contribute to the housework because 'they was the boss, you see, then, fathers were the bosses. Mother used to do all the struggling.'[73] Mr B4B, born 1920, felt his father's authority went unchallenged even by the Second World War; he noted that when he returned, by which time Mr B4B had married and moved out of the family home, 'he was the boss when he came home. Oh yes, he was used to commanding men and he expected you to do what you were told.'[74] This continued right through the period; Mrs R1P, born 1945, remembered arguments within her family, recollecting how 'my dad would never argue, because he was the boss and that was it'.[75]

Yet, in examining the ways in which both parents and children discussed men's authority and position within the home, it becomes clear that there were subtle signs of a growing intolerance for the idea of the father as an authoritarian figure, tying in with a new emphasis on increasingly informal parent–child relationships. Mr P6B, for example, born in 1950, reflected that his father was more influential than his mother in terms of family decision-making, but when questioned about whether his father was 'fairly dominant', he replied 'Not really, he just managed to get his own way I'd say. He didn't go and thump her or anything he just seemed to manage to get his own way somehow.'[76] Intergenerational comparisons were again present: Mr G1P, born 1903, was asked who was the boss when he was a child, and responded 'Mother always! Father thinks he is but he is not! There's only one boss in a house, isn't there?' and added 'It will never alter, will it?', indicating a perceived timelessness in gender power relations within the home. Yet in terms of how strict parents were, he highlighted change, using the example of the family's furniture to depict authority: 'now we don't bother, if anybody comes in you sit where you want. Now my father and mother always had a chair and they were made for them and they had different arms on. My father's had two and my mother's had only plain arms.'[77] In his autobiography, Jim Bullock similarly

---

[70] Mr S1P, ERA, Preston 1890–1940, p. 24.
[71] Mrs B1P, ERA, Preston 1890–1940, pp. 9, 13, 22.
[72] Mrs P2P, ERA, Preston 1890–1940, p. 15; Mr I2L, ERA, 1940–70, p. 7.
[73] Arthur Wood, Int163, *Families*, UKDA, p. 12. Also see Mrs M1P, ERA, Preston 1890–1940, p. 65.
[74] Mr B4B, ERA, 1940–70, p. 49   [75] Mrs R1P, ERA, 1940–70, p. 40.
[76] Mr P5B, ERA, 1940–70, p. 20.
[77] Mr G1P, ERA, Preston 1890–1940, pp. 22, 27.

spoke of the ritual of his father sitting in his armchair at the head of the dinner table, with his mother opposite at the other end. He added 'No one would ever have dreamed of sitting in my father's chair, whether he was in the house or not.'[78] Here, we can see how much the use of space within the family home could be intimately linked with power relations.[79] Likewise, Mrs W6B, born 1936, noted that 'My father was head of the house and what father said was law. My family haven't been brought up that way.'[80] Mr G3L, born 1937, noted that it was his mother who was the 'boss' in his family, and he was, in contrast, not quite as strict with his own children, born in the 1960s.[81] As Roberts notes, ideas of open discussion between parents and children became increasingly common; she cites Mr N2L's description of how he listened to his children's opinions, even if the power of decision-making ultimately lay with him.[82]

The unashamed authority of a father was no longer accepted amongst these individuals. George Ryder, though describing himself as 'head of household', clearly felt this to be a duty rather than a privileged position, as he felt keenly the need to provide properly for his family.[83] Ted Cunningham, who became a father in the 1930s in the north-east of England, discussed his own father and compared him to himself. He stated that 'he was a father in the sense that he had brought me on to this earth but he was never a father', and recalled how 'he punished us just to let us know that he was the man of the house'. Ted rejected such behaviour, worked as hard as he could for his family, and tried to give them all the things he never had himself.[84] Geordie Todd, too, born in 1912 in North Shields, spoke of his father as 'king of the house', who 'ruled with an iron rod', though only after his mother had died, as she was initially the 'ruling element' within their household. Yet, in contrast, when Geordie himself became a father in 1938, he worked as hard as possible to provide for his young son, and wanted to be closer to him.[85] That men were 'heads' of their families remained a common idea, but both the framing and perception of this was subtly changing. An automatic sense of authority was no longer invested so readily in the status of father; instead, the responsibilities as well as rights of a father's position were emphasized, and the benevolence of fatherly power was highlighted.

It is very difficult to ascertain whether these intergenerational contrasts reflect a real shift in behaviour or simply a difference in perception on the part of parents and children. There are certainly signs of more informal interaction between fathers and children, which suggests authority-driven relationships were becoming less common; J. S. Mathews' letters to his children during the Second World

[78] Bullock, *Bowers Row*, pp. 6, 16.

[79] On a discussion of this in the nineteenth century, see Doolittle, 'Time, Space', pp. 251–6; Julie-Marie Strange, 'Fatherhood, Providing, and Attachment in Late Victorian and Edwardian Working-Class Families', *Historical Journal* 55:4 (2012), p. 1016.

[80] Mrs W6B, ERA, 1940–70, p. 25.   [81] Mr G3L, ERA, 1940–70, pp. 29,62.

[82] Roberts, *Women and Families*, p. 43. Also see Mr N2L, ERA, 1940–70, p. 41.

[83] George Ryder, 'A Man's World', roll 135, p. 54.

[84] Ted Cunningham, 'A Man's World', roll 91, pp. 23–6; roll 93, p. 82.

[85] Geordie Todd, 'A Man's World', roll 94, pp. 6–7; rolls 100–102, pp. 135–60.

War are illustrative of a happy and open relationship despite the difficult circumstances. As well as describing the affection he felt for his children evacuated away
in America, in letters in 1943 he teased his son for starting to shave and joked
with his daughters about them forgetting about him and his wife at home. His
son also alluded to their playful relationship in his reaction to being asked about
a girlfriend in 1941: 'Whats [sic] this about me saying I had a girl friend. Please
straighten this out because I am being kidded out of my mind and I am sure
have said nothing about one in my letters. Mummy asked me for a picture?????'
He also teased his father in return in a letter of 1942, noting 'We received a letter from Daddy yesterday. Has the 34th hair grown back on that superb Welsh
mustache [sic]. When I first saw the picture I thought it was a smudge that had
accidentally gotten there and I tried to rub it off. (My apologies to the "grower").'[86]
Indeed, those who became parents from the 1930s onwards were likely to intimate
a difference in authority between themselves and their own mothers and fathers.
Furthermore, whilst ideas about authority have changed considerably across the
twentieth century, the very nature of the parent–child relationship, as guardian
and minor, means that there is always an asymmetry in power relations. As noted
in Chapter 4, there were signs of more informal and relaxed relations between
parents and children and a decline in the domineering patriarch whose word was
law. Yet throughout the period interviewees described their parents as strict, and
a sense of strong parental authority figures, most notably embodied in fatherhood but also on the part of mothers, emerges from accounts of childhood in all
decades. Whilst recollections of authority and strictness on the part of parents is
almost bound to vary between parents and children, and there remained a strong
diversity in behaviour throughout this period, a rejection of 'Victorian' attitudes,
less emphasis on men's status as undisputed king-like figures, and a suggestion
of change between different generations at least indicate signs of somewhat more
egalitarian relationships emerging, in ideals if not always practice.

AUTHORITY AND THE FAMILY BUDGET

Throughout discussions in popular culture and amongst individuals, then, came
widespread discussion in terms of who within the family should and did hold the
most authority, and whether this was changing. Interviewees pondered on whether
their mothers or fathers were in charge of the family, and who was stricter, but
were less likely to explicitly discuss shifts in the legal position of fatherhood. One
way in which interviewees did discuss power relations within their families, both
as children and parents, was through a consideration of money within family life.
This was particularly prevalent in the Elizabeth Roberts Archive, as in numerous
of her interviews, respondents were asked whether the father of the family handed

---

[86] Private Papers of J. S. Mathews, Imperial War Museum Archive (IWMA), Documents.16403,
letter to Cliff dated 29 September 1943, letter to Sheila and Dinah dated 12 December 1943, letters
from Cliff dated 19 July 1941 and 4 January 1942.

over his intact wage packet or gave his wife a certain amount for 'housekeeping'. This was an important matter in working-class families, in which a weekly wage for the husband was the norm; middle-class families were more likely to have a more joint approach to spending the family budget. Furthermore, respect for family money was expected more of men with children, though this was part of being a 'good' husband too. This was increased by the fact that women were less likely to take on work outside the home after having children, rendering them more vulnerable to a man who wasted his money. What father did with his pay was occasionally discussed in the press; in the *Daily Mirror* in 1949, handing over a pay packet but taking no other responsibility within family life was a minimum standard of behaviour expected, as set out in the quiz 'Am I a Good Husband?' Doing so was one of three possible scenarios describing men's behaviour, with the others representing more involvement in family life and therefore attracting more 'good husband' points.[87] Yet, as will be discussed later in this chapter, the interview evidence suggests that numerous men throughout the period did not conform to this standard. In another *Mirror* article of 1953, also addressing husbands, the opening of the pay packet was linked directly to men's authority within the home. This piece, by agony aunt Mary Brown, started 'If a man wants to be a happy king in his home he must EARN his title. The mere physical fact of his manhood and his legal status as husband and father do not automatically ensure his kingship or his happiness.' Brown continued by discussing different types of bad husbands, noting 'The MEAN man's wife never knows what is in her husband's pay packet. He spends plenty on himself but doles her out a weekly pittance just enough to keep them out of debt. *His wife is not a partner, she is an unpaid servant and she knows it.*'[88]

Amongst interviewees, there was a spread in terms of those men who handed over an unopened wage packet and those who chose to apportion a certain amount of housekeeping; Roberts found that in her earlier study, of working-class life between 1890 and 1940, almost all women controlled the family budget.[89] However, across all the interviews, it is clear that there was a division between those who handed over their wages unopened and those who handed over the majority of them. Gorer believed there was a north/south divide, with those in northern England more likely to hand over an unopened wage packet; indeed, most respondents, interviewed for projects other than that of Elizabeth Roberts, who said this happened in their family were from the north or the Midlands, though there was substantial diversity across all regions.[90] Zweig suggested the handing over of the whole wage packet was also more common amongst Welsh and Irish families.[91] By the latter part of the period, Roberts found that women

---

[87] *Daily Mirror*, 4 October 1949, p. 4. For a fuller discussion of this and other quizzes in the press, see Laura King, 'Hidden Fathers? The Significance of Fatherhood in Mid- Twentieth-Century Britain', *Contemporary British History* 26:1 (2012), pp. 25–46.

[88] *Daily Mirror*, 29 April 1953, p. 4. Original emphasis.

[89] Elizabeth Roberts, *A Woman's Place: An Oral History of Working-Class Women, 1890–1940* (Oxford, 1984), p. 110.

[90] Gorer, *Exploring*, pp. 131–2.   [91] Zweig, *The Worker*, p. 35.

had lost some of the control of budgeting, with a stronger division between 'his' and 'her' money, in part because of the rise in numbers of women working. This way of thinking could actually lead to a more difficult situation for women, as they lost out in terms of both power and money.[92]

Across all the interview collections, of 149 interviewees who recalled the division of the wage packet, eighty-two noted that they, their husbands, or their fathers handed over an amount of housekeeping, and fifty-five suggested the man of the house 'tipped up' his entire wages, with a small minority highlighting other, more joint, arrangements. Those interviewed for projects other than Elizabeth Roberts' did not always discuss money management. But here too, there was a diversity in experience across the whole period. In some families, fathers were more dominant in money matters;[93] in others, women handled the budget.[94] Some discussed this explicitly in terms of authority, with Edith Broadway, for example, noting that her husband, like most men, 'wanted to be the boss. He was not going to be subject to bringing his pay packet home and giving it to me so I was allocated a certain amount for housekeeping.'[95] Mr C1P, a millworker who married in 1915, felt he was lucky as he handed over his wages and did not have to worry about money, as his wife was a good manager, yet added that 'some women are careful and some are wasteful and some men are careful and some men are wasteful so there's no one rule that would apply to every case, is there?'[96] Some men, furthermore, were reluctant to explicitly discuss with their wives how much they earned.[97] In Joyce Pounds' family, in Wales in the 1930s and 1940s, the lack of knowledge of her father's wages did not mean her mother was not in charge. She noted,

> I'm making my mother out to be such an ogre, but she was . . . the boss of the family, so I mean . . . on the other hand, she never knew how much money my father earned, and he gave her housekeeping, but she sorted everything out and she paid all the bills[.][98]

Patterns of behaviour did not always fall along class lines, though they could intersect with occupational status. The father of Margret Povey, born 1936, was a shop manager, something she referred to when discussing who controlled the family budget: 'My father was the business manager and he organised the money.'[99]

In examining Roberts' interviewees alongside those interviewed for other projects, it is clear that the move away from the handing over of the intact or

---

[92] Roberts, *Women and Families*, pp. 90–2.

[93] For example Brian Huston, Int073, *Families*, UKDA, p. 12; Trevor Welham, Int156, *Families*, UKDA, p. 12; William Dykes, Int053, *Families*, UKDA, pp. 19–20.

[94] For example Mary Lear, Int084, *Families*, UKDA, p. 23; Roy Hubbard, Int069, *Families*, UKDA, pp. 22–3; Margaret Beckwith, Int009, *Families*, UKDA, p. 39.

[95] Edith Broadway, quoted in Steve Humphries and Pamela Gordon (eds), *A Labour of Love: The Experience of Parenthood in Britain 1900–1950* (London, 1993), pp. 95–6.

[96] Mr C1P, ERA, Preston 1890–1940, p. 69.

[97] Ian Canning, Int026, *Families*, UKDA, p. 15; Rosemary Vincent, Int147, *Families*, UKDA, p. 29; Isabelle Eddington, Int054, *Families*, UKDA, p. 13. Also see Tom Brennan, *Reshaping a City* (Glasgow, 1959), p. 101.

[98] Joyce Mary Pounds, Int114, *Families*, UKDA, p. 17.

[99] Margret Povey, Int115, *Families*, UKDA, p. 21.

near-complete wage packet could have both negative and positive consequences. In some cases, couples took on a joint approach to money, which could lead to a loss of power or status for the mother, but could also reflect a more equal and companionate partnership. Dealing with the family money could invest that person with authority, but could also be seen as an unwanted responsibility.[100] Carefully managing his own wages could signify an emotional investment in family life, as was the case in the family of Ted Walker, born 1934, whose father distributed his money between various tins for insurance, clothing, and so on, as well as Ted's '*Start-In-Life*'.[101] For some couples, sharing the burden of money management could be a sign of the emotional sharing identified by Szreter and Fisher as signifying a good marriage in this period.[102] Elaine Rickwood, born in 1946 to a father who was a fitter in a colliery, then in the RAF, and a mother who worked in a mill reflected on her parents' shared approach to money, noting, 'My father was very open about what he had. He didn't hand over his wage packet, but together they would . . . this is when mum wasn't working—they would decide together—well that was for saving, that was for the gas and so on and so forth.' They also had joint and respective individual savings accounts.[103] The exchange between Kate Morrissey, born 1951, and her mother is noteworthy in this sense. Kate noted that her mother, a cost clerk, managed the family budget with little input from her father, a postman. She discussed how this changed, and her father took responsibility for bills. At this point, her mother intervened in the interview, explaining 'I got fed-up of it. I kept paying out these bills and he's going off and not a care in the world. So I put my foot down. He happily took it on.'[104] In contrast to her parents, Joyce Pounds noted that though her husband, who she married in 1951, handed over a proportion of housekeeping for certain items, she felt that 'It was considered our money, it wasn't considered his money or my money, it was just our money.'[105] Mr K1B, a joiner with a family business who married in 1944, highlighted how he and his wife had a joint bank account, yet 'I wrote the cheques, it was just a question of what did we want and we both agreed it and that was it you know. But my wife could have written a cheque, but she left it to me to do and to square them up.'[106] Others, particularly those from more middle-class backgrounds like Allean Cleveland and her husband, married in 1935, simply shared family budgeting because they had set up a joint account on marrying.[107] Indeed, the move towards receiving a salary through bank accounts rather than a

[100] Kate Fisher also makes this point in terms of responsibility for birth control. Kate Fisher, *Birth Control, Sex and Marriage in Britain 1918–1960* (Oxford, 2006), p. 229.

[101] Ted Walker, *The High Path* (London, 1982), p. 16.

[102] Simon Szreter and Kate Fisher, *Sex before the Sexual Revolution: Intimate Life in England 1918–1963* (Cambridge, 2010), pp. 212–3.

[103] Elaine Rickwood, Int117, *Families*, UKDA, pp. 18–19.

[104] Kate Morrissey, Int094, *Families*, UKDA, pp. 10–11. Also see May Welham, Int155, *Families*, UKDA, p. 76; Mary Walter, Int151, *Families*, UKDA, p. 20.

[105] Joyce Mary Pounds, Int114, *Families*, UKDA, p. 32.

[106] Mr K1B, ERA, 1940–70, p. 21.

[107] Allean Cleveland, Int031, *Families*, UKDA, p. 18. Also see Laura Millard, Int090, *Families*, UKDA, p. 33.

packet of cash wages could lessen women's input into spending, as Roberts high-lights.[108] Mr Fides, a self-employed businessman born in 1929, suggested that he and his wife, in common with their parents, pooled all their earnings from the start: 'we both came home on Friday night, opened the wage packets, tipped 'em on the table, counted it all up and said well, that's our money . . . It was never hers and his, it was theirs.'[109] For him and a substantial number of others, this shared approach was positive.

In the context of men's growing involvement in the traditionally feminine sphere of child-rearing and domestic housework, this question of a joint approach to family management becomes even more complex. As Roberts notes, some women went as far as to reject men's help, carefully guarding 'their' area of domestic expertise.[110] As Szreter and Fisher have shown, men of all social classes were care-ful to respect their wife's expertise, even if they were loving and involved fathers.[111] A respect for the different spheres of authority remained in many families in this period.[112] Some discourses, such as romance fiction, further promoted the idea of ideal men as responsible for 'taking care' of women's needs, and romance authors tended to infantilize women and invest men with a benign, gentle authority over them.[113] Yet at the same time as this persistence of strong gendered ideals around family roles, there were hints at a more joint approach to all family matters. Indeed, by examining shifting ideals about the family budget through the prism of more active fatherhood, a slightly different picture emerges. Hilda Lovejoy, born 1917 and married aged 23, explained that her husband gave her a proportion of his wages, and increased this when he did overtime, but also noted that 'when [the children] wanted anything, he was paying'.[114] Indeed, couples were more likely to discuss child-rearing and all family matters as a joint responsibility by the 1950s. In Bott's study of London families, all couples were said to consider child-rearing as a joint affair, even if household tasks were, to different extents, divided by gen-der,[115] and in Young and Willmott's study of Woodford, they commented that as well as some degree of sharing of certain household chores, 'Naturally enough, the couple also share the work, worry and pleasure of the children.'[116] Zweig too noted the shared approach to both child-rearing and money amongst numerous couples, especially if the wife worked.[117] Indeed, in a number of oral history interviews, there was a shift in language; interviewees parenting at the end of this period were

---

[108] Roberts, *Women and Families*, p. 92.

[109] Mr Fides, Int167, *Families*, UKDA, p. 21.

[110] Elizabeth Bott [1957], *Family and Social Network: Roles, Norms, and External Relationships in Ordinary Urban Families* (London, 1971), p. 80; Roberts, *Women and Families*, p. 39. Also see Mr G3L, ERA, 1940–70, p. 26.

[111] Szreter and Fisher, *Sex*, p. 206.

[112] Bott, *Family*, p. 64; Newson and Newson, *Patterns*, p. 222; Szreter and Fisher, *Sex*, ch.5.

[113] King, 'The Perfect Man'.   [114] Hilda Lovejoy, Int085, *Families*, UKDA, p. 18.

[115] Bott, *Family*, p. 80.

[116] Peter Willmott and Michael Young, *Family and Class in a London Suburb* (London, 1960), p. 22. Also see Michael Young and Peter Willmott [1957], *Family and Kinship in East London* (Harmondsworth, 1967), p. 27.

[117] Zweig, *The Worker*, pp. 23, 36.

more likely to discuss child-rearing and decision-making in the first person plural. For some this was explicit; Emily Norton highlighted that in terms of looking after the children, she and her husband 'did it together. We did everything together.'[118] In this sense, a move towards joint budgeting of the family income can be seen as part of a growing move towards numerous couples wanting to share the benefits and difficulties of managing family life.

THE FATHER AND THE FAMILY HIERARCHY

The evidence of history supported the power of men within the domestic sphere, as heads of household in a legal, economic, and social sense. Though it continued in some discourses throughout this period, the framing of the father's position shifted in significant ways, and a notable minority of families started to embrace more genuinely joint approaches to money management and childcare. The idea that the father had lost his authority became increasingly common alongside the consideration of a father as the 'head' of a family, a development that was portrayed as positive in the post-Second World War period. The construction of the family power hierarchy also underwent substantial change in this period. As the father's authority was being questioned, the prioritization of the child's interests and well-being was promoted. As Deborah Thom notes, direct authority moved away from the father, and greater notice was taken of the child's point of view.[119] Furthermore, certain discourses emphasized a new equality between family members, rejecting entirely the idea of hierarchical relationships. The available evidence indicates that such models of power relationships were reflective of developments in terms of family life, as increasing numbers of parents sought to build more egalitarian relationships with their own children than they themselves had experienced.

Present in the press, and in other cultural sources, was the assertion that the father had lost all his authority, and this was initially a source of mockery. Again, this portrayal differed in terms of class: as A. James Hammerton suggests, the lower-middle-class man was frequently the subject of satire in the early twentieth century, and indeed, this continued in the interwar period.[120] The paterfamilias, moreover, had a history as a subject of parody: as Andrew Spicer notes, this continued in music hall in the first half of the twentieth century. Yet, after the war, the qualities that were initially mocked were deemed heroic. In films especially, the ordinary man's courage was highlighted and praised.[121] The press also capitalized

---

[118] Emily Norton, Int100, *Families*, UKDA, p. 20.

[119] Deborah Thom, ' "Beating Children Is Wrong": Domestic Life, Psychological Thinking and the Permissive Turn', in L. Delap, B. Griffin, and A. Wills (eds), *The Politics of Domestic Authority in Britain since 1800* (Basingstoke, 2009), pp. 277–8.

[120] A. James Hammerton, 'The English Weakness? Gender, Satire and Moral Manliness in the Lower Middle Class, 1870–1920', in A. Kidd and D. Nicholls (eds), *Gender, Civic Culture, and Consumerism: Middle-Class Identity in Britain, 1800–1940* (Manchester, 1999), pp. 164–5.

[121] Andrew Spicer, *Typical Men: The Representation of Masculinity in Popular British Cinema* (new edn, London, 2003), p. 17.

on this tradition of satire, as cartoons and other satirical pieces used the contrast of the Victorian patriarch to illustrate the interwar father's lack of authority. Yet the use of historical imagery to illustrate what was good and bad about father-hood could also, and increasingly, be found in more negative terms: the Victorian father was also portrayed as an autocrat who abused his position, as Kate Fisher notes.[122] Similarly, Tim Fisher has demonstrated how the 'fathercraft father' was constructed partly in opposition to his Victorian predecessor.[123]

The press seized on this theme. Cartoons of the 1920s exploited the declining authority of the father, particularly those in the *Daily Mirror*. In 1922, for exam-ple, the *Mirror* published a cartoon by W. K. Haselden entitled 'The schoolboy and his report: past and present'. The schoolboy of the 'past', who cowered at his father's disgust at his rather bad school report, was contrasted with the schoolboy of the 'present'. He, conversely, reproaches his father for questioning the report at all, resulting in his father apologising for failing to be proud of him. The father stated, 'Sorry, old boy, it's only my ignorance—I didn't mean to offend you!' The perception of a shift of power was clearly articulated here, and the father of the day was portrayed as a rather pitiful figure.[124] Similarly, in February 1924, 'Papa' of the past was compared with the interwar, 'modern' father in another Haselden cartoon (Figure 5.1). Whilst servants and children weep at the anger of the nineteenth-century 'Papa', their interwar counterparts laugh and mock the father in their family; even the maid present is depicted smiling. The caption below this cartoon reinforced the applicability of its message to reality: 'Our read-ers tell us that the old dictatorial type of husband and father has died out. At any rate, he seems to have lost his authority.'[125] This mockery continued into the 1930s: in the *Daily Mirror*'s 'Rummy' cartoon of 10 April 1937, a boy is depicted spanking his father's behind with a paddle of some sort for failing to do his son's homework properly, suggesting a literal role reversal and also a more metaphorical reversal of power relations within the father–child relationship.[126]

This idea was considered, in both a light-hearted and a serious way, in other articles, editorials, and letters across the press. The *Daily Mirror*, for example, featured an article in January 1919 about the state of fatherhood after the war, entitled 'The Abdication of the Pre-War "Pa"', with the subheading 'Will the authority of the "heavy father" return?' The author, Eleanor Maclean, contended that the heavy father had 'one rule of life on which he held with an iron grip': that 'every man is master in his own house'. Such a father was described as a 'tyrant of the teatable, the despot at dinner time, and general autocrat of the home', but per-haps now obsolete, as even his control of money had been lost through the war as both his children and his wife could work for themselves. Because of this change, the author stated, he should not assume he could return to his pre-war position: 'Paterfamilias will find his string shortened when his brood return to the nest.'[127]

---

[122] Fisher, *Birth Control*, p. 228.
[123] Fisher, 'Fatherhood and the Experience', p. 123.
[124] *Daily Mirror*, 27 July 1922, p. 5.   [125] *Daily Mirror*, 7 February 1924, p. 5.
[126] *Daily Mirror*, 10 April 1937, p. 18.
[127] *Daily Mirror*, 11 January 1919, p. 5.

Fig. 5.1. W. K. Haselden cartoon, *Daily Mirror*, 7 February 1924, p. 5. Reprinted with permission, © Mirrorpix.

Such sentiments continued in this and other newspapers throughout the 1920s, some in sympathy with the tyrannical father, others celebrating his demise. In January 1922, the *Manchester Guardian* printed an article about 'The decline of the parent', in which a difference in generations was discussed. It was suggested that parents of the day, including the author, remembered a time when a father was an 'acknowledged head of household' and a 'parent's word carried weight'. Yet there had apparently been a 'complete reversal' of this order, and 'parental prestige' had disappeared, a sad state of affairs in the eyes of that writer.[128] Another *Mirror* article, published in 1929, discussed Bertrand Russell's assertion that 'paternal authority is declining', to which the author responded that though the extent of such a decline may be exaggerated, the father's 'forced abdication is no cause for grief'.[129] This decline in authority could be a source of mockery, a cause of sympathy for the father, or even a reason for celebration—at least in the less conservative *Manchester Guardian* and *Daily Mirror*—although *The Times* in particular held onto a respect for traditional patriarchal authority figures.

The use of the term 'Victorian' became increasingly negative in its cultural representation, to denote a tyrannical figure who abused his disproportionate authority. Oral history interviewees also employed this term: Frank Davies, who grew up in the interwar period, described his father as 'one of the old school', on the 'back end of the Victorian era' in discussing his father's lack of interest in himself and his siblings.[130] Likewise, Margret Rawe, married in 1951, was asked about her ideas about child-rearing, and responded 'I think I knew—not strict in the sense of being Victorian strict, but I've always felt children needed discipline. A lot of love and a little discipline, that's what I think about children.'[131] The term also pervaded academic research: Elizabeth Bott, in her interviews with families in her study of London in the 1950s, observed that all respondents contrasted their ideals relating to the family and marriage with 'those of the older generation and "Victorian families"'.[132] Ferdynand Zweig, too, noted that several of his interviewees discussed 'old-fashioned' and 'Victorian' ideas in contrast with their own views.[133]

Such an image of the Victorian father could also be found in most newspapers, and certainly the *Daily Mirror*: in 1956, for example, an article was printed

---

[128] *Manchester Guardian*, 25 January 1922, p. 12. James Marchant, in another *Daily Mirror* article, agreed, suggesting 'these are bad times for fathers'. *Daily Mirror*, 3 September 1924, p. 5. Letters, too, highlighted this: in 1929, for example, under the title 'Fatherhood in Eclipse', the *Daily Express* printed a letter from 'F.W.A.' claiming that whilst the father used to be the 'pivot of the home' with 'absolute authority', in both theory and practice in 'Victorian times', fathers were now experiencing a loss of authority. *Daily Express*, 17 June 1929, p. 10. Also see *Daily Express*, 23 April 1927, p. 8; *Daily Mirror*, 30 January 1928, p. 7; *The Times*, 5 March 1930, p. 15.

[129] *Daily Mirror*, 23 October 1929, p. 9.

[130] Frank Davies, 'A Man's World', roll 75, pp. 1–4. Also see George Aberdou, Int165, *Families*, UKDA, p. 35; Mrs P2P, ERA, Preston 1890–1940, p. 15; Mr I2L, ERA, 1940–70, p. 7.

[131] Margret Rawe, Int116, *Families*, UKDA, p. 37.   [132] Bott, *Family*, p. 206.

[133] Zweig, *The Worker*, pp. 32, 180. Also see R. F. Delderfield, *Bird's Eye View* (London, 1954), p. 24; Nigel Gray, *The Worst of Times: An Oral History of the Great Depression in Britain* (London, 1985), p. 180.

tackling the subject of 'Happy Families'. This discussed the greater openness and equality between family members and suggested, 'Gone (and good riddance to him) is the Victorian father who thought he was God'; as discussed at the start of this chapter, the link between familial and religious authority was increasingly questioned. Instead, the fact that mothers, fathers, and their children were now more like 'good pals' was celebrated.[134] In a very different context, a headline of 12 April 1958 gave details of a case in which ' "Victorian Dad" must pay £350'. This term was a direct quotation from the judge in the case, who condemned this father's violence towards his daughter and her boyfriend.[135] The toppling of the Victorian autocrat, of whom children were scared, was largely deemed positive for family life.

A FAMILY MEMBER?

This celebration of the toppling of the autocratic father was part of the wider trend which celebrated the father as an equal member of the family, rather than the head of it. As part of this, fathers were portrayed as subordinating their own interests to those of their children, as well as spending as much time with their families as they could. As such, it can be argued that the family hierarchy became reordered. Between husbands and wives there was a greater emphasis on their different but equally important contributions to the family, thus preserving a gendered binary, but also promoting the idea of equality.[136] Additionally, the parent–child relationship was also constructed as more equal: as discussed earlier in this chapter, the press portrayed the running of the household and the activities of the family as increasingly revolving around children rather than parents, reminding fathers that there were limits to their authority. The idea of a greater understanding, sympathy, and friendship between the generations became idealized in popular culture, and lived out in some families' experiences. There were tensions here: this equality between parents and children could challenge the idea that fathers were supposed to discipline and set a good example to children. Yet the father was increasingly idealized as a gentle guiding figure: more of a benevolent older brother than a dictatorial authority figure. Zweig believed this new role for fathers was becoming increasingly common practice, noting that 'There is little doubt that the image of the stern, bullying, dominating and self-assertive father or of the absent father who took no interest in the children, leaving them to the mother, is fast disappearing, and the new image of a benevolent, friendly and brotherly father is emerging.'[137] It is clear that this did not represent a wholesale

---

[134] *Daily Mirror*, 2 February 1956, p. 2. This article is also discussed at the start of this book.
[135] *Daily Mirror*, 12 April 1958, p. 5.
[136] Collins argues the emphasis on equality was arguably distinctive to twentieth-century notions of companionate marriage. Marcus Collins, *Modern Love: An Intimate History of Men and Women in Twentieth-Century Britain* (London, 2003), pp. 90–3.
[137] Zweig, *The Worker*, p. 23.

change across society, yet Zweig highlights the increasing possibility of the father embracing a newly accepted role within family life that rejected dictatorial modes of authority over his wife and children.

The relationship between mother and father in terms of power within the home is also central to understanding the hierarchy of authority within the family. Much of the time, it was claimed that mother and father had different 'spheres' of authority, and, as such, the authority of the man could be coupled with respect for the woman and her expertise in terms of domestic matters. This view could be found throughout the period: in a light-hearted piece in the *Daily Mirror* in 1919, for example, writer Keith Campbell compared the family hierarchy to that of the Army, with the father as head, an 'unostentatious boss'—the general staff—and mother as manager of supplies—the quartermaster staff. Through this understanding of the family hierarchy, and the assignation of complementary roles, compromise and, consequently 'domestic happiness' could be achieved.[138] Such a depiction of power relations in the family allowed for father as 'boss' but also portrayed family harmony, as each parent had their separate realm of authority. Fathers' superiority was also implied in articles which reminded readers of the never-ending work of mothers, in contrast to fathers who were often able to have a restful evening after their day's work had been done, a reflection of the *Mirror*'s majority female readership. In the children's page of the *Daily Mirror* in October 1935, for example, the regular letter from the children's editor 'Uncle Dick' focused on mothers, and suggested that mothers 'are never, like father, "off duty" '.[139] Another *Mirror* article, a couple of months later, argued that the support that women gave to men as wives and mothers directly contributed to their success in the outside world.[140] Similar opinions were voiced during and after the Second World War, as the perceived importance and celebration of the mother grew;[141] yet this actually served to create a sense of equality in difference between mother and father. Whilst at the start of the twentieth century the father was still portrayed as inherently superior, by the middle of the century individuals were more reluctant to suggest this so explicitly, and, as such, a greater emphasis was placed on the equality born out of difference in terms of male and female parenting.

This shift in understandings of the family hierarchy was reinforced by the growing belief that fathers were equal family members, who should not be prioritized over their wives or children, but who could also enjoy the benefits of emotionally close and intimate family life. Fathers were also increasingly portrayed as equally responsible for the well-being of their children. An article in *The Times* in

---

[138] *Daily Mirror*, 29 October 1919, p. 5.   [139] *Daily Mirror*, 9 October 1935, p. 20.
[140] *Daily Mirror*, 28 January 1936, p. 23.
[141] Abrams, 'There Was Nobody', pp. 219–42; Alston, *The Family*, p. 22; Davidoff, Doolittle, Fink, and Holden, *The Family Story*, p. 210; Janet Finch and Penny Summerfield, 'Social Reconstruction and the Emergence of Companionate Marriage, 1945–59', in D. Clark (ed.), *Marriage, Domestic Life and Social Change* (London, 1991), pp. 7–12; Grey, 'Discourses', p. 26; Jane Lewis, *The Politics of Motherhood: Child and Maternal Welfare in England, 1900–1939* (London, 1980); Diane Richardson, *Women, Motherhood and Childrearing* (Basingstoke, 1993), pp. 29–48.

1946 typified this change, presenting the father as equally important, as children were the 'joint responsibility of a partnership which includes father as well as mother'.[142] Again, as was demonstrated previously, situating the father as a natural member of the family, and likewise families as incomplete without a father, was a crucial aspect of the discourse that surrounded men's return from war. Such discourses were contradicted by an acknowledgment of women's ability to cope without their husbands during the war. Furthermore, this emphasis on the centrality of men to their families could isolate those outside the nuclear family structure. However, the priority of reconstructing the nation physically and emotionally privileged the focus on the family as the unit of social order which would take Britain into the future. Such an emphasis was fuelled by wartime concerns of marital adultery and 'illegitimate' children; through situating men at the hearts of their families, questions about the biological paternity of children born in the war could be put aside. Finally, the need and desire to celebrate the men who had been fighting could also be answered through the location of men at the hearts of families, as this was portrayed as the ultimate prize for their sacrifices as soldiers. The return to normal family life in peacetime was a frequently problematic transition,[143] yet the supposed healing nature of the family for individual men was used to promote the recovery of the nation from the scars of war.

The involvement of the father in family life, as a full and active member, was endorsed in the press before the Second World War. Advertising, for example, capitalized on the contented picture of family life to promote products and services, from Selfridges department store to pianos. Indeed, in both of these particular examples, the product advertised was attributed with bringing father into the heart of the family.[144] Another example can be drawn from the *Manchester Guardian* in 1925, in which the teaching of housecraft was discussed. Within this article, men's duties as family members were assessed, and the impact of men involving themselves more in their families was celebrated.[145] However, after the Second World War, the desire to locate fathers as full family members took on a new urgency and extent, and, moreover, was a theme common to the more popular lowbrow newspapers, as such participation was deemed to be appropriate for fathers of all social classes. Some articles explicitly discussed the greater happiness that the reunion of the whole family had brought. In the *Daily Mirror* in 1946, for instance, it was noted that cases referred to the NSPCC had reduced dramatically since the end of the war, as 'the family circle is complete again'. Though other reasons for this decline were acknowledged, their coverage was brief, and the article focused almost exclusively on the happiness ensuing from the family reunions.[146] This article demonstrates the wish to focus on the family

---

[142] *The Times*, 6 August 1946, p. 5.

[143] Martin Francis, 'A Flight from Commitment? Domesticity, Adventure and the Masculine Imaginary in Britain after the Second World War', *Gender and History* 19:1 (2007), p. 167.

[144] *The Times*, 16 November 1921, p. 6; *The Times*, 23 June 1924, p. 10.

[145] *Manchester Guardian*, 29 September 1925, p. 6.

[146] *Daily Mirror*, 23 September 1946, p. 3.

as part of a successful and happy social reconstruction. Others commented upon the changes that had taken place; in the *Manchester Guardian* in 1954, for example, recent sociological research was discussed which noted the disappearance of 'vigorous communal life', where doors were left open for gossip and 'father was very much the head of the family'.[147] Many articles, of course, concluded otherwise, as was discussed earlier in this chapter. Yet the desire to encompass all forms of behaviour in terms of father's involvement as a family member arguably won out. In the *Daily Mirror* particularly, a positive outlook on how fathers were behaving was promoted.

Some letter-writers and interviewees also voiced this belief; S. Bensinger, writing to his wife whilst serving in the First World War in 1917, hoped for a peaceful conclusion to the war soon 'so that I can take my place again beside you my dear & our kiddies & so on'.[148] Florrie Dukes was a mother of one son born in 1940, and her husband was sent to fight abroad between 1942 and 1945. She discussed the emotional difficulty of this time, and stated that all she wanted was for her husband to return home, so they could 'be a family together again'.[149] Additionally, Robert Williamson, who also fought in the Second World War, longed to get home to his wife and daughter. He claimed that he felt more emotion towards his family than some men, stating 'I was a family man—it's as simple as that and I wanted to get back to my family.'[150] For Geordie Todd, who also served in the Second World War, his son's initial rejection of him was incredibly difficult, yet when he managed to develop a stronger relationship with him after some months back home, he recalled that 'I thought now we are a family, we were a happy family and we did everything together, which we had never done before.'[151] For many families, the readjustment to 'normal' family life after both wars was incredibly problematic; the opening story of Allport's *Demobbed*, of a man who stabbed his wife because she was pregnant with an Italian prisoner-of-war's child, illustrates this.[152] Barry Turner and Tony Rennell's book *When Daddy Came Home* supplies further evidence of these difficulties in family life.[153] Mathew Thomson highlights the difficulties produced by the war on a collective as well as an individual level, though suggests these remained remarkably little discussed at the time.[154] Others hinted at a less dramatic but very difficult break in family relationships; Pamela Pittuck, for example, born in 1930, noted that on her father's return from serving in the Navy during the Second World War she felt 'he was an alien to me really',

---

[147] *Manchester Guardian*, 3 July 1954, p. 3.

[148] Private Papers of S. Bensinger, IWMA, Documents.16579, letter to wife dated 23 October 1917.

[149] Florrie Dukes, quoted in Humphries and Gordon, *A Labour*, p. 260.

[150] Robert Williamson, 'A Labour of Love', roll 160, p. 134.

[151] Geordie Todd, 'A Man's World', roll 102, p. 160.

[152] Alan Allport, *Demobbed: Coming Home after the Second World War* (New Haven, CT, and London, 2009), pp. 1–2.

[153] Barry Turner and Tony Rennell, *When Daddy Came Home: How Family Life Changed Forever in 1945* (London, 1995).

[154] Mathew Thomson, *Lost Freedom: The Landscape of the Child and the British Post-War Settlement* (Oxford, 2013), pp. 47–78.

and added 'not having had a father for all those years, I sort of didn't want him. It's quite a shame really.'[155] As Allport notes, the return of fathers could be a rather unwelcome disruption of family life, particularly for young children who had had very little contact with their fathers. The moment of homecoming could be a 'rude awakening'.[156]

Large parts of the press insisted on papering over these potential cracks in family life. The editorial line of promoting men's situation at the heart rather than head of their families could be found in all parts of newspapers, and within this, the interests of families were prioritized. For example, in her advice column in 1956, Mary Brown responded to the letter of a sailor who could not decide whether he should sign up to five more years in the Navy, which would earn him a promotion, or stay at home with his family. Brown wrote in support of the wife, who believed her husband belonged at home, in part because 'a little boy needs his Daddy', stating that his wife wanted 'the comfort of his everyday presence for herself and her little son', all 'simple and natural desires'.[157] The position of fathers as involved family members was also reinforced through the discussion of various situations in which this was not the case. Firstly, readers were reminded that families were incomplete without fathers. For example, in the *Daily Mirror* in 1948, a 'woman doctor' wrote to the 'half a million women in this country between the ages of twenty-five and fifty-four [who] have no prospects of marriage and children'. The author adopted a child as a solution to her spinsterhood, and she advised others about such possibilities. Yet, while presenting this as a solution to the assumed unhappiness of single women, it was made clear that this situation was inferior to normal family life: 'there is still something missing in a home where there is no father'.[158] Additionally, those families that discouraged fathers' active involvement as a family member were criticized. In 1950, for example, an article written by the Reverend Mervyn Stockwood was published in the *Daily Mirror*, in which it was argued that large families were undesirable, in part because they resulted in father 'keeping out of the way' and 'spending his evenings at the pub or the dogs'.[159] Furthermore, circumstances which forced young couples to live with their parents were also condemned because of the effects they had on fathers' participation as family members. Due to the crowded living conditions, such a father was said to 'forget his delight' at the newborn baby and 'find solace' elsewhere.[160] As with the promotion of various ideals relating to family life in the press, the positive promotion of a mode of behaviour was matched by negative portrayals of those who failed to meet such standards.

Many social researchers, including Newson and Newson, stressed the sense of partnership between husband and wife, and argued that the conception of the father as an equal family member was an accurate depiction of family life.[161] Yet

---

[155] Pamela Pittuck, Int108, *Families*, UKDA, p. 25.   [156] Allport, *Demobbed*, p. 69.
[157] *Daily Mirror*, 3 December 1956, p. 12.
[158] *Daily Mirror*, 13 November 1948, p. 2. Also see *Daily Mirror*, 22 December 1952, p. 8.
[159] *Daily Mirror*, 4 April 1950, p. 2.   [160] *Daily Mirror*, 11 December 1950, pp. 4–5.
[161] Newson and Newson, *Patterns*, p. 219.

their discussion of a father's needs as paramount in working-class households is also revealing; they suggested that this was largely due to the fact that many working-class fathers actually felt *more* naturally part of domestic life than their middle- or upper-class counterparts. Most working-class men were able to take time off work, for example if their wife was having a baby, and shift working patterns frequently meant that men spent much of the day, when children were awake, at home.[162] Indeed, whilst there was an ongoing reframing of men's involvement in family life in this period, and there is a substantial amount of evidence of fathers taking their roles more seriously, as Lawrence notes, it is also important to recognize a 'broad spectrum of working-class masculinities', with home-centric masculine identities accepted within numerous working-class communities before as well as after the Second World War.[163] The changing context of acceptability of involved fatherhood within notions of masculinity, and lack of tolerance of entirely distant men, further cemented this home-centric identity within working-class culture. Again, focusing on the relationship between mother and father is important: as Newson and Newson also argued, the mother was often highly regarded in the working-class home, the 'queen' to the father's 'king'.[164] This is a significant point, and it is vital not to fall back on stereotyped visions of a father dominating his household in a brutal and violent way. Though the father could be conceived as superior to the rest of the family, this was frequently not enacted in day-to-day family life. Instead of the mother being an inferior figure, most couples strongly endorsed the complementary nature of their individual roles within the family. This was certainly so in Bott's study of London families in the 1950s.[165]

Though couples differed in their behaviour along the lines of class, and, as Newson and Newson noted, because of the dynamic of the marital relationship and the individual personalities of wife and husband, these differences were exaggerated in many analyses. Whilst some researchers seized upon the conception of the father as 'master', others highlighted how his authority remained complementary to the mother's role. Yet, though there were differences, there were also signs that behaviour was converging around a norm of increasingly shared authority. Whilst the rhetoric both in popular culture and from individuals themselves surrounding the father's status could vary between classes, the shift in terms of the prioritization of children's interests and the involvement of men in family life could be found across various social groups. Frank Davies, a father of one from a working-class area of Salford, for example, discussed how he always put his family first, before his relationships with others, and in this he contrasted himself with his own father, of whom he was afraid.[166] Geordie Todd, furthermore, a fisherman from County Durham, only felt that his family could truly be defined as such after he had returned from the war and built a relationship with his son.[167] Many of these men discussed how they worked hard

---

[162] Newson and Newson, *Patterns*, pp. 216–18.   [163] Lawrence, 'Class', p. 285.
[164] Newson and Newson, *Patterns*, p. 222.   [165] For example, Bott, *Family*, p. 64.
[166] Frank Davies, 'A Man's World', rolls 75–84, 158.
[167] Geordie Todd, 'A Man's World', roll 102, p. 160.

to earn for their family and consequently prioritized the needs of their families over themselves.

To further illustrate this change in the perception of the family hierarchy, a final example of food will be explored. Decisions made regarding who was given the best of the food and, as such, prioritized within the family were of significance in both a practical and a more metaphorical way. As Ann Alston highlights, the importance of food as a signifier can be seen in twentieth-century children's literature: the consumption of meals together round a dinner table as a family was a significant marker of the 'good' family.[168] Indeed, individuals also used the specific example of food in discussing their ideas about power within the family. Numerous interviewees noted that their fathers got the best food, but with it the power to bestow favour on their children through giving them choice titbits from their plates. As Strange notes, the giving of food in times of need or scarcity could also have emotional significance.[169] Esther Peel, born in 1907, told of how her father used to have the only egg, but would give her a toast 'soldier' dipped in the yolk. She added 'But, of course, the husband always had to be fed first.'[170] Others, such as Ted Walker, hinted at the emotional meaning of these treats.[171] Mrs M1P, born 1913, discussed how the family would argue over who got the small portion of sheep's brains, a prized part of the meal:

> Usually it was father, of course, there was only a little tiny portion. If the boys wanted any he would give them a little each. Of course, father was the mainstay and his resistance had to be kept up. You see he was the worker and he had to come first.[172]

Frank Davies, mentioned earlier in this chapter, recalled fathers' entitlement to the best of the food available when he was growing up, as in the interwar period:

> Well me father—all fathers I should say—they were all the same—we used to compare notes as kids, but them being the breadwinner he was entitled to the biggest share of the grub . . . we'd had ours, we'd sit and watch him and you know, hoping he'd leave some and him knowing this of course he'd say D'you want some of this and he'd scrape a bit onto your plate.[173]

Frank's behaviour and attitudes when he was himself a father in the 1950s were quite consciously in contrast to those of his father. Robert Roberts summed up such attitudes in his overview of working-class Salford life in the first quarter of the century, reflecting that even in times of financial hardship, 'What "luxuries"

[168] Alston, *The Family*, pp. 131–2.

[169] Julie-Marie Strange, *Fatherhood and the British Working Class, 1865–1914* (Cambridge, forthcoming 2014), ch. 2.

[170] Esther Peel, quoted in Humphries and Gordon, *A Labour*, pp. 128–9.

[171] Walker, *The High Path*, p. 15. Also see Bullock, *Bowers Row*, p. 6; Robert Morgan, *My Lamp Still Burns* (Llandysul, 1981), p. 17; Phyllis Willmott, *Growing Up in a London Village: Family Life between the Wars* (Halifax, 1979), p. 11.

[172] Mrs M1P, ERA, Preston 1890–1940, p. 26.

[173] Frank Davies, 'A Man's World', roll 76, pp. 28–9. Also see Sean Harold Smith, 'A Man's World', roll 49, pp. 65–6; Mr M10L, ERA, 1940–70, p. 116.

people bought at a corner shop often figured only in the father's diet, and his alone.' However, this prioritizing of men in sharing out protein and sweet foods was 'not usually due to greed or selfishness: a man simply had to store energy against a sudden call to do some casual job'.[174]

Others insisted that children got fed as well as their parents, and this became increasingly common as the period progressed, across all social classes. Mrs B5P, married in the mid-1920s, said that 'The children could eat as much as their dad' if they wanted.[175] Diana Kellard found it difficult to reconcile her recollections of her childhood in the 1930s and 1940s with her mother's, noting 'I can more remember bread and butter and jam type tea and I can remember my dad having a dinner but now my mother says that she didn't do that. She said Ooh no, we'd have all had the same meal.' Diana's mother's recollections hinted at the shifting acceptability of men being entitled to the best food.[176] Indeed, some children like G. A. W. Tomlinson, who grew up in Nottinghamshire in the early decades of the twentieth century, highlighted how their fathers sacrificed their own needs in this sense: 'I cannot forget that many times he went to the pit without a bite of "snap" so that I might have something to eat during the day.'[177] This theme was also present in social research: in the Pilgrim Trust survey of unemployment in the 1930s, it was noted that all families refused to economize on food and clothing for children, 'even in Liverpool'.[178] Furthermore, in Seebohm Rowntree's study of families in York in 1941, participants were asked to keep diaries and budgets relating to their activities. Rowntree found no reference to any man eating differently to his family, indicating both Rowntree's initial assumption and the evidence to the contrary.[179] This finding was replicated in Michael Young and Peter Willmott's study of Essex and London. The father, they stated, 'no longer gets the first pick of everything', and in support of this statement they quoted a Mrs Glass from Bethnal Green as saying 'Now it's the children who get the best of it. If there's one pork chop left, the kiddy gets it.'[180] Newson and Newson also stressed change here: 'It seems no longer the case that father, the breadwinner, has the meat while the children make do with potatoes and gravy', and concluded that infants were fed better now than ever before.[181] This change was underlined during and after the Second World War, when government schemes provided orange juice and extra milk for children, thus serving to demonstrate that their nutritional needs should be prioritized on both an individual and a national level.

---

[174] Robert Roberts, *The Classic Slum*, pp. 80, 85.

[175] Mrs B5P, ERA, Preston 1890–1940, p. 25.

[176] Diana Kellard, Int077, *Families*, UKDA, p. 25.

[177] G. A. W. Tomlinson, *Coal-Miner* (London, c.1937), p. 170.

[178] Pilgrim Trust, *Men without Work: A Report Made to the Pilgrim Trust* (Cambridge, 1938), p. 126.

[179] B. Seebohm Rowntree, *Poverty and Progress: A Second Social Survey of York* (London, 1941), p. 188.

[180] Young and Willmott, *Family and Kinship*, p. 28.

[181] Newson and Newson, *Patterns*, p. 63.

CONCLUSION

Fathers were consequently understood as much more active family members by the end of this period than in previous decades, and their position within the family hierarchy had shifted. However, this change was in tension with more negative conceptions of the father, which reiterated his potentially dangerous side. This tension limited the extent to which the father could be portrayed as a full-fledged family participant, and so the active encouragement of fathers to put their families first and identify themselves with their families, as will be discussed in Chapter 6, was constrained. Fathers also remained ambivalent to family life, with many maintaining a distance and others unwilling to take on more unpleasant responsibilities. Furthermore, certain discourses, such as romantic literature, promoted the idea of men's benign authority as attractive to women.[182] However, even where contradictory, discussions in the press continued to question the father's authority and dominant position in the family hierarchy. In both popular culture and the attitudes of individuals there was a growing belief that this challenge to fathers' status was a positive development, and there was a rejection of the all-powerful Victorian patriarch and the values he symbolized. As Zweig noted, there had been a change in the positioning of the father within the family: 'The father is there to assist and help, to give guidance; but he is no more the master with the big stick.'[183] These developments were not without consequences; in marital relationships, power and responsibility were intertwined, and helping one's spouse manage their own specialist, gendered area of responsibility could also disempower that person.[184] In the case of parenting, this dynamic becomes even more complex. Within the parent–child relationship, in modern society there has always been a necessary imbalance of authority. When considering power between mother, father, and child, there is further complication, as mothers and fathers could hold power over children in different ways. Indeed, in some respects, children could find it easier to develop a positive relationship with the parent who was less powerful in terms of their involvement of the running of family and home, whether that be mother or father.

Differences in social classes are notable here. Though there was a growing assertion of an emerging classlessness, there was also an acceptance that ideas about paternal authority could and did differ between social groups. The working-class father was accepted as a head of the family, to be treated with respect, whilst the middle- or upper-class father was deemed to be more approachable and respectful to the needs of his wife and children. Fletcher suggested that change had occurred in the middle classes too, noting 'The "authoritarian" family of the earlier middle classes has gone, and in its place has developed the small, planned, democratically managed family.'[185] Indeed, further study of testimony has suggested that this

---

[182] King, 'The Perfect Man'.　　　[183] Zweig, *The Worker*, p. 207.

[184] Roberts, *Women and Families*, pp. 84–94; Szreter and Fisher, *Sex*, ch. 5.

[185] Ronald Fletcher, *Britain in the Sixties: The Family and Marriage: An Analysis and Moral Assessment* (Harmondsworth, 1962), p. 110.

may have been more of a rhetorical than behavioural difference in terms of class, with the continued suggestion of working-class men as heads of their families often more a ceremonial conception of position than a determinant of family practices. The final exploration of how food was shared between family members forms one way of tracing this reality more precisely and examining the changes in how family members were situated within a hierarchy of power. More than any other area, the discussion of men's authority within the sphere of family life was riddled with contradictions in both popular culture and individuals' attitudes.

6

Performing Fatherhood and Masculinity: Parenting and Gender Identities

The balance of power and authority within the family was a highly significant aspect of familial dynamics and relationships, and important to the construction of gender identities. For men throughout the nineteenth and twentieth centuries, a degree of authority over but also responsibility towards dependent women and children could be an important milestone towards adult masculine status.[1] Yet the context of how parenting and gender identities were interlinked shifted in this period. In the press at least, it was frequently suggested that the sexes were converging in the first half of the twentieth century.[2] In comparison to later periods, however, the division between men's and women's paid work, labour in the home, and indeed male and female parenting, remained profound. The twentieth century should be seen as one of gradual and not always linear change. Whilst as Lynne Segal posits, gendered divisions of labour within and outside the home remained largely constant,[3] this did not mean that change did not occur. That gender is a relational construct is fundamental to the recent literature on gender history, and research into gender more broadly.[4] Yet the focus on power and the relationship between masculinity and femininity should not obscure change occurring within each gender as well as between the two binaries.

Margaret and Patrice Higonnet's use of a double helix to represent gendered divisions and change in wartime is useful here. Within this double helix, women could take on what were previously male roles, such as working or, in wartime, serving in the Armed Forces, without threatening the status of men whose own position was also elevated.[5] This model is a useful way of conceptualizing change in terms of men's and women's roles and identities without a concurrent shift in

[1] John Tosh, *Manliness and Masculinities in Nineteenth-Century Britain: Essays on Gender, Family and Empire* (Harlow, 2005), pp. 131–3.

[2] Adrian Bingham, *Gender, Modernity, and the Popular Press in Inter-War Britain* (Oxford, 2004), p. 242.

[3] Lynne Segal, *Slow Motion: Changing Masculinities, Changing Men* (3rd edn, Basingstoke, 2007), p. 4.

[4] Joan W. Scott, 'Gender: A Useful Category for Historical Analysis', *American Historical Review* 91:5 (1986), pp. 1053–75.

[5] Margaret R. Higonnet and Patrice L. Higonnet, 'The Double Helix', in M. R. Higonnet, J. Jenson, S. Michel, and M. Collins (eds), *Behind the Lines: Gender and the Two World Wars* (New Haven, CT, and London, 1987), pp. 34–5.

the division between men and women. In the post-Second World War period, there was an initial retreat back along the double helix, but the model still applies. As men's wages rose and they achieved their breadwinner status more readily in a post-war boom, it was acceptable for women to work as well; their earnings were substantially less than those of men and were seen as extra disposable income for the family rather than a central breadwinner wage.[6] The traditional gender order thus remained in place, and though men were increasingly active as fathers, their principal work remained outside the home. Whilst the hierarchical relationship between masculinity and femininity, and men and women, remained, there was also fluctuating and significant change.

The relationship between fatherhood and masculinity was a complex one in this period, as the ideal of the new 'family man' became increasingly prominent along-side other, more traditional, forms of masculine identity.[7] Fatherhood could both prove and threaten manly and masculine ideals. However, as discussed elsewhere, separating out men's involvement in parenting from their position as husbands and relationship to the home itself is crucial. Here, the concept of 'domestic masculinity' has unhelpfully conflated these categories. What this period witnessed was a flourishing of 'family-orientated', rather than domestic, masculinity in both cultural ideals and social practice.[8] The national context in which masculinity was constructed frequently encouraged and reinforced this trend. Normative masculinity was juxtaposed against perceptions of hyper-manliness in other countries, particularly during wartime.[9] In cultural representation, as Martin Francis notes, for RAF men at least, 'the domestic domain remained a critical reference-point in the lives of men, even when they were sequestered from that world' by the practicalities of military service.[10] In victory, the prizing of such qualities continued, and these were highly compatible with involved fatherhood and the characteristics it indicated. A family-orientated construction of masculinity was an important dimension to the focus on happy family life within post-war reconstruction.[11] Men's

---

[6] Dolly Smith-Wilson, 'A New Look at the Affluent Worker: The Good Working Mother in Post-War Britain', *Twentieth Century British History* 17:2 (2006), pp. 225–6; Penny Summerfield, 'Women in Britain since 1945: Companionate Marriage and the Double Burden', in J. Obelkevich and P. Catterall (eds), *Understanding Post-War British Society* (London, 1994), p. 63.

[7] Segal, *Slow Motion*, p. 16.

[8] Laura King, 'Hidden Fathers? The Significance of Fatherhood in Mid-Twentieth-Century Britain', *Contemporary British History* 26:1 (2012), pp. 26–7; Laura King '"Now You See a Great Many Men Pushing Their Pram Proudly": Family-Orientated Masculinity Represented and Experienced in Mid-Twentieth-Century Britain', *Cultural and Social History* 10:4 (2013), p. 600.

[9] R. W. Connell, *Masculinities* (2nd edn, Cambridge, 2005), p. 193; Sonya O. Rose, 'Temperate Heroes: Concepts of Masculinity in Second World War Britain', in S. Dudink, K. Hagemann, and J. Tosh (eds), *Masculinities in Politics and War: Gendering Modern History* (Manchester, 2004), pp. 177, 186.

[10] Martin Francis, *The Flyer: British Culture and the Royal Air Force, 1939–1945* (Oxford and New York, 2008), p. 97.

[11] On the focus on the family in reconstruction, see Angela Davis, 'A Critical Perspective on British Social Surveys and Community Studies and Their Accounts of Married Life c.1945–1970', *Cultural and Social History* 6:1 (2009), pp. 57–8; Janet Fink and Katherine Holden, 'Pictures from the Margins of Marriage: Representations of Spinsters and Single Mothers in the Mid-Victorian Novel, Inter-War Hollywood Melodrama and British Film of the 1950s and 1960s', *Gender and*

return home to their families was often difficult,[12] and, as such, the endorsement of and increased significance placed on involved fatherhood and family-orientated masculinity was used to help the return to 'normality', at least on a discursive level. This was reinforced by powerful cultural institutions such as the Church; as Sue Morgan notes, certain voices within the Church argued that fatherhood was central to men's lives and identities in the interwar periods and beyond.[13] As Stephen Brooke and Lesley Hall have demonstrated, the 1950s were, in many ways, a decade of instability in gender identities, as, for example, a more aggressive masculinity was also celebrated.[14] The mid-twentieth century was thus a crucial moment in the history of masculinity.

PROVING MASCULINITY BY PROVIDING

Fatherhood could both prove and challenge a man's masculine identity and sense of manliness. Some aspects of parenting, such as breadwinning, allowed men to secure adult masculinity, whereas other aspects of fatherhood, such as the intimate care of children, could prove problematic, due to their association with the feminine sphere of family and caring. There was a fine line for men to negotiate, and indeed men performed their masculine identities differently in public and in private. Economic provision was the fundamental core of fatherhood: there was a simple equation between economic provision for a dependent wife and children and fulfilling one's duties 'as a man'.[15] Alongside earning a substantial wage himself, maintaining a full-time housewife and even daughters at home could further prove masculinity in certain communities and amongst the upper and middle classes, though this became less common by the end of this period, as increasing numbers of women worked.[16] There was an assumption that men were the

History 11:2 (1999), p. 237; Martin Francis, 'The Domestication of the Male? Recent Research on Nineteenth- and Twentieth-Century British Masculinity', *Historical Journal* 45:3 (2002), p. 644; Michael Peplar, *Family Matters: A History of Ideas about Family since 1945* (London, 2002), pp. 25–6.

[12] Martin Francis, 'A Flight from Commitment? Domesticity, Adventure and the Masculine Imaginary in Britain after the Second World War', *Gender and History* 19:1 (2007), p. 167.

[13] Sue Morgan, '"Iron Strength and Infinite Tenderness": Herbert Gray and the Making of Christian Masculinities at War and at Home, 1900–1940', in L. Delap and S. Morgan (eds), *Men, Masculinities and Religious Change in Twentieth-Century Britain* (Basingstoke, 2013), p. 188.

[14] Stephen Brooke, 'Gender and Working Class Identity in Britain during the 1950s', *Journal of Social History* 34:4 (2001), pp. 773–95; Lesley Hall, *Sex, Gender and Social Change in Britain since 1880* (Basingstoke, 2000), p. 166.

[15] Connell, *Masculinities*, pp. 28–9; Wally Seccombe, 'Patriarchy Stabilized: The Construction of the Male Breadwinner Wage Norm in Nineteenth-Century Britain', *Social History* 11:1 (1986), pp. 53–75.

[16] Alva Myrdal and Viola Klein, *Women's Two Roles: Home and Work* (London, 1956), pp. 5–6; Jane Lewis, *The Politics of Motherhood: Child and Maternal Welfare in England, 1900–1939* (London, 1980), p. 224; Elizabeth Roberts, *A Woman's Place: An Oral History of Working-Class Women, 1890–1940* (Oxford, 1984), p. 40; Selina Todd, *Young Women, Work, and Family in England 1918–1950* (Oxford, 2005), p. 59.

automatic providers for their families within government policy and thinking.[17] The father and man of this period was also, of course, a worker, and these identities were closely tied together.

Evidence from oral history interviews illustrates this amply. Indeed, though male selfishness was not unusual and some families suffered extreme poverty, as discussed in Chapter 2, only a handful of individuals highlighted explicitly that their fathers or husbands chose not to fulfil this masculine role to at least a basic standard.[18] Mrs O1P, born 1902, referred to the unusual scenario in her family, where her father 'wouldn't work at all. He would say, "I'll look after Matt", he used to call me Matt. She used to give him, my mother used to give him so much money a week to look after me.'[19] Kathleen Musgrave, born 1918, when questioned whether her husband minded her going out to work, responded 'Well I had to dear because unfortunately he was—a drinker. You see. I had quite a hard life with him.'[20] Yet most men saw breadwinning as central to their gendered identities. Mr B1B, for example, born in Barrow-in-Furness in 1897, was asked what he thought made a 'real gentleman', in terms of both his father's generation and his own. He stated, 'I think it was more of the moral line as to how you were as a parent such as he's a good man is Mr X, gives his wife his pay packet', and suggested that a good man 'would rather see that he had something for the children and then go out on Friday night when he gets his pay'.[21] Edith Broadway, who had three children in the 1930s and 1940s, discussed her husband's reluctance to let her work, as he wanted to be the sole breadwinner: 'If the wife went out to work it wasn't the case, he wasn't keeping her, and it went against the grain.'[22] Elizabeth Arnold, born in 1935 and married aged 24, highlighted a similar situation in her marriage, and those in her local community in London, noting that 'Whilst you're at home, the man is the breadwinner. [Women] used to sneak this home work and hide it. But then when he started drinking, I really had to get a job.' Elizabeth's situation shows how the insistence on solely male breadwinning coupled with irresponsibility with the family finances could be particularly problematic.[23]

Yet whilst in most families women remained the principal carers and men the principal wage-earners, some couples questioned the rigidity of the gendered division of labour within and outside the home. John Buck, for example, became a

---

[17] Susan Pedersen, *Family, Dependence, and the Origins of the Welfare State: Britain and France, 1914–1945* (Cambridge and New York, 1993), esp. pp. 341–3.

[18] For example, Mrs H8P, Elizabeth Roberts Archive (ERA), Preston 1890–1940, p. 11; Mrs T5P, ERA, Preston 1890–1940, pp. 13–14; Mr N3L, ERA, 1940–70, p. 25; Jean Bates, Int007, P. Thompson and H. Newby, *Families, Social Mobility and Ageing, an Intergenerational Approach, 1900–1988 [computer file]*. Colchester, Essex: UK Data Archive (UKDA) [distributor], July 2005. SN: 4938, p.10; Pat O'Mara, *The Autobiography of a Liverpool Irish Slummy* (London, 1934), p. 37.

[19] Mrs O1P, ERA, Preston 1890–1940, p. 12.

[20] Kathleen Musgrave, Int096, *Families*, UKDA, p. 19.

[21] Mr B1B, ERA, Barrow/Lancaster 1890–1940, p. 83. Also see George Ryder, 'A Man's World', British Film Institute Archive, roll 134, pp. 43–5; Henry Curd, Int042, *Families*, UKDA, p. 43.

[22] Edith Broadway, quoted in Steve Humphries and Pamela Gordon (eds), *A Labour of Love: The Experience of Parenthood in Britain 1900–1950* (London, 1993), pp. 95–6.

[23] Elizabeth Arnold, Int002, *Families*, UKDA, p. 62.

father right at the end of the period, and noted that he and his wife discussed whether she should start part-time work after having a child in the early 1960s. They agreed, because his wife was 'getting like a cabbage' at home, and they wanted extra disposable income. John noted that 'Some people say a woman's place is at the kitchen sink, and that the husband is the wage earner. I think that's wrong. You're both equal. And that's the reason, because we wanted a car, and we were going to pay cash for this car.'[24] Here, the combination of the questioning of traditional gender roles alongside more practical, consumerist desires led to a different gender balance, for the Buck family at least. The assumed normality of the male-breadwinner model family was also present in almost all social surveys into the family in this period, as researchers subscribed to views prevalent in the societies they studied. In his study of a rural Scottish parish, the sociologist James Littlejohn branded the nuclear family as 'normal', constituting over half of the houses studied.[25] Only some feminists started to question the accepted model. Researching women's dual role in work and home, Alva Myrdal and Viola Klein argued that a greater partnership between men and women was required, as women were contributing to the family budget, and thus men should share the home-making role. They called for a recognition that 'the patriarchal family . . . has outlived its day'.[26]

For many fathers in the 1930s, breadwinning was particularly difficult, and the thousands who suffered long-term unemployment experienced a blow to their sense of manhood. Chapter 2 highlighted the consequences of unemployment for fathers in terms of their breadwinner roles, and Chapter 3 explored the possibilities for greater involvement in other parenting duties. Beyond the practicalities of child-rearing, high unemployment levels had consequences for understanding masculine identity on an individual and national level. Neil Penlington found that, as a means to combat the detrimental effects that unemployment had on manliness, men found alternative means of provision to fulfil this role, such as growing produce on allotments, keeping animals, and procuring coal, often illegally.[27] As Sally Alexander highlights, a worker 'felt less of a man' if he did not have a job, and as Adrian Bingham notes, concerns about manliness were prominent in the interwar press.[28] Such debates were particularly prevalent in the *Manchester Guardian*. An article from 1932, for example, commented upon the 'intolerable position' in an unnamed town where women worked in the 'booming' textile trade, whilst husbands kept the house.[29] An article from 1936 introduced

[24] John Buck, Int022, *Families*, UKDA, pp. 47–8.

[25] James Littlejohn, *Westrigg: The Sociology of a Cheviot Parish* (London, 1963), pp. 25–6.

[26] Myrdal and Klein, *Women's Two Roles*, p. 161.

[27] Neil Penlington, 'Masculinity and Domesticity in 1930s South Wales: Did Unemployment Change the Domestic Division of Labour?', *Twentieth Century British History* 21:3 (2010), pp. 289–93. Also see Sally Alexander, 'Men's Fears and Women's Work: Responses to Unemployment in London between the Wars', *Gender and History* 12:2 (2000), p. 411. For an example of this, see G. A. W. Tomlinson, *Coal-Miner* (London, c.1937), p. 185.

[28] Alexander, 'Men's Fears', pp. 404, 411; Bingham, *Gender*, p. 217.

[29] *Manchester Guardian*, 18 February 1932, p. 6.

a psychological context, suggesting that children blamed their father if he could not get work, causing rifts between parents and children.[30] The shame men felt was demonstrated by a letter published in the *Daily Mirror* in 1938, in which a father apologised to his sons for his inability to be a proper father and provider to them. In it, he described the hopes he had for their futures, which were 'unattainable' now 'Daddy has no job'. The publication of this letter demonstrates a desire to evoke sympathy for unemployed men.[31]

This problem was explored in the novel and film *Love on the Dole* by Walter Greenwood, in which the daughter of the family, Sally Hardcastle, earns money whilst her father and brother are unemployed. The parallel situations of father and son highlight the dire nature of mass unemployment. Mr Hardcastle is desperate because he cannot provide for his family. His son, Harry, is also unable to find work, a plight worsened when he becomes a father. In the film, his landlady summarizes this when she throws him and his wife out, reminding him that he, not his wife, should be providing. Finally, Sally's unwilling romantic and sexual involvement with a local bookmaker, Sam Grundy, leads to employment for her brother and father, further demonstrating how badly men were emasculated by their inability to perform their duty and provide.[32] The setting portrayed in *Love on the Dole* was based on Salford in the 1930s, and indeed the potential power of the film due to its realism was indicated the British Board of Film Censors' ban of the film until 1941, when the effects of mass unemployment had largely been reversed.[33]

Examples of similar situations can be found in contemporary research into unemployment. Men were often unable to find work whilst their wives and daughters could. In a Pilgrim Trust report, this was found to be a particularly important factor influencing men's attitudes to their masculinity. The result of this situation was universally deemed to be unhappiness. In fact, women gave up paid work to improve the 'wild' mental states of their husbands, and men worked for less income than dole money could bring for the sake of their self-esteem.[34] The study also noted that the home remained an important symbol of independence, and indeed earning a wage was explicitly linked with the attainment of self-respect and worth.[35] The authors concluded that the key assumption of Western individualism for the past three and a half centuries had been that a man was responsible for maintaining himself and his family. Unemployment, they contested, was undermining this state of affairs, and in turn, state maintenance meant the unemployed man was 'losing his citizenship'.[36] A similar situation was depicted by E. Wight Bakke in his survey of

---

[30] *Manchester Guardian*, 29 August 1936, p. 10.

[31] *Daily Mirror*, 17 September 1938, p. 9.   [32] *Love on the Dole* (John Baxter, 1941).

[33] Sarah Street, *British Cinema in Documents* (London, 2000), p. 23.

[34] Pilgrim Trust, *Men without Work: A Report Made to the Pilgrim Trust* (Cambridge, 1938), pp. 147, 165–7.

[35] Pilgrim Trust, *Men without Work*, pp. 189, 195.

[36] Pilgrim Trust, *Men without Work*, pp. 199–200. Also see Wal Hannington, *The Problem of the Distressed Areas* (London, 1937), p. 163.

unemployed men in Greenwich, in which he stated, 'practically every man who had a family showed evidence of the blow his self-confidence had suffered from the fact that the traditional head of the family was not able to perform his normal function'.[37]

Whilst it was rare for social researchers in the 1930s to discuss the effects of unemployment on masculinity explicitly, it is possible to gain an understanding of this situation through their use of terms such as 'self-confidence', 'character', 'independence', 'status', and 'citizenship'. These concepts were linked strongly to normative masculinity, and the adverse effect unemployment had on these understandings of self, by the individual and others, clearly had an impact on individuals' masculinity, and vice versa. Indeed, such concerns were also prevalent in the House of Commons. Mr Ellis Smith, MP for Stoke-on-Trent South, contended in 1936 that fathers were walking 'with their heads down' and considering suicide because their children were keeping them.[38] A doctor, writing in Beales and Lambert's collection of men's accounts of unemployment in this period, noted that unemployment not only caused mental illness, but also irreversibly 'undermines the character of the affected individual'.[39] Such difficult circumstances, and the emotions that went with them, were experienced by a small number of those respondents and autobiographers researched for this study. George Short, for example, was a father of two from County Durham. Previously a miner, he was unemployed for most of the 1930s. He discussed the frustration of unemployment for men like him:

> The average man, particularly the men of my class, they always believed that they were the breadwinner and the fact that the wife got a job didn't help, because that helped to take away from the man the sense of importance which was his. I saw people become completely demoralized and their sense of manliness began to deteriorate just because they had not got a job and because they weren't able to provide the things that they believed their family was entitled to.[40]

Mr D2P, who married in the mid-1930s, felt extremely concerned when he was laid off work, and discussed this in terms of the threat it posed to his masculinity: 'The Friday after we were married it snowed quite hard and this put outside workers off work. I was stopped to make room for an older man. I nearly cried, maybe after all we would have to live on my wife's earnings. How unmanly this makes you feel.'[41] Ron Barnes, who was married with one child after the

---

[37] E. Wight Bakke, *The Unemployed Man: A Social Study* (London, 1933), p. 70.

[38] Hansard, HC, vol. 313, cc.1482–1483, 22 June 1936. Also see speeches by Mr Lawson and Mr White, Hansard, HC, vol. 313, cc.1441, 1451, 22 June 1936; speeches by Mr Arthur Greenwood and Mr Mander, Hansard, HC, vol. 315, cc.326, 378–379, 21 July 1936; speech by Mr Maclay, Hansard, HC, vol. 315, c.765, 22 July 1936; speech by Mr Lipson, Hansard, HC, vol. 342, c.3162, 22 December 1938; speech by Mr Greenfell, Hansard, HC, vol. 355, c.1108, 12 December 1939.

[39] Morris Robb, 'The Psychology of the Unemployed from the Medical Point of View', in H. L. Beales and R. S. Lambert (eds) [1934], *Memoirs of the Unemployed* (Wakefield, 1973), p. 274.

[40] George Short, quoted in Steve Humphries and Pamela Gordon (eds), *A Man's World: From Boyhood to Manhood, 1900–1960* (London, 1996), p. 108.

[41] Mr D2P, ERA, Preston 1890–1940 (letter from Mr D2P), p. 50. Also see Mrs A1P, ERA, Preston 1890–1940, pp. 5–6.

Second World War, when employment levels were much higher, experienced a period of six months out of work due to ill health. He took on the housework whilst his wife was employed in a factory, and felt that 'The shortage of money, the reversal of our roles as husband and wife did a lot to damage our marriage.' He added that 'being unemployed is worse than imprisonment', and 'lost status' could become 'apathy'.[42] A 'skilled wire drawer', writing in Beales and Lambert's collection, noted the difficulties he experienced because his wife worked. He explained that 'Our child is still too young to realise that it is her mother who works. We carefully keep her from knowing it', and reflected on his life in gendered terms: 'I do the housework after my wife has left home at half-past seven in the morning, I read, I play with the child, I go out for walks in the evening after my wife has returned at half-past six. Is this a man's life?'[43] Similarly, Kenneth Maher of Caerphilly recalled an incident where one unemployed man reacted violently against an under-manager, explaining 'I can't be a man to put up with this.'[44] Whether men were active fathers or not, their loss of status as a provider for dependents was felt and understood to be very damaging.

As noted in Chapter 3, despite the difficulties presented by unemployment, some men welcomed the opportunity to develop more intense relationships with their children.[45] Unemployment was thus a point at which the relationship between fatherhood and masculinity was brought into focus. The possibilities for a more active fatherhood were there, but by taking such opportunities, a man's masculinity, already compromised by lack of status as a breadwinner, could be seriously threatened. For men like Phyllis Willmott's father, unemployment did not change their understanding of what it was appropriate for men to do within the home. She noted that 'However long the weeks off work dragged on, Dad did not expect to be asked to help with household chores. Not even when Mum, desperate and against his wishes, took on a morning charring job.' There were some small tasks that were permissible in terms of childcare, such as mending the children's shoes and cutting their hair, as these were 'jobs which were appropriate for men'. Furthermore, Phyllis highlighted that their father's lack of work was positive for the children, as he would stay at home more, listening to the wireless and playing games with them.[46] Unemployment brought about a situation in which a choice between either fatherhood and masculinity could be made, on both a national and an individual level.

---

[42] Ron Barnes, *Coronation Cups and Jam Jars* (London, 1976), p. 195. Also see A Colliery Banksmen, 'Frustration and Bitterness', in Beales and Lambert, *Memoirs*, p. 91.

[43] A Skilled Wire Drawer, 'The Wife Works While I Look after the Home', in Beales and Lambert, *Memoirs*, p. 180.

[44] Kenneth Maher, 'Caerphilly', in Nigel Gray (ed.), *The Worst of Times: An Oral History of the Great Depression in Britain* (London, 1985), p. 33.

[45] For example George Short, quoted in Humphries and Gordon, *A Man's World*, pp. 108, 182; Robert Williamson, 'A Labour of Love', British Library, roll 157, p. 10.

[46] Phyllis Willmott, *Growing Up in a London Village: Family Life between the Wars* (Halifax, 1979), pp. 144–5.

THE IDENTITIES OF FATHERHOOD
IN PRIVATE AND PUBLIC

As breadwinners, men also acted as mediators between the outside world and the relative privacy of the home. Part of this public-facing masculine identity was the idea of protecting women and children. As Tosh notes of the latter half of the nineteenth century, protection of dependents from the outside world could operate in both a literal and figurative sense, a notable example of which was the defence of daughters' virginity.[47] This notion of a father as a figurative protector remained important to masculinity in the twentieth century, and whilst it was perhaps less prominent in discussions about fatherhood, the idea of protecting the virtue of one's daughters remained. In Mary Moran's account of her family life in Luton in the 1950s onwards, fatherly protection was explicitly linked to affection; she felt that her daughters were somewhat closer than her sons to their stepfather 'because in a way he protected the girls, you know, if anyone did anything wrong to the girls, he was there'.[48] Throughout the whole period, there were numerous accounts of fathers acting more protectively to daughters than sons; this sort of protectiveness invoked both positive and negative reactions from the daughters themselves.[49]

The idea of fathers as protectors was not a particularly dominant theme in press discussions of fatherhood, though some advertisers capitalized on this idea. Lifebuoy soap positioned the father as a protector of health in advertising their soaps,[50] whilst the wool company Chilprufe highlighted the idea that father should insist on their products for his offspring, adding 'Family protection is his life's work'.[51] The NSPCC, likewise, made an appeal for orphaned children in 1941 on the basis that they had lost 'daddy's protection'.[52] Similarly, advertising for life insurance in the *Manchester Guardian* in 1954 emphasized the need to assure fathers' protection for the future.[53] Here, provision and protection were inextricably intertwined. By the end of the period, there are hints that the term 'protective' became imbued with more negative connotations. In a report of a court case in the *Daily Mirror* in 1955, for example, the presiding judge reprimanded the father involved for his overprotectiveness towards his daughter. The judge was reported as advising 'Let the girl seek her own way in the world. We can guard our lambs too much.'[54]

---

[47] John Tosh, *A Man's Place: Masculinity and the Middle-Class Home in Victorian England* (New Haven, CT, and London, 1999), pp. 85–6.

[48] Mary Moran, Int092, *Families*, UKDA, p. 61. Also see Julie-Marie Strange, 'Fatherhood, Providing, and Attachment in Late Victorian and Edwardian Working-Class Families', *Historical Journal* 55:4 (2012), p. 1021.

[49] For example, Mrs B2P, ERA, Preston 1890–1940, p. 28; Mrs B10P, ERA, 1940–70, p. 28; Mrs E2P, ERA, 1940–70, p. 18; Mrs H5L, ERA, 1940–70, pp. 29–31; Mrs L5B, ERA, 1940–70, p. 29.

[50] *Manchester Guardian*, 10 February 1926, p. 6; *Daily Mirror*, 12 February 1926, p. 12; *Daily Mirror*, 27 September 1927, p. 16.

[51] *The Times*, 21 November 1938, p. 15.   [52] *The Times*, 11 December 1941, p. 7.

[53] *Manchester Guardian*, 19 January 1954, p. 11.

[54] *Daily Mirror*, 18 January 1955, p. 6.

Yet both world wars brought this conception of masculine identity to the fore, and protection of families and the country at large were often strongly linked. Numerous articles in the press suggested that, in order to achieve a normative masculinity, men should be protecting their families, and to do this, men should be fighting for their country. This was, of course, a convenient way of encouraging the enlistment of married men. A debate in the *Daily Mirror* in June 1915 reflected wider concerns about whether married men should fight; there was much disagreement on this point. Whilst some accused those signing up of being selfish,[55] other letter-writers linked men's choice to fight with their position as family protector. 'Married, Not Engaged' wrote that men should embrace 'fighting for [women's] honour, which to a woman and to all men, excepting Huns, is the most sacred thing on God's earth'.[56] The same debates about whether men should stay with their families in order to fulfil their duties as father or fight for their country were also prominent in the press in the Second World War. In August 1944, for example, agony aunt Ann Tower commented on a letter she had received from a widowed serviceman, who had two sons. He had chosen to enlist when the war broke out, despite his age, and ensured his sons were happily living with their grandmother and were adequately provided for. Yet this man also worried that he was 'failing in my love for my children' and had been criticized by others for leaving his family. Tower neatly reconnected good fatherhood with active military service, stating 'No man who had so strong a sense of duty towards his country could possibly fail in his responsibilities as a father.'[57] In this sense, protecting family and country were rendered one and the same, and Tower situated good citizenship as intimately connected with good fatherhood.

Newspapers also seized on the potential for human-interest stories created by men's departure overseas, and the soldier was frequently coupled with a baby or child, underlining reasons for fighting.[58] An article from the *Daily Mirror* in March 1940 pictured a soldier saying goodbye to his young baby, under the head-line 'Cheerio, Old Son'. The caption explained that 'he hopes (and we hope) [the war] will ensure that the future of his son shall be set in the quiet pastures of peace and liberty'.[59] Advertising for war savings also tapped into ideas about male protection of their families. Adverts addressing fathers underlined the risk of being 'too casual' about the potential for invasion, and noted that 'Money is wanted to remove that risk from our womenfolk and youngsters.'[60] Another advert encouraging saving featured a sketch of a soldier greeting his family, Mother, Sheila, and Peter, on embarkation leave, plus a short poem which ended with the lines 'Dad is going to fight for England/ For a world where men are free/ Better times for all but—mostly/ He'll be fighting for these three.'[61] The connection between

[55] *Daily Mirror*, 11 June 1915, p. 5; *Daily Mirror*, 17 June 1915, p. 5.
[56] *Daily Mirror*, 7 June 1915, p. 7.   [57] *Daily Mirror*, 29 August 1944, p. 7.
[58] Laura King, 'The Perfect Man: Fatherhood, Masculinity and Romance in Popular Culture in Mid-Twentieth-Century Britain', in Alana Harris and Timothy Jones (eds), *Love and Romance in Britain, 1918–1970* (Basingstoke, forthcoming 2014).
[59] *Daily Mirror*, 1 March 1940, p. 3.
[60] *The Observer*, 8 March 1942, p. 2. Also see *Manchester Guardian*, 3 March 1942, p. 1.
[61] *Manchester Guardian*, 15 March 1944, p. 3.

protection for country and family also continued in other contexts. In the *Daily Mirror* in 1950, journalist Claud Morris discussed his feelings about the Korean War through the prism of fatherhood. He noted that he had fought in the Second World War to help achieve peace, and for 'A chance to live and breathe and plan and have kids', and his stake in the current war was 'a seven-week-old son named William. A gurgling baby, just beginning to give his first few smiles, and look at the world I've introduced him to.'[62] As an identity, fatherhood was not only connected closely with masculinity, but also (male) citizenship; fighting for family, home, and nation were closely connected and fatherhood could symbolize a greater stake in the nation's future and welfare.

A small number of individual testimonies reflected this same reasoning. For some, like Mr B1B, the experience of warfare was instrumental in achieving full masculine status.[63] C. Jones, writing to his wife during the First World War, noted that:

Each day that passes without you is so much happiness missed that can never be regained a loss I should regret my beloved were I not satisfied that my duty to you requires my presence on this side. I have no sympathy even now with the young married men who hide behind their wives skirts [sic] and protest that single men should go first. If a woman is worth having she is worth fighting for. What do you say?[64]

Mr D2P, furthermore, discussed his decision to volunteer to fight in the Second World War. He recalled his feelings at the time:

Why had I volunteered? Could I live without my wife and son? But the War I would fight in would save my son. We would see that there would be no more wars and the Germans would never be allowed to arm again. So, for David's sake it would be worth it. God bless him I thought.[65]

This way of thinking about fighting was not, however, particularly prominent in the sample of letters between serving men and their families, apart from Jones' letter to his wife, just quoted; the idea of masculinity as based around protecting one's family and country was arguably a public construction that gave way to more personal sentiments in private letters.

Throughout this period, men were increasingly publicly identified as fathers, and fatherhood became a primary part of men's identities, as imposed on them by others and as defined by themselves. A desirable version of masculinity was consistently promoted in the press through the image of the 'family man', and was used to articulate positive versions of masculinity by individuals as well. Segal highlights the prominence of this identity in the 1950s, alongside that of the 'old wartime hero', as the two opposed faces of masculinity in this period.[66] It

---

[62] *Daily Mirror*, 11 July 1950, p. 2.

[63] Mr B1B, ERA, Barrow/Lancaster 1890–1940, p. 89.

[64] Private Papers of C. Jones, Imperial War Museum Archive (IWMA), Documents.11085, p. 305.

[65] Mr D2P, ERA, Preston 1890–1940 (letter from Mr D2P), p. 64. Also see William Woodruff [2003], *Beyond Nab End* (London, 2008), p. 300.

[66] Segal, *Slow Motion*, p. 16.

is unclear why these two forms of masculinity are considered to be 'opposed', as much evidence linked the wartime hero to the family by stressing that men were fighting for families across Britain, and that men's reward when they returned was to enjoy family life.[67] However the two identities were linked, it must be remembered that both could have been, and were, present in individual constructions of masculine identity. Indeed, the idea of the 'family man' was extremely important to understandings of masculinity in the post-war period, but, as yet, this concept has not been interrogated or researched in any meaningful way.[68]

Indeed, the idea of the 'family man' as a positive identity was used to structure quizzes for men. A quiz in the *Daily Mirror* in January 1945 presented an easy possibility of defining oneself as such, and, in its scoring of men into different categories, it reaffirmed the idea that women would positively want to marry a 'family man'.[69] This image was also frequently drawn upon in readers' letters; identifying themselves as family men could support an argument and induce sympathy. In *The Times* in 1927, for example, a letter was published from 'A Family Man', who started the letter attacking unfair death duties: 'My case is typical of that of many thousands of family men who have worked hard.'[70] In a different context, in the *Daily Mirror* in 1946, this status was again used to reinforce authority. A 'Men Talking' section reproduced the discussion of a disobedient child by a group of men in a pub, and the wisest words came from 'Pat, who's a family man'.[71] This piece also demonstrates the acceptability of fatherhood within normative masculinity in this newspaper by depicting men discussing the problems that dads could face in traditionally masculine space of the pub: a clear message that open discussion about fatherhood between men was promoted. Finally, this identity was also associated with celebrity fathers: in the *Daily Express* in 1953, a photograph was published of Ted Ray, the comedian, watching his son in a military parade. The accompanying article told readers that he was present 'as a family man and distinctly proud father'.[72] Likewise, the *Daily Mirror* in 1955 featured a large photograph and story about Burt Lancaster taking his family to the circus, under the headline 'A family man takes his children for a "treat"'.[73]

Several oral history interviewees also drew on this positive discourse. Mrs H6L, born 1933, discussed her 'marvellous father', who was a 'real family man', enjoying time with his young family before the Second World War. Unfortunately, this changed as her mother and father grew apart in the wake of war and the changes it had brought upon them.[74] Geordie Todd, a fisherman from North Shields, spoke extensively of his delight on becoming a father during the war.

---

[67] See, for example, Francis' analysis of RAF men. Francis, *The Flyer*, e.g. p. 85

[68] Francis, 'The Domestication', p. 645; Francis, 'A Flight', p. 164; Segal, *Slow Motion*, p. 16.

[69] *Daily Mirror*, 11 January 1945, p. 7. Also see *Daily Mirror*, 16 March 1956, p. 9. For a lengthier discussion of this and other quizzes, see King, 'Hidden Fathers', p. 30.

[70] *The Times*, 15 October 1927, p. 13.   [71] *Daily Mirror*, 7 January 1946, p. 2.

[72] *Daily Express*, 5 December 1953, p. 5.

[73] *Daily Mirror*, 10 September 1955, p. 9. For a lengthier discussion of celebrity fathers, see King, 'The Perfect Man'.

[74] Mrs H6L, ERA, 1940–70, pp. 20–1.

He stated, 'Well I was a family man and my wife and I wanted a family.'[75] This construction indicates the growing use of 'family man' as a chosen identity rather than a description of whether one had children or not. Mr Knight, born 1946, portrayed this as an 'ordinary' but stable identity, noting that he thought he had ended up as an 'ordinary family man', something of which his mother approved.[76] The identity of a 'family man' was understood to be positive in both representation and experience. Indeed, the identities associated with fatherhood most commonly in the first part of the twentieth century and earlier, such as provider or protector, were 'inward-looking'; in other words, provision and protection were about negotiating the line between the outside world and the private space of the family. Yet the newly prominent identity of the 'family man' was constructed the other way round and was more 'outward-looking'; the private space of the family came first, and a man's status in terms of family life helped define his identity in a more public sphere.

MASCULINE STATUS: VIRILITY, PATERNITY, AND SEXUALITY

Fatherhood also contributed to the achievement of masculinity in other ways. Being head of a family could enhance status. Additionally, adult children, and especially sons, could reflect well on a man, providing a legacy and continuing a family name. Sons were even understood as a sort of 'other self' for men, and their achievements could add to or make up for fathers' lack thereof. Tosh suggests this was particularly important amongst the middle classes in the nineteenth century. Fatherhood provided the 'ultimate demonstration of virility', with sons providing 'symbolic immortality', whilst husbands without children suffered a 'loss of masculine status'.[77] This view certainly continued into the twentieth century. Christine Heward found that a fundamental aspect of the relationship between father and son was that of model/imitator, and many sons studied followed their fathers' career paths.[78] Further, with regard to the early part of the twentieth century, Frank Mort identifies the conception of fatherhood as central to masculinity in the views of eugenicists, youth leaders, and other experts and officials, who believed to remain without children was 'unmanly', as it broke the 'patriarchal chain'.[79] This trend became less significant in the middle decades of the twentieth century, as the ethos of individuality

---

[75] Geordie Todd, 'A Man's World', roll 100, p. 130. Also see Robert Williamson, 'A Labour of Love', roll 160, p. 34.

[76] Mr Knight, Int079, *Families*, UKDA, p. 5.

[77] Tosh, *A Man's Place*, pp. 80, 114–5; Tosh, *Manliness*, pp. 131–3.

[78] Christine Heward, 'Like Father, Like Son: Parental Models and Influences in the Making of Masculinity at an English Public School, 1929–1950', *Women's Studies International Forum* 13:1/2 (1990), p. 146.

[79] Frank Mort, *Dangerous Sexualities: Medico-Moral Politics in England since 1830* (2nd edn, London, 2000), p. 153.

and emphasis on the child's personality became more prominent. Sons were less likely to follow their fathers' career paths in most circumstances. However, this conception of children as a credit to their fathers in particular, though to mothers too, remained strong, reinforced by historical tradition and growing ambitions for children in general terms.

This idea is central to Warwick Deeping's *Sorrell and Son*. A focal question in the book is whether Sorrell's desire to see his son, Christopher, succeed is inherently selfish. The timing of Sorrell's death, when his son has become a successful doctor and has married, testifies to the fact that Christopher's well-being is Sorrell's one aim, and that he has largely lived through his son. This is further illustrated by the fact that Sorrell does not seek medical treatment, accepting his fate: he has nothing left to strive for now Christopher has achieved all that Sorrell deems necessary in life.[80] The traditional idea of sons as an 'other self' was reflected by its frequent appearance in *Men Only*, a magazine with a rather conservative perspective on masculinity.[81] An article from 1945, for example, on the topic of boxing, suggested that a father felt the same highs and lows as the son who was actually experiencing the fight.[82] In an article about cricket, entitled 'Fathers and Sons', the author noted that fathers whose sons also became cricketers must be 'greatly gratified', whilst those sons who followed their fathers' cricketing careers were demonstrating their adoration.[83] However, the individuality of children was seen to be of great importance, even before the Second World War. In an article of 1936, the author recognized a change in fathers' approach to the individuality of children, arguing that parents who forced sons to follow in their footsteps were in the wrong, and that since the war, fathers had become more sensible.[84]

Such debates were also present in newspapers, which reinforced the connection between virility and masculinity. A front-page story of the *Daily Mirror* in 1958, for example, featured an exceptionally old father. The headline read 'The twins' proud dad—age 86' and the first line of the article reinforced this sentiment: 'DAVID RAMSAY, aged EIGHTY-SIX, was a proud man as he bounced two baby girls on his knees yesterday . . . proud because the girls are TWINS, and David is their FATHER.'[85] The press also focused on the significance of naming children. An article in the *Daily Mirror* in 1919 explored this theme from a father's point of view. The author used an anecdote about two parents-to-be to discuss whether father or mother should have the privilege of choosing the baby's name. In this story, the mother had assumed she would choose it if the child were a boy and her husband would select a name for a daughter. However, her husband objected: 'to a man the name of his son is of much greater importance than his

[80] Warwick Deeping [1925], *Sorrell and Son* (Harmondsworth, 1984).

[81] Jill Greenfield, Sean O'Connell, and Chris Reid, 'Fashioning Masculinity: *Men Only*, Consumption and the Development of Marketing in the 1930s', *Twentieth Century British History* 10:4 (1999), p. 458.

[82] *Men Only* 30:118, September 1945, pp. 61–2.

[83] *Men Only* 41:164, August 1949, p. 46.   [84] *Men Only* 1:4, March 1936, pp. 9–12.

[85] *Daily Mirror*, 24 March 1958, p. 1. Original emphasis.

daughter's'. The author supported the father's perspective: 'there is something fine about handing down a treasured name from father to son, even if it is only John Smith'.[86]

The continuation of the family surname was very important to many men, and indeed, as some of the oral history interviews demonstrate, sons felt this pressure. Nelson Fowler was a farmer from Devon, born in 1904. He had three sisters but no brothers, and as such, took over the family farm from his father in 1939. When asked about carrying on the family name, Nelson stated that his father wanted a grandson: 'he'd say ah, I 'ope you have a boy, he said, I hope you have a son'.[87] This was also the tradition in the rural Scottish borders; shepherd Andrew Purves described in his autobiography how he 'was named after my grandfather, in the time-honoured fashion followed by most Scots families'.[88] Another interviewee, Tony Kildwick, born to a relatively wealthy Yorkshire family in the 1920s, high-lighted the pressure to continue the family name. As he was homosexual, this was not a welcome prospect, but he simply assumed that he would have a family. Describing his attitudes to marriage when he was a young man, he thought, 'I shall do my duty and become a father.'[89] The importance attributed to names, however, was also being questioned through this period. In their study of Bethnal Green and an Essex housing estate in 1957, Michael Young and Peter Willmott found a much greater variety of names given to children than previously. A new mass media had 'created new aspirations and new ideals' and so the names most commonly given to children, they stated, were 'unknown to ancestors christened before the dawn of Hollywood'.[90]

The elevated status of fatherhood shifted in this period, with a decline in the perception of sons as an 'other self' of the father, and a decrease in the trend of naming children after their parents. However, the credit that children could bring to their parents continued. Additionally, parenthood, and particularly father-hood, was used as a legitimating tool when putting forward an argument. Already by the nineteenth century, as Siân Pooley has shown in her study of Burnley in the late nineteenth and early twentieth centuries, men and women used their parental status to increase the power of what they were saying in the local press, signing letters as fathers or mothers.[91] This practice was also in evidence in the national newspapers researched here. In *The Times*, for example, a letter was pub-lished in 1920 from a 'Father of Three', whose status as a father was used to give greater weight to his views on the situation regarding India.[92] In contributing to an ongoing debate about grammar school places in the *Manchester Guardian* in

---

[86] *Daily Mirror*, 9 July 1919, p. 7.

[87] Nelson Fowler, 'A Man's World', roll 141, p. 10.

[88] Andrew Purves, *A Shepherd Remembers: Reminiscences of a Border Shepherd* (East Lothian, 2001), p. 8.

[89] Tony Kildwick, quoted in Humphries and Gordon, *A Man's World*, pp. 162–3.

[90] Michael Young and Peter Willmott [1957], *Family and Kinship in East London* (Harmondsworth, 1967), p. 25.

[91] Siân K. Pooley, 'Parenthood and Child-Rearing in England, c.1860–1910', PhD Thesis (University of Cambridge, 2009), pp. 254–5.

[92] *The Times*, 7 April 1920, p. 9.

1945, a headmaster identified himself as a father before specifying his occupation, starting the letter 'As a father of three and a headmaster' and signing the letter 'Parent-cum-teacher'.[93] Whilst parental status was often pertinent to the debate, on education or state family policy, for instance, it was frequently invoked to support a stance on some quite different and more general issue, relating to world politics or foreign policy. This was certainly the case in the article by Claud Morris on the Korean War, discussed earlier in this chapter; his fatherhood was used to give his opinions on the war greater authority.[94]

For numerous interviewees and autobiographers, there was a clear connection between virility and paternity, and demonstrating manliness. Being sexually active was an important aspect of adult manliness. This connection between masculinity and sexuality was demonstrated in a doctor's essay in Beales and Lambert's collection. The writer discussed how unemployment could become emasculating, in that men might initially be more interested in sexual activity because of their lack of occupation, but 'As the feeling of insecurity grows, it encroaches on sexual function, leading to fear of sexual congress and relative or complete impotence.' Alternatively, sex could provide an outlet for the expression of 'compensatory phantasies' around hate and power.[95] Indeed, some autobiographers even highlighted how aware they were of their father's sexuality. Edward Blishen, a writer born in 1920 to a middle-class family, noted the inherent contradiction in his father's identity: 'The curious thing—and I'd felt the oppression of it very strongly, as a boy—was that the force of his sexuality was matched only by the dreadful negative power of his official puritanism.' Indeed, his father had another child outside marriage, and though he paid a paternity order, he denied his other son's existence altogether.[96] For some, producing children, rather than sexual activity in itself, was a significant marker of masculinity. Jim Bullock, born 1903, recollected the definite ideas around virility and masculinity in the mining village of Bowers Row in Yorkshire. He described:

> The first child was conceived as soon as was decently possible, for the young husband had to prove his manhood. If a year passed without a child—or the outward sign of one being on the way—this man was taunted by his mates both at work and on the street corner by such cruel remarks.[97]

Furthermore, he was expected to share in his wife's physical symptoms of pregnancy, experiencing morning sickness, toothache, and so on, and 'Men were supposed to lose weight in ratio to the women gaining it.' If this was not the case, it

---

[93] *Manchester Guardian*, 30 July 1945, p. 4. Also see *Daily Mirror*, 17 March 1936, p. 11; *Daily Mirror*, 10 September 1959, p. 11.

[94] *Daily Mirror*, 11 July 1950, p. 2.

[95] Morris Robb, 'The Psychology', *Memoirs*, p. 277.

[96] Edward Blishen, *Shaky Relations: An Autobiography* (London, 1981), pp. 30, 117. For an earlier example, also see William Bowyer, *Brought Out in Evidence: An Autobiographical Summing Up* (London, 1941), p. 110.

[97] Jim Bullock, *Bowers Row: Recollections of a Mining Village* (Wakefield, 1976), pp. 62–3.

was assumed that 'either he did not love her, or he was unfaithful, or he could be guilty of both'.[98]

Likewise, A. H. Wright wrote to his wife in June 1944 about his joy at their new baby, noting that those he was serving with were impressed at his achievements: 'When I tell them it weighed 9¼ lbs. they are amazed and laugh and congratulate me all round.' Yet writing in April 1945, he was also keen to distance himself from older patriarchal ideals: 'when talking of Gillian to others, I always say "*my* daughter", but hasten to say not in the sense that some fathers use as if to imply their wives are merely an instrument of production'.[99] For Mary Siddall's husband, conception was where his duties as a father largely ended. She noted that they argued about how little he helped her with their ten children, born between 1921 and 1944, stating 'He says, well I, you know I'm not like that, you see, I can't, not like people taking the babies in prams, he says. I weren't born to be like that. I said, no you were born to make em.'[100] Mathew Meret, discussing becoming a father in the late 1950s, also described his feelings on learning he was going to become a father. In describing his reaction, he drew on a gendered discourse: 'Oh—great. Yeah—fantastic. A typical chauvinist. Met with various comments from work, like. People I knew, you know. Very good friends. Like You dozy bugger and things like that. But other than that.'[101] Ron Barnes, born in the mid-1930s, also highlighted another connection between masculinity, virility, and sexuality in discussing his wife's first pregnancy, in his autobiography. He noted: 'It's strange how women seem to look more attractive when they are carrying.'[102]

During both world wars, conceptions of masculinity were brought into focus, and the connection between masculinity, sexuality, and paternity was scrutinized.[103] There was widespread concern about sexual promiscuity, and throughout both wars, fears that men were fathering children with women to whom they were not married.[104] As Nicole Crockett and Penny Summerfield, and Sonya Rose, point out, such concerns were heavily gendered and full of double standards, with women understood to be responsible for the preservation of

---

[98] Bullock, *Bowers Row*, pp. 63–4.

[99] Private Papers of A. H. Wright, IWMA, Documents.13285, letters dated 5 June 1944, 22 April 1945.

[100] Mary Siddall, 'A Labour of Love', roll 42, p. 22.

[101] Mathew Meret, Int089, *Families*, UKDA, p. 65.

[102] Barnes, *Coronation Cups*, p. 177.

[103] For a more extensive discussion of masculinity and war, see John Horne, 'Masculinity in Politics and War in the Age of Nation-States and World Wars, 1850–1950', in Dudink, Hagemann, and Tosh (eds), *Masculinities*, pp. 22–40.

[104] Hall, *Sex, Gender*, pp. 92–5; Antonia Lant, 'Prologue: Mobile Femininity', in Christine Gledhill and Gillian Swanson (eds), *Nationalising Femininity: Culture, Sexuality and British Cinema in the Second World War* (Manchester, 1996), pp. 19–20; Roy Porter and Lesley Hall, *The Facts of Life: The Creation of Sexual Knowledge in Britain, 1650–1950* (New Haven, CT, and London, 1995), p. 208; Sonya O. Rose, 'Sex, Citizenship, and the Nation in World War II Britain', *American Historical Review* 103:4 (1998), pp. 1147, 1164–5; Sally Sokoloff, '"How Are They at Home?" Community, State, and Servicemen's Wives in England, 1939–45', *Women's History Review* 8:1 (1999), pp. 28, 34, 39.

sexual morality, on an individual level and in terms of the nation as a whole.[105] Indeed, whilst the association of femininity and sexuality could be morally problematic, there was less concern about male sexual activity during the Second World War, which was seen as more acceptable within a masculine gendered identity. Indeed, men were provided with condoms when they were sent abroad on service.[106] As Sally Sokoloff points out, older ideas about sex and marriage did not by any means fall by the wayside, and indeed extramarital affairs could be covered up, with 'illegitimate' children being passed off as the husband's offspring.[107] Some remembered this situation in more positive or even nostalgic terms; W. H. Barrett, for example, in his autobiography, recalled the fun had by some in the First World War: 'Married women, being off the chain since they had freedom while their husbands were away, mothered a lot of lonely soldiers stationed near by; these soldiers, in turn, fathered a lot of kids and everyone was merry and bright.'[108] Indeed, in some places, such as Warcop, a village in Cumbria where Edward Short grew up, there was not as much stigma around illegitimacy as might have been expected; he noted that 'Three of my best friends were without fathers.'[109] In other areas, such as the Scottish borders as described in Andrew Purves' autobiography, in the interwar period, 'Unmarried mothers were sorely looked down upon', with a rapid marriage before the birth largely resolving the issue and a paternity order providing some restitution but leaving the young mother with the 'stigma of single parenthood'.[110] However, during both wars and in peacetime, it is nigh on impossible to get any but the vaguest impression of how common paternity outside marriage actually was.[111]

Whilst sexuality and the potential for 'illegitimate' children were brought into focus during both world wars, there was a longer tradition of associating the achievement of adult masculinity not only with sexual activity but also with producing children. The relationship between masculinity, sexuality, and parenting fluctuated throughout this period. Sexual activity remained one way of demonstrating masculinity, but as Helen Smith has demonstrated, at least amongst working-class communities, heterosexual virility was only one of numerous ways in which manliness could be proved.[112] Whilst the growth in ideas of family limitation and the slow increase in use of birth control did change the context of having children in this period, particularly by the 1950s, sexual intercourse and

---

[105] Penny Summerfield and Nicole Crockett, '"You Weren't Taught That with the Welding": Lessons in Sexuality in the Second World War', *Women's History Review* 1:3 (1992), p. 435; Sonya O. Rose, *Which People's War? National Identity and Citizenship in Wartime Britain 1939–1945* (Oxford, 2003), pp. 118–19.

[106] Rose, *Which People's War?*, p. 119.   [107] Sokoloff, 'How Are They', p. 34.

[108] W. H. Barrett, *A Fenman's Story* (London, 1965), p. 32.

[109] Edward Short, *I Knew My Place* (London, 1983), p. 134.

[110] Purves, *A Shepherd*, pp. 242–3.

[111] Alan Allport, *Demobbed: Coming Home after the Second World War* (New Haven, CT, and London, 2009), pp. 93–4.

[112] Helen Smith, 'A Study of Working-Class Men Who Desired Other Men in the North of England, c.1895–1957', PhD Thesis (University of Sheffield, 2013), p. 234.

fertility remained strongly related.[113] There was a substantial increase in the numbers of couples using birth control, and family size fell throughout the first half of the twentieth century.[114] Indeed, for many women, relative sexual abstinence on the part of their husbands was prized, certainly in the earlier part of the period in question.[115] Marcus Collins argues that it was in the 1960s and 1970s that masculinity and sexuality became more closely connected in an age of greater permissiveness. Indeed, change throughout this period and beyond was by no means linear, and male dominance was reasserted following the war.[116] Yet sex, marriage, and parenting remained culturally almost inseparable, even if they were no longer necessarily linked because of the spread of information and technologies of birth control.

Many interviewees discussed their desire to have children, and the reasons behind this. As in interviews conducted for Fisher's project, a large proportion of parents were apparently unlikely to discuss family planning explicitly or at length with each other when embarking on married life, and men were as much or more involved in birth control as women.[117] For example, Frank Jonston, a factory worker who had his first child in 1959, described in the course of the interview how he and his wife had discussed starting a family. Initially, he stated that they 'didn't plan children when we first got married', then added that they simply expected children, noting 'When we were first married, children—we thought that would come.' Yet both husband and wife were keen to stress that 'They weren't mistakes.'[118] Edward and Jean Winn talked about planning their family in a similar way. They clearly gave some thought to having children, noting that they did not want to have an only child, but there was not any clear discussion of limiting the family size. Jean reflected on how things had changed since they married in 1942: 'It's awfully difficult to go back to those days from modern times, you know, everything's out in the open nowadays, you didn't even talk about things then so much, I don't suppose.'[119] Furthermore, some interviewees also alluded to the greater knowledge and responsibility of men for birth control and reproduction, as again found by Fisher.[120] Mrs B1P, born in 1900, described how her husband had to explain the mechanics of birth to her when she went into labour, though such ignorance was becoming less common as the period progressed.[121]

---

[113] Hera Cook, 'Demography', in H. G. Cocks and Matt Houlbrook (eds), *Palgrave Advances in the Modern History of Sexuality* (Basingstoke, 2006), p. 25; Hall, *Sex, Gender*, pp. 152, 156.

[114] Kate Fisher, *Birth Control, Sex and Marriage in Britain 1918–1960* (Oxford, 2006), p. 1.

[115] Ross McKibbin, *Classes and Cultures: England 1918–1951* (Oxford, 1998), pp. 297–8. Also see John M. Mogey, *Family and Neighbourhood: Two Studies in Oxford* (Oxford, 1956), p. 62.

[116] Hera Cook, *The Long Sexual Revolution: English Women, Sex, and Contraception, 1800–1975* (Oxford, 2004), pp. 184–5. Also see King, 'The Perfect Man'.

[117] Fisher, *Birth Control*, pp. 7–8, 12.

[118] Frank Jonston, Int076, *Families*, UKDA, p. 30.

[119] Edward/Jean Winn, Int159, *Families*, UKDA, p. 20.

[120] Kate Fisher, 'Uncertain Aims and Tacit Negotiation: Birth Control Practices in Britain, 1925–50', *Population and Development Review* 26:2 (2000), pp. 309–11.

[121] Mrs B1P, ERA, Preston 1890–1940, p. 46. Elizabeth Roberts, *Women and Families: An Oral History, 1940–1970* (Oxford, 1995), p. 59.

Lily Wells, for example, married in 1935, recalled how her husband insisted that they did not have too many children, and 'he always said it was a man's—more of a man's to blame for having children than it was a woman, so, and I agreed with him. I know it takes two but the man is the most dominant I think and he never wanted a lot of children.'[122]

For numerous interviewees throughout the period, particularly men, the reasons behind starting a family were difficult to articulate. John Buck, a railway worker who had his first child in 1960, was asked what influenced him in his decision to start a family, and he responded, 'Nothing. I suppose really, what you get married for is to have a family.' He added that it was a case of 'Pure ignorance' for him and his wife, neither of whom had apparently even heard of birth control.[123] Likewise, George Aberdou, a manuals engineer who married in 1952, when asked about how many children he wanted, responded 'I don't think I thought about it. I felt maybe that that was the next thing. And whether I took matters into my own hands or not I don't know.'[124] Indeed, for some couples, it was the husband who was in favour of having (more) children than the wife.[125] Marriage remained inextricably linked with children; as a woman wrote to Marie Stopes in 1929, 'there was no reason for marriage unless we intended having a family'. She asked for advice, as, though her husband had agreed theirs would be a 'proper marriage', they no longer had sexual relations.[126]

CHALLENGING MASCULINITY: GENDER BOUNDARIES OF PARENTING

Whilst conceiving children could help achieve a certain masculine status, and virility and sexuality were important aspects of adult masculinity, a disassociation from the birth of the child was usual in terms of maintaining manly ideals. As Stephen Frosh notes, masculinity had and has no secure base itself; instead, it was and is constructed through separation from the other, the mother and infant.[127] David Swift, born 1930, made this point explicitly, noting:

> It was there for women to have babies and men to have no part in it, all they had part in was making 'em, no part in seeing them born or being involved in the birth, no part in waking up at night, no part in bathing them, no part in all your job was to go to work and bring home money to keep them, that was, and provide them with warmth and clothing, that was, I was told that was my job.[128]

---

[122] Lily Wells, 'A Labour of Love', roll 102, p. 11.

[123] John Buck, Int022, *Families*, UKDA, pp. 52, 62. Also see Brian Huston, Int073, *Families*, UKDA, p. 41.

[124] George Aberdou, Int165, *Families*, UKDA, p. 94.

[125] Terrence O'Farrell, Int103, *Families*, UKDA, pp. 31–2; Margret Wall, Int149, *Families*, UKDA, pp. 7, 48–9.

[126] Marie Stopes Letters, vol. 6, ADD.58675, 1929–31, pp. 7–11 (c) The British Library Board.

[127] Stephen Frosh, *Sexual Difference: Masculinity and Psychoanalysis* (London and New York, 1994), p. 109.

[128] David Swift, 'A Man's World', roll 88, pp. 83–4.

The explicit association of men with making children but not getting too involved in the rearing of them was an important means by which some men could assert their manliness, and apparently secure their masculine identity. Robert Roberts, discussing life in Salford in the first quarter of the twentieth century, referred to this connection between virility and household labour: 'Men in the lower working class, aping their social betters, displayed their virility by never performing any task in or about the home which was considered by tradition to be women's work.'[129] As we have seen in other chapters, many men were increasingly involved in family life and childcare, yet the preservation of a gendered binary of work within and outside the home remained important, at the very least in rhetorical terms.

The role and position of men during childbirth is worth considering here, as an important point at which concerns about masculinity were revealed. The presence of men at the births of their children has become almost universal, yet this is a new development—few men would have attended childbirth even in the early 1960s, the end of the period in question here.[130] It was simply not considered an option for the vast majority of men. Tosh, in his research into masculinity in the nineteenth century, found that upper-class and some middle-class men were present during childbirth by the 1840s, following the example of Prince Albert.[131] Yet this became extremely rare in the twentieth century, only to be found amongst the most wealthy and upper-class families.[132] As in America, men were starting to become more involved in childbirth by the end of the 1950s.[133] The reason given for not wanting or considering being present during childbirth was frequently connected to norms of masculinity.

In the press, the role of fathers during childbirth was not a prominent matter for discussion until the post-Second World War period, at which point the *Daily Mirror* focused on it as a possibility and matter of interest for its readers. Before this, there appeared only the occasional story about the very rare father who had to help his wife during birth because there was no one else available. In 1939, for example, an article spread across the front page of the *Mirror* told the tale of a father who had to 'act as midwife' because he was 'unable to get a doctor or a nurse in time'.[134] This served to remind readers of the rarity of such an event. However, before the war had ended, the *Daily Mirror* instructed fathers-to-be to read its

---

[129] Robert Roberts, *The Classic Slum: Salford Life in the First Quarter of the Century* (Manchester, 1971), p. 36.

[130] Julie Smith, 'The First Intruder: Fatherhood, a Historical Perspective', in P. Moss (ed.), *Father Figures: Fathers in the Families of the 1990s* (Edinburgh, 1995), pp. 17–25; Hiranthi Jayaweera, Heather Joshi, Alison Macfarlane, Denise Hawkes, and Neville Butler, 'Pregnancy and Childbirth', in S. Dex and H. Joshi (eds), *Children of the 21st Century: From Birth to Nine Months* (Bristol, 2005), pp. 109–32.

[131] Tosh, *A Man's Place*, pp. 81–2.

[132] See, for example, the interview with Lord Riverdale, 'A Man's World', rolls 176–183, and an article from the *Daily Mirror* in which this is discussed: *Daily Mirror*, 5 October 1953, p. 7.

[133] Judith Walzer Leavitt, *Make Room for Daddy: The Journey from Waiting Room to Birthing Room* (Chapel Hill, NC, 2009).

[134] *Daily Mirror*, 4 January 1939, p. 1.

article and, in turn, to take 'an intelligent and helpful' interest in his wife's pregnancy.[135] After the war, the role fathers could play as helpers to their wives during pregnancy was more frequently discussed.

In the 1950s, positive coverage of fathers attending childbirth became increasingly common in the *Daily Mirror*.[136] Indeed, the case of a father who delivered his child without medical help was treated very differently in 1959 in comparison with the story from 1939. In the article from 1959, again featured on the front page of the newspaper, the couple were said to have decided they wanted the father to be present during the birth, but their doctor would not permit it. Consequently, the father delivered the baby himself at home, and, according to the newspaper, faced criminal charges as a result. The perspective of the new parents dominated the article, with only a very short statement from a doctor included at the end, perhaps indicating the support of the *Mirror* for the parents' right to make their own decision.[137] However, this article clearly demonstrates the variety of opinions about the possibility of fathers attending their children's births. Other articles also encouraged a cautious approach, or suggested that there was some degree of controversy surrounding this idea. In an article published in the *Daily Mirror* in 1958, both perspectives on the matter were discussed in reaction to a debate on the presence of fathers at their children's births at the British Medical Association (BMA). The headline ' "Let father see the birth? *No*, he's a pest!" ' arguably indicated the view taken here, although it was reported that the members of the BMA voted in overwhelming numbers for the involvement of fathers during normal childbirth.[138] Other articles recorded stories of fathers unable to cope when they were present, and the (usually female) views of those against this development.[139] However, such articles reinforced the view that a father should at least be interested and extremely proud when his children were born.[140]

By the end of this period, there is evidence fathers' attendance at childbirth was becoming a possibility, if not common: Newson and Newson recorded 13 per cent of fathers in their sample group as present during births in the home.[141] An historical sociology project found that 5 per cent of those interviewed, all mothers in the Avon area, said their husband or partner was present during their children's births in the 1950s, in contrast to 97 per cent in the 1990s.[142] The subject formed the feature of two *Daily Mail* cartoons in 1960, which accompanied an article entitled 'Today one Father in 10 is in at the Birth'.[143] Whilst the proportion of

[135] *Daily Mirror*, 19 February 1945, p. 7.
[136] See, for example, *Daily Mirror*, 17 November 1954, p. 5; *Daily Mirror*, 12 September 1955, p. 2; *Daily Mirror*, 16 September 1955, p. 6; *Daily Mirror*, 3 June 1956, p. 7; *Daily Mirror*, 25 August 1958, p. 12.
[137] *Daily Mirror*, 16 January 1959, p. 1.   [138] *Daily Mirror*, 17 July 1958, p. 9.
[139] *Daily Mirror*, 13 July 1954, p. 2; *Daily Mirror*, 25 January 1956, p. 7.
[140] See, for example, *Daily Mirror*, 20 August 1955, p. 2; *Daily Mirror*, 25 November 1957, p. 7; *Daily Mirror*, 8 September 1958, p. 6.
[141] John and Elizabeth Newson [1963], *Patterns of Infant Care in an Urban Community* (Harmondsworth, 1974), p. 29.
[142] Smith, 'The First Intruder', pp. 17–25.
[143] *Daily Mail*, 2 June 1960. From the cartoon archive (www.cartoons.ac.uk), reference numbers MW0712 and MW0713 [accessed 15 June 2011].

men attending birth in the space of the home seemed to be increasing at the very end of this period, reaching somewhere in the region of 10 per cent, it is clear that most men were still very reluctant to witness childbirth due to normative ideas of manliness.

Out of the interviews conducted with fathers, there were twenty-four cases in which it was clear whether the father had attended or otherwise, for births up until 1960. Only one father attended the delivery, and two reported being there during some part of the labour.[144] Somewhat surprisingly, Harry Tillett—the only father who attended the delivery of his child, in 1953—said that he did so because the midwife who attended the delivery at home 'was an old-fashioned one'. Harry's wife described the midwife's attitude in more detail, and how it transpired that her husband ended up staying with her:

> she went downstairs and she said to him 'Get up there with your wife. It's as much your fault as hers', like, you know—it's as much your responsibility as hers. You go and sit with her and she sat down with me mother and they sat knitting and drinking tea and whatnot—apparently. And then me labour pains got worse and he just happened to be there holding me hand and there he stayed, like, and that was it. But if she'd have said to me then 'Do you want your husband with you?' I'd have said no. And if she'd have said to him 'Do you want to be with your wife?', he'd have probably said no.

She clarified that this was because 'It just wasn't done in them days. Men just weren't with their wives, were they, to have babies.'[145] Most oral history interviewees highlighted that a birthing room, whether in hospital or at home, was not a 'man's place'.[146] David Swift, a labourer in 1950s Nottingham, said he did not want to be present 'because it wasn't manly'.[147] John Caldwell, whose wife unusually asked for him to be present, was very much relieved when the midwife would not agree to this. In response to a question about what 'put him off' witnessing the birth, John replied:

> Well I'll tell you what put me off. I always thought well a man is a man and I was manly . . . I was very muscular and I thought No that's no place for me like you know there even though she requested it. I thought that's no place for me I'm a man I'm not one of those shilly shally blokes you know want to be in on something that they shouldn't be in on.[148]

Even Frank Davies, who helped his wife with most aspects of childcare, stated that it was 'unheard of' and 'taboo' for fathers to be present during childbirth.[149]

---

[144] Mr N2L, ERA, 1940–70, pp. 60–1; Terrence O'Farrell, Int103, *Families*, UKDA, p. 32; Harry Tillett, Int140, *Families*, UKDA, pp. 74–5.

[145] Harry Tillett, Int140, *Families*, UKDA, pp. 74–5

[146] For example, Mr B1B, ERA, Barrow/Lancaster 1890–1940, pp. 24–5; Mr P6B, ERA, 1940–70, p. 51; John Buck, Int022, *Families*, UKDA, pp. 63–4; Marion Thomas, Int168, *Families*, UKDA, pp. 46–7.

[147] David Swift, 'A Man's World', roll 88, pp. 83–4.

[148] John Caldwell, 'A Labour of Love', roll 69, pp. 2–3.

[149] Frank Davies, 'A Man's World', roll 82, p. 171. Also see George Ryder, 'A Man's World', roll 134, pp. 37–8.

There was a continued separation of what roles were appropriate for men and women to undertake. Though a substantial and growing number of fathers were increasingly involved in not only childcare, but even the care of babies, this remained strictly defined by gendered norms. Certain labour within the home was by nature 'women's work', whether men helped with it or not, as discussed in Chapter 3.[150] In some families, like Ian Crewe's as he grew up in the 1940s and 1950s, this also meant that daughters were expected to contribute to domestic work but sons were not.[151] This fact did not mean that men did not contribute to any household tasks, with domestic repairs and, increasingly, 'do-it-yourself' seen as a man's domain. For Joyce Mary Pound's mother, gardening was part of a man's role; she noted that 'Mother said it was a sign of a good husband if he dug the garden. He used to dig the garden and grow vegetables', referring to their family life in interwar Wales.[152] Some, such as Mrs M1P, noted how much ideas had changed in comparison to the time when they were interviewed; she explained 'You didn't see men doing anything like [cleaning and cooking], that would be the mother's jobs. My son-in-law does all sorts of things but they both go out to work and he has to.'[153]

Indeed, a small number of men interviewed went as far as to label their attitudes as 'chauvinist'; this word was notably common in interviewees' accounts. Mr N2L, for example, who married in the early 1940s, did not mind describing himself in these terms, as this exchange with the interviewer demonstrates:

R: Oh me, me. I always made the decision, I've always been what do they call these men? Not dogmatic.
LB: Authoritarian?
R: Chauvinistic.
LB: I see.[154]

George Aberdou, furthermore, who became a father in the late 1950s, reflected on his behaviour in the light of more modern attitudes:

I mean compared to what I believe now—in terms of my sympathies for women—I must have been—your average male chauvinistic pig. To some extent, not completely. But I think I—played a role and so did she, without even being conscious of the roles that we were playing.[155]

---

[150] For example, Mr B9P, ERA, Preston 1890–1940, p. 21; Mr D2P, ERA, Preston 1890–1940 (letter from Mr D2P), p. 61; Mrs B2B, ERA, 1940–70, p. 14; Mrs C8L, ERA, 1940–70, p. 23; Mr M12B, ERA, 1940–70, p. 27; John Bostock, Int014, *Families*, UKDA, p. 42; Ceridwen Brook, Int016, *Families*, UKDA, pp. 9–10; Kathleen Lunan, Int086, *Families*, UKDA, p. 27; Mrs Schlarman, Int128, *Families*, UKDA, p. 9; Edward/Jean Winn, Int159, *Families*, UKDA, p. 21; Arthur Wood, Int163, *Families*, UKDA, p. 12; Mr Fides, Int167, *Families*, UKDA, pp. 8–9; Ray Rochford, 'A Labour of Love', roll 48, pp. 11–12.
[151] Ian Crewe, Int040, *Families*, UKDA, p. 12.
[152] Joyce Mary Pounds, Int114, *Families*, UKDA, p. 24.
[153] Mrs M1P, ERA, Preston 1890–1940, p. 62.
[154] Mr N3L, ERA, 1940–70, p. 107. Also see Mr L5B, ERA, 1940–70, p. 17; Mr K2P, ERA, 1940–70, p. 120.
[155] George Aberdou, Int165, *Families*, UKDA, p. 94.

As quoted earlier, for Mathew Meret, his pride in his child's birth rendered him a 'typical chauvinist'.[156] In contrast, Mr W6L, born 1931, said his father 'wasn't one of them chauvanists [sic] you know, he couldn't be could he, my mother was the gaffer'.[157] Ian Canning, born 1945, also saw this as a negative term, noting that he lost respect for his father because he was adamant about not letting his wife see his wage packet, an act that could be very symbolically important, as discussed in Chapter 5. He described his father's attitude: 'It's the old sort of male chauvinist bit I think. A little bit of secrecy.'[158] For Patricia Dowden, born 1930, it was also a negative term, and whilst such behaviour was apparently becoming less common, it was part of her family life. On being asked whether her father looked after her on her own, she replied, 'I don't think he did, no, no. One of the—last of the chauvinists, I think, my father. Yes. No, no, my husband is the last. Yes.'[159] This discourse was clearly changing in its meaning and in its acceptability in both the period of study and decades since; reflecting its more common use from the 1970s onwards in the wake of second-wave feminism, interviewees sought to negotiate contemporary and previous attitudes. Yet the use of the term underlines the fundamentality of the division between 'men's work' and 'women's work', in both childcare and housework. Whilst interviewees recognized changing ideas about gender roles, they highlighted gender difference and underlined masculine identity on an individual and collective level.

In Preston, Barrow, and Lancaster, where all of Elizabeth Roberts' largely working-class interviewees lived, many men allowed themselves to get involved in certain household work and childcare, if it fell within the limits of what could be seen as legitimately masculine work and if it was conceived as 'help'.[160] More obvious examples of this included anything that was physically challenging, such as fetching fuel for fires and carrying large loads of washing, or employed traditionally masculine skills, such as mending shoes.[161] Men also frequently cut children's hair and were involved in preparing home remedies and medicine if children were ill.[162] Many childcare tasks could fall within both gendered parenting boundaries. For example, in his description of who took on what tasks around the house, Mr F1P, born 1907, noted that his father 'could do anything. He could cook and clean and he would wash clothes and darn and sew.' Yet, when pushed further about the idea of his father sharing the jobs with his mother, he simply replied 'If mother was ill he could take over.'[163] Likewise, John Buck reflected on his involvement in his new baby's care in 1960: 'usually . . . what can I say . . . I was there if needed, like, you know, another pair of hands'.[164] Hilda Lovejoy was very pleased with

---

[156] Mathew Meret, Int089, *Families*, UKDA, p. 65.

[157] Mr W6L, ERA, 1940–70, p. 22

[158] Ian Canning, Int026, *Families*, UKDA, p. 15.

[159] Patricia Dowden, Int051, *Families*, UKDA, p. 17.

[160] Roberts, *Women and Families*, p. 37.

[161] See for example, Mr S4B, ERA, 1940–70, p. 53; Mrs L2L, ERA, 1940–70, p. 16; Peter Coverley (Snr), Int037, *Families*, UKDA, p. 10.

[162] See for example, Mrs M3P, ERA, Preston 1890–1940, p. 16; Bullock, *Bowers Row*, p. 43.

[163] Mr F1P, ERA, Preston 1890–1940, pp. 45–6.

[164] John Buck, Int022, *Families*, UKDA, p. 65.

her husband in this sense, as for her such help meant he was a marvellous husband and father; on being asked who did the housework after their marriage in the early 1940s, she replied 'Do you know, you'll think—he helped? He was marvellous.'[165] Martin Jack's discussion of men's involvement in childcare revealed the generational change commented on by a number of interviewees. Martin, a physiotherapist, born in 1931, recollected how his father, a farmer and postman in Oldham, tended to help with more traditionally masculine tasks such as gardening, whilst in the mid-1950s, when Martin himself became a father, he noted he was happy to feed and bathe his children and could 'change a nappy like the best of 'em', though shopping and cooking remained largely his wife's responsibility.[166]

This gendered boundary in acceptable behaviour remained powerful and it was important for maintaining gendered identities for both men and women, even where men did take on tasks which could be seen as 'women's work'. As such, discussions of what was appropriate for men and women did not always match up to behaviour. Yet some interviewees also questioned this gendered division, encouraged by the fact that women were being employed in paid work in increasing numbers, if only usually in part-time and often low-skilled roles. Mrs A1P, born in 1910, contrasted her own experiences to those of her mother: 'my mother was at home, she didn't go to work but I really think that when you work they should pull their weight with the housework because they are benefiting from your money'. Yet, tellingly, again, in the example of cleaning, she focused on the rhetoric of male help, explaining that 'He helped me he didn't do it all.' She thought this was common practice, noting that, of her female colleagues' husbands, 'I think more or less they all had to pull their weight.'[167] Other practical circumstances also meant this division was weakened in some families; Mrs T4B, born 1948, recalled how her father took on a lot of housework and childcare, partly because her mother suffered from ill health; furthermore, 'he had been brought up in a family of lads' and so 'thought no shame to doing jobs like that anyway'.[168] Whilst Roy Hubbard, born 1939, did not question this division per se, he did describe the tasks his mother and father undertook as largely dictated by practical factors, and thought that 'There didn't seem to be any division in [domestic work], [it was] really because of the time factor.'[169]

When it came to childcare activities, the boundaries were more frequently blurred. Taking on certain childcare activities was more acceptable than cleaning, washing, or cooking. To align with accepted gendered boundaries, the age of the children mattered here. Nappies could be a particularly vexed issue for men, with the messiness and interaction with a small baby considered too 'feminine' for some.[170] As noted in Chapter 3, Newson and Newson found that 57 per cent

---

[165] Hilda Lovejoy, Int085, *Families*, UKDA, p. 19.
[166] Martin Jack, Int075, *Families*, UKDA, pp. 17, 69.
[167] Mrs A1P, ERA, Preston 1890–1940, pp. 52–3.
[168] Mrs T4B, ERA, 1940–70, p. 37.
[169] Roy Hubbard, Int069, *Families*, UKDA, p. 12.
[170] For example, Mrs W5B, ERA, 1940–70, p. 77; Mrs H3P, ERA, 1940–70, p. 52; Marion Dilworth, Int050, *Families*, UKDA, p. 33; Frank Jonston, Int076, *Families*, UKDA, p. 31; Mrs Laughton, Int083, *Families*, UKDA, p. 23; Sidney Sorell, Int132, *Families*, UKDA, p. 26.

of fathers in their study group changed nappies sometimes or often, with 43 per cent never doing so.[171] Mrs O1B, who married in 1939, described her husband's attitude: 'Oh odd times he would change her nappy, oh yes he often fed her, but like most men he wasn't too keen on changing nappies.'[172] Indeed, when it came to caring for babies, another means in which gender difference could be maintained was an insistence that men were too clumsy for some tasks, such as bathing. Edward Byrne, who became a father in 1939 and was separated from his children for long periods when they were young, described feeling 'a bit of a na-na at first, like men do, especially with the first one'.[173] Middle-class men seem to have been more willing to get involved in tasks such as nappy-changing through-out the period.[174] However, by the late 1950s and early 1960s some working-class men also appeared to be more willing to deal with nappies and similar tasks, indi-cating a changing notion of masculine identity within the home, though there remained much diversity in this area.[175] Mr K2P was happy to change nappies but, like many men, pointed out that his wife usually took on this task.[176] Yet, as noted earlier in this chapter, Martin Jack took pride in his proficiency in this area, noting 'Can change a nappy like the best of 'em, me.'[177]

In this sense, even in the privacy of the home, there remained a great deal of diversity in behaviour across different social groups, with expectations about acceptable masculine behaviour remaining important in how men navigated their new status as fathers. Again, the active family-orientated masculinity, as pro-moted in newspapers like the *Daily Mirror*, arguably helped widen the boundaries of normative masculinity to encompass nappy-changing within an increasingly prominent 'family man' identity. The comedy derived from fathers' potential participation in childcare and domestic labour remained a substantial theme of popular culture. This facilitated and normalized such involvement by maintain-ing fathers' incompetence, which reasserted the gendered understanding of par-enting in which mothers were constructed as the 'naturally' able parent. In the press, a prime example of this came in the form of cartoons, such as those printed in the *Daily Mirror*'s 'Newlyweds' series in the mid-1920s.[178] In 1925, a father was depicted putting the baby to sleep, and then inadvertently waking him up again [Figure 6.1].[179] Indeed, this role was even presented in *Men Only*, which paid lit-tle heed to fatherhood as a part of manhood and men's lives. In a somewhat rare

---

[171] Newson and Newson, *Patterns*, p. 137.   [172] Mrs O1B, ERA, 1940–70, p. 38.

[173] Edward Byrne, Int019, *Families*, UKDA, p. 49. Also see Frank Jonston, Int076, *Families*, UKDA, p. 31; Laura Millard, Int090, *Families*, UKDA, pp. 34–5; Mike Walters, quoted in Humphries and Gordon, *A Man's World*, pp. 170–1.

[174] For example, Owlen Farrand, Int055, *Families*, UKDA, p. 34.

[175] For example, Mrs W6B, ERA, 1940–70, p. 51; Margaret Beckwith, Int009, *Families*, UKDA, pp. 118–9; Mary Lear, Int084, *Families*, UKDA, p. 90; Terrence O'Farrell, *Families*, UKDA, p. 33; Margret Rawe, Int116, *Families*, UKDA, p. 35.

[176] Mr K2P, ERA, 1940–70, p. 13. Also see Norah Austin, Int003, *Families*, UKDA, p. 19.

[177] Martin Jack, Int075, *Families*, UKDA, p. 69.

[178] On the theme of childcare, see *Daily Mirror*, 7 November 1925, p. 12; *Daily Mirror*, 16 November 1925, p. 14; *Daily Mirror*, 4 January 1926, p. 14.

[179] *Daily Mirror*, 7 November 1925, p. 12.

Fig. 6.1. Newlyweds cartoon, *Daily Mirror*, 7 November 1925, p. 12. Reprinted with permission, © Mirrorpix.

reference to men's relationships with their children, a cartoon from 1958 satirized a father's role at bedtime. An exhausted-looking father was depicting returning downstairs with a storybook in one hand, telling his wife 'I thought he'd never go to sleep', yet the child in question is, unbeknownst to his father, following him, looking wide-eyed and alert.[180]

Articles too explored this theme: an article in the *Manchester Guardian* in 1928 entitled 'A Day at Home' detailed a father's day off, in which he had to mind his two sons. The expectations of the father were contrasted with the reality of looking after two small boys, and the final thought of this father was that he was looking forward to getting back to the office tomorrow: 'It will be quiet there, and I shall finish reading the paper at lunch.'[181] Some articles maintained that men would find nappy-changing and other baby-care tasks unpleasant as well as difficult; in July 1951, for example, Tom Cowie wrote about being left alone with his 4-year-old son and 10-month-old baby overnight, in an article entitled 'And I thought I could cope with the kiddies!' The article ended with his escape for a recuperative drink in the local pub, and the 'ordeal' of nappy-changing was described as such: 'With an arm lock on his wriggling form, I firmly groped with the other hand for safety pins and talcum powder.' Indeed, the language here is notable, with the 'arm lock' approach and the use of 'firmly' underlining masculine strength; this was no gentle, feminine approach to nappy-changing.[182] It is also clear that the article was aimed at female readers, emphasizing their heroism in being able to cope so well with the demands of home and children. Yet, though the whole escapade underlined the difference between men and women, the willingness of a father of two young boys to look after them alone for thirty-six hours and describe it in a national newspaper was a very modern phenomenon. At the end of the same month, another letter-writer pointed out that something was awry in a recently printed photograph of a marine changing the nappy of his young baby: 'Stanley M. Tew (Father of Two)' highlighted the fact that the father depicted was unwisely using a blanket, rather than nappy, pin.[183] Here again, the acceptability of men not only changing nappies, but discussing it in public, was encouraged.

As in other areas, fathers who failed in their duties were, by the 1950s, censured. The views of official figures were reported, praising fathers who helped in the house and criticizing those who did not. A *Daily Mirror* article in 1951 focused on an American father who beat his wife when she asked him to help with nappy-changing. The judge was reported as saying that changing nappies was 'a task befitting a husband as much as a mother'.[184] This was also demonstrated in another article from the *Daily Mirror* in 1952, in which a magistrate discussed a father's role. The line was clearly drawn between what a father should do and what jobs should be left to mother, in the views of this magistrate and in the article.

---

[180] *Men Only* 68:270, June 1958, p. 270.
[181] *Manchester Guardian*, 15 June 1928, p. 8.
[182] *Daily Mirror*, 3 July 1951, p. 8. Also see *Daily Mirror*, 9 July 1951, p. 2.
[183] *Daily Mirror*, 30 July 1951, p. 2.   [184] *Daily Mirror*, 25 June 1951, p. 1.

'Taking baby out' was seen as appropriate for fathers, whilst 'bathing baby' and 'washing nappies' should be left to the mother. However, it was emphasized that a father should be 'willing and trained' to do anything if needs be.[185] Childcare advice authors also advocated this view, and though many focused on the mother, they also discussed the father's role as a support to his wife in her parenting. Frankenburg, for example, highlighted that 'The increasing help and interest of fathers is valuable in many ways', and recommended an evening bath, as 'Father also has time to help if he wishes to do so.'[186] Spock insisted that regarding childcare as the mother's sole responsibility was 'the wrong idea', and suggested it was 'fine' for the father to change nappies and give bottles occasionally.[187] In a new and enlarged edition of 1958, he added, 'a man can be a warm father and a real man at the same time'.[188] Winnicott and others also consistently reiterated the value of a father's help, particularly in the first few months of a child's life.[189] Thus, whilst there was a lack of consensus as to the exact jobs appropriate for men, there was a common expectation amongst various sources that fathers should take on some parenting duties. The idea of men wanting to help their wives in the home became normalized, then, in popular culture, though there were definite limits.[190]

Indeed, the depiction of a marine changing his baby's nappy, as just discussed, was part of a coupling of military men with active fatherhood.[191] The *Daily Mirror* was again especially keen on this formula, and, for example, also printed a photograph of 'Able Seaman Albert Weeks, 21' arriving home from the West Indies to greet his new baby. He was reported as commenting that 'I'm home for twenty-eight days' leave, so I'd better get used to nappy-changing', and it was reported that 'he changed one then and there'.[192] Advertising for Rinso washing powder products in 1954 also encouraged men to involve themselves in this aspect of childcare, though it underlined that men were not naturally able to take on this task, with women 'the expert' in this case.[193] Another Rinso advert in 1957 stressed this point even more strongly with the line, 'The menfolk are only too happy to agree that "mother knows best".'[194] Here again, an audience of both men and women was presumably taken into account, in retaining a certain degree of masculine separation from caring for babies, but also appealing to women's pride in their expertise in this role.

[185] *Daily Mirror*, 7 April 1952, p. 3.
[186] Mrs S. Frankenburg (C.U.) [1922], *Common Sense in the Nursery* (Kingswood, 1954), pp. vi, 89.
[187] Benjamin Spock, *Baby and Child Care* (London, 1955), p. 12. Indeed, the section on 'The Father's Part' was much extended in the 1958 edition, disproportionately more than other sections. Benjamin Spock, *Baby and Child Care* (2nd edn, London, 1958).
[188] Spock, *Baby and Child Care* (2nd edn), p. 29.
[189] Mary Truby King [1934], *Mothercraft* (Sydney, 1937), pp. 26, 28; D. W. Winnicott, *Getting to Know Your Baby* (pamphlet, London, 1945), pp. 18–19; D. W. Winnicott, *The Ordinary Devoted Mother and Her Baby: Nine Broadcast Talks* (pamphlet, London, 1949), p. 8; D. W. Winnicott, *The Child and the Family: First Relationships* (London, 1957), pp. 13–14, 81–2.
[190] In films, for example, men take on such activities as washing-up in *The Passionate Friends* (David Lean and Ronald Neame, 1949); *This Happy Breed* (David Lean and Noël Coward, 1944); *The Scamp* (Wolf Rilla and James Lawrie, 1957).
[191] King, 'The Perfect Man'.   [192] *Daily Mirror*, 20 February 1954, p. 8.
[193] *Daily Mirror*, 19 March 1954, p. 5   [194] *Daily Mirror*, 10 December 1957, p. 16.

MASCULINITY IN PRIVATE AND PUBLIC

As such, the maintenance of gender difference mattered even when the activity in question, such as nappy-changing, took place within the private sphere of the home. The performance of the gendered identity of fatherhood became potentially even more contentious when in public. As noted in Chapter 3, taking children out for outings was frequently understood to be a key part of a father's role; this could have important consequences for the enactment of masculinity. Carrying a young baby or wheeling a pram remained controversial for many men throughout this period.[195]

Two fathers out of the sample went as far as to refuse to acknowledge their children in public. Mrs H5L, born 1931 and from Lancaster, and Patricia Brotherston, born 1935 and from London, both described how their fathers refused to speak to them in the street. Mrs H5L's father was a bus conductor and would not acknowledge his children whilst working, perhaps indicating a reluctance to mix the worlds of work and family. She recalled how 'he used to ignore us. If we ever got on his bus we hadn't to let on that he was our dad.'[196] Likewise, Patricia stated that she did not speak to her father much at all, though he was better in the house compared to in public: 'My father wouldn't talk to any of us in the street. I don't know why. He got on the same bus with us and he could totally ignore us. You wouldn't even know it was your father.'[197] Mrs R1P, born 1945 and from Preston, also noted that her father 'never went anywhere with us'.[198] This was unusual though, and eighty interviewees noted their fathers went out with them at least occasionally, with only eight suggesting this never happened. Of the fathers, twenty-seven recalled taking their children out at least sometimes, and no father said he did not do this. For Jim Bullock, born 1903, the walk to chapel was about a public display of familial authority: 'We usually all went together [to chapel], my father and mother first, with father just slightly in the lead. I suppose this was to show his authority.'[199] One or two others hinted at how outings with father meant proudly displaying or even showing off his offspring; Richard Church, growing up in what he called a lower-middle-class family in early twentieth-century London, noted the 'sentimental pride' associated with his father taking him out.[200] George Hewins, furthermore, discussing the birth of his son in a similar period, though in a more working-class context, described how he took his baby out to meet relatives and friends as soon as it was allowed out after a traditional period of six weeks spent at home under a veil, away from the wider community, clearly to display his pride in producing a child.[201] Mr G1P highlighted the fact there was a change in acceptability around the time of the First World War, after which time for most fathers

---

[195] King, 'Now You See', pp. 599–617.   [196] Mrs H5L, ERA, 1940–70, p. 3.

[197] Patrica Brotherston, Int017, *Families*, UKDA, p. 11.

[198] Mrs R1P, ERA, 1940–70, p. 20.   [199] Bullock, *Bowers Row*, p. 20.

[200] Richard Church, *Over the Bridge: An Essay in Autobiography* (London, 1955), p. 2.

[201] George Hewins, *The Dillen: Memories of a Man of Stratford-Upon-Avon*, ed. A. Hewins (London, 1981), p. 67.

taking children out occasionally, as long as they were old enough to walk, was not a controversial action, or felt to be in tension with their masculinity.[202]

Yet for many fathers, especially from the interwar period, the meaning of outings was quite different; weekend free time meant more informal walks with the children whilst female members of the household prepared food or completed other domestic work. This trend was highlighted in novels such as *The Family from One End Street*, published in 1937, in which the father's 'great ambition' is to get enough money together to take his family to London one bank holiday, and in R. C. Sheriff's *Fortnight in September*, in which the father performs a 'celebratory waltz' at the thought of their family holiday.[203] In the press too, some articles emphasized family days out were tiring,[204] whilst others highlighted the positive nature of outings and holidays for fathers and children.[205] In doing so, there was an ongoing implicit recognition of the ambivalence of fathers towards their roles, and the mix of pleasure and lack of interest that an individual parent could feel. For those like Mr L3P, born 1919, this came naturally to them as fathers, as they had experienced the same as children. He noted of his childhood, 'he used to take me all over did dad. He was a pretty good walker.' When he became a father, 'I used to use a lot of time then, though with the children walking. I walked miles. And they never knew where they were going, and I never knew.'[206] Andrew Purves, a shepherd who grew up in the Scottish borders in the interwar period, also had positive memories of childhood walks, and suggested there was an intergenerational timelessness to this experience. He noted that 'nothing delighted me more than to be allowed at times to accompany father in the fields. I recall how he often used to carry me on his back over the thistly patches, or when my small legs grew tired. Many, many years later I did the same for my own sons when they were small.'[207]

The account of Mr P6B, who became a father in 1942, demonstrated how normal taking children out had become by the Second World War. He noted that he spent a lot of time with his sons when they were little and added 'I don't think I ever went out without one of them.'[208] Some interviewees were more explicit about how this had changed over time. Mr L3P, as discussed earlier in this section, noted that his father would take them out, but this was not particularly common when he was growing up shortly after the First World War, and in turn he took his children out and educated them about the area in which they lived. He also reflected on how things had changed, saying that previously 'The woman was left to bring the child up until he got as able he could happen walk, I think and then the father might take him a walk. But not until then.' He also commented on

[202] Mr G1P, ERA, Preston 1890–1940, p. 47.

[203] Eve Garnett [1942], *The Family from One End Street* (London, 1981), pp. 143–73; R. C. Sheriff, *The Fortnight in September* (Leipzig, 1932), p. 24.

[204] *Daily Mirror*, 17 May 1921, p. 5; *Daily Mirror*, 12 August 1924, p. 11; *Daily Mirror*, 6 August 1928, p. 9; *Manchester Guardian*, 26 July 1922, p. 4; *Manchester Guardian*, 9 August 1923, p. 4.

[205] *Daily Mirror*, 27 July 1921, p. 2; *Daily Mirror*, 30 July 1953, p. 7; *Daily Mirror*, 22 April 1954, p. 1; *Daily Mirror*, 22 May 1956, p. 13; *Daily Mirror*, 3 August 1957, p. 7.

[206] Mr L3P, ERA, 1940–70, pp. 23–4, 106.   [207] Purves, *A Shepherd*, p. 30.

[208] Mr P6B, ERA, 1940–70, p. 54.

the change before and after the Second World War, when he was asked whether he pushed his children in their pram: 'After the war yes, but not before.'[209] Martin Jack remembered his childhood with fondness, recalling: 'we lived an entirely different way of life in those days to what you do now. I mean, people didn't have cars, so you went out for long walks and the Sunday afternoon walk, I mean, everybody who was anybody walked on Sunday afternoon.'[210] For some fathers, such as Mr S9P, who started a family in the late 1940s, this was clearly a highlight of their free time. He discussed at length the many trips he and his children took together, and humorously described the fanciful tales he used to tell them.[211]

Though many fathers regularly took their children out, there were certain boundaries of acceptability to this. A few fathers were still reluctant to go out alone with their child.[212] A large number of children and fathers referred to walking and other 'active' activities, most of which were in some way 'masculine', such as sports, and this was particularly the case for sons. Just before the start of this period, Mr B4P, born 1896, did not go out alone with his father 'unless we went somewhere they were shooting or rabbit coursing. Then perhaps he would take us.'[213] Others explained that outings with their father meant football, cricket or other sports matches, or activities that could be constructed as in some way 'masculine' in their nature.[214] Mr K2P, married in 1957, said that he took his six sons to watch and take part in a whole range of sporting activities, and 'used to do a lot with the kids', though he regretted that his work patterns meant he had had less time to spend with his youngest son.[215] For Martin Jack, who became a father in the mid-1950s, outings initially meant taking his young baby in the pram to the local pub for a drink of beer.[216] For Mr L5B, born in 1950, there was disagreement between himself and his father as to how much time they spent together outside the family home. This discussion was centred on football; Mr L5B noted:

> I upset my father just a few years ago when we were talking about the lack of time he spent with me when I was a kid. And he said, 'Oh I used to play football with you!' And I said, 'Yeh, I remember you playing football with me one Sunday at the bank.' And he said, 'Oh I used to do it regular', and I said, 'Well if you used to do it regular why do I remember that one occasion, why does it stand out in my mind?'[217]

[209] Mr L3P, ERA, 1940–70, pp. 23–4, 106, 150.
[210] Martin Jack, Int075, *Families*, UKDA, p. 20. Also see Mrs Laughton, Int083, *Families*, UKDA, p. 16–17; Hilda Lovejoy, Int085, *Families*, UKDA, p. 10.
[211] Mr S9P, ERA, 1940–70, pp. 21, 70–1.
[212] Mrs Roy, Int122, *Families*, UKDA, p. 25.
[213] Mr B4P, ERA, Preston 1890–1940, p. 38.
[214] For example, Mr S4P, ERA, Preston 1890–1940, p. 26; Mr T2P, ERA, Preston 1890–1940, p. 70; Edward Byrne, Int019, *Families*, UKDA, p. 10; Martin Byrne, Int020, *Families*, UKDA, p. 10; John Burrell, Int024, p. 25; Marion Dilworth, Int050, *Families*, UKDA, p. 33; Michael Fell, Int057, *Families*, UKDA, p. 15–16; Diana Kellard, Int077, *Families*, UKDA, p. 32; Leslie Lane, Int081, *Families*, UKDA, p. 23; David Roy, Int123, *Families*, UKDA, p. 13; Mr Fides, Int167, *Families*, UKDA, p. 17. Also see Willmott, *Growing Up*, p. 20; B. L. Coombes, *These Poor Hands: The Autobiography of a Miner Working in South Wales* (London, 1939), p. 146.
[215] Mr K2P, ERA, 1940–70, p. 16; Alan Parks, Int106, *Families*, UKDA, p. 26.
[216] Martin Jack, Int075, *Families*, UKDA, pp. 68–9.
[217] Mr L5B, ERA, 1940–70, p. 19.

Here we can see the subjectivity of individual memory at work, and perhaps tensions not only between a father's and son's memories but also in cultural expectations, both in the 1950s and at the time of interview, around how much time men spent with children and what happened in reality. Fathers might invest significance in the time they spent with their children in ways their offspring did not, or did not recall. One or two middle-class fathers took their children to different sorts of activities: Marion Thomas, born 1909, spent a lot of time with her father, the manager of a mill, and she recalled that 'we used to go to lectures—at that time there were lots of sort of public lectures you know. Or sometimes we'd go to the theatre in Manchester, Liverpool you know.'[218] Patricia Robertson, born 1940, similarly recalled that her father, an engineer, 'used to take me out a lot. He used to take me to the ballet, and the opera a lot, and the theatre.'[219]

Furthermore, an outing with father was, to a large extent, dependent on the age of the child. Mr T3P, who married in 1909, was not alone when he stated, 'I have taken [the children] out many a time but I would never wheel a carriage and I would never carry them. They had to be walking before I took them.'[220] Mrs P1P's husband likewise took their children out only 'when they had got over the pram stage'.[221] Mr W5L, whose son was born much later, in 1960, agreed, stating that, in terms of outings with his son, 'it wasn't until he was toddling and getting about that I—Well that's when I got interested in him to be perfectly honest.' He did, however, take him out in his pushchair.[222] Some interviewees also highlighted the fact that fathers might not look after children alone in the domestic space of the home, but would do so outside; Margaret Beckwith, for example, born to a mining family in 1942, when asked whether her father looked after them, replied 'Not in the—house. I cannot remember. Took we out. Every Sunday morning, we used to get all dressed up and he used to take us for a walk every Sunday morning.'[223]

There are a number of ways in which we can interpret men's increasing willingness to spend time with their children outside the family home. Firstly, it proved a relatively easy way in which men could enact their role as a helper to their wives and an entertainer to children, and provided a way of investing in the emotional relationship with their children if they wanted to do so. Hymy Weatherall, who had children from both his first marriage in 1929 and his second in 1946, indeed connected taking children out with being a good parent. He stated, 'I did look after them. I was—I wheeled them about in the park. I was a good parent—a close parent—I did the dutiful things that parents do.'[224] Pram-pushing became increasingly common even if it still did not fit entirely naturally within dominant, normative ideas of masculinity.[225] Displaying their fatherhood in public could be a

[218] Marion Thomas, Int168, *Families*, UKDA, p. 21.
[219] Patricia Robertson, Int119, *Families*, UKDA, p. 5.
[220] Mr T3P, ERA, Preston 1890–1940, p. 70.
[221] Mrs P1P, ERA, Preston 1890–1940, p. 37.   [222] Mr W5L, ERA, 1940–70, p. 61.
[223] Margaret Beckwith, Int009, *Families*, UKDA, p. 43. Also see David Cleveland, Int032, *Families*, UKDA, p. 13.
[224] Hymy Weatherall, Int154, *Families*, UKDA, p. 24.
[225] King, 'Now You See', pp. 599–617.

way for men to prove they were embodying some of the new ideals of active father-hood as discussed throughout this book. Yet men, particularly those from tradi-tional working-class areas, often helped more in terms of childcare and domestic work than they let on in public.[226] The gendered differentiation between what men and women should have done and were good at doing remained, although the rhetoric of 'help' allowed for some blurring of the boundaries. For some men, spending time with children outside the home might not only have been more practical in terms of helping their wives, but also sat more easily within gendered norms. As fatherhood was changing in its meaning, taking on childcare outside the home was perfectly possible, as it could not be understood as domestic labour in itself. Childcare, defined as minding children, was a different sort of task to washing nappies, cooking, cleaning, and so on. In this sense, the long tradition of the gendered separate spheres of the home were crucial, even if, as with most peri-ods in history, both men and women frequently crossed the gendered divide.[227] Whilst the idea of gendered, separate spheres may not enhance understanding of what men and women were doing, it is valuable in understanding ideas about identity, even if these did not always match up neatly to behaviour.

CONCLUSION

It is clear, then, that changes to fatherhood and masculinity took place towards the end of this period, but that the boundaries of both acceptable fatherhood and acceptable masculinity remained debated, uncertain, and, at times, contradictory. Fatherhood offered a means to prove masculinity, primarily through demonstrat-ing the ability to provide for dependants, the status it offered as a protector of women and children, and the proof a family gave of a man's sexual activity and fecundity. However, it also brought about challenges to manliness, as men had to negotiate involved fatherhood, which was increasingly encouraged, and ideas of masculinity, which were also in flux. Local community norms remained impor-tant, yet newspapers and other public voices increasingly prescribed what was good and bad fatherhood, and encouraged men to push prams, change nappies, and read bedtime stories.

It becomes clear that fatherhood and masculinity could be combined closely and more easily in the post-Second World War era than previously. Whilst sexual activity and virility in terms of producing children, and subsequently providing for and protecting them, were crucial components of masculinity, more positive aspects of fatherhood also came to the fore in this period. The 'family man' iden-tity signifies a modified relationship between masculinity and fatherhood. Zweig

---

[226] Joanna Bourke, *Working Class Cultures in Britain 1890–1960: Gender, Class, and Ethnicity* (London, 1994), p. 94.

[227] On this debate, see Amanda Vickery, 'Golden Age to Separate Spheres? A Review of the Categories and Chronology of English Women's History', *Historical Journal* 36:2 (1993), pp. 383–414. On the crossing of spheres, see, for example, Tosh, *A Man's Place*, pp. 2–3.

even contested that the worker was becoming 'feminized'.[228] Indeed, fathers were featured in the press like never before, in a range of different types of articles, as well as cartoons, letters, and advertising. Men wrote of their pride in their families and children were portrayed as a credit to their fathers. Though some of the challenges that fatherhood could present to masculinity were still present, the press minimized these, suggesting an active version of fatherhood to be encompassed in family-orientated masculinity. In men's experiences, of course, this combination of the ideals of physical masculinity with the changing of nappies could be more problematic, but the growth in acceptance of men's involvement in what were traditionally seen as 'women's jobs' was not just confined to prescription. As long as the gendered divide remained, at least rhetorically, men from all social backgrounds became increasingly happy to include their children and families as part of their identities. As John Goldthorpe and David Lockwood noted, husbands from both white-collar and manual backgrounds were equally 'family-centred'.[229] Indeed, it is possible to argue that the growing encouragement of a more child-friendly version of masculinity in the press helped bring about the acceptance and even expectation of these sorts of identities for 'ordinary' men. The constant bombardment of images of happy and involved fathers in the press, as discussed throughout this book, thus helped to encourage lived masculine identities that more comfortably included involved fatherhood. It also must be remembered that, within any one individual, masculine identity was always multifaceted and complex. Mr Fides, born 1929, discussed how his father and himself, who were both boxers, combined both gentle and 'manly' attributes: 'My father was one of the gentlest men you could ever meet and yet he was a boxer which is the same as me, you know. I wouldn't say that I was gentle, but I can sit and watch a film and it'll make me cry.'[230]

The causes for such a change by the 1950s are manifold. The idealization of home and family following the Second World War, for children and parents, helped promote a more family-orientated masculinity, which was arguably most notable within working-class culture.[231] Indeed, as Brooke has pointed out, changes to gender and class were very much intertwined, and he suggests that changes to working-class values were responsible in part for changes to ideals of masculinity.[232] Further, the affluence of the post-war years meant providing sufficiently for one's family became much easier than in previous difficult economic times. Men could therefore achieve the masculine obligations of breadwinning, and perhaps because of this, felt secure enough in their masculine identities to become more involved in day-to-day family life. As Smith has demonstrated in

[228] Ferdynand Zweig, *The Worker in Affluent Society: Family Life and Industry* (London, 1961), p. 208.

[229] John H. Goldthorpe, David Lockwood, Frank Bechhofer, and Jennifer Platt [1968], *The Affluent Worker in the Class Structure* (Cambridge, 1969), p. 106.

[230] Mr Fides, Int167, *Families*, UKDA, p. 16.

[231] On the idealization of home in the context of child development, see Mathew Thomson, *Lost Freedom: The Landscape of the Child and the British Post-War Settlement* (Oxford, 2013), p. 48.

[232] Brooke, 'Gender', pp. 773–95.

respect to working-class culture in the north, the practical benefits of increased affluence also helped to shift the emphasis of men's identities to family and home, and away from public spaces and friends.[233] The male breadwinner ideal was still fundamental to masculinity, and this did not change until much later. Yet its continuance should not mask the real transformations that were taking place—though the centrality of breadwinning had not altered, the framing of it had, and many men took great pride in providing an improved standard of living for their families. The idealization of the nuclear family as a close-knit unit and the shift to a more family-orientated masculinity thus go hand in hand; both trends were accelerated by the Second World War, and grew in significance during the 1950s. Indeed, the 1950s can be pinpointed as a moment of transformation in masculinity—it is clear that there were tensions and controversies surrounding this change, and that by no means all men embraced it, but a new, if fragile, family-orientated masculinity came to prominence in this period.

---

[233] Smith, 'A Study', pp. 226–7.

Conclusion: Changing Fathers, Changing Men?

Fatherhood is currently a widely discussed and controversial issue, as paternity and parental leave, fathers' rights to custody, and 'feckless fathers' continue to provoke debate. Assertions of what fathers did and did not do in the past are constantly invoked to support interpretations about the state of fatherhood today and the need for change in the future.[1] This process happened as much in the period discussed in this book as now; the 'Victorian' father was contrasted with contemporary practices. Throughout the twentieth century in Britain, and before, on both an individual and a collective level, there has been a continual rejection of assumed past modes of behaviour, and a reiteration of the novelty of fatherhood practices in the present. *Family Men* has demonstrated the complexity and diversity of understandings and experiences of fatherhood, and highlights the need for a different chronology of fathering in twentieth-century Britain. It provides a case study for understanding the relationship between cultural ideals, individual attitudes, and social experience, and has wider implications for the historiographies of class, the family, the nation, and community in the twentieth century.[2]

FATHERHOOD AND MASCULINITY

Family Men has set out to shed new light on ideas and experiences of fatherhood. It aims to help us move away from generalizations about fathers in the past, which have been all too common in the limited research on the twentieth century that has existed up to now. The book therefore challenges Lynne Segal's claim that 'questions of men's relationship to childcare . . . were not on the conceptual, let alone the

---

[1] For examples of the lack of complexity credited to fatherhood in the past in academic research, see Louie Burghes, Lynda Clarke, and Natalie Cronin, *Fathers and Fatherhood in Britain* (London, 1997), p. 9; Peter Moss, 'Introduction', in P. Moss (ed.), *Father Figures: Fathers in the Families of the 1990s* (Edinburgh, 1995), p. xi.

[2] As Childers, Pooley, and Vincent note of the different contexts of twentieth-century France, nineteenth-century England, and twentieth-century Spain respectively, ideas about parenting were strongly connected to conceptions of citizenship, authority, and responsibility. Kristen Stromberg Childers, *Fathers, Families, and the State in France, 1914–1945* (Ithaca, NY, and London, 2003), p. 3; Siân K. Pooley, 'Parenthood and Child-Rearing in England, c.1860–1910', PhD Thesis (University of Cambridge, 2009), p. 1; Mary Vincent, 'The Martyrs and the Saints: Masculinity and the Construction of the Francoist Crusade', *History Workshop Journal* 47 (1999), pp. 82–3.

political, agenda' in the period from the First World War to the end of the 1950s.[3] Throughout all types of source materials used, the evidence for such an assertion is tenuous. Even in the case of parenting advice literature, which doubted men's interest in children and focused on the mother, the question of what fathers should and should not be doing was a concern. As this book has demonstrated throughout, there was much more debate about fatherhood than has been recognized, and fathers and children were the subjects of scrutiny in a similar way, if not to the same extent, as mothers.[4] Fatherhood was invested with increased psychological, social, and cultural significance as the period progressed, and there is much evidence to suggest that this shift could be seen in the behaviour of individuals and families, as well as in popular debate. Expectations of a father's duties were raised in this period, as the meanings attributed to his roles of providing, entertaining, guiding his children, and helping his wife changed, and the bar for 'good' fatherhood was raised from the interwar period onwards. The relationship between fathers and children was seen as deeply meaningful and influential by the 1940s, as the emphasis on the influence of parenting became an accepted and popular notion throughout the media and in the attitudes of individuals. A new perspective on the father's position within the family reinforced this view, as the authoritarian Victorian patriarch was rejected in favour of a more friendly and accessible parent, a development that was greeted in increasingly positive terms in the aftermath of the Second World War. Finally, the end of the period witnessed a redefinition of the relationship between fatherhood and masculinity, as tensions between the two came to the fore, and a new family-orientated masculinity became an accepted part of normative masculine identity. What was acceptable for men to do in private and in public altered, and older, working-class stereotypes about manliness were weakening in their hold.[5]

The period, then, can be understood as one of 'equality in difference' in terms of gender relations. This is illustrated by the 1925 Guardianship of Infants Act, of which the intention and result was to secure equality between mother and father. The twentieth century was by no means a time of linear progression towards a convergence of the sexes; whilst many questions were raised about this matter, the emphasis on the differentiation between male and female parenting remained. The double helix is thus more useful here as a depiction of change than a Venn diagram of motherhood/fatherhood or masculinity/femininity.[6] In particular, though there was enormous diversity in people's experiences, there was also an emphasis on and

[3] Lynne Segal, *Slow Motion: Changing Masculinities, Changing Men* (3rd edn, Basingstoke, 2007), p. 20.

[4] See Angela Davis, 'A Critical Perspective on British Social Surveys and Community Studies and Their Accounts of Married Life c.1945–1970', *Cultural and Social History* 6:1 (2009), pp. 47–64.

[5] Jon Lawrence, 'Class, "Affluence" and the Study of Everyday Life in Britain, c.1930–64', *Cultural and Social History* 10:2 (2013), p. 285.

[6] Higonnet and Higonnet use the double helix in their research, whereas Fisher includes Venn diagrams in his thesis on fatherhood to encapsulate change. The former is more convincing. Margaret R. Higonnet and Patrice L. R. Higonnet, 'The Double Helix', in M. R. Higonnet, J. Jenson, S. Michel, and M. Collins (eds), *Behind the Lines: Gender and the Two World Wars* (New Haven, CT, and London, 1987), pp. 31–47; Timothy J. Fisher, 'Fatherhood and the Experience of Working-Class Fathers in Britain, 1900–1939', PhD Thesis (University of Edinburgh, 2004), e.g. p. 50.

awareness of change in both popular culture and the testimonies of individuals. As in Abrams', Szreter, and Fisher's and Williamson's research, there appears to be a particular shift in ideas from the 1930s and 1940s.[7] Change was occurring around the era of the Second World War, but had its roots in the interwar period.

The causes of this transformation originate in the interwar period, and it was around the middle of the 1930s that there were some substantial developments in terms of understandings of fatherhood. Two parallel trends arguably form the root causes of this shift: a newly popularized psychology led to a continual stress on the influence of parents, and rising living standards and the resulting raised aspirations of many families worked together to increase the perceived significance of fatherhood particularly and parenting generally. The greater hopes and expectations that all sorts of parents had for their children meant that the increased psychological importance placed on childhood and parent–child relationships was seen as a positive development: according to this body of theory, parents did have a real influence on their children, and through rising living standards could practically, as well as theoretically, exert such influence. The involved father was one construction of masculinity that was newly promoted and glorified by the press, and such constructions were arguably internalized and encompassed in the identities of many, though not all, men. The Second World War and its aftermath were crucial within this process; the family formed a fundamental reason for fighting and was also the logic behind much reconstruction rhetoric. Situating the father at the heart of the family was essential to promoting the future of the nation.

A NATIONAL, PRESCRIPTIVE, AND PSYCHOLOGY-INFLUENCED CULTURE

This book has also considered the relationship between cultural norms and prescription, and the experiences of individuals and families. It is argued here that a consideration of popular culture, such as the press, is crucial to understanding the relationship between experts and cultural authorities, and the attitudes and behaviour of individuals. The shift in fatherhood, then, relates to social changes noted in the previous section, but was arguably brought about, in large part, by a national culture which changed in both nature and extent, alongside individuals' reactions to their own parents' child-rearing styles and individuals' experiences of childhood. This national popular culture was new to this period in terms of its reach, and it is here that parenting culture must be understood to be quite different to that of the late nineteenth century.[8] A homogenous, classless version of

---

[7] Lynn Abrams, '"There Was Nobody Like My Daddy": Fathers, the Family and the Marginalisation of Men in Modern Scotland', *Scottish Historical Review* 78:2 (1999), p. 233; Simon Szreter and Kate Fisher, *Sex before the Sexual Revolution: Intimate Life in England 1918–1963* (Cambridge, 2010), p. 204; Margaret Williamson, '"He Was Good with the Bairns": Fatherhood in an Ironstone Mining Community, 1918–1960', *North East History* 32 (1998), p. 95.

[8] As Pooley found in her thesis, parenting cultures remained profoundly local into the early twentieth century. Pooley, 'Parenthood', p. 290.

family life was promoted, and in the press, a newly prescriptive tone and emphasis strengthened the influence of what was espoused. The cumulative effect of the daily newspaper also contributed to the power of this medium, and the increasingly prominent 'expert' voice established authority. New psychological modes of thinking further reinforced the influence of parenting for healthy children and a strong nation, and such ideas became increasingly prominent in popular culture throughout the period. The growth of a consumerist society, particularly important at the end of this period as a new age of affluence was emerging, is also key to understanding the impact of this increasingly significant popular culture.

It is argued here, then, that a more powerful and proactive press helped bring about a certain version of fatherhood and family life. This was a trend not without contradiction; as Adrian Bingham notes, the 'family newspaper' was increasingly filled with sexualized content, and editors had to tread a fine line in balancing these two preoccupations.[9] The picture painted of the post-war family could be equally contradictory, balancing a wholeheartedly positive view of men's (potential) involvement in family life with the need to retain a strong sense of gender difference in parenting roles and identities. It is near impossible to find direct evidence relating to the complex relationship between individuals and public debates, and to establish the direction of cause and effect. Yet this book has shown a substantial degree of correlation between individual attitudes and behaviour and norms established and reinforced in popular culture. Where there was discrepancy, such as in regard to the corporal punishment of children, individuals' attitudes tended to lag behind public ideals. In analysing specific tropes, such as food within the family, ideas around discipline and the phrase 'wait till your father comes home', and nappy-changing, we can approach a fuller understanding of this relationship.[10] Furthermore, as a newly powerful national culture was emerging in this period,[11] there is evidence of greater homogeneity across different social groups and regions.[12] Whilst causation in this area can never be proven, it seems highly likely that popular cultural authorities were an important force within the shaping of the boundaries of individual attitudes and behaviour. Whether men and women agreed with their own upbringings or not, they reacted

[9] Adrian Bingham, *Family Newspapers? Sex, Private Life, and the British Popular Press 1918–1978* (Oxford, 2009), p. 263.

[10] Laura King, ' "Now You See a Great Many Men Pushing Their Pram Proudly": Family-Orientated Masculinity Represented and Experienced in Mid-Twentieth-Century Britain', *Cultural and Social History* 10:4 (2013), p. 601.

[11] Both Pooley and Doolittle found signs of a new public discussion of fatherhood and family life in latter half of the nineteenth century; by this period the predominance of the national over the local in social and cultural terms was new, and intensified from the interwar period onwards. Megan Doolittle, 'Missing Fathers: Assembling a History of Fatherhood in Mid-Nineteenth Century England', PhD Thesis (University of Essex, 1996), p. 230; Pooley, 'Parenthood', p. 287

[12] Ronald Fletcher, *Britain in the Sixties: The Family and Marriage: An Analysis and Moral Assessment* (Harmondsworth, 1962), p. 127; Geoffrey Gorer, *Exploring English Character* (London, 1955), pp. 297, 303; Richard Hoggart [1957], *The Uses of Literacy: Aspects of Working-Class Life with Special Reference to Publications and Entertainments* (Harmondsworth, 1971), p. 342; Peter Willmott and Michael Young, *Family and Class in a London Suburb* (London, 1960), p. 122. Also see Davis, 'A Critical Perspective', p. 54; Szreter and Fisher, *Sex*, p. 29.

to their parents' parenting styles and the parameters of acceptable behaviour at a community and national level when making decisions about parenting. As Szreter and Fisher note, intergenerational relations changed significantly in the interwar period,[13] and shifting understandings of power and authority between parents and children helped bring about a culture in which men and women could more freely react against their own family backgrounds.

As was highlighted in the introduction of this chapter, there was, of course, a wide spectrum of behaviour across society. Yet the focus on the 'ordinary family' in newspapers and films, and, to an extent, literature, created a rhetoric of homogeneity in terms of the experiences of different social groups, even where differences between parts of society remained.[14] A common understanding of certain standards of behaviour was emerging, even if variety in practice remained. The values of upper-working- and lower-middle-class communities were brought to the fore as never before. Again, the context of the Second World War and the welfare state was crucial: the celebration of the ordinary family was essential to minimize social division and unite the nation, at least in theory, behind the war and reconstruction efforts.[15] This did not mean that a classless society emerged, but that social conditions were drawing together the ways of life of different social and economic groups, and popular cultural media sought to appeal to a wide section of the population.[16] The increase in the electorate in 1918 and 1928 and the victory of the Labour Party in 1945, and the subsequent effect this had on British politics, cemented the centrality of working-class values to debates about the family and beyond. The importance of women to these debates is also noteworthy; as a predominant part of the electorate by 1928, their ideas and concerns came to figure much more strongly in both politics and culture, and, as such, more attention was paid to familial and domestic matters. Fatherhood, in this sense, provided an opportunity for politicians, journalists, and the like. By stressing the importance of men to their families, they spoke to the concerns and problems of women. Yet, by focusing on the crucial role of men, even within the traditionally feminine world of the family, it was possible to uphold patriarchal beliefs and avoid undermining the traditional gender order.[17] A new focus on fatherhood responded to women but reasserted the importance of men.[18]

---

[13] Szreter and Fisher, *Sex*, pp. 29–30.   [14] King, 'Now You See', pp. 610–11.

[15] On the emphasis on happy family life and unity across class and race boundaries in the United States in the aftermath of the war, see Elaine Tyler May, *Homeward Bound: American Families in the Cold War Era* (2nd edn, New York, 1999), esp. p. xvii.

[16] See Hoggart, *The Uses*, pp. 342–3.

[17] This was particularly evident in the *Daily Mirror*, the only major newspaper with a predominantly female readership. Mass-Observation File Report 1339, 'Daily Express Readership' (June 1942), p. 3; Mass-Observation File Report 3063, 'Report on Newspaper Reading, 1947–48' (November 1949), ch.xvii. Also see Adrian Bingham, *Gender, Modernity, and the Popular Press in Inter-War Britain* (Oxford, 2004), pp. 34–37.

[18] Laura King, 'The Perfect Man: Fatherhood, Masculinity and Romance in Popular Culture in Mid-Twentieth-Century Britain', in Alana Harris and Timothy Jones (eds), *Love and Romance in Britain, 1918–1970* (Basingstoke, forthcoming 2014).

FAMILY AND SOCIETY

This appeal to the ordinary family in popular culture reflects a wider debate about the advent of a classless society. This is crucial here, as this book has sought to understand similarities and differences between the family lives of those from various class backgrounds. Child-rearing practices are one means of distinguishing between class groups.[19] It is argued here that class differences, and inequalities, persisted through this period and beyond, but the extent and nature of such differences were changing. James Obelkevich suggests that by the post-Second World War period, the spread of affluence did 'significantly reduce' class differences, though not 'eliminate' them.[20] Stephen Brooke has noted that the coherence of working-class identity was affected greatly by the prosperity of this period, but believes that claims about the 'death' of working-class consciousness have been 'greatly exaggerated'.[21] As Jon Lawrence highlights, class categories were much less clear-cut in reality than rhetoric, and there was a wider spectrum of class-based living conditions in both the pre- and post-Second World War periods than has been hitherto acknowledged.[22] Changes in terms of class were indeed strongly connected to changes in understandings of gender. As Brooke also contests, an aggressive masculinity and a nostalgic vision of working-class family life emerged as a result of these shifts.[23] Indeed, as was noted in Chapter 6, the 1950s in particular did form a period of uncertainty in terms of gender identity, and should be viewed as an important moment in the history of masculinity.[24]

There was a broad range of social experience in this period; what is posited here is that this diversity should not always be understood through the dimension of class. Emerging from the social research evidence, problematic though it is, is a more homogenous experience of family life across class boundaries.[25] This was by no means because of a simple 'embourgeoisement' of class values, but due more to a process of something like 'normative convergence', to use John Goldthorpe and David Lockwood's term.[26] The spectrum of understandings of family life was thus narrower for the majority of people, as cultural values converged on a national

[19] As Pooley notes, parenthood was 'not just fundamentally shaped by class, but...experiences of rearing children were also constitutive of class inequalities and identities'. Pooley, 'Parenthood', p. 280. Furthermore, in John and Elizabeth Newson's study of Nottingham families, they suggested that, whilst measuring class through a father's occupation was clearly flawed, considering different ways of rearing children might provide a 'safer guide' to classifying individuals and families in this way. John and Elizabeth Newson [1963], *Patterns of Infant Care in an Urban Community* (Harmondsworth, 1974), p. 152.

[20] James Obelkevich, 'Consumption', in J. Obelkevich and P. Catterall (eds), *Understanding Post-War British Society* (London, 1994), p. 149.

[21] Stephen Brooke, 'Gender and Working Class Identity in Britain during the 1950s', *Journal of Social History* 34:4 (2001), p. 773.

[22] Lawrence, 'Class', pp. 275–6.   [23] Brooke, 'Gender', p. 775.

[24] Brooke, 'Gender', pp. 773–95. Also see Lesley Hall, *Sex, Gender and Social Change in Britain since 1880* (Basingstoke, 2000), p. 166.

[25] Davis, 'A Critical Perspective', p. 54.

[26] John H. Goldthorpe, David Lockwood, Frank Bechhofer, and Jennifer Platt [1968], *The Affluent Worker in the Class Structure* (Cambridge, 1969), p. 163.

level, certainly in terms of family life. This was a long, complicated, and uneven process, throughout this period and beyond.[27] As Geoffrey Gorer noted, attitudes to child-rearing were remarkably consensual across different regions of England, much more so than attitudes to other matters, such as religion.[28] Class and region still mattered then, but the markers of class were becoming increasingly blurred. In this particular area of family life and parenting, both attitudes and experiences were becoming closer across class groups, as a national culture both unified and provided a pattern for both opinions and behaviour. The living spaces and conditions of families from different social backgrounds were becoming more alike, which had important effects on the ways families behaved. Yet, as Lawrence suggests, self-conscious working-class values also diminished in importance as a different set of ideals became prominent at a national level.[29] As fatherhood became imbued with cultural and social significance, those numerous men who were engaged in family life were better able to display their active fathering and family-orientated masculinity. The greater affluence of the post-Second World War era, as discussed by Langhamer and Lawrence, was enabling rather than, in itself, transformative.[30]

The 1930s, 1940s, and 1950s constituted an important period of change for the family: the smaller family was now the norm across all social classes, the family was becoming more of a self-contained and independent unit, and marriages were increasingly idealized as companionate. Changes in leisure time were also crucial, as were the spaces which families inhabited. Families were now spending their leisure time together, taking trips in an increasingly affordable family car or watching television together by the 1950s—and the father could also take part due to decreases in working hours. The cleaner, warmer, and more spacious homes that were becoming a reality for increasing numbers of families also made it easier for family members to spend time enjoying each other's company. This trend was linked to rising aspirations, for the next generation in particular.[31] The conception of the family enjoying time together as a single unit was a relatively new development in this period, as demonstrated by Pooley's work on the family between 1860 and 1910. As she indicates, spending such time together was not an accurate picture of most families in the earlier period, and was by no means assumed to be positive.[32] The middle decades of the twentieth century, then, witnessed a new

---

[27] This is a point not always recognized by the researchers. Thanks to Jon Lawrence for a stimulating discussion about this study, for highlighting the problems with Goldthorpe and Lockwood's use of the term, and for sharing unpublished material on the topic.

[28] Gorer, *Exploring*, p. 162.   [29] Lawrence, 'Class', p. 285.

[30] Claire Langhamer, 'Love, Selfhood and Authenticity in Post-War Britain', *Cultural and Social History* 9:2 (2012), pp. 292–3; Lawrence, 'Class', p. 285.

[31] On these shifts, see Abrams, 'There Was Nobody', p. 233; Joanna Bourke, *Working Class Cultures in Britain 1890–1960: Gender, Class, and Ethnicity* (London, 1994), pp. 81–6; Brooke, 'Gender', p. 773; Judy Giles, *Women, Identity and Private Life in Britain, 1900–50* (Basingstoke, 1995), pp. 68–71; Lesley A. Hall, *Hidden Anxieties: Male Sexuality 1900–1950* (Cambridge, 1991), e.g. p. 76; Ross McKibbin, *Classes and Cultures: England 1918–1951* (Oxford, 1998), pp. 518–20; Obelkevich, 'Consumption', p. 141.

[32] Pooley, 'Parenthood', pp. 191–2.

hegemony of the coherent and self-sufficient nuclear family unit, which spanned class and region.

FATHERHOOD IN THE TWENTIETH CENTURY AND BEYOND

The period studied here is thus crucial to understanding the culture and experience of parenting, family, gender, and class across the twentieth century. As Pooley has argued, parenting has implications for and is constitutive of conceptions of class, gender, welfare, place, and nationhood.[33] By the 1950s, a period of uncertainty in terms of gender identities, a new understanding of fathering had emerged, as a serious and influential endeavour, and a new normative family-orientated masculinity had come to the fore. This development was by no means a simple stepping stone on a gradual path of gender convergence. Whilst there was much discussion of this matter, understandings of male and female parenting continued to be rather distinct, and fathers remained inferior in their status as parents in comparison to mothers. Many fathers remained indifferent to and distant from family life. However, newly popularized psychological modes of understanding, coupled with greater affluence for more families, led to a new understanding of the emotional power of fatherhood. The Second World War and its aftermath, with its focus on the nuclear family unit as the means of ensuring the nation's future, furthered this trend and brought a cohesiveness to the relationship between fatherhood and masculinity.[34] The new emphasis on the family unit as strong and self-contained was closely associated with this change. The power of these trends was also reinforced by the perception of a new classless society, which is significant in its rhetoric if not its description of reality. What this book has shown, however, is that in both attitudes and experiences, there was some movement towards a more homogenous experience between families of different classes, and greater overlap in both behaviour and ideas. That this all took place at a national level forms another new development not witnessed before the First World War. Much more research into fatherhood in the twentieth century is required; *Family Men* provides a starting point for a new development of this historiography. In particular, more is needed on the subtleties of class and regional similarity and difference, on ethnicity and religion, on fatherhood in less normative family forms, on the material culture of fatherhood and family life, on parenting policy, and on the emotional nature of fatherhood and masculinity over time.

---

[33] Pooley, 'Parenthood', p. 1.

[34] On the link between the wellbeing of the future family and nation in post-war France and Germany, see Luc Capdevila, 'The Quest for Masculinity in a Defeated France, 1940–1945', *Contemporary European History* 10:3 (2001), p. 428; Till van Rahden, 'Fatherhood, Rechristianization, and the Quest for Democracy in Postwar Germany', in D. Schumann (ed.), *Raising Citizens in 'the Century of the Child': The United States and German Central Europe in Comparative Perspective* (New York, 2010), p. 142.

Much did, of course, change after the end of the 1950s, and there are many contrasts to draw between fatherhood as understood in the twenty-first century and in the period studied here. A shift in thinking about child welfare had important consequences for understandings of parenting and a general positivity about the family in the 1960s, with revelations about child abuse and neglect instigated by the Kempe Report.[35] Furthermore, new ways of thinking about gender and the family emerged with and in the wake of second-wave feminism, and the continued shifting relationship of the state and individual also raised questions relating to the family and fatherhood. Partly because of this, there were more important developments in conceptions of fatherhood from the mid-1970s particularly, as the foundation of Families Need Fathers in 1974 indicated the start of a movement for fathers' rights. The 1990s also witnessed a 'reassessment' of fatherhood and its meanings, as 'traditional' roles disappeared and increasing numbers of single-parent families further brought into focus what fatherhood should and did mean.[36] If families could and were operating entirely without a father (or mother), a whole new set of questions about the meanings of parenting, and the gendered differentiation between motherhood and fatherhood, was raised. A resurgent discourse on understandings of fatherhood emerged at this time, and particular groups of fathers were increasingly portrayed in negative terms, as fatherhood itself was being imbued with ever more significance.[37]

What perhaps changed most radically after this period was the balance between fatherhood in private and in public. In the period in question here, the 1910s to the 1960s, barriers to men's involvement with their children outside the home decreased, with more money to spend on leisure activities and less stigma about active fatherhood. Beyond this period, as the public display of fatherhood has become increasingly prized, the shift between male parenting within and outside the home has altered. There has been a significant shift in the acceptability of men displaying strong emotions. Whilst many men in the first half of the twentieth century sought to hide their involvement in childcare chores, and gradually men were more likely to take their children out when old enough to walk, it seems that a public display of strong engagement with children, through pram-pushing and the like, could be used to absolve men of chores within the home. Whilst fatherhood has been remodelled continually and radically from the 1970s onwards, the increasing prominence of emotionally involved fatherhood has not generally been matched with such a substantial shift in the gendered division of domestic labour and childcare; mother remains the primary parent for most children. Taking children out and playing with them in public has provided a common way of fathers interacting with their sons and daughters throughout the twentieth century and beyond, yet, whilst fathers may have had to face mockery to do this in the first

[35] See Harry Hendrick, *Child Welfare: England 1872–1989* (London, 1994), pp. 242–57; Mathew Thomson, *Lost Freedom: The Landscape of the Child and the British Post-War Settlement* (Oxford, 2013), pp. 103–4.
[36] See Moss, 'Introduction', pp. xi–xxiv.
[37] See Burghes, Clarke, and Cronin, *Fathers*, p. 7.

half of the century, men are praised for doing so today. In this sense, the past hundred years constitute a period of both continuity and change, and by no means steady or linear progression towards gender equality. This book demonstrates that fathers have been more involved in family life and parenting in the past than is usually assumed. This is not to say that those children who grew up in this period were not subject to much stricter regimes and less emotionally open relationships; however, the practices of the period must be set in their contemporary context as well as contrasted with present values. As history is so inherent to understandings of fatherhood, there is a need for a fuller understanding of men in the past. It is hoped that the findings of this book will contribute towards a situation in which men are not congratulated for taking on childcare labour and an involved or even equal role in their children's lives as women, but that this is expected; yet likewise, those fathers who do want to play a more active role in their families can look towards history to provide evidence that such engagement is not new.

APPENDIX

LIST OF INTERVIEWS USED

Transcripts
Elizabeth Roberts Archive, transcripts held at Centre for North-West Regional Studies,
Lancaster University
Preston 1890–1940

Mr C1P, born 1884
Mr T3P, born 1886
Mr B4P, born 1896
Mrs B4P, husband born 1896/married 1925
Mr B8P, born 1896
Mr T1P, born 1897
Mrs B5P, born 1898
Mrs M3P, born 1898
Mrs P1P, born 1899
Mrs W1P, born 1899
Mr S1P, born 1900
Mr W3P, born 1900
Mrs B1P, born 1900
Mrs O1P, born 1902
Mr G1P, born 1903
Mr T2P, born 1903
Mrs H8P, born 1903
Mr B7P, born 1904
Mrs M6P, born 1904
Mrs D3P, born 1905
Mrs T5P, born 1905
Mr F1P, born 1906
Mrs P2P, born 1907
Mrs D1P, born 1908
Mr D2P, born 1910
Mrs A1P, born 1910
Mrs A2P, born 1910
Mrs J1P, born 1911
Miss T4P, born 1912
Mrs M1P, born 1913
Mrs S7P, born 1914
Mr S4P, born 1915
Mrs B2P, born 1916
Mrs H7P, born 1916
Mrs C5P, born 1919
Mr B9P, born 1927

Barrow/Lancaster 1890–1940

Mrs B1L, born 1888
Mr B1B, born 1897
Mr F2B, born 1900
Mr A2B, born 1904
Mrs A2B, born c.1904
Mrs H3L, born 1904
Mr M3L, born 1906
Mrs M3L, born 1917

1940–70

Mr P6B, born 1909
Mrs M11B, born 1914
Mrs Y2P, born 1915
Mrs O1B, born 1916
Mr F1L, born 1917
Mr L3P, born 1919
Mrs N3L, born 1919
Mr B4B, born 1920
Mrs L3B, born 1920
Mr K1B, born 1921
Mr N3L, born 1921
Mrs F1L, born 1921
Mrs P6B, born 1921
Mrs L3P, born 1922
Mr M7P, born 1922
Mr S4B, born 1922
Mrs W4L, born 1923
Mr S9P, born 1925
Mrs C7L, born 1926
Mr M13B, born 1927
Mrs R3P, born 1927
Mrs S3B, born 1927
Mrs Y1L, born 1927
Mr C8P, born1928
Mrs B3B, born 1928
Mr K2P, born 1930
Mrs K2P, husband born 1930/married 1957
Mr I2L, born 1930
Mr W6L, born 1931
Mr B2B, born 1931
Mr L4B, born 1931
Mr M14B, born 1931
Mr N2L, born 1931
Mr R3B, born 1931
Mr R3P, born 1931
Mrs B2B, born 1931
Mrs H3P, born 1931

Mrs H5L, born 1931
Mr S7L, born 1932
Mrs A4L, born 1932
Mrs J1B, born 1932
Mrs T2L, born 1932
Mr M12B, born 1933
Mrs H6L, born 1933
Mrs W5B, born 1933
Mrs B4L, born 1936
Mrs B11P, born 1936
Mrs M12B, born 1936
Mrs R4B, born 1936
Mrs W6B, born 1936
Mrs W6L, born 1937
Mr B11P, born 1937
Mr G3L, born 1937
Mrs E2P, born 1937
Mrs C8P, born 1940
Mr W5L, born 1940
Mr W7P, born 1940
Mrs L2L, born 1941
Mrs C8L, born 1942
Mrs L5B, born 1943
Mr R1P, born 1944
Mrs A3L, born 1944
Mr W7B, born 1945
Mrs R1P, born 1945
Mr F2L, born 1946
Mr H7L, born 1947
Mrs B10P, born 1947
Mrs T4B, born 1948
Mr M10L, born 1948
Mr Y1P, born 1948
Mrs P3L, born 1948
Mrs S6L, born 1948
Mr T4B, born 1949
Mr W8P, born 1949
Mr L5B, born 1950
Mr P5B, born 1950

'100 Families' online archive, P. Thompson and H. Newby, Families, Social Mobility and Ageing, an Intergenerational Approach, 1900–1988 [computer file]. Colchester, Essex: UK Data Archive [distributor], July 2005. SN: 4938

126/Sidney Sadler, born 1899
131/Ernest Shiell, born 1901
131/Daisy Shiell, husband born 1901
019/Edward Byrne, born 1904
118/Mrs Robertson, born 1904

153/Florence Warner, born 1906
154/Hymy Weatherall, born 1906
031/Allean Cleveland, born 1907
105/Emily Parker, born 1907
014/John Bostock, born 1908
168/Marion Thomas, born 1909
124/Mrs Ross, born 1910
122/Mrs Roy, born 1911
046/Ivor Davies, born 1912
163/Arthur Wood, 1912
155/May Welham, born 1913
055/Owlen Farrand, born 1914
146/Ron Vincent, born 1914
027/Ella Carey, born 1915
037/Peter Coverley (Snr), born 1915
042/Henry Curd, born 1915
042/Elsie Curd, husband born 1915/married 1938
086/Kathleen Lunan, born 1916
151/Mary Walter, born 1916
025/Leonard Canning, born 1917
083/Mrs Laughton, born 1917
085/Hilda Lovejoy, born 1917
159/Edward Winn, born 1917
080/Phyllis Lane, born 1918
096/Kathleen Musgrave, born 1918
132/Sidney Sorell, born 1918
157/Agnes Welham, born 1918
159/Jean Winn, born 1920
100/Emily Norton, born 1921
100/Walter Norton, wife born 1921
098/Jean Nedwell, born 1922
062/Irene Handley, born 1924
062/Albert Handley, born 1921
026/Margaret Corner, born 1926
087/J Mann, born 1926
003/Norah Austin, born 1927
092/Mary Moran, born 1928
090/Laura Millard, born 1929
127/George Sadler, born 1929
134/Vera Spencer, born 1929
134/Leonard Spencer, wife born 1929/married 1946
140/Harry Tillett, born 1929
145/Geoffrey Turner, born 1929
149/Margret Wall, born 1929
167/Mr Fides, born 1929
051/Patricia Dowden, born 1930
108/Pamela Pittuck, born 1930
116/Margret Rawe, born 1930
165/George Aberdou, born 1930

056/Mrs Fell, born 1931
073/Brian Huston, born 1931
075/Martin Jack, born 1931
089/Mathew Meret, born 1931
058/Arnold Roy Fitzsimmons, born 1932
078/Mohamed Asdiq Kholeif, born 1932
114/Joyce Mary Pounds, born 1932
076/Frank Jonston, born 1933
084/Mary Lear, born 1933
103/Terrence O'Farrell, born 1933
113/Victor Powers, born 1933
142/Ruth Tilley, born 1933
002/Elizabeth Arnold, born 1935
017/Patrica Brotherston, born 1935
022/John Buck, born 1935
006/Roy Barrow, born 1936
050/Marion Dilworth, born 1936
115/Margret Povey, born 1936
037/Jill Hunter, born 1937
047/Kenneth Davies, born 1937
077/Diana Kellard, born 1938
130/Mr Sell, born 1938
161/John Wilson, born 1938
166/David John Darbishire, born 1938
020/Martin Byrne, born 1939
032/David Cleveland, born 1939
069/Roy Hubbard, born 1939
001/Doreen Angus, born 1940
007/Jean Bates, born 1940
064/George Hindley, born 1940
119/Patricia Robertson, born 1940
024/John Burrell, born 1941
123/David Roy, born 1941
004/Sheila Barlow, born 1942
009/Margaret Beckwith, born 1942
0013/Christine Boyle, born 1942
040/Ian Crewe, born 1942
133/Alan Sorrell, born 1942
160/Arthur Winn, born 1942
016/Ceridwen Brook, born 1943
034/Sonia Colbeck, born 1943
104/Colin Osbourne, born 1943
162/Mary Wood, born 1943
049/John Dennis, born 1944
125/Angela Ross, born 1944
135/Glenda Speed, born 1944
156/Trevor Welham, born 1944
026/Ian Canning, born 1945
060/Margret Hallum, born 1945

147/Rosemary Vincent, born 1945
046/Martin Curd, born 1946
054/Isabelle Eddington, born 1946
066/Barbara Hirbert, born 1946
079/Mr Knight, born 1946
081/Leslie Lane, born 1946
117/Elaine Rickwood, born 1946
128/Mrs Schlarman, born 1946
011/Derek Benjamin, born 1947
057/Michael Fell, born 1947
095/Kathleen Murray, born 1948
049/Michael Cudmore, born 1949
137/Harry Stainer, born 1949
150/Michael Wall, born 1949
158/Brian Welham, born 1949
038/Peter Coverley (Jnr), born 1950
063/Gerald Handley, born 1950
093/Mrs J Morris, born 1951
094/Kate Morrissey, born 1951
106/Alan Parks, born 1951
101/Henry Offord, born 1952
053/William Dykes, born 1953
141/Steve Tillett, born 1953
152/Terrence Walter, born 1953
099/Elaine Nelson, born 1954

'A Labour of Love' Collection (Testimony Films), transcripts held at the British Library, London

Lucy Bayliss, married in First World War
Hilda Bennett, born 1897
Mary Siddall, born 1899
Ivy Summers, born 1901
Alf Short, born 1903
John Caldwell, born 1908
Lily Wells, married 1935
James Hardie, born 1910
Robert Williamson, born 1910
Verna Brennan, born 1918
Mary Cole, born 1918
Hilda Caldwell, born 1919
Ray Rochford, born 1925
Florence Siddall, born c.1921
Valerie Cole, born 1941

'A Man's World Collection' (Testimony Films), transcripts held at the British Film Institute Archive, London

Lord Riverdale, married 1925
Nelson Fowler, born 1904
Ted Cunningham, married 1932

Bert Barnes, first child born 1931
Sidney Ling, born 1910
George Ryder, born c.1911
Tom Hopkins, born c.1912
Geordie Todd, born 1912
Humphrey Gillett, born c.1913
Richard Nesbitt, born c.1919
Glyn Davies, married 1946
Frank Davies, born 1921
Joan Davies, married 1949
Alec Gunn, schoolboy in 1930s/served in Second World War
Joe Phillips, born 1927
Sean Harold Smith, born 1927
Roy Booth, born c.1929
Ron McGill, born c.1930
Danny Slattery, born c.1930
David Swift, born 1930
Irene Swift, husband born 1930

Recordings
'A Labour of Love' Collection (Testimony Films), held at the British Library, London

John Caldwell recording, C590/01/322 C1
Ray Rochford recording, C590/01/300 C2-303 C1
Alf Short recording, C590/01/465-468 C1
Robert Williamson recording, C590/01/410-417 C1

Bibliography

UNPUBLISHED PRIMARY SOURCES

Letters
Imperial War Museum Letters, held at Imperial War Museum, London

Private Papers of E. G. Ball, Documents.13 449
Private Papers of S. Bensinger, Documents.16 579
Private Papers of P. A. Buchanan, Documents.1044
Private Papers of E.G. Buckeridge, Documents.13 267
Private Papers of G. and E. Butling, Documents.2423
Private Papers of M. Canty, Documents.13 575
Private Papers of D. S. Cave, Documents.6443
Private Papers of Mrs H. L. Dockrill, Documents.11 743
Private Papers of J. Evans, Documents.16 621
Private Papers of C. D. Fuller, Documents.16 408
Private Papers of H. W. Hicks, Documents.15 335
Private Papers of C. Jones, Documents.11 085
Private Papers of T. D. Laidlaw, Documents.11 018
Private Papers of J. S. Mathews, Documents.16 403
Private Papers of J. Mott, Documents.15 587
Private Papers of J. W. Mudd, Documents.1174
Private Papers of D. E. Parker, Documents.1926
Private Papers of F. I. Williams, Documents.17 022
Private Papers of P. A. Wise, Documents.1131
Private Papers of A. H. Wright, Documents.13 285

Marie Stopes Letters (c) The British Library Board, London

Vol 1 ADD.Ms.58670, 1918–1919
Vol 6 ADD.Ms.58675, 1929–1931
Vol 9 ADD.Ms.58678, 1940–1958

MASS-OBSERVATION FILE REPORTS

A.11. 'Motives and Methods of Newspaper Reading', December 1938
38A. 'Newspaper Reading Habits', February 1940
48. 'Selection and Taste in Book Reading', January–February 1940
57. 'Film Report', March 1940
66. 'Film Response', April 1940
90. 'Morale', April 1940
96. 'Children's Reading at Fulham Library', February 1940
113. 'Press Space Analysis', May 1940
126. 'Report on the Press', May 1940
129. 'Summary of News Belief and Disbelief', May 1940
343. 'What People Think about the Press', August 1940
470. 'The Social Function of the Press', October 1940

1222. 'Book Reading Survey', March–April 1942
1231. 'Daily Mirror Warning and News Relief', April 1942
1252. 'Radio II', May 1942
1273. 'Forces Family Allowances', May 1942
1282. 'Family Allowances at the Labour Party Conference', May 1942
1330A. 'Daily Express', June 1942
1332. 'Books and the Public', July 1942
1339. 'Daily Express Readership', June 1942
1341. 'Social Climbing', July 1942
1871. 'The Cinema and the Public', July 1943
1960. 'Daily Express Housing', November 1943
1963. 'What Makes a Marriage Successful?', November 1943
1967. 'The Foundations of a Successful Marriage', November 1943
2015. 'Why People Marry', February 1944
2018. 'Books and the Public', February 1944
2086. 'Childhood Reading', May 1944
2111. 'Population Problems', June 1944
2120. 'The Film and Family Life', June 1944
2285. 'Women's Reasons for Having Small Families', September 1945
2429. 'The Cinema and the Public', 1946
2473. 'Report on Juvenile Delinquency', April 1947
2474. 'Note on Juvenile Delinquency', April 1947
2492. 'Book Buying Habits', May 1947
2557. 'Attitudes to Daily Newspapers', January 1948
3063. 'Report on Newspaper Reading, 1947–48, November 1949
3107. 'A Survey of the Ideal Family', April 1949

OFFICIAL DOCUMENTS

Cabinet Documents, available at http://www.nationalarchives.gov.uk/documentsonline/
cabinetpapers.asp [accessed 30/8/2013]

CAB 24/133
CAB 24/165
CAB 24/166
CAB 24/171
CAB/65/49/26
CAB/195/3

PUBLISHED PRIMARY SOURCES

Press
Newspapers and magazines

Daily Express
Daily Mirror
Lilliput
The Listener
Manchester Guardian

Men Only
Observer
The Times

Internet Sources
The National Cartoon Archive, University of Kent
(http://www.cartoons.ac.uk/[last accessed 30/08/2013])

TELEVISION PROGRAMMES AND FILMS REFERRED TO

'A Man's World: The Father', BBC2, broadcast 27 March 1996, held at British Film Institute Archive, London

Love on the Dole (John Baxter, 1941)
Sally in our Alley (Maurice Elvey and Basil Dean, 1931)
The Briggs Family (Herbert Mason and A.M. Salomon, 1940)
The Passionate Friends (David Lean and Ronald Neame, 1949)
The Scamp (Wolf Rilla and James Lawrie, 1957)
This Happy Breed (David Lean and Noël Coward, 1944)

ADVICE LITERATURE

Frankenburg, Mrs S. (C.U.) [1922], *Common Sense in the Nursery* (Kingswood, 1954).

Illingworth, R. S. and Illingworth, C. M., *Babies and Young Children: Feeding, Management and Care* (London, 1954).

Isaacs, S. [1929], *The Nursery Years: The Mind of the Child from Birth to Six Years* (London, 1956).

Isaacs, S. (ed.), *Fatherless Children: A Contribution to the Understanding of their Needs* (London, 1945).

Isaacs, S., 'Fatherless Children', in S. Isaacs (ed.), *Fatherless Children: A Contribution to the Understanding of Their Needs* (London, 1945), pp. 1–14.

King, F. T., *The Expectant Mother and Baby's First Month* (London, 1924).

King, F. T., *Feeding and Care of Baby* (London, 1937).

King, M. T. [1934], *Mothercraft* (Sydney, 1937).

Riviere, J., 'The Bereaved Wife', in S. Isaacs (ed.), *Fatherless Children: A Contribution to the Understanding of Their Needs* (London, 1945), pp. 15–22.

Sharpe, E. F., 'What the Father Means to the Child', in S. Isaacs (ed.), *Fatherless Children: A Contribution to the Understanding of Their Needs* (London, 1945), pp. 23–9.

Spock, B., *Baby and Child Care* (London, 1955).

Spock, B., *Baby and Child Care* (2nd edn, London, 1958).

Stopes, M. [1918], *Married Love: A New Contribution to the Solution of Sex Difficulties* (London, 1923).

Valentine, C. W., *Parents and Children: A First Book on the Psychology of Child Development and Training* (London, 1953).

Willcock, C. (ed.), *The Man's Book* (London, 1958).

Winnicott, D. W., *Getting to Know Your Baby* (pamphlet, London, 1945).

Winnicott, D. W., *The Ordinary Devoted Mother and Her Baby: Nine Broadcast Talks* (pamphlet, London, 1949).

Winnicott, D. W., *The Child and the Family: First Relationships* (London, 1957).

FICTIONAL TEXTS REFERRED TO

Ballard, P. B., *The Bargerys* (London, 1934).

Blyton, E. [1942], *Five on a Treasure Island* (London, 2001).

Blyton, E. [1942], *Five Go Adventuring Again* (London, 1993).

Blyton, E. [1945], *The Caravan Family*, published in *The Family Collection* (London, 2002).

Blyton, E. [1947], *The Saucy Jane Family*, published in *The Family Collection* (London, 2002).

Blyton, E. [1949], *Five Get into Trouble* (Leicester, 1975).

Blyton, E. [1950], *The Pole Star Family*, published in *The Family Collection* (London, 2002).

Blyton, E. [1950], *The Seaside Family*, published in *The Family Collection* (London, 2002).

Blyton, E. [1951], *The Queen Elizabeth Family*, published in *The Family Collection* (London, 2002).

Blyton, E. [1951], *The Buttercup Farm Family*, published in *The Family Collection* (London, 2002).

Blyton, E. [1952], *Five Have a Wonderful Time* (London, 1986).

Blyton, E. [1954], *Five Have Plenty of Fun* (London, 1991).

Blyton, E. [1955], *The River of Adventure*, published with *The Circus of Adventure* (London, 2002).

Blyton, E. [1956], *Five on a Secret Trail* (London 1985).

Brisley, J. L. [1928], *Milly-Molly-Mandy Stories* (Harmondsworth, 1972).

Crompton, R. [1922], *Just William* (London, 1990).

Crompton, R. [1922], *More William* (online, 2005, available at http://manybooks.net [last accessed 30/08/2013]).

Deeping, W. [1925], *Sorrell and Son* (Harmondsworth, 1984).

Garnett, E. [1942], *The Family from One End Street* (London, 1981).

Hall, R. [1928], *The Well of Loneliness* (London, 1983).

Lawrence, D. H., *Sons and Lovers* (New York, 1913).

Monckton, E., *The Gates Family* (London, 1934).

Nesbit, E. [1906], *The Railway Children* (London, 1995).

Sheriff, R. C., *The Fortnight in September* (Leipzig, 1932).

Woolf, V. [1927], *To the Lighthouse* (Harmondsworth, 1964).

AUTOBIOGRAPHIES

Ackerley, J. R. [1968], *My Father and Myself* (New York, 1999).

Barnes, R., *Coronation Cups and Jam Jars* (London, 1976).

Barrett, W. H., *A Fenman's Story* (London, 1965).

Beavis, D., *What Price Happiness? My Life from Coal Hewer to Shop Steward* (Whitley Bay, 1980).

Blishen, E., *Shaky Relations: An Autobiography* (London, 1981).

Bowyer, W., *Brought Out in Evidence: An Autobiographical Summing Up* (London 1941).

Boyle, J., *A Sense of Freedom* (Edinburgh, 1977).

Bullock, J., *Bowers Row: Recollections of a Mining Village* (Wakefield, 1976).

Church, R., *Over the Bridge: An Essay in Autobiography* (London, 1955).

Clarke, S., *Sam, an East End Cabinet-Maker* (London, n.d. c.1983).

Cook, G., *A Hackney Memory Chest* (London, 1983).

Coombes, B. L., *These Poor Hands: The Autobiography of a Miner Working in South Wales* (London, 1939).

Cowan, E. [1974], *Spring Remembered: A Scottish Jewish Childhood* (London, 1990).

Crozier, F. P., *A Brass Hat in No Man's Land* (London, 1930).

Daley, H., *This Small Cloud: A Personal Memoir* (London, 1986).

Dayus, K., *Her People* (London, 1982).

Delderfield, R. F., *Bird's Eye View* (London, 1954).

Edwin, J., *I'm Going–What Then?* (Bognor Regis, 1978).

Finn, R. L., *Spring in Aldgate* (London, 1968).

Foley, W. [1977/1978/1981], *Shiny Pennies and Grubby Pinafores: How We Overcame Hardship to Raise a Happy Family in the 1950s* (London, 2010).

Forman, C., *Industrial Town: Self Portrait of St Helens in the 1920s* (London, 1979).

Haythorne, E., *On Earth to Make the Numbers Up* (Castleford, 1991).

Healey, B., *Hard Times and Easy Terms, and Other Tales by a Queen's Park Cockney* (Brighton, 1980).

Hewins, G., *The Dillen: Memories of a Man of Stratford-Upon-Avon*, ed. A. Hewins (London, 1981).

Hitchin, G., *Pit-Yacker* (London, 1962).

Hughes, M. [1940], *A London Family between the Wars* (Oxford, 1979).

Jobson, A., *The Creeping Hours of Time* (London, 1977).

Johnson, P., *The Vanished Landscape: A 1930s Childhood in the Potteries* (London, 2004).

Lawson, J. [1932], *A Man's Life* (London, 1949).

Magee, B. [2003], *Clouds of Glory: A Hoxton Childhood* (London, 2004).

Morgan, R., *My Lamp Still Burns* (Llandysul, 1981).

O'Mara, P., *The Autobiography of a Liverpool Irish Slummy* (London, 1934).

Purves, A., *A Shepherd Remembers: Reminiscences of a Border Shepherd* (East Lothian, 2001).

Roberts, R., *The Classic Slum: Salford Life in the First Quarter of the Century* (Manchester, 1971).

Short, E., *I Knew My Place* (London, 1983).

Tomlinson, G. A. W., *Coal-Miner* (London, c.1937).

Walker, T., *The High Path* (London, 1982).

Weir, M. [1970], *Shoes Were for Sunday* (London, 1973).

Willmott, P., *Growing Up in a London Village: Family Life between the Wars* (Halifax, 1979).

Woodruff, W. [1993], *The Road to Nab End: An Extraordinary Northern Childhood* (London, 2008).

Woodruff, W. [2003], *Beyond Nab End* (London, 2008).

Worboyes, S., *East End Girl: Growing Up the Hard Way* (London, 2006).

ORAL HISTORY AND MEMOIR COLLECTIONS

A Colliery Banksman, 'Frustration and Bitterness', in H. L. Beales and R. S. Lambert (eds) [1934], *Memoirs of the Unemployed* (Wakefield, 1973), pp. 89–98.

A Skilled Wire Drawer, 'The Wife Works While I Look after the Home', in H. L. Beales and R. S. Lambert (eds) [1934], *Memoirs of the Unemployed* (Wakefield, 1973), pp. 175–81.

Allen, H., 'Leicestershire', in N. Gray (ed.), *The Worst of Times: An Oral History of the Great Depression in Britain* (London, 1985), pp. 138–46.

Beales, H. L., and Lambert, R. S. (eds) [1934], *Memoirs of the Unemployed* (Wakefield, 1973).

Common, J. (ed.) [1938], *Seven Shifts* (Wakefield, 1978).

Farrington, J., 'Manchester', in N. Gray (ed.), *The Worst of Times: An Oral History of the Great Depression in Britain* (London, 1985), pp. 10–26.

French, S., *Fatherhood: Men Writing about Fathering* (London, 1992).

Gray, N., *The Worst of Times: An Oral History of the Great Depression in Britain* (London, 1985).

Hoyland, J. (ed.), *Fathers and Sons* (London, 1992).

Humphries, S. and Gordon, P. (eds), *A Labour of Love: The Experience of Parenthood in Britain, 1900–1950* (London, 1993).

Humphries, S. and Gordon, P. (eds) *A Man's World: From Boyhood to Manhood, 1900–1960* (London, 1996).

Maher, K., 'Caerphilly' in N. Gray (ed.), *The Worst of Times: An Oral History of the Great Depression in Britain* (London, 1985), p. 27–53.

Owen, U. (ed.) [1983], *Fathers: Reflections by Daughters* (London, 1994).

Robb, M., 'The Psychology of the Unemployed from the Medical Point of View', in H. L. Beales and R. S. Lambert (eds) [1934], *Memoirs of the Unemployed* (Wakefield, 1973), pp. 271–87.

SOCIAL RESEARCH

Arensberg, C. M. and Kimball, S. T. [1940], *Family and Community in Ireland* (Cambridge, MA, 1968).

Bakke, E. W., *The Unemployed Man: A Social Study* (London, 1933).

Baldamus, W. and Timms, N., 'The Problem Family: A Sociological Approach', *The British Journal of Sociology* 6:4 (1955), pp. 318–27.

Banks, J. A., *Prosperity and Parenthood: A Study Family Planning among the Victorian Middle Classes* (London, 1954).

Bell, C., *Middle Class Families: Social and Geographical Mobility* (London, 1968).

Black, E. I. and Simey, T. S. (eds), *Neighbourhood and Community: An Enquiry into Social Relationships on Housing Estates in Liverpool and Sheffield* (Liverpool, 1954).

Bott, E. [1957], *Family and Social Network: Roles, Norms, and External Relationships in Ordinary Urban Families* (London, 1971).

Bowlby, J., *Child Care and the Growth of Love* (Harmondsworth, 1953).

Bowley, A. H. [1946], *Problems of Family Life: An Environmental Study* (Edinburgh, 1948).

Brennan, T., *Reshaping a City* (Glasgow and London, 1959).

Cauter, T. and Downham, J. S., *The Communication of Ideas: A Study of Contemporary Influences on Urban Life* (London, 1954).

Dennis, N., Henriques, F., and Slaughter, C. [1956], *Coal Is Our Life: An Analysis of a Yorkshire Mining Community* (London, 1969).

Firth, R. (ed.), *Two Studies of Kinship in London* (London, 1956).

Firth, R., 'Family and Kin Ties in Britain and Their Social Implications: Introduction', *The British Journal of Sociology* 12:4 (1961), pp. 305–9.

Firth, R., Hubert, J., and Forge, A., *Families and Their Relatives: Kinship in a Middle-Class Sector of London: An Anthropological Study* (London, 1969).

Fletcher, R., *Britain in the Sixties: The Family and Marriage: An Analysis and Moral Assessment* (Harmondsworth, 1962).

Goldthorpe, J. H., Lockwood, D., Bechhofer, F., and Platt, J. [1968], *The Affluent Worker in the Class Structure* (Cambridge, 1969).

Gorer, G., *Exploring English Character* (London, 1955).

Hannington, W., *The Problem of the Distressed Areas* (London, 1937).

Harris, C. C., *The Family: An Introduction* (London, 1969).

Hoggart, R. [1957], *The Uses of Literacy: Aspects of Working-Class Life with Special Reference to Publications and Entertainments* (Harmondsworth, 1971).

Hubert, J., 'Kinship and Geographical Mobility in a Sample from a London Middle-Class Area', *International Journal of Comparative Sociology* 6 (1965), pp. 61–80.

Jackson, B. and Marsden, D. [1962], *Education and the Working Class* (Harmondsworth, 1970).

Kempe, R. S. and Kempe, C. H., *Child Abuse* (London, 1978).

Klein, V., *Britain's Married Women Workers* (London, 1965).

Lancaster, L., 'Some Conceptual Problems in the Study of Family and Kin Ties in the British Isles', *The British Journal of Sociology* 12:4 (1961), pp. 317–33.

Littlejohn, J., *Westrigg: The Sociology of a Cheviot Parish* (London, 1963).

Loudon, J. B., 'Kinship and Crisis in South Wales', *The British Journal of Sociology* 12:4 (1961), pp. 333–50.

Marchant, J. (ed.), *Rebuilding Family Life in the Post-War World: An Enquiry with Recommendations* (London, c.1944).

Mass-Observation, *Britain and Her Birth-Rate* (London, 1945).

Mays, J. B. [1954], *Growing Up in the City: A Study of Juvenile Delinquency in an Urban Neighbourhood* (Liverpool, 1964).

McGregor, O. R., 'Some Research Possibilities and Historical Materials for Family and Kinship Study in Britain', *The British Journal of Sociology* 12:4 (1961), pp. 310–17.

Mogey, J. M., *Rural Life in Northern Ireland: Five Regional Studies Made for the Northern Ireland Council of Social Service* (London, 1947).

Mogey, J. M., 'Changes in Family Life Experienced by English Workers Moving from Slums to Housing Estates', *Marriage and Family Living* 17:2 (1955), pp. 123–8.

Mogey, J. M., *Family and Neighbourhood: Two Studies in Oxford* (Oxford, 1956).

Mogey, J. M., 'A Century of Declining Paternal Authority', *Marriage and Family Living* 19:3 (1957), pp. 234–9.

Myrdal, A. and Klein, V., *Women's Two Roles: Home and Work* (London, 1956).

Newson, J. and Newson, E. [1963], *Patterns of Infant Care in an Urban Community* (Harmondsworth, 1974).

Pierce, R. M., 'Marriage in the Fifties', *Sociological Review* 11 (1963), pp. 215–40.

Pilgrim Trust, *Men without Work: A Report Made to the Pilgrim Trust* (Cambridge, 1938).

Rosser, C. and Harris, C., *The Family and Social Change: A Study of Family and Kinship in a South Wales Town* (London, 1965).

Rowntree, B. S., *Poverty and Progress: A Second Social Survey of York* (London, 1941).

Shaw, L. A., 'Impressions of Family Life in a London Suburb', *Sociological Review* 2 (1954), pp. 179–94.

Slater, E. and Woodside, M., *Patterns of Marriage: A Study of Marriage Relationships in the Urban Working Classes* (London, 1951).

Spring-Rice, M., *Working-Class Wives: Their Health and Conditions* (Harmondsworth, 1939).

St Philip's Settlement Education and Economics Research Society, *The Equipment of the Workers* (London, 1919).

Titmuss, R. and Titmuss, K., *Parents Revolt: A Study of the Declining Birth-Rate in Acquisitive Societies* (London, 1942).

Willmott, P. and Young, M., *Family and Class in a London Suburb* (London, 1960).

Women's Group on Public Welfare, *The Neglected Child and His Family* (London, 1948).

Wynn, M., *Fatherless Families: A Study of Families Deprived of a Father by Death, Divorce, Separation or Desertion before or after Marriage* (London, 1964).

Young, M. and Willmott, P. [1957], *Family and Kinship in East London* (Harmondsworth, 1967).

Zweig, F., *The Worker in Affluent Society: Family Life and Industry* (London, 1961).

OFFICIAL DOCUMENTS

Hansard, *Parliamentary Debates of the Houses of Commons and Lords.*

Royal Commission on Population, *Report*, Command Number 7695 (London, 1949).

Other published materials

Bromley, P. M. [1957], *Family Law* (London, 1962).

Cudlipp, H., *Publish and Be Damned! The Astonishing Story of the Daily Mirror* (London, 1953).

Graveson, R. H. and Crane, F. R. (eds), *A Century of Family Law, 1857–1957* (London, 1957).

James, T. E., 'The Illegitimate and Deprived Child: Legitimation and Adoption', in R. H. Graveson and F. R. Crane (eds), *A Century of Family Law, 1857–1957* (London, 1957), pp. 39–55.

Mayer, J. P., *British Cinema and Their Audiences* (London, 1948).

Pettit, P. H., 'Parental Control and Guardianship', in H. Graveson and F. R. Crane (eds), *A Century of Family Law, 1857–1957* (London, 1957), pp. 56–87.

Richards, J. and Sheridan, D. (eds), *Mass-Observation at the Movies* (London, 1987).

Selected Secondary Sources

Abbott, M., *Family Ties: English Families 1540–1920* (London, 1993).

Abbott, M., *Family Affairs: A History of the Family in Twentieth Century England* (London, 2003).

Abrams, L., '"There Was Nobody Like My Daddy": Fathers, the Family and the Marginalisation of Men in Modern Scotland', *Scottish Historical Review* 78:2 (1999), pp. 219–42.

Aldgate, A. and Richards, J., *Best of British: Cinema and Society from 1930 to the Present* (2nd edn, London, 1999).

Alexander, S., 'Becoming a Woman in London in the 1920s and 1930s', in D. Feldman and G. Stedman Jones (eds), *Metropolis-London: Histories and Representations since 1800* (London, 1989), pp. 245–71.

Alexander, S., 'Men's Fears and Women's Work: Responses to Unemployment in London between the Wars', *Gender and History* 12:2 (2000), pp. 401–25.

Allport, A., *Demobbed: Coming Home after the Second World War* (New Haven CT, and London, 2009).

Alston, A., *The Family in English Children's Literature* (London and New York, 2008).

Anderson, B., *Imagined Communities: Reflections on the Origin and Spread of Nationalism* (Rev. edn, London and New York, 2006).

Anderson, M., 'The Emergence of the Modern Life Cycle in Britain', *Social History* 10:1 (1985), pp. 69–87.

Anderson, M., 'Highly Restricted Fertility: Very Small Families in the British Fertility Decline', *Population Studies* 52:2 (1998), pp. 177–99.

Armstrong, N., 'Father(ing) Christmas: Fatherhood, Gender and Modernity in Victorian and Edwardian England', in T. L. Broughton and H. Rogers (eds), *Gender and Fatherhood in the Nineteenth Century* (Basingstoke, 2007), pp. 96–110.

Arnold, J. H. and Brady, S. (eds), *What Is Masculinity? Historical Dynamics from Antiquity to the Contemporary World* (Basingstoke, 2011).

Arnold, J. H. and Brady, S., 'Introduction', in J. H. Arnold and S. Brady (eds), *What is Masculinity? Historical Dynamics from Antiquity to the Contemporary World* (Basingstoke, 2011), pp. 1–14.

Bailey, J., '"A Very Sensible Man": Imagining Fatherhood in England c.1750–1830', *History* 95:319 (2010), pp. 267–92.

Bailey, J., 'Masculinity and Fatherhood in England c.1760–1830', in J. H. Arnold and S. Brady (eds), *What Is Masculinity? Historical Dynamics from Antiquity to the Contemporary World* (Basingstoke, 2011), pp. 167–86.

Bailey, J., *Parenting in England, 1760–1830* (Oxford, 2012).

Bengry, J., 'Courting the Pink Pound: *Men Only* and the Queer Consumer, 1935–39' *History Workshop Journal* 68:1 (2009), pp. 122–48.

Bertaux, D. and Thompson, P. (eds), *Between Generations: Family Models, Myths and Memories* (2nd edn, Somerset, NJ, 2005).

Bertaux, D. and Thompson, P., 'Introduction', in D. Bertaux and P. Thompson (eds), *Between Generations: Family Models, Myths and Memories* (2nd edn, Somerset, NJ, 2005), pp. 1–12.

Bibbings, L., 'Image of Manliness: The Portrayal of Soldiers and Conscientious Objectors in the Great War', *Social and Legal Studies* 12:3 (2003), pp. 335–58.

Bingham, A., *Gender, Modernity, and the Popular Press in Inter-War Britain* (Oxford, 2004).

Bingham, A., *Family Newspapers? Sex, Private Life, and the British Popular Press 1918–1978* (Oxford, 2009).

Bingham, A., 'The Digitization of Newspaper Archives: Opportunities and Challenges for Historians', *Twentieth Century British History* 21:2 (2010), pp. 225–31.

Bloom, C., *Bestsellers: Popular Fiction since 1900* (2nd edn, Basingstoke, 2008).

Bourke, J., *Working Class Cultures in Britain 1890–1960: Gender, Class, and Ethnicity* (London, 1994).

Bourke, J., *Dismembering the Male: Men's Bodies, Britain and the Great War* (London, 1996).

Bourke, J., 'Effeminacy, Ethnicity and the End of Trauma: The Sufferings of "Shell-Shocked" Men in Great Britain and Ireland, 1914–39', *Journal of Contemporary History* 35:1 (2000), pp. 57–69.

Brannen, J. and Nilsen, A., 'From Fatherhood to Fathering: Transmission and Change among British Fathers in Four-generation Families', *Sociology* 40 (2006), pp. 335–52.

Brooke, S., 'Gender and Working Class Identity in Britain during the 1950s', *Journal of Social History* 34:4 (2001), pp. 773–95.

Broughton, T. L. and Rogers, H. (eds), *Gender and Fatherhood in the Nineteenth Century* (Basingstoke, 2007).

Broughton, T. L. and Rogers, H., 'Introduction: The Empire of the Father', in T. L. Broughton and H. Rogers (eds), *Gender and Fatherhood in the Nineteenth Century* (Basingstoke, 2007), pp. 1–28.

Bruley, S., '*The Love of an Unknown Soldier*: A Story of Mystery, Myth and Masculinity in World War One', *Contemporary British History* 19:4 (2005), pp. 459–79.

Bruzzi, S., *Bringing Up Daddy: Fatherhood and Masculinity in Post-War Hollywood* (London, 2005).

Buettner, E., 'Fatherhood Real, Imagined, Denied: British Men in Imperial India', in T. L. Broughton and H. Rogers (eds), *Gender and Fatherhood in the Nineteenth Century* (Basingstoke, 2007), pp. 178–89.

Bulmer, M. (ed.), *Essays on the History of British Sociological Research* (Cambridge, 1985).

Bulmer, M., 'The Development of Sociology and of Empirical Social Research in Britain', in M. Bulmer (ed.), *Essays on the History of British Sociological Research* (Cambridge, 1985), pp. 3–36.

Bulmer, M., Bales, K., and Sklar, K. K. (eds), *The Social Survey in Historical Perspective, 1880–1940* (Cambridge, 1991).

Bulmer, M., Bales, K., and Sklar, K. K., 'Preface', in M. Bulmer, K. Bales, and K. K. Sklar (eds), *The Social Survey in Historical Perspective, 1880–1940* (Cambridge, 1991), pp. xvii–xix.

Bulmer, M., Bales, K., and Sklar, K. K., 'The Social Survey in Historical Perspective', in M. Bulmer, K. Bales, and K. K. Sklar (eds), *The Social Survey in Historical Perspective, 1880–1940* (Cambridge, 1991), pp. 1–48.

Burghes, L., Clarke, L., and Cronin, N., *Fathers and Fatherhood in Britain* (London, 1997).

Burgess, A., *Fatherhood Reclaimed: The Making of the Modern Father* (London, 1997).

Burnett, J., *Idle Hands: The Experience of Unemployment, 1790–1990* (London, 1994).

Calder, A., 'Mass-Observation 1937–1949', in M. Bulmer (ed.), *Essays on the History of British Sociological Research* (Cambridge, 1985), pp. 121–36.

Capdevila, L., 'The Quest for Masculinity in a Defeated France, 1940–1945', *Contemporary European History* 10:3 (2001), pp. 423–45.

Childers, K. S., *Fathers, Families, and the State in France, 1914–1945* (Ithaca, NY, and London, 2003).

Clark, D. (ed.), *Marriage, Domestic Life and Social Change* (London, 1991).

Clark, D., 'Introduction', in D. Clark (ed.), *Marriage, Domestic Life and Social Change* (London, 1991), pp. 3–6.

Coleman, D., 'Population and Family', in A. H. Halsey (ed.), *Twentieth-Century British Social Trends* (3rd edn, Basingstoke 2000), pp. 27–93.

Collins, M., 'The Pornography of Permissiveness: Men's Sexuality and Women's Emancipation in Mid-Twentieth Century Britain', *History Workshop Journal* 47 (1999), pp. 99–120.

Collins, M., 'Pride and Prejudice: West Indian Men in Mid-Twentieth-Century Britain', *Journal of British Studies* 40:3 (2001), pp. 391–418.

Collins, M., *Modern Love: An Intimate History of Men and Women in Twentieth-Century Britain* (London, 2003).

Connell, R. W., *Masculinities* (2nd edn, Cambridge, 2005).

Cook, H., *The Long Sexual Revolution: English Women, Sex, and Contraception, 1800–1975* (Oxford, 2004).

Cook, H., 'Demography', in H. G. Cocks and M. Houlbrook (eds), *Palgrave Advances in the Modern History of Sexuality* (Basingstoke, 2006), pp. 19–40.

Cooter, R. (ed.), *In the Name of the Child: Health and Welfare, 1880–1940* (London and New York, 1992).

Curran, J. and Seaton, J., *Power without Responsibility: The Press, Broadcasting and New Media in Britain* (6th edn, London, 2003).

Davidoff, L., Doolittle, M., Fink, J., and Holden, K., *The Family Story: Blood, Contract and Intimacy, 1830–1939* (Harlow, 1999).

Davidoff, L. and Hall, C., *Family Fortunes: Men and Women of the English Middle Class, 1780–1850* (2nd edn, London, 2002).

Dawson, G., *Soldier Heroes: British Adventure, Empire and the Imagining of Masculinities* (London and New York, 1994).

Davis, A., 'A Critical Perspective on British Social Surveys and Community Studies and Their Accounts of Married Life c.1945–1970', *Cultural and Social History* 6:1 (2009), pp. 47–64.

Davis, A., *Modern Motherhood: Women and Family in England, 1945–2000* (Manchester, 2012).

Day, G. (ed.), *Literature and Culture in Modern Britain, Volume Two: 1930–1955* (Harlow, 1997).

De Grazia, V., 'Establishing the Modern Consumer Household: Introduction', in V. De Grazia and E. Furlough (eds), *The Sex of Things: Gender and Consumption in Historical Perspective* (London, 1996), pp. 151–61.

Delap, L., '"Be Strong and Play the Man": Anglican Mascunities in the Twentieth Century', in Lucy Delap and Sue Morgan (eds), *Men, Masculinities and Religious Change in Twentieth-Century Britain* (Basingstoke, 2013), pp. 119–45.

Delap, L., Griffin, B., and Wills, A. (eds), *The Politics of Domestic Authority in Britain since 1800* (Basingstoke, 2009).

Delap, L. and Morgan, S. (eds), *Men, Masculinities and Religious Change in Twentieth-Century Britain* (Basingstoke, 2013).

Dermott, E., *Intimate Fatherhood: A Sociological Analysis* (London, 2008).

Doolittle, M., 'Fatherhood, Religious Belief and the Protection of Children in Nineteenth-Century English Families', in T. L. Broughton and H. Rogers (eds), *Gender and Fatherhood in the Nineteenth Century* (Basingstoke, 2007), pp. 31–42.

Doolittle, M., 'Time, Space and Memories: The Father's Chair and Grandfather Clocks in Victorian Working Class Domestic Lives', *Home Cultures* 8:3 (2011), pp. 245–54.

Dudink, S., Hagemann, K., and Tosh, J. (eds), *Masculinities in Politics and War: Gendering Modern History* (Manchester, 2004).

Dyhouse, C., 'Mothers and Daughters in the Middle-Class Home, c.1870–1914', in J. Lewis (ed.), *Labour and Love: Women's Experiences of Home and Family, 1850–1940* (Oxford, 1986), pp. 27–47.

Dyhouse, C., *Feminism and the Family in England, 1880–1939* (Oxford, 1989).

Finch, J. and Summerfield, P., 'Social Reconstruction and the Emergence of Companionate Marriage, 1945–59', in D. Clark (ed.), *Marriage, Domestic Life and Social Change* (London, 1991), pp. 7–32.

Fink, J. and Holden, K., 'Pictures from the Margins of Marriage: Representations of Spinsters and Single Mothers in the Mid-Victorian Novel, Inter-War Hollywood Melodrama and British Film of the 1950s and 1960s', *Gender and History* 11:2 (1999), pp. 233–55.

Fisher, K., '"She Was Quite Satisfied with the Arrangements I Made": Gender and Birth Control in Britain 1920–1950', *Past and Present* 169 (2000), pp. 161–93.

Fisher, K., 'Uncertain Aims and Tacit Negotiation: Birth Control Practices in Britain, 1925–1950', *Population and Development Review* 26:2 (2000), pp. 295–317.

Fisher, K., *Birth Control, Sex and Marriage in Britain 1918–1960* (Oxford, 2006).

Fisher, K. and Szreter, S., '"They Prefer Withdrawal": The Choice of Birth Control in Britain, 1918–1950', *Journal of Interdisciplinary History* 34:2 (2003), pp. 263–91.

Fisher, T., 'Fatherhood and the British Fathercraft Movement, 1919–1939', *Gender and History* 17:2 (2005), pp. 441–62.

Francis, M., 'The Domestication of the Male? Recent Research on Nineteenth- and Twentieth-Century British Masculinity', *Historical Journal* 45:3 (2002), pp. 637–52.

Francis, M., 'A Flight from Commitment? Domesticity, Adventure and the Masculine Imaginary in Britain after the Second World War', *Gender and History* 19:1 (2007), pp. 163–85.

Francis, M., *The Flyer: British Culture and the Royal Air Force, 1939–1945* (Oxford and New York, 2008).

Frosh, S., *Sexual Difference: Masculinity and Psychoanalysis* (London and New York, 1994).

Gallie, D., 'The Labour Force', in A. H. Halsey (ed.), *Twentieth-Century British Social Trends* (3rd edn, Basingstoke, 2000), pp. 281–323.

Gallwey, A., 'The Rewards of Using Archived Oral Histories in Research: The Case of the Millennium Memory Bank', *Oral History* 41:1 (2013), pp. 37–50.

Giles, J., *Women, Identity and Private Life in Britain, 1900–50* (Basingstoke, 1995).

Gillis, J. R., *For Better, For Worse: British Marriages, 1600 to the Present* (Oxford, 1985).

Gittins, D., *Fair Sex: Family Size and Structure 1900–39* (London, 1982).

Gledhill, C. and Swanson, G. (eds), *Nationalising Femininity: Culture, Sexuality, and British Cinema in the Second World War* (Manchester, 1996).

Gordon, E. and Nair, G., 'Domestic Fathers and the Victorian Parental Role', *Women's History Review* 15:4 (2006), pp. 551–9.

Green, J., *All Dressed Up: The Sixties and the Counterculture* (London, 1999).

Greenfield, J., O'Connell, S., and Reid, C., 'Fashioning Masculinity: *Men Only*, Consumption and the Development of Marketing in the 1930s', *Twentieth Century British History* 10:4 (1999), pp. 457–76.

Greenfield, J., O'Connell, S., and Reid, C., 'Gender, Consumer Culture and the Middle-Class Male, 1918–39', in A. Kidd and D. Nicholls (eds.), *Gender, Civic Culture, and Consumerism: Middle-Class Identity in Britain, 1800–1940* (Manchester, 1999), pp. 183–97.

Grey, D., 'Women's Policy Networks and the Infanticide Act 1922', *Twentieth Century British History* 21:4 (2010), pp. 441–63.

Griffin, B., Delap, L., and Wills, A., 'Introduction: The Politics of Domestic Authority in Britain since 1800', in L. Delap, B. Griffin, and A. Wills (eds), *The Politics of Domestic Authority in Britain since 1800* (Basingstoke, 2009), pp. 1–24.

Griswold, R. L., 'Introduction to the Special Issue on Fatherhood', *Journal of Family History* 24:3 (1999), pp. 251–4.

Hall, L. A., *Hidden Anxieties: Male Sexuality 1900–1950* (Cambridge, 1991).

Hall, L. A., *Sex, Gender and Social Change in Britain since 1880* (Basingstoke, 2000).

Hall, S., 'Encoding, Decoding', in S. During (ed.), *The Cultural Studies Reader* (London, 1993), pp. 90–103.

Halsey, A. H. (ed.), *Twentieth-Century British Social Trends* (3rd edn, Basingstoke, 2000).

Hammerton, A. J., 'The English Weakness? Gender, Satire and Moral Manliness in the Lower Middle Class, 1870–1920', in A. Kidd and D. Nicholls (eds.), *Gender, Civic Culture, and Consumerism: Middle-Class Identity in Britain, 1800–1940* (Manchester, 1999), pp. 164–82.

Harris, A., '"A Paradise on Earth, a Foretaste of Heaven": English Catholic Understandings of Domesticity and Marriage, 1945–1965', in L. Delap, B. Griffin, and A. Wills (eds), *The Politics of Domestic Authority in Britain since 1800* (Basingstoke, 2009), pp. 155–81.

Harris, A., '"The People of God Dressed for Dinner and Dancing"? English Catholic Masculinity, Religious Sociability and the Catenian Association', in Lucy Delap and Sue Morgan (eds), *Men, Masculinities and Religious Change in Twentieth-Century Britain* (Basingstoke, 2013), pp. 54–89.

Harris, A. and Jones, T. (eds), *Love and Romance in Britain, 1918–1970* (Basingstoke, forthcoming 2014).

Harris, C., 'The Family in Post-War Britain', in J. Obelkevich and P. Catterall (eds), *Understanding Post-War British Society* (London, 1994), pp. 45–57.

Harris, J., 'Social Planning in War-time: Some Aspects of the Beveridge Report', in J. M. Winter (ed.), *War and Economic Development* (Cambridge, 1975), pp. 239–256.

Hart, N., 'Gender and the Rise and Fall of Class Politics', *New Left Review* 175 (1989), pp. 19–47.

Harvey, K. and Shepard, A., 'What Have Historians Done with Masculinity? Reflections on Five Centuries of British History, circa 1500–1950', *Journal of British Studies* 44 (2005), pp. 274–80.

Haywood, I., *Working-Class Fiction: From Chartism to Trainspotting* (Plymouth, 1997).

Hendrick, H., *Child Welfare: England 1872–1989* (London, 1994).

Heward, C., 'Like Father, Like Son: Parental Models and Influences in the Making of Masculinity at an English Public School, 1929–1950', *Women's Studies International Forum* 13:1/2 (1990), pp. 139–49.

Higonnet, M. R. and Higonnet, P. L. R., 'The Double Helix', in M. R. Higonnet, J. Jenson, S. Michel, and M. Collins (eds), *Behind the Lines: Gender and the Two World Wars* (New Haven, CT, and London, 1987), pp. 31–47.

Higonnet, M. R., Jenson, J., Michel, S., and Collins, M. (eds), *Behind the Lines: Gender and the Two World Wars* (New Haven, CT, and London, 1987).

Higonnet, M. R., Jenson, J., Michel, S., and Collins, M., 'Introduction', in M. R. Higonnet, J. Jenson, S. Michel, and M. Collins (eds), *Behind the Lines: Gender and the Two World Wars* (New Haven, CT, and London, 1987), pp. 1–17.

Holden, K., *The Shadow of Marriage: Singleness in England, 1914–1960* (Manchester, 2007).

Horne, J., 'Masculinity in Politics and War in the Age of Nation-States and World Wars, 1850–1950', in S. Dudink, K. Hagemann, and J. Tosh (eds), *Masculinities in Politics and War: Gendering Modern History* (Manchester, 2004), pp. 22–40.

Houlbrook, M., *Queer London: Perils and Pleasures in the Sexual Metropolis, 1918-1957* (Chicago, ILL, 2005).

Hubble, N., *Mass-Observation and Everyday Life: Culture, History, Theory* (Basingstoke, 2006).

Jackson, B., *Fatherhood* (London, 1984).

Jayaweera, H., Joshi, H., Macfarlane, A., Hawkes, D., and Butler, N., 'Pregnancy and Childbirth', in S. Dex and H. Joshi (eds), *Children of the 21st Century: From Birth to Nine Months* (Bristol, 2005), pp. 109–32.

Jones, B., 'The Uses of Nostalgia: Autobiography, Community Publishing and Working Class Neighbourhoods in Post-War England', *Cultural and Social History* 7:3 (2010), pp. 355–74.

Jones, T., 'Love, Honour, and Obey? Romance, Subordination and Marital Subjectivity in Interwar Britain', in Timothy Jones and Alana Harris (eds), *Love and Romance in Britain, 1918–1970* (Basingstoke, forthcoming 2014).

Kent, R., 'The Emergence of the Sociological Survey, 1887–1939', in M. Bulmer (ed.), *Essays on the History of British Sociological Research* (Cambridge, 1985), pp. 52–69.

Kent, S. K., *Making Peace: The Reconstruction of Gender in Interwar Britain* (Princeton, NJ, 1993).

Kent, S. K., *Gender and Power in Britain, 1640–1990* (London, 1999).

Kidd, A. and Nicholls, D. (eds), *Gender, Civic Culture, and Consumerism: Middle-Class I dentity in Britain, 1800–1940* (Manchester, 1999).

King, L., 'Hidden Fathers? The Significance of Fatherhood in Mid-Twentieth-Century Britain', *Contemporary British History*, 26:1 (2012), pp. 25–46.

King, L., '"Now You See a Great Many Men Pushing Their Pram Proudly": Family-Orientated Masculinity Represented and Experienced in Mid-Twentieth-Century Britain', *Cultural and Social History* 10:4 (2013), pp. 599–617.

King, L., 'The Perfect Man: Fatherhood, Masculinity and Romance in Popular Culture in Mid-Twentieth-Century Britain', in Timothy Jones and Alana Harris (eds), *Love and Romance in Britain, 1918–1970* (Basingstoke, forthcoming 2014).

Kynaston, D., *Austerity Britain, 1945–51* (London, 2007).

Kynaston, D., *Family Britain, 1951–57* (London, 2009).

Landy, M., *British Genres: Cinema and Society, 1930–1960* (Princeton, NJ, 1991).

Langhamer, C., 'The Meanings of Home in Postwar Britain', *Journal of Contemporary History* 40:2 (2005), pp. 341–62.

Langhamer, C., 'Love and Courtship in Mid-Twentieth-Century England', *Historical Journal* 50:1 (2007), pp. 173–96.

Langhamer, C., 'Love, Selfhood and Authenticity in Post-War Britain', *Cultural and Social History* 9:2 (2012), pp. 277–97.

Lant, A., 'Prologue: Mobile Femininity', in C. Gledhill and G. Swanson (eds), *Nationalising Femininity: Culture, Sexuality and British Cinema in the Second World War* (Manchester, 1996), pp. 13–32.

LaRossa, R., *The Modernization of Fatherhood: A Social and Political History* (Chicago, IL, and London, 1997).

LaRossa, R., 'The Historical Study of Fatherhood: Theoretical and Methodological Considerations', in Mechtild Oeschsle, Ursula Müller, and Sabine Hess (eds), *Fatherhood in Late Modernity: Cultural Images, Social Practices, Structural Frames* (Leverkusen, 2012), pp. 37–58.

Lawrence, J., 'Class, "Affluence" and the Study of Everyday Life in Britain, c.1930–64', *Cultural and Social History* 10:2 (2013), pp. 273–99.

Leavitt, J. W., *Make Room for Daddy: The Journey from Waiting Room to Birthing Room* (Chapel Hill, NC, 2009).

Levine-Clark, M., 'The Politics of Preference: Masculinity, Marital Status and Unemployment Relief in Post-First World War Britain', *Cultural and Social History* 7:2 (2010), pp. 233–52.

Lewis, C., *Becoming a Father* (Milton Keynes, 1986).

Lewis, J., 'The Ideology and Politics of Birth Control in Inter-War England', *Women's Studies International Quarterly* 2:1 (1979), pp. 33–48.

Lewis, J., *The Politics of Motherhood: Child and Maternal Welfare in England, 1900–1939* (London, 1980).

Lewis, J., *Women in England 1870–1950: Sexual Divisions and Social Change* (London and New York, 1984).

Lewis, J. (ed.), *Labour and Love: Women's Experiences of Home and Family, 1850–1940* (Oxford, 1986).

Lewis, J., 'Introduction: Reconstructing Women's Experiences of Home and Family', in J. Lewis (ed.), *Labour and Love: Women's Experiences of Home and Family, 1850–1940* (Oxford, 1986), pp. 1–24.

Light, A., *Forever England: Femininity, Literature and Conservatism between the Wars* (London, 1991).

Lowe, N. V., 'The Legal Status of Fathers: Past and Present', in L. McKee and M. O'Brien (eds), *The Father Figure* (London, 1982), pp. 26–42.

Lummis, T., 'The Historical Dimension of Fatherhood: A Case Study 1890–1914', in L. McKee and M. O'Brien (eds), *The Father Figure* (London, 1982), pp. 43–56.

Lupton, D. and Barclay, L., *Constructing Fatherhood: Discourses and Experiences* (London, 1997).

Macnicol, J., *The Movement for Family Allowances, 1918–45: A Study in Social Policy Development* (London, 1980).

Macnicol, J., 'The Effect of the Evacuation of Schoolchildren on Official Attitudes to State Intervention', in H. L. Smith (ed.), *War and Social Change* (Manchester, 1986), pp. 3–31.

Mandler, P., 'The Problem with Cultural History', *Cultural and Social History* 1:1 (2004), pp. 94–117.

May, E. T., *Homeward Bound: American Families in the Cold War Era* (2nd edn, New York, 1999).

McAleer, J., *Popular Reading and Publishing in Britain, 1914–50* (Oxford, 1992).

McKee, L. and O'Brien, M. (eds), *The Father Figure* (London, 1982).

McKee, L. and O'Brien, M., 'The Father Figure: Some Current Orientations and Historical Perspectives', in L. McKee and M. O'Brien (eds), *The Father Figure* (London, 1982), pp. 1–25.

McKibbin, R., *Classes and Cultures: England 1918–1951* (Oxford, 1998).

Meyer, J., *Men of War: Masculinity and the First World War in Britain* (Basingstoke, 2009).

Meyer, J., 'Separating the Men from the Boys: Masculinity and Maturity in Understandings of Shell Shock in Britain', *Twentieth Century British History* 20:1 (2009), pp. 1–22.

Morgan, D., 'Masculinity, Autobiography and History', *Gender and History* 2:1 (1990), pp. 34–9.

Morgan, S., '"Iron Strength and Infinite Tenderness": Herbert Gray and the Making of Christian Masculinities at War and at Home, 1900-1940', in L. Delap and S. Morgan (eds), *Men, Masculinities and Religious Change in Twentieth-Century Britain* (Basingstoke, 2013), pp. 168–196.

Mort, F., 'Crisis Points: Masculinities in History and Social Theory', *Gender and History* 6:1 (1994), pp. 124–130.

Mort, F., 'Social and Symbolic Fathers and Sons in Postwar Britain', *Journal of British Studies* 38:3 (1999), pp. 353–84.

Mort, F., *Dangerous Sexualities: Medico-Moral Politics in England since 1830* (2nd edn, London, 2000).

Moss, P. (ed.), *Father Figures: Fathers in the Families of the 1990s* (Edinburgh, 1995).

Moss, P., 'Introduction', in P. Moss (ed.), *Father Figures: Fathers in the Families of the 1990s* (Edinburgh, 1995), pp. xi–xxiv.

Mosse, G. L., *The Image of Man: The Creation of Modern Masculinity* (Oxford and New York, 1996).

Nelson, C., *Invisible Men: Fatherhood in Victorian Periodicals, 1850–1910* (Athens, GA, and London, 1995).

Noakes, L., *War and the British: Gender, Memory and National Identity* (London, 1998).

Obelkevich, J. and Catterall, P. (eds), *Understanding Post-War British Society* (London, 1994).

Obelkevich, J., 'Consumption', in J. Obelkevich and P. Catterall (eds), *Understanding Post-War British Society* (London, 1994), pp. 141–54.

Parker, C., 'Introduction', in C. Parker (ed.), *Gender Roles and Sexuality in Victorian Literature* (Aldershot, 1995), pp. 1–24.

Pedersen, S., *Family, Dependence, and the Origins of the Welfare State: Britain and France, 1914–1945* (Cambridge and New York, 1993).

Peniston-Bird, C., 'Classifying the Body in the Second World War: British Men In and Out of Uniform', *Body and Society* 9:4 (2003), pp. 31–48.

Penlington, N., 'Masculinity and Domesticity in 1930s South Wales: Did Unemployment Change the Domestic Division of Labour?', *Twentieth Century British History* 21:3 (2010), pp. 281–99.

Peplar, M., *Family Matters: A History of Ideas about Family since 1945* (London, 2002).

Porter, R. and Hall, L., *The Facts of Life: The Creation of Sexual Knowledge in Britain, 1650–1950* (New Haven, CT, 1995).

Pugh, M., *We Danced All Night: A Social History of Britain between the Wars* (London, 2009).

van Rahden, T., 'Fatherhood, Rechristianization, and the Quest for Democracy in Postwar Germany', in D. Schumann (ed.), *Raising Citizens in 'the Century of the Child': The United States and German Central Europe in Comparative Perspective* (New York, 2010), pp. 141–64.

Richardson, D., *Women, Motherhood and Childrearing* (Basingstoke, 1993).

Riley, D., *War in the Nursery: Theories of the Child and Mother* (London, 1983).

Robb, M., 'Exploring Fatherhood: Masculinity and Inter-Subjectivity in the Research Process', *Journal of Social Work Practice* 18:3 (2004), pp. 395–406.

Roberts, E., *A Woman's Place: An Oral History of Working-Class Women, 1890–1940* (Oxford, 1984).

Roberts, E., *Women and Families: An Oral History, 1940–1970* (Oxford, 1995).

Roper, L., 'Beyond Discourse Theory', *Women's History Review* 19:2 (2010), pp. 307–19.

Roper, M., 'Maternal Relations: Moral Manliness and Emotional Survival in Letters Home during the First World War', in S. Dudink, K. Hagemann, and J. Tosh (eds), *Masculinities in Politics and War: Gendering Modern History* (Manchester, 2004), pp. 295–315.

Roper, M., 'Between Manliness and Masculinity: The "War Generation" and the Psychology of Fear in Britain, 1914–1950', *Journal of British Studies* 44:2 (2005), pp. 343–63.

Roper, M., 'Slipping Out of View: Subjectivity and Emotion in Gender History', *History Workshop Journal* 59:1 (2005), pp. 57–72.

Roper, M., *The Secret Battle: Emotional Survival in the Great War* (Manchester, 2009).

Roper, M. and Tosh, J. (eds), *Manful Assertions: Masculinities in Britain since 1800* (London, 1991).

Roper, M. and Tosh, J., 'Introduction: Historians and the Politics of Masculinity', in M. Roper and J. Tosh (eds), *Manful Assertions: Masculinities in Britain since 1800* (London, 1991), pp. 1–24.

Rose, J., *The Intellectual Life of the British Working Classes* (New Haven, CT, and London, 2001).

Rose, N., *The Psychological Complex: Psychology, Politics and Society in England, 1869–1939* (London, 1985).

Rose, N., *Governing the Soul: The Shaping of the Private Self* (London, 1989).

Rose, S. O., 'Sex, Citizenship, and the Nation in World War II Britain', *The American Historical Review* 103:4 (1998), pp. 1147–76.

Rose, S. O., *Which People's War? National Identity and Citizenship in Wartime Britain 1939–1945* (Oxford, 2003).

Rose, S. O., 'Temperate Heroes: Concepts of Masculinity in Second World War Britain', in S. Dudink, K. Hagemann, and J. Tosh (eds), *Masculinities in Politics and War: Gendering Modern History* (Manchester, 2004), pp. 177–97.

Sanders, V., '"What Do You Want to Know about Next?" Charles Kingsley's Model of Educational Fatherhood', in T. L. Broughton and H. Rogers (eds), *Gender and Fatherhood in the Nineteenth Century* (Basingstoke, 2007), pp. 55–67.

Savage, M., *Identities and Social Change in Britain since 1940: The Politics of Method* (Oxford, 2010).

Scott, J. W., 'Gender: A Useful Category for Historical Analysis', *The American Historical Review* 91:5 (1986), pp. 1053–75.

Scott, J. W., 'Rewriting History', in M. R. Higonnet, J. Jenson, S. Michel, and M. Collins (eds), *Behind the Lines: Gender and the Two World Wars* (New Haven, CT, and London, 1987), pp. 21–30.

Scott, J. W., *Gender and the Politics of History* (New York, 1988).

Scott, J. W., 'The Evidence of Experience', *Critical Inquiry* 17:4 (1991), pp. 773–97.

Seccombe, W., 'Patriarchy Stabilized: The Construction of the Male Breadwinner Wage Norm in Nineteenth-Century Britain', *Social History* 11:1 (1986), pp. 53–76.

Segal, L., *Slow Motion: Changing Masculinities, Changing Men* (3rd edn, Basingstoke, 2007).

Seymour-Ure, C., *The British Press and Broadcasting since 1945* (2nd edn, Oxford, 1996).

Shepard, A. and Walker, G., 'Gender, Change and Periodisation', *Gender and History* 20:3 (2008), pp. 453–62.

Showalter, E., 'Rivers and Sassoon: The Inscription of Male Gender Anxieties', in M. R. Higonnet, J. Jenson, S. Michel, and M. Collins (eds), *Behind the Lines: Gender and the Two World Wars* (New Haven, CT, and London, 1987), pp. 61–9.

Smith, G., 'Schools', in A. H. Halsey (ed.), *Twentieth-Century British Social Trends* (3rd edn, Basingstoke, 2000), pp. 179–220.

Smith, J., 'The First Intruder: Fatherhood, a Historical Perspective', in P. Moss (ed.), *Father Figures: Fathers in the Families of the 1990s* (Edinburgh, 1995), pp. 17–25.

Smith-Wilson, D., 'A New Look at the Affluent Worker: The Good Working Mother in Post-War Britain', *Twentieth Century British History* 17:2 (2006), pp. 206–29.

Sokoloff, S., '"How Are They at Home?" Community, State, and Servicemen's Wives in England, 1939–45', *Women's History Review* 8:1 (1999), pp. 27–52.

Soloway, R. A., *Birth Control and the Population Question in England 1877–1930* (Chapel Hill, NC, 1982).

Spicer, A., *Typical Men: The Representation of Masculinity in Popular British Cinema* (New edn, London, 2003).

Stevenson, J., *British Society, 1914–1945* (Harmondsworth, 1984).

Steedman, C., *Landscape for a Good Woman: A Story of Two Lives* (London, 1986).

Strange, J. M., '"Speechless with Grief": Bereavement and the Working-Class Father, c.1880–1914', in T. L. Broughton and H. Rogers (eds), *Gender and Fatherhood in the Nineteenth Century* (Basingstoke, 2007), pp. 138–49.

Strange, J. M., 'Fatherhood, Providing, and Attachment in Late Victorian and Edwardian Working-Class Families', *Historical Journal* 55:4 (2012), pp. 1007–27.

Strange, J. M., *Fatherhood and the British Working Class, 1865–1914* (Cambridge, forthcoming 2014).

Street, S., *British National Cinema* (London and New York, 1997).

Street, S., *British Cinema in Documents* (London, 2000).

Summerfield, P., 'Mass-Observation: Social Research or Social Movement?', *Journal of Contemporary History* 20:3 (1985), pp. 439–52.

Summerfield, P., 'Approaches to Women and Social Change in the Second World War', in B. Brivati and H. Jones (eds), *What Difference Did the War Make?* (Leicester, 1993), pp. 63–79.

Summerfield, P., 'Women in Britain since 1945: Companionate Marriage and the Double Burden', in J. Obelkevich and P. Catterall (eds), *Understanding Post-War British Society* (London, 1994), pp. 58–72.

Summerfield, P. and Crockett, N., '"You Weren't Taught That with the Welding": Lessons in Sexuality in the Second World War', *Women's History Review* 1:3 (1992), pp. 435–54.

Szreter, S., *Fertility, Class and Gender in Britain, 1860–1940* (Cambridge, 1996).

Szreter, S. and Fisher, K., 'Love and Authority in Mid-Twentieth-Century Marriages: Sharing and Caring', in L. Delap, B. Griffin, and A. Wills (eds), *The Politics of Domestic Authority in Britain since 1800* (Basingstoke, 2009), pp. 132–54.

Szreter, S. and Fisher, K., *Sex before the Sexual Revolution: Intimate Life in England 1918–1963* (Cambridge, 2010).

Thane, P., *Foundations of the Welfare State* (2nd edn, Harlow, 1996).

Thane, P., 'Women and Political Participation in England, 1918–1970', in E. Breitenbach and P. Thane (eds), *Women and Citizenship in Britain and Ireland in the Twentieth Century: What Difference Did the Vote Make?* (London and New York, 2010), pp. 11–28.

Thane, P., 'Unmarried Motherhood in Twentieth-Century England', *Women's History Review* 20:1 (2011), pp. 11–29.

Thom, D., 'Wishes, Anxieties, Play, and Gestures: Child Guidance in Inter-War England', in R. Cooter (ed.), *In the Name of the Child: Health and Welfare, 1880–1940* (London and New York, 1992), pp. 200–19.

Thom, D., '"Beating Children Is Wrong": Domestic Life, Psychological Thinking and the Permissive Turn', in L. Delap, B. Griffin, and A. Wills (eds), *The Politics of Domestic Authority in Britain since 1800* (Basingstoke, 2009), pp. 261–83.

Thompson, P., *The Voice of the Past* (3rd edn, Oxford, 2000).

Thompson, P., 'Family Myth, Models, and Denials in the Shaping of Individual Life Paths', in D. Bertaux and P. Thompson (eds), *Between Generations: Family Models, Myths and Memories* (2nd edn, Somerset, NJ, 2005), pp. 13–38.

Thomson, M., 'Psychology and the "Consciousness of Modernity" in Early Twentieth-Century Britain', in M. Daunton and B. Rieger (eds), *Meanings of Modernity: Britain from the Late-Victorian Era to World War II* (Oxford and New York, 2001), pp. 97–115.

Thomson, M., *Psychological Subjects: Identity, Culture, and Health in Twentieth-Century Britain* (Oxford, 2006).

Thomson, M., *Lost Freedom: The Landscape of the Child and the British Post-War Settlement* (Oxford, 2013).

Todd, S., *Young Women, Work, and Family in England 1918–1950* (Oxford, 2005).

Todd, S., 'Breadwinners and Dependants: Working-Class Young People in England, 1918–1955', *International Review of Social History* 52 (2007), pp. 57–87.

Todd, S., 'Affluence, Class and Crown Street: Reinvestigating the Post-War Working Class', *Contemporary British History* 50:1 (2008), pp. 501–18.

Tosh, J., 'Domesticity and Manliness in the Victorian Middle Class: The Family of Edward White Benson', in M. Roper and J. Tosh (eds), *Manful Assertions: Masculinities in Britain since 1800* (London, 1991), pp. 44–73.

Tosh, J., 'What Should Historians Do with Masculinity? Reflections on Nineteenth Century Britain', *History Workshop Journal* 38 (1994), pp. 179–202.

Tosh, J., *A Man's Place: Masculinity and the Middle-Class Home in Victorian England* (New Haven, CT, and London, 1999).

Tosh, J., 'Hegemonic Masculinity and the History of Gender', in S. Dudink, K. Hagemann, and J. Tosh (eds), *Masculinities in Politics and War: Gendering Modern History* (Manchester, 2004), pp. 41–58.

Tosh, J., *Manliness and Masculinities in Nineteenth-Century Britain: Essays on Gender, Family and Empire* (Harlow, 2005).

Tosh, J., 'Masculinities in an Industrializing Society: Britain 1800–1914', *Journal of British Studies* 44:2 (2005), pp. 330–42.

Tosh, J., 'The History of Masculinity: An Outdated Concept?', in J. H. Arnold and S. Brady (eds), *What Is Masculinity? Historical Dynamics from Antiquity to the Contemporary World* (Basingstoke, 2011), pp. 17–34.

Turner, B. and Rennell, T., *When Daddy Came Home: How Family Life Changed Forever in 1945* (London, 1995).

Urwin, C. and Sharland, E., 'From Bodies to Minds in Childcare Literature: Advice to Parents in Inter-War Britain', in R. Cooter (ed.), *In the Name of the Child: Health and Welfare, 1880–1940* (London and New York, 1992), pp. 174–99.

Vickery, A., 'Golden Age to Separate Spheres? A Review of the Categories and Chronology of English Women's History', *Historical Journal* 36:2 (1993), pp. 383–414.

Vincent, M., 'The Martyrs and the Saints: Masculinity and the Construction of the Francoist Crusade', *History Workshop Journal* 47 (1999), pp. 69–98.

Wahrman, D., 'Change and the Corporeal in Seventeenth- and Eighteenth-Century Gender History: Or, Can Cultural History Be Rigorous?', *Gender and History* 20:3 (2008), pp. 584–602.

Weeks, J., *Sex, Politics and Society: The Regulation of Sexuality since 1800* (2nd edn, New York, 1989).

Weiss, J., '"A Drop-In Catering Job": Middle-Class Women and Fatherhood, 1950–1980', *Journal of Family History* 24:3 (1999), pp. 374–90.

Williamson, M., '"He Was Good with the Bairns": Fatherhood in an Ironstone Mining Community, 1918–1960', *North East History* 32 (1998), pp. 87–108.

Willmott, P., 'The Institute of Community Studies', in M. Bulmer (ed.), *Essays on the History of British Sociological Research* (Cambridge, 1985), pp. 137–50.

Wills, A., 'Delinquency, Masculinity and Citizenship in England 1950–1970', *Past and Present* 187 (2005), pp. 157–85.

Young, H., 'Being a Man: Everyday Masculinities', in L. Abrams and C. G. Brown (eds), *A History of Everyday Life in Twentieth-Century Scotland* (Edinburgh, 2010), pp. 131–52.

Young, M., interviewed by P. Thompson, 'Reflections on Researching *Family and Kinship in East London*', *International Journal of Social Research Methodology* 7:1 (2004), pp. 35–44.

UNPUBLISHED THESES AND DISSERTATIONS

Doolittle, M., 'Missing Fathers: Assembling a History of Fatherhood in Mid-Nineteenth Century England', PhD Thesis (University of Essex, 1996).

Fisher, T. J., 'Fatherhood and the Experience of Working-Class Fathers in Britain, 1900–1939', PhD Thesis (University of Edinburgh, 2004).

Grey, D. J. R., 'Discourses of Infanticide in England, 1880–1922', PhD Thesis (Roehampton University, 2009).

Pooley, S. K., 'Parenthood and Child-Rearing in England, c.1860–1910', PhD Thesis (University of Cambridge, 2009).

Smith, H., 'A Study of Working-Class Men Who Desired Other Men in the North of England, c.1895–1957', PhD Thesis (University of Sheffield, 2013).

Index

Printed and bound by CPI Group (UK) Ltd, Croydon, CR0 4YY